SkillPath

Business Communication Style Guide

The Practical Guide to Clarity, Readability
and Correctness in Business Writing

Poley and Crocker

SkillPath Publications
Mission, Kansas

ISBN: 978-1-608114-74-0

Printed in the United States of America

◆ CREDITS

Project Editor: Bill Cowles

Editorial Support: Theresa Morgan
Debra Karr
Maggie Wagner
Marie Davis
Kristen Jones

Book Design: Dusty Crocker
Stephanie Butler

Cover Design: Stephanie Butler

Book Layout
and Prepress: Chad Pio
Dusty Crocker
Stephanie Butler
Willa Sleyster
Danielle Horn

◆ DEDICATIONS

Michelle Fairfield Poley—

For Eleanor, Michael, Jonathan, Robin and Jeremy—with so much love

And for Chris—now it's your turn

Dusty Crocker—

To my wife, Sally, and our three boys: Patrick, Jonathan and Baer

Thanks for all of your support and understanding

◆ PREFACE

The inspiration of SkillPath founders Jerry Brown and Denise Dudley has been a driving force in creating a tool that everyone who uses words in their work can use to work more productively, more effectively and certainly more happily. Evidence of Jerry and Denise's "work hard, play hard" philosophy can be found in the way we express many of the rules, do's, and don'ts of business communication.

We believe that some style and structure points are important, and that some are not so important, in the grand scheme of life. When you use this as a guide to better communication, and not as an enforcer of arbitrary rules, you'll gain greater freedom for the ways you express yourself. Have fun with it.

This book was written based on American-English style and usage. Our friends and colleagues in Canada, Australia, New Zealand and the United Kingdom will surely want to temper our advice with their own cultural and language preferences.

— The Editors

◆ TABLE OF CONTENTS

BUSINESS WRITING

Model Business Documents

GRAPHICS

Graphics

Prepress and Printing

CAREER SUCCESS

Career Success Handbook

SkillPath

Business Communication Style Guide

2

CLARITY, READABILITY AND CORRECTNESS

CLARITY

For decades, business writing experts have said that your number one goal as a writer must be *clarity*. Your writing must be so clear that no reader can make a mistake about its meaning. Of course, you may say, that's a tall order, and one that discounts the work a reader should be doing to understand your written message—but it's reality.

Your reader can't always be trusted to have the time, inclination or (sadly, in a few cases) the intelligence to devote much attention to your writing. It is always the writer's responsibility to make the message so easily understood that the reader could have no excuse for missing it.

Rules

The rules for clarity are easy to follow:

1. Begin every document with an overview statement or bottom line.
2. Use familiar words every time you can.
3. Keep most sentences short and simple.
4. Use the most conventional sentence structures and verb forms.
5. Use visual formatting strategies to communicate difficult information.
6. Edit carefully to guarantee clarity.

Explanations and Examples

1. Begin every document with an overview statement or bottom line.

Beginning every document with an overview statement, or the bottom line, helps the reader to frame your message. And it is advice that has been used in the business and peak achievement arenas for years. Stephen Covey, the well-known and well-respected author of *The 7 Habits of Highly Effective People,* actually mainstreamed this advice to millions when he made it his Habit #2: Begin with the end in mind.

Public speakers have also used this advice for years; do you remember the simple formula for any speech?

1. Tell them what you're going to tell them.
2. Tell it to them.
3. Then tell them what you told them.

By beginning your document with the overview or bottom line, you are telling your readers what you are going to be telling them. This allows them to hang imaginary hooks in their heads for the ideas you will soon express. And they can sort while they read, instead of having to read, then sort. In fact, most busy readers *won't* come back a second time to analyze your document. What they don't get the first time through they are most likely *never* going to get.

Compare these two short memos:

> Short words and simple sentences are important to your readers because they don't take too much energy to read. Why use the word *facilitate* when you could have used the word *lead*? What about those 40+ word sentences that show up in so many of the professional journals these days? Who could possibly understand them? Just reading them wears readers out so much they can't possibly have enough energy left to understand what was being said!
>
> The passive voice is another issue. When your reader has to imagine a scene in the reverse order from how it actually happened, that reader can't help but get confused. Do everything you can as a writer to help your readers paint a picture logically.
>
> Grammar errors make your writing hard to understand as well. Make sure you are using a current style guide that has been written for the type of writing you do.

◀ *Memo 1*

Memo 2 ▶ As a writer, your number one goal is *clarity*—the certainty that your reader can and will easily and precisely understand every word of your writing. There are four main tools you can use to guarantee clarity: short words, simple sentences, active voice verbs and correct grammar.

Short words and simple sentences are important to your readers because they don't take too much energy to read. Why use the word *facilitate* when you could have used the word *lead*? To say nothing about those 40+ word sentences that show up in so many of the professional journals these days. Who could possibly understand them? Just reading them wears readers out so much they can't possibly have enough energy left to understand what was being said!

The passive voice is another issue. When your reader has to imagine a scene in the reverse order from how it actually happened, that reader can't help but get confused. Do everything you can as a writer to help your readers paint a picture logically.

Grammar errors make your writing hard to understand as well. Make sure you are using a current style guide that has been written for the type of writing you are engaged in.

Memo 2 gives the reader clear direction of where it is headed from the very beginning. Before even finishing the first paragraph, the reader knows what is ahead. This allows that reader to read more quickly and confidently. Memo 1 forces the reader to carefully consider every word and sentence in the hope of eventually finding some unifying point. If asked for the four main points, do you think the reader of Memo 1 could easily recount them after one reading? It's doubtful.

2. Use familiar words every time you can.

Certainly, you will need some large words and probably even some words that are not easily understood by many readers. That's okay, as long as your readers understand the words. To overcomplicate a message by adding words like *facilitate*, *utilize* and *paradigm* when the words *help*, *lead* and *model* are accurate is showing discourtesy to your busy reader. You don't need to impress your readers with how many multi-syllable words you can string together into one sentence if you can impress them with the clarity and intelligence of your ideas.

Compare these examples:

> Commence the operation by altering the temperature 50 degrees to the negative.
>
> To facilitate the implementation of modifications agreed upon Thursday, the engineers will reactivate the system after depressing the red button.
>
> **OR**
>
> Start the operation by reducing the temperature 50 degrees.
>
> To help make the changes agreed upon Thursday, the engineers will turn on the system after they press the red button.

3. Keep most sentences short and simple.

And whenever possible, both.

In business writing, no sentence should be longer than 32 words, although a sentence can be as short as one word. (Stop. Look. Listen.) Even more important, aim to keep your average sentence length somewhere between 10 – 17 words.

To figure average sentence length, count the number of words in all the sentences in a document, then divide that total by the number of sentences those words were in. In ideally clear and readable business writing, your answer should be somewhere between 10 – 17 words.

4

Business Writing

Even more important than how many words you put into a sentence is how many ideas that sentence contains. A simple sentence is one that contains only one major idea. Ever since you and your reader were small children, you have been reading—and understanding—simple sentences. From your first primary reader and its fascinating stories about Dick, Jane and Spot, all the way through Dr. Seuss, A.A. Milne and one fairy tale after another, simple sentences communicated images to you, and they did it quickly, clearly and powerfully. (Okay, maybe not so powerfully in the case of Dick, Jane and Spot.)

Grammatically speaking, a simple sentence is defined as a sentence that contains one major idea, usually in a form that contains one subject and one verb. It is possible, though, to have a compound subject or a compound verb.

Here are some examples of simple sentences:

> The project failed miserably.
>
> Sam and Janet spent most of the department's entertainment budget on the Christmas party.
>
> Marilu and Larry copied, collated, stapled and stuffed the shareholder reports until lunchtime.

Compare those sentences to these ▶

> The project that had been worked on by every member of the sales department sometime over the course of the past six months to no avail failed miserably.
>
> Sam and Janet spent most of the department's entertainment budget, which had only recently received enough donations from all of us to be useable at all, on the Christmas party.
>
> Marilu and Larry, now in their second month of secretly seeing each other socially after work most nights and on weekends, copied, collated, stapled and stuffed the shareholder reports until lunchtime.

Notice that each of the simple sentences conveys a clear and unambiguous picture. Even when Marilu and Larry were doing four different things with those shareholder reports, the picture you (the reader) got was clear.

It's not that the more complex sentences can't be understood. It's just that your busy reader would have to work harder to do it—especially if they appeared one after another in a longer document. Albert Joseph, author of the best-selling business writing training program *Put It in Writing*, calls it "collective overload."

When there are too many words, too many ideas, too many commas or semicolons and too few periods, your reader's energy level just breaks down. Be thoughtful of your readers. Make sure that each of your important ideas merits its own sentence. When you have a less important (known in grammar as *subordinate*) idea that goes with your major idea, it is fine to include it in the same sentence. Just make sure that the structure and punctuation of the sentence make clear which idea is the major one.

The more quickly your reader can read and understand, the more likely it is your reader will keep reading and understanding. Think about the difficult reading you have done—especially difficult reading that you stuck with. What made you keep reading? Wasn't it the fact that there was going to be a test? (Or in the case of legal documents, a potentially unpleasant resolution to a case?)

Face it, your business reader is under no obligation or duress to read what you write—and you aren't allowed to make that reader take an exam. Everything you can do to make the reading go more easily and quickly for that reader is like an insurance policy that pays you in your reader's willingness to keep reading—and to keep understanding.

4. Use the most conventional sentence structures and verb forms.

Simply put, those would include the standard English sentence where a Subject does a Verb at, to, for, with or near an Object. Sometimes even other Objects are involved, as in Indirect Objects and Objects of Prepositions.

First, let's discuss the standard English sentence. No adult, except maybe a third grade English teacher, needs to know how to diagram a sentence. But those old diagrams made it easy to see the standard English sentence.

Jake and I	returned	the	financial statements	to the client's file	last Friday.
subject	verb		direct object	prepositional phrase	adverbial phrase
				(indirect objects)	

Subject-Verb-Direct Object-Indirect Object(s) is the structure of most of the sentences you have read in your lifetime. Because it is so familiar, it is also the easiest and quickest structure to read for understanding.

Every once in a while, of course, the reader's needs can be even better served by a less common structure. For example, when you want to emphasize *when* those financial statements were returned to the client's file:

> Last Friday, Jake and I returned the financial statements to the client's file.

In this case, even though it is an adverbial phrase serving as an indirect object, it appears first in the sentence. People tend to notice and remember best what they read first in a sentence. But can you imagine making sense out of this?

> Returned the financial statements, Jake and I to the client's file last Friday.

Huh? That's the way Yoda, the Jedi Master in the *Star Wars* movies, talks!

The moral? Use the most conventional writing structures and styles you can so your reader doesn't need to spend too much time deciphering the syntax. This way, the reader can spend all of his or her available energy on your meaning. After all, that's what clarity demands.

Your other concern for simplicity's sake is the voice of your verbs.

Now that grammar checking software is a part of almost every word processing program, more adults are aware of a verb's voice. Voice is the property of the verb that shows whether the subject is acting or being acted upon.

As mentioned earlier, most English sentences are written in the order of a Subject doing a Verb at, to, for, with or near an Object. These sentences are written in the active voice. The subject is "acting" the verb:

> The dog buried a bone.
> Luke just published the quarterly report on our Web page.
> Our clients have given the Mega-500 great reviews.

Do you see how easy it is to follow the meaning in these sentences? As you read, you first see a dog, then that dog is digging a hole and finally, the dog drops a bone into the hole! How convenient! You see Luke, then you see him publishing a report and finally, you see it published on a Web page. Easy to read, easy to see.

Compare them to the less direct versions here ▶

> A bone was buried by the dog.
> The quarterly report was published on our Web page by Luke.
> The Mega-500 has been given great reviews by our clients.

To see these, you have to move from back to front. First, you see a bone. Then, as though rewinding your mind, you now have to create a hole that the bone is being put in and finally, you see that it is a dog doing the burying. Same thing with the quarterly report. First, you see it published, then on a Web page and finally, by Luke.

These sentences are difficult for your busy readers because they cause those readers to slow down their reading to understand. Ultimately, readers who are slowed end up pushing the document aside and reading someone else's document—not yours.

And what about more complicated ideas, not as simple as bones being buried and Web pages being published? Or worse yet, what about the careless writer who instinctively senses that he or she has written a complete sentence and just leaves out the "by whom" altogether?

> A bone was buried.

By whom? Sometimes it matters. If I am writing to convince you to buy a new Mega-500 from our company, which sentence would move you more?

> Our clients have given the Mega-500 great reviews.
> **OR**
> The Mega-500 has been given great reviews.

The clients are more persuasive than some unnamed group, right?

To make matters even worse, some irresponsible writers purposely use the passive voice to avoid responsibility. And unfortunately, they have ruined it for the rest of us. Now, many sensitive or intelligent readers are rightly suspect of the passive voice.

Notice this sentence ▶ Your performance has been found to be unsatisfactory.

By whom? Your boss? Your jealous co-worker? The CEO? A cranky janitor who got hold of some of your company's expensive letterhead? As a reader, you don't know. And if a reader can't know something for sure, how clear is it? No one is taking responsibility for criticizing your performance.

Aim to keep most of your writing in the active voice. It's easier to read, quicker to understand and more clear and responsible.

5. **Use visual formatting strategies to communicate difficult information.**

Any ideas that you actually produce on paper or in e-mail are going to be easier to understand than the exact same ideas presented in a speech. Why? Because when you write, you have access to formatting changes like those seen to the right.

Traditionally, language is thought of as a means of communication that one person speaks (referred to as vocal) and another person hears (referred to as auditory). Writing adds a visual dimension. And the good news for you, a business writer, is that most of your readers are visually oriented.

Perhaps you've heard of the three different learning styles educators now recognize: visual, auditory and kinesthetic. Visual people tend to learn and understand ideas best by seeing them; auditory people tend to learn and understand ideas best by hearing them; and kinesthetic people tend to learn and understand ideas best by doing or touching them. Most people are able to use all three styles, but one tends to be stronger. In today's society, there are more visual people than auditory or kinesthetic. By showing your readers your thoughts, your transitions and the relationships among your important points, you can't help but communicate clearly.

boldface

underlining

italics

• bulleted lists

DIFFERENT FONTS

white space

▲

These visual strategies help your reader quickly see your ideas and the relationships among them

> **Writer's Tips:**
> For a full explanation of the
> active and passive voice,
> see Passive Voice, page 134.

Perhaps you can think of an example of your own visual preferences. Maybe a team member was trying to explain some statistics about your project to you and they made no sense—until that team member flipped open a laptop computer and produced a PowerPoint® graph. You got it immediately. The same thing happens for your reader when you make your points visually as well as verbally.

Charts, graphs and bulleted lists help your readers quickly see information that would be difficult to understand in paragraph form.

6. Edit carefully to guarantee clarity.

That is the topic to which the bulk of this book is devoted. You will see sections covering the most common grammar problems business writers face. You will find sections explaining the correct rules for using every punctuation mark. There are sections about wordiness and how to avoid it, readability and how to enhance it—as well as many, many other topics of interest.

We have also included a large selection of samples to guide you in preparing the clearest and most readable documents possible.

Browse through all the pages of this book sometime soon. Become familiar with what's here. Then rest easy and know that you have the reference you need, every time you need it.

READABILITY

Readability is the characteristic of your writing that determines how quickly and easily your readers will be able to comprehend your message. In today's often over-busy, overworked and overstressed workplace, it could well be the single most important characteristic in determining whether your document will get a fair reading or not.

Your readers are busy. They probably think they get too much mail. Assume that they are looking for reasons to put some of that mail aside. When a document:

- Has no connection to the reader
- Sounds stuffy or overly formal
- Is not visually appealing
- Just appears to be a blob of information with no clear bottom line
- Has the reader's name misspelled or not used
- Has an author who has a reputation for sending too much junk mail

How could you expect a busy reader to find time to carefully read?

As a business writer, writing in a highly readable style is the main thing separating you from many other kinds of writers. Academic writers, most notably, don't need to be quite as concerned about how easily their documents can be read because in most cases the people doing the reading have a vested interest in getting the information—no matter how difficult or time consuming.

In the world of work, your readers are generally under no such obligation or duress.

Rules

Your writing must be engaging—capable of grabbing and keeping your reader's attention as well as capable of positively influencing that reader. To that end, follow these guidelines:

1. Know your reader and your reader's environment.
2. Use the conversational tone you would use if you were speaking to this reader.
3. Always use the reader's preferred name and title, spelled correctly.
4. Make the document appealing at first glance.
5. In e-mail, always write a clear and inviting subject line.
6. Guard your reputation as a writer with your life—in both e-mail and on paper.

Explanations and Examples

1. Know your reader and your reader's environment.

In other words, your readers need to know you care—about them. How many times have you received a piece of mail that made you scratch your head and ask, "Why are they writing this to me?"

It is always the writer's job to make clear to the reader from the very beginning just what is in it for that reader to keep reading. It is never the reader's job to figure it out on his or her own.

When you, as a writer, take the time to research your reader's interests, needs and environment—and then use that information as you write—you will be rewarded with your reader's attention and gratitude. Ask questions like the ones in this reader analysis checklist:

Reader Analysis Checklist

WHO?
Job title, department, responsibilities
Length of time with company
Educational background, specialty
Personal: Age, gender, attitudes, hobbies

WHAT?
What does the reader already know about the subject?
What else does the reader need to know?
What will the reader do about this message (decide, delegate, transmit, do)?
What's in it for the reader? Benefits? Risks?

WHEN?
When will the reader read this message?
How much time will the reader spend on it?
When does the reader have to act?

WHERE?
Where in the company hierarchy is this reader located?
Where is most of the reader's work done?
Where else in the company does the reader have to go for approval to act?

HOW?
How interested is the reader in this message?
How will the reader feel about this message?
How will the reader's job, workload or life be affected by this message?

WHY?
Why am I writing?
Why should the reader respond?

---

2. Use the conversational tone you would use if you were speaking to this reader.

If you have ever owned more than one grammar or style guide at the same time, you probably are already aware that writing experts are not always in agreement. In fact, writing experts disagree about many small or picky things. In this book, we have highlighted many disagreements and have provided options for you to make your own choice.

But there is one principle that all business writing experts agree on. If you write more like you speak, you will be a great business writer.

There are three reasons to write the way you speak:

- You will write more quickly. When you write the way you speak, you are using the vocabulary that you are most comfortable with, therefore you will write more quickly. The side benefit is that you will rarely write yourself into the middle of a sentence that you can't write your way out of. (Admit it: it's happened to you.)

- You will write more clearly. When you write the way you speak, you are using words that you use most often. Because you use them so often their meanings are more definite in your mind. And most likely, they will also be more definite in your readers' minds.

- You will write with more rapport. When you use conversational language in your writing, readers can't help but notice that you write like they speak as well. This lets them know that you are a living, breathing, warm human being—as opposed to a nameless bureaucracy or a computer.

Consider the fact that all of us have four working vocabularies. They are (in descending order):

- Reading vocabulary
- Listening vocabulary
- Writing vocabulary
- Speaking vocabulary

The single largest vocabulary most of us would claim is our reading vocabulary. Aren't there many words we have read that we ourselves would never use in speaking or writing? Words that when we read them in the context of a sentence or a paragraph made enough sense that we didn't find it necessary to stop to look them up? But are we confident enough to use them ourselves? Do we even know their correct pronunciation?

Our second largest vocabulary would be our listening vocabulary. When others talk to us, they occasionally use words that we either have never heard before or would never use ourselves. But we—as in reading—understand them because of their context.

Our third largest vocabulary is our writing vocabulary. While nowhere near as large as our reading or listening vocabularies, many people freely use words in writing that they would never consider speaking over a table to a friend in a crowded restaurant. Here's an example:

As per our conversation of the 20th, please be advised that the foreclosure agreement entered into by all parties will expire at midnight of the third day following final approval and signature.

What? No one would ever say that over lunch! But many of us don't think twice when it comes to putting it in writing.

At this point, maybe you have a question: Yes, I understand that writing as I speak would be more casual and easier to read, but what if I am writing to someone who is important, or not familiar to me?

Certainly, we are not suggesting that when you write to your bosses and clients you should use slang or inappropriate language. Just imagine yourself sitting across a table at lunch from your reader and imagine what words you would use to tell that reader your ideas.

Our smallest vocabulary, then, is our speaking vocabulary. This is the one we are so comfortable with it is second nature to us. When we use this speaking vocabulary in our writing, our readers don't experience the kind of overload they do when we use the larger, less familiar words of our reading and listening vocabularies.

3. **Always use the reader's preferred name and title, spelled correctly.**

Do you read every word of every piece of mail you get? Of course not. Have you ever noticed the first stages of sorting you do on your incoming pile? Have you ever put something aside because it wasn't addressed directly to you, only to "To Whom it May Concern" or to "Dear Sir"? Have you ever put something aside because your name was misspelled, or because you were addressed as a Mr. instead of a Ms. or a Ms. instead of a Dr.?

Remember: it is *always* the writer's job to keep the reader interested and to keep the reader reading. If you are unsure of the name, the title or the spelling of the name of your reader, make a phone call or do the research to find out.

We can almost guarantee you that if you use your reader's name and accurate title—spelled correctly—that reader will read at least the first paragraph of your document. And in today's overcommunicated workplace, isn't that a guarantee you can't turn down?

When writing to multiple readers, or when there is no way to find out the reader's name, address your readers by the most accurate title you can think of

Dear Voter:
Dear Student:
Dear Parent:
Dear Customer Service Representative:

Writer's Tips:
For more information, see
Salutations, page 178.

9

Business Writing

4. Make the document appealing at first glance.

This principle applies to both e-mail and paper. Remember that your readers are looking for things to put aside, lighten their workloads. And if your document or e-mail looks like it is overwhelming, messy or just too much to read, it is likely that your reader will put it in a later pile. (Of course, you know when "later" comes—never.) In the case of e-mail, your reader may just delete it at first glance.

In e-mail, make sure you follow conventional style rules. Use traditional capitalization rules—never send an e-mail in ALL CAPS: that looks like yelling. But remember to use some capital letters—at the beginning of sentences and at the beginning of proper nouns.

Also in e-mail, make sure that your readers see at least one paragraph break in the initial window before they scroll. This makes your e-mail look less overwhelming and easier to read.

On paper, make sure the print is dark and even. Include bulleted lists and never have a paragraph longer than ten printed lines. But vary the length of your paragraphs—some long, some short—to give your reader variety. For your letters, use a beautiful letterhead and for memos and reports, make sure that your format is inviting and logical. Paper must be clean and of good quality.

You may wonder about how fair it is that your important meaning can fall victim to aesthetics. No one is saying it is fair that it happens, we are just reminding you: it does.

5. In e-mail, always write a clear and inviting subject line.

Face it, we're all getting more and more e-mail every day. And face this as well: most readers delete a good portion of their e-mail before they ever open it.

A clear, accurate and positive subject line will get you more attention from even your busiest readers. Beware of a subject line that includes more than one RE:, for example. Yet every time you hit the Reply button on some e-mail programs, a RE: automatically appears in your outgoing subject line. Realize that if you are replying to a reply that was itself a reply to a reply, you might just be sending a subject line that is all RE: RE: RE:. RE's across the line aren't too interesting or helpful to your reader.

Be as specific and as complete as possible.

Company Picnic
Company Picnic Postponed to June 30
Brown Project
Brown Project Ahead of Schedule

Use a subject line that contains a summary of the most important information your reader needs. Here are some examples of e-mail subject lines. Which ones are more helpful to you as a reader?

6. Guard your reputation as a writer with your life—in both e-mail and on paper.

As a responsible writer, you need to assume that no one is forcing your reader to read your document. Therefore, your reputation as a writer who communicates in a positive and clear way—and as a writer who communicates only when necessary—helps your reader look forward to the e-mail and paper he or she receives from you.

How about in your experience? Have you ever deleted an e-mail message unread just because you saw the screen name of the person who sent it to you? And you knew it was likely to be junk—just because you have received so much junk from that person in the past?

Don't risk it. If you have only one screen name at work, do not forward junk mail with that screen name. If there is something so funny or so interesting you find in junk mail that you do want to forward it to people, send it to yourself at a home e-mail address first and forward it from that address. This way, you won't run the risk of ruining the reputation you have with the screen name you use at work.

Also, make a point to send only information that is useful to your readers. And try not to send too many e-mails in one day to the same person—unless, of course, the two of you are having an ongoing discussion about a certain topic.

Here's another thought: Consider sending a daily or weekly update e-mail instead of many e-mails throughout that day or week, just to keep your reader's workload down.

And, of course—whether sending a document on paper or through e-mail, stay positive and warm in your tone. Your reader needs to feel a human connection with you in order to care much about your message. Follow the rest of the tips listed in this section, and also in the section on Clarity (page 2), and you are sure to impress and inform your readers.

CORRECTNESS

Your readers judge your credibility and intelligence—and the credibility and intelligence of your ideas—based on clarity, readability and correctness. This is an issue we will emphasize again and again in this style guide.

But for some reason, when you make basic errors of accuracy, whether in your content or in your usage of the English language, your readers can be most unforgiving. You must safeguard your credibility, your reputation and your content by doing everything within your power to make sure every document you write and send is both absolutely accurate and unfailingly correct.

Rules

That is why we recommend these six principles of correctness and accuracy:

1. Use a spell-checker, and then proofread anyway.
2. As often as possible, have a good friend (or a good editor) proofread for you.
3. When proofreading your own writing, do what you can to separate yourself from it first.
4. Learn what you can about grammar, punctuation and usage.
5. Have a good style guide available as a reference.
6. Double-check all dates, times, specifications and names—for both accuracy and correct spelling—before sending anything.

Explanations and Examples

1. Use a spell-checker, and then proofread anyway.

The spell-checker in your computer's word processing program catches so many errors that you could otherwise miss, and takes such a small amount of time, it really makes sense to use it. If you have prepared a document in a word processing program, run the spell-checker on it before you print it out to proofread it and certainly before you print it out to send it.

Even your e-mail program probably now contains a spell-checker that is good enough and quick enough that you can spell-check your e-mail before pressing the Send button.

Trust us: it's worth the time and it's worth the bother. Your readers judge your credibility, your intelligence and the quality of your ideas based on many things—not the least of which is the accuracy of your spelling.

A note of caution: When adding words to your spell-checker, be wary of a psychological tendency wired into us humans. We want to be right. We sometimes want to be right so much that our brains fool us into believing we are—even when we're not. Before adding any word to your spell-checker, make sure to look at it twice and be certain that you are adding the correct spelling of that word.

A second note of caution: Of course, your computer's spell-checker is not reading your documents for their intended meaning. That spell-checker is just making sure that each individual word matches up with a word or a logarithm programmed into the software. Words that are words, just the wrong words (like *form* instead of *from*) won't be flagged by your spell-checking software. That's why we offer you the second half of this tip:

Then proofread anyway. If you know that you are predisposed toward certain misspellings or typos, use the Find command in your word processor to locate all of the potential misspellings. For example, if your common typo is indeed *form* for *from*, use your Find command to find the word *form*, then the word *from* throughout your document. Double-check each one as your software presents it to you.

2. As often as possible, have a good friend (or a good editor) proofread for you.

It is a cognitive reality that a writer cannot accurately see the errors in something he or she has just finished typing. You see, as you type, your brain is making a picture of what you are typing—not a picture of what you are really typing, but a picture of what you want to be typing. Then, when you read over that typing in the same place you just finished typing it (for example, on your computer screen), your brain superimposes the image it created over the image you are seeing with your eyes. Has it happened to you? A friend or a co-worker reads your document over your shoulder and laughs at a simple error you still cannot see.

While it may not always be possible to have a second pair of eyes proofread your writing, do everything you can to find someone other than yourself to read your most important documents. This proofreader/editor doesn't need to be your assistant or your boss—a co-worker who writes as much as you do is a good candidate. Offer to share the proofreading job: you can proofread their writing; they can proofread yours.

It's important to note that even if you think you know more about your subject or even more about grammar, punctuation and usage, another reader will always be able to find errors you might miss—just because of the cognitive psychology involved.

3. When proofreading your own writing, do what you can to separate yourself from it first.

When you do not have another reader available to do your editing and proofreading, you must help your brain detach itself from what it just wrote. Here are some strategies for doing that:

Take a break. Ideally, a long break—like a whole day. If you can afford the time, write the document on Day One and proofread it on Day Two. But even if you can afford only a few minutes between the writing and proofreading of a particular document, make sure to truly take a break from it. Get up from where you had been sitting when you wrote it and stretch your legs. Walk down a hall or look out a window or perhaps even make a phone call—but a phone call about something besides the topic you just finished writing about.

Make a hard copy of it. Never proofread a document in the same place you just typed it. For most of us businesspeople today, that means never proofread a document on your computer screen. That's where your brain expects to see it. So that's where it is easiest for your brain to manipulate cognitively what it sees and turn it into what it wants to see. Always make a printout on paper to proofread whenever possible. This is something you should consider doing even for some e-mail—the most important pieces of your e-mail. Never forget: Your reader judges your credibility based on how error-filled or error-free your writing is.

Enlarge that hard copy, or print it using a different font. To separate yourself even further from your writing, change the font size to half again as large, e.g., change 12 point to 18 point or try changing the font before you proofread. Anything you can do that makes your document look less like what your brain expects to see will take you a long way toward accuracy. What you are dealing with here is your comfort zone. You need to break out of it.

Proofread aloud. Proofreading aloud is an especially good tip for finding two specific kinds of errors. The first would be punctuation errors. We don't recommend the suggestion "Use a comma anytime you would pause in speech" as your first rule of punctuation. But if you do have difficulty figuring out how much or which punctuation to use, sometimes the sound of the sentence can help you correctly decide. If you find yourself breathing or pausing too much while you read, that is a good sign you have overdone it. If you, on the other hand, feel out of breath while you read your writing, you can probably assume you need more periods or commas.

A second error that is often hard to see until you read aloud is missing words. Many of us, as writers, can think and type so quickly that we accidentally leave words out of our typing, even if we were thinking them as we wrote. Yet when proofreading silently, in our heads, we can read just as quickly as we think. And that is too fast to notice those missing words. On the other hand, by slowing down enough to actually breathe in, breathe out and enunciate words, the missing words jump out at us. This tip works especially well if you also follow the words you are reading with your finger.

Proofread backwards. Before we all had spell-checking software, this was the way we were told to proofread for spelling. Now that most of us do have spell-checkers, it is probably not necessary to do this. But we offer it for your consideration just in case you ever need to proofread something that is not in a computer file you have immediate spell-checking access to. Here's why it works:

Most of us have been readers since we were five or six. And ever since we began learning to read, we were told to read from a capital letter to a period for the main idea of the sentence. So, if we can read it for meaning, we do. When reading the phrase *Chairman of the Board*, we understand it—in fact we recognize it. So we are likely to pay considerable attention to what we consider the important words in that phrase: *Chairman* and *Board*. As for the *of* and *the*? Well, we have the tendency to assume they must be okay. When reading backwards, right to left instead of left to right, we give better attention to the words we might otherwise be assuming are correct because we can't understand the meaning of the phrases and sentences. Board the of Chairman makes no sense, therefore we focus better on the mechanics.

Proofread line by line. The theory here is the same as the theory with reading backwards. When you read just small groups of words, rather than full sentences, you tend to focus better on the individual components and the mechanics.

Once you read the whole sentence, your brain can't help it—it attempts to understand the meaning of the sentence, not the correctness of each component. Use a ruler or a blank sheet of paper to guide your eye down a page, line by line.

Proofread it in a different place. A different place than the place you were in when you wrote it, that is. Get away from your writing area. Perhaps you could borrow someone else's office or a conference room down the hall. Or maybe it is a nice day and you could go outside and proofread it there. Even if you just move your chair from the side of the desk you were sitting on when you wrote it—just move it to the opposite side of your desk and proofread it there—that can be a very powerful change. Because now, everything is backwards. Maybe the door to your office is now behind you instead of in front of you, your window is on your left instead of your right. Believe it, your brain will notice these changes and help you take less for granted in your writing.

4. **Learn what you can about grammar, punctuation and usage.**

   While no one can know all the rules governing American English (there are just too many), it is a timesaving idea to learn the ones you use frequently.

   Any native speaker of a language knows much about how that language works and is able to make the correct choices in grammar, punctuation and usage quite often, almost instinctively. The downside of being a native speaker is that we sometimes don't know why we do what we do. When we run into trouble, when we have questions about a picky detail, we may not even know what the questions are about, let alone where to look for answers.

   Have you ever studied a foreign language? If so, do you remember how becoming aware of details about that language involving things like tenses and gender caused you to realize—maybe for the first time—that a lot of those things existed in English too?

   When you find yourself questioning the same thing over and over, take the time to look it up and learn it. Save yourself some time. In some cases, you may even want to consider enrolling in a class or seminar to polish those skills.

   On the other hand, don't worry too much about learning the details that you only need occasionally. Your brain space is valuable! That's what a reference guide like this is for.

5. **Have a good style guide available as a reference.**

   And that is exactly what you have done by purchasing this book. Now that you own it, make sure you keep it available. Keep the CD-ROM version near the computer at which you do most of your writing and keep the book itself within easy reach. As a matter of fact, make a point of spending 30 minutes or so browsing through it before you actually need it as a tool. Become familiar with it now so you can save yourself time when you are in need of a particular piece of information quickly.

   Plus, there's another benefit of having a comprehensive style guide. When you make changes to someone else's writing, you get to blame the style guide. It's much more tactful than saying, "Hey, I changed this because you have never known what you were doing with commas." See? Listen to how much better it sounds when you say: "According to page 150 of the *Business Communication Style Guide*, …"

6. **Double-check all dates, times, specifications and names—for both accuracy and correct spelling—before sending anything.**

   Accuracy is a proofreading issue that is slightly different from correctness. Accuracy is about whether August 21 is really August 21—or was it supposed to be August 12?

   Before sending any document, be a responsible writer. Double-check all dates, times, instructions and names for accuracy. Be especially sensitive to the accuracy of names and titles—as discussed in our Readability section; misspelling your reader's name is one sure way to convince that reader your document is not important enough to read. And it is obvious that if you are conveying information that is in itself inaccurate or incorrect, your reader can't know that until the bad information gets him or her into a jam.

   These six principles of correctness will help you guard your reputation as a writer—the reputation that your reader will value enough to keep reading not just this document but everything else you may send in the future.

   There are more pages of this book devoted to the issue of correctness than any other topic. Look up the things you need as you need them. Spend time with this book learning what you'd like to remember. And all our best to you as you become a more credible and powerful writer than ever before.

BUSINESS GRAMMAR AND USAGE

ABBREVIATIONS, ACRONYMS AND INITIALS

Most people call both abbreviations and what more accurately should be called initials by one name: *abbreviations*. Those same people generally know that *acronyms* are a special kind of what they would call an abbreviation. But here's the difference among the three of them (for discriminating users of the English language):

Abbreviations are shortened forms of words, like *lb.* for pound and *Ave.* for Avenue. Their correct forms are commonly listed in dictionaries as a part of the entry for the words they abbreviate.

Acronyms are abbreviations of phrases or names, usually composed of the first letters of all the important words in the phrase or name. Acronyms are almost always pronounced as words themselves, as in *DOS* (disk operating system) and *UNICEF* (United Nations International Children's Emergency Fund). Thorough dictionaries often list them as entries—paperback or less thorough ones don't.

Initials are also abbreviations of phrases or names, composed of the first (also referred to as initial—get it?) letters of all the important words in the phrase. Initials, however, are not pronounced as the words they spell but as the letters that make up those words. Some examples are *FBI* and *USA*. Again, complete dictionaries tend to list the more common ones.

The rules governing the use of abbreviations, acronyms and initials are similar but not always the same:

Abbreviations always end with a period. If the original word was capitalized, then the abbreviation is also capitalized. Check a current dictionary or an on-line dictionary (like *www.mydictionary.com*) to find the correct abbreviation for any word.

Acronyms should not contain any periods, because they would interfere with the pronunciation of the word. Compare the readability of *A.I.D.S.* and AIDS (acquired immune deficiency syndrome). Remember: In business writing, readability is one of your most important goals. All the letters of an acronym are capitalized, even when they aren't normally capitalized in the full spelling of the phrase. Very occasionally, though, an acronym crosses over into becoming a word itself (*radar* and *laser* are good examples) and then it becomes unnecessary to capitalize the letters. When in doubt, check your dictionary for correct usage.

Initials can either have periods between the letters or not. This choice is up to you, the writer. But please—be consistent. Three things to consider in making this important choice:

1. Are the initials clearly and easily understood without the periods, or is there a chance your reader could misread them as words?

2. In the case of company or organization names, how do the companies or organizations themselves present their initials? You can check their letterhead and envelopes to see.

Examples ▶

US	United States OR the word us, meaning me and someone else?
AM	Morning OR a state of being (I am)?

3. Aside from these two considerations, it is usually more readable to leave out the extra periods. As a rule, punctuation that is not necessary to the meaning of your writing should be avoided.

Rules

1. Always use a period at the end of the standard abbreviation for a single word.

2. Eliminate periods between the letters of acronyms—they interfere with your reader's ability to quickly and clearly understand your meaning.

3. Use periods between the letters of initials only if they will help the reader understand the meaning more clearly or more quickly.

4. Abbreviate titles only when they are before names.

5. Abbreviate the names of familiar organizations or institutions, very famous people and universally familiar objects when you can be certain your reader will understand your meaning.

6. If you are unsure of your reader's familiarity with a particular abbreviation (or acronym or set of initials), place the unabbreviated form in parentheses after your first use of the abbreviation in your writing.

7. Abbreviate units of measure, references to time and mathematical terms when they are used with numbers. Do not add an *s* to the abbreviation, even if it is plural.

8. Use the article *a* before an acronym or set of initials that begins with the sound of a consonant; use the article *an* before an acronym or set of initials that begins with the sound of a vowel.

9. Only use the most common and standard abbreviations of single words in the body of a document and avoid using all abbreviations in headings and titles.

10. When an abbreviation, acronym or set of initials ends a sentence, use only one period to end the sentence. If the abbreviation, acronym or set of initials requires a punctuation mark in addition to a period after it, use that punctuation mark immediately after the final period of the abbreviation or the last capitalized letter of the acronym.

11. Never abbreviate people's names, words connected to other words with a hyphen or words at the beginning of a sentence.

12. Use the two-letter state codes designated by the U.S. Postal Service on all correspondence to the states and territories of the United States.

13. Check a dictionary for the correct plural form of any abbreviation of a single word. If an abbreviated word becomes possessive, spell out the word before making it possessive. Follow conventional rules for making acronyms and initials plural and possessive.

14. Whatever you do, remember that consistency and clarity must be your watchwords. Use abbreviations, acronyms and initials to communicate, not to impress.

Examples and Explanations

1. **Always use a period at the end of the standard abbreviation for a single word.**

   When using the standard (meaning, the form a dictionary indicates as correct) abbreviation of any word, always use a period at the end of the abbreviation. This period tells the reader that the word is indeed abbreviated.

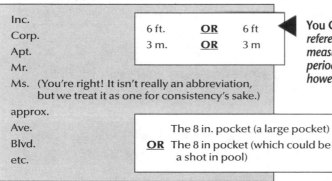

Inc.
Corp.
Apt.
Mr.
Ms.   (You're right! It isn't really an abbreviation, but we treat it as one for consistency's sake.)
approx.
Ave.
Blvd.
etc.

6 ft.   **OR**   6 ft
3 m.   **OR**   3 m

You Choose: *Most dictionaries and writing reference guides agree that even units of measure, when abbreviated, should have periods at the end. Some technical guides, however, suggest that they should not.*

The 8 in. pocket (a large pocket)
OR The 8 in pocket (which could be a shot in pool)

Funny enough, even the technical guides generally agree that the abbreviation for inches *should always have a period at the end so the reader doesn't mistake it for the word* in

If this sounds inconsistent, don't be surprised. It is!

Your choice really depends on the environment you are writing in (do most of the other writers in your organization favor one style over the other?) and the environment you are writing to (do your readers have a technical background?).

Our recommendation? If you aren't a technical writer with a technical audience, stick with the periods. The general reader expects them.

2. **Eliminate periods between the letters of acronyms—they interfere with your reader's ability to quickly and clearly understand your meaning.**

   Any style guide for the world of work would be remiss if it didn't emphasize readability (the ease with which a reader can read and clearly understand a piece of writing). And ever since most of us were small children we were taught that a period means stop. Don't confuse your readers by asking them to stop in the middle of what they recognize as a word.

NASA	DOS	RAM	AIDS

Business Writing

3. **Use periods between the letters of initials only if they will help the reader understand the meaning more clearly or more quickly.**

Busy readers could confuse some sets of initials with other words—as with the time designation for morning, a.m. Without periods it just looks too much like the word *am*. And to be consistent, this means we should also use those periods in the time designation for afternoon, p.m.

It is also true that some organizations include the periods in their own initials—in which case it would be a good idea for a writer attempting to influence that organization in some way to use those periods as well. When in Rome …

FBI	AAA	USA
JFK	NFL	AMA
DVD	TV	

When the letters are all capitalized, your reader will have an easier time reading without the periods

4. **Abbreviate titles only when they are before names.**

Certainly we use abbreviations in forms of address every day:

| Mr. Williams | Ms. O'Rourke |
| Dr. Greene | Prof. Hernandez |

But it is not appropriate to use those same abbreviations in the middle of sentences, separated from people's names, as replacements for the words they abbreviate.

Incorrect: Mary and her Dr. attended last week's conference.
Correct: Mary and her doctor attended last week's conference.

INSTEAD OF: Prof. Joe Hernandez   **USE**: Professor Joe Hernandez
Pres. Linda Hardy   President Linda Hardy

And although all the rule books (including this one) tell you it is okay to abbreviate a title before a person's name, sometimes it can be just a touch more elegant to spell it out fully—and perhaps even flattering to the person who worked long and hard to earn that title

Note: There are also some abbreviations we commonly use after names:

Just be careful to avoid being redundant: Dr. Laura M. Greene, M.D.

Ross P. Williams, Jr.
Laura M. Greene, M.D.

5. **Abbreviate the names of familiar organizations or institutions, very famous people and universally familiar objects when you can be certain your reader will understand your meaning.**

Most people refer freely to organizations such as the FBI, the CIA, 3M and IBM. In fact, some people probably couldn't tell you what those initials stand for! (Okay, because you begged: Federal Bureau of Investigation, Central Intelligence Agency, Minnesota Mining and Manufacturing and International Business Machines.)

The same is true of FDR, JFK and LBJ (Franklin Delano Roosevelt, John Fitzgerald Kennedy and Lyndon Baines Johnson). And can you imagine asking a spouse or roommate:

Would you record that television show I like so much on the Digital Video Recorder?

It's much more natural to say:

Of course, remember that *clarity* is your watchword. Be certain your reader will understand you. This can become especially important if you use many abbreviations and acronyms in your organization. It's easy to assume that everyone speaks your language just because you speak it so regularly.

> Would you DVR that TV show I like so much?

> *Writer's Tips:*
> *See our section on Jargon for more information, page 107.*

6. **If you are unsure of your reader's familiarity with a particular abbreviation (or acronym or set of initials), place the unabbreviated form in parentheses after your first use of the abbreviation in your writing.**

Better safe than sorry, and clarity is your number one goal. Once you have defined your abbreviation, acronym or set of initials the first time you can freely use it throughout the document. Unless the document is more than 35 pages long—then reiterate the initials in each major section.

> Lorenzo and Max have both been working in our IST (Information Services Technology) department for over three years. In fact, they are the senior members of that department and have trained the rest of our current IST professionals.

Something to Consider. If you are writing a long or very technical document with many abbreviations, acronyms and sets of initials that need explanation, do one of three things:

- Include the parenthetical definitions each time you use the abbreviated form OR
- Restate the abbreviated form at the first use in each major section OR
- Provide a glossary of all terms at the end of your report or document. This way, your reader won't feel overwhelmed with a need to learn too many terms too quickly. If you choose to provide a glossary, make it clear to your readers at the beginning of your document so they will know where to look.

7. **Abbreviate units of measure, references to time and mathematical terms when they are used with numbers.**
   Do not add an *s* to the abbreviation, even if it is plural.

> Jeremy weighed 7 lb. 12 oz. when he was born.
> Newborn babies' weights in the US are measured in pounds and ounces.

8. **Use the article *a* before an acronym or set of initials that begins with the sound of a consonant; use the article *an* before an acronym or set of initials that begins with the sound of a vowel.**

a UNICEF worker	**NOT**	an UNICEF worker
an FBI agent	**NOT**	a FBI agent

The articles *a* and *an* have the same function—the only difference between them is meant to ease the pronunciation of a group of words. Therefore, in the case of initials and acronyms, it is better to choose the article that sounds best.

Initials that begin with the letters below should be introduced with the article *an*.

> A, E, F, H, I, L, M, N, O, R, S, and X ◀ *Here are the letters that, when spoken, begin with the sound of a vowel*

Use the article *a* before initials that begin with these letters.

> B, C, D, G, J, K, P, Q, T, U, V, W, Y and Z ◀ *These letters, when spoken, begin with the sound of a consonant*

It is true that many of us were taught as children to use the article *a* in front of consonants and the article *an* in front of vowels, period. And although it is true that generally a reader is not reading our writing aloud, remember that we all have a silent voice in our heads as we read. That silent voice has just as much trouble quickly reading and pronouncing a FBI agent and an UNICEF worker as a speaking voice would. As you can see, the suggestion to use the sound the letter begins with as your guide has a lot to do with readability.

9. **Only use the most common and standard abbreviations of single words in the body of a document and avoid using all abbreviations in headings and titles.**

   This rule applies to e-mail as well as to documents printed on paper. Informal abbreviations like *thru* for *through* are definitely off limits, but also be judicious in your use of even standard abbreviations. They can make you look lazy and they interfere with the smooth flow of words your reader was enjoying.

   > **Instead of**: Tues. was the most productive day we've yet seen in Oct.
   >
   > **Use**: Tuesday was the most productive day we've yet seen in October.

10. **When an abbreviation, acronym or set of initials ends a sentence, use only one period to end the sentence. If the abbreviation, acronym or set of initials requires a punctuation mark in addition to a period after it, use that punctuation mark immediately after the final period of the abbreviation or the last capitalized letter of the acronym.**

    Here's what this rule boils down to: You never need more than one period to end a sentence. ("Never" is a strong word, and when you study parentheses you will see there is an exception there. But it is the only exception.)

    If you use an abbreviation or a set of initials (with periods between the letters) at the end of a sentence, the period at the end of the abbreviation or after the last initial will serve double-duty and also end the sentence.

    > For the past ten years our company has been based in the U.S.
    >
    > The vinyl you requested is available in every shade of brown imaginable: tan, beige, sienna, burnt sienna, toasted sienna, etc.

    If you use an abbreviation or set of initials with periods and an additional punctuation mark is needed, first use the period that is required in the abbreviation or initials, then (without skipping a space) type the needed punctuation mark.

    > How long has your company been based in the U.S.?
    >
    > Her address is: 123 Main St., Cleveland, OH 44102.

11. **Never abbreviate people's names, words connected to other words with a hyphen or words at the beginning of a sentence.**

    > **NOT**: Chas. and Frank finished the project a week ahead of schedule.
    >
    > **BUT**: Charles and Frank finished the project a week ahead of schedule.
    >
    > **NOT**: Eight in. routing circuit
    >
    > **BUT**: Eight inch routing circuit

12. **Use the two-letter state codes designated by the U.S. Postal Service on all correspondence to the states and territories of the United States.**

    If you happen to remember them, do not use the old formal abbreviations for the states on anything that will be sent through the mail. (Here are some to remind you: Miss., Minn., Calif.)

    Instead, use the postal codes established by the U.S. Postal Service. These postal codes have become so common that they are often also used as abbreviations for the states and territories in charts and graphs. Certainly for most Americans, they are more recognizable (and therefore more readable) than the older standard abbreviations. However, the state name must be spelled out in the body of the document.

The postal codes established by the U.S. Postal Service

▼

Alabama	AL	Louisiana	LA	Oregon	OR		
Alaska	AK	Maine	ME	Pennsylvania	PA		
Arizona	AZ	Maryland	MD	Puerto Rico	PR		
Arkansas	AR	Massachusetts	MA	Rhode Island	RI		
California	CA	Michigan	MI	American Samoa	AS		
Colorado	CO	Minnesota	MN	South Carolina	SC		
Connecticut	CT	Mississippi	MS	South Dakota	SD		
Delaware	DE	Missouri	MO	Tennessee	TN		
District of Columbia	DC	Montana	MT	Texas	TX		
Florida	FL	Nebraska	NE	Utah	UT		
Georgia	GA	Nevada	NV	Vermont	VT		
Guam	GU	New Hampshire	NH	Virginia	VA		
Hawaii	HI	New Jersey	NJ	Virgin Islands	VI		
Idaho	ID	New Mexico	NM	Washington	WA		
Illinois	IL	New York	NY	West Virginia	WV		
Indiana	IN	North Carolina	NC	Wisconsin	WI		
Iowa	IA	North Dakota	ND	Wyoming	WY		
Kansas	KS	Ohio	OH				
Kentucky	KY	Oklahoma	OK				

13. **Check a dictionary for the correct plural form of any abbreviation of a single word. If an abbreviated word becomes possessive, spell out the word before making it possessive. Follow conventional rules for making acronyms and initials plural and possessive.**

To make a word plural, add an *s*. To make an abbreviation plural, check with your dictionary. It is true that usually the plural form will be the same as the singular with the addition of a final *s*.

Apartments	Apts.
Avenues	Aves.
Professors	Profs.

Units of measure are exceptions ▶

Inches	In.
Feet	Ft.
Meters	M.

It's best to check a dictionary.

As for possessives of abbreviations, just don't do it.

NOT:	the bldg.'s demolition	**BUT:**	the building's demolition
	the Lt.'s office		the Lieutenant's office
	FL's vote		Florida's vote

In the case of acronyms and initials, the rules are more predictable. If an acronym or set of initials is to be made plural, simply add a lowercase *s* to the end. (If initials are to be made plural or possessive, never use periods in them.)

Does your son know his *ABCs* yet?

How many OKs do we need before we proceed with this?

Our new PCs will be here any day.

When making a plural of a single letter, use an apostrophe before the s to help your reader avoid confusion

> **USE:** The Oakland A's
> **NOT:** The Oakland As

To be consistent, this rule extends to all other single letters, not just the ones that form a real word with the s at the end

> My daughter got three B's on her last report card.
> Make sure to cross the t's and dot the i's.

Possessives are also made in the standard way. Add 's.

> NAFTA's impact has already been felt in the auto industry.
> The FBI's hiring guidelines are incredibly strict.
> My PC's screen keeps getting fuzzy in the middle of the day.

The only thing that is a little different from the standard rules is that there are hardly any exceptions. As you will discover in the possessives section of this book, when a regular word ends in *s*, we advise that the best way to make it possessive is to just add an apostrophe (boss' desk). With acronyms and initials, we advise you to add both the apostrophe and an *s*. You may ask why—would it help to know that it just looks better that way?

The NAS's membership is growing.	**instead of**	The NAS' membership is growing.
UPS's delivery time is good for us.	**instead of**	UPS' delivery time is good for us.

14. **Whatever you do, remember that consistency and clarity must be your watchwords. Use abbreviations, acronyms and initials to communicate, not to impress.**

You and your reader don't have to make every stylistic choice in exactly the same way to understand each other clearly. Your reader knows as well as you do that styles can differ. What your reader can't understand is if you use one style in your first paragraph and a different style in your second. Choose your style—like whether or not you use periods in initials—and stick with it.

And don't forget your main reason for writing: to clearly and accurately communicate your message to your reader. If you are unsure whether your reader will understand an abbreviation, acronym or set of initials you want to use, *spell it out.*

Some common abbreviations and acronyms are included here, as well as a list of foreign (especially Latin) abbreviations that have standard meanings. For readability's sake, use those sparingly.

General Abbreviation and Initials List

AA	administrative assistant OR Alcoholics Anonymous OR associate in arts	act.	active
		A.D.	after the birth of Christ (from Latin: *anno Domini*)
AAA	American Automobile Association	Ad hoc	for a particular purpose
		addl.	additional
A.B.	Bachelor of Arts (from Latin: *artium baccalaureus*)	adj.	adjective
abbr.	abbreviation	adv.	adverb
abr.	abridged OR abridgment	a.k.a.	also known as
abs.	absolute OR absent OR absence OR abstract	A.M.	Master of Arts (from Latin: *artium magister*) OR M.A.
acct.	account OR accountant	A.M. or a.m.	morning (from Latin: *ante meridiem*)
ACE	after the common era		
ack.	acknowledge	Amer.	American OR America

amt.	amount
anon.	anonymous
ant.	antonym
AP	accounts payable
app.	appendix
approx.	approximately
APR	annual percentage rate
AR	accounts receivable
arch.	archaic
art.	article
ASAP	as soon as possible
assn.	association
assoc.	associate OR associated
asst.	assistant
att.	attachment
attrib.	attributed to
Attn.	Attention
aux.	auxiliary
Ave.	Avenue
avg.	average
b.	born
B.A.	Bachelor of Arts
bal.	balance
B.C.	before Christ
BCE	before the common era
bf	boldface
bibliog.	bibliography
biog.	biography
bk.	book
bldg.	building
Blvd.	Boulevard
BO	back order
B.S.	Bachelor of Science
c OR c.	copy OR circa OR around (used with dates: c. 1946)
C	Celsius
cap.	capital OR capitalize
cc	copies
CD	compact disc
CEO	Chief Executive Officer
Cf	confer, meaning compare
CFO	Chief Financial Officer
ch. (or chap.)	chapter
chg.	charge
CIO	Chief Information Officer

cit.	citation
cl.	clause
Co.	company
c/o	care of
c.o.d.	cash on delivery
col.	column
COLA	cost of living adjustment
colloq.	colloquial
conf.	conference
Cong.	Congress
conj.	conjunction
cont.	contents OR continued
(contd.)	continued
COO	Chief Operating Officer
Corp.	Corporation
CPA	certified public accountant
cpi	characters per inch
CPI	Consumer Price Index
cr.	credit
CST	Central Standard Time
Ct.	court
ctn.	carton
d.	died
DA	district attorney
d.b.a.	doing business as
DC	direct current
DDS	doctor of dental surgery
def.	definition
dept.	department
dev.	development OR developed by
dict.	dictionary
dir.	director OR directed by
dis.	discount
dist.	district
distr.	distributor OR distributed by
div.	division
DJIA	Dow Jones Industrial Average
DOA	dead on arrival
doc.	document
doz.	dozen
dr.	debtor
Dr.	Doctor
DST	daylight savings time
dtd.	dated
DVD	digital videodisc

E.	east	GMAT	Graduate Management Admission Test
ea.	each	GMT	Greenwich Mean Time
EAP	Employee Assistance Program	GNP	gross national product
ed.	editor OR edited OR edition	Gov.	governor
EEO	Equal Employment Opportunity	govt.	government
e.g.	for example (from Latin: *exempli gratia*)	GPO	Government Printing Office
enl.	enlarged	GPS	global positioning system
e.o.m.	end of month	gr. wt.	gross weight
esp.	especially	GRE	Graduate Records Examination
Esq.	Esquire	GSA	General Services Administration
EST	Eastern Standard Time	hdlg.	handling
et al.	and others (from Latin: *et alii, et aliae*)	HF	high frequency
etc.	and so forth (from Latin: *et cetera*)	HHS	Department of Health and Human Services
ETA	estimated time of arrival	HMO	Health Management Organization
ETD	estimated time of departure	HMS	his (her) majesty's ship
ex.	example	HOV	high-occupancy vehicle
exec.	executive	hp	horsepower
F	Fahrenheit	HQ	headquarters
f.	female OR frequency	hr.	hour(s)
f., ff.	and following, pages following	HR	(with number) House Bill
FAA	Federal Aviation Administration	HRH	his (her) royal highness
facsim.	facsimile	HUD	Department of Housing and Urban Development
FBI	Federal Bureau of Investigation		
FCC	Federal Communications Commission	Hz	hertz (a unit of frequency)
FDA	Food and Drug Administration	I- (as in I-70)	Interstate 70
FDIC	Federal Deposit Insurance Corporation	ibid.	in the same place (from Latin: *ibidem*)
Fed.	federal	ID	identification
FHA	Federal Housing Authority	i.e.	that is (from Latin: *id est*)
FICA	Federal Insurance Contributions Act (social security)	IF	intermediate frequency
FIFO	first in, first out	illus.	illustration
fig.	figure	IMF	International Monetary Fund
fr.	from	inc.	including
f/t	full time	Inc.	Incorporated
FTC	Federal Trade Commission	incl.	including
fwd.	forwarded OR foreword	ins.	insurance
f/x	special effects (movies)	INS	Immigration and Naturalization Service
FY	fiscal year	intl.	international
FYI	for your information	intro.	introduction OR introduced by
GAO	General Accounting Office	inv.	invoice
gen.	general	IOU	I owe you
GM	general manager		

IPO	initial public offering (of stock)
IQ	intelligence quotient
IRA	individual retirement account
irreg.	irregular
ISBN	International Standard Book Number
J.D.	doctor of law (from Latin: *juris doctor*)
jour.	journal
Jr.	Junior
KB	kilobyte
kHz	kilohertz
l., ll.	line, lines
lang.	language
lat.	latitude
LOC	Library of Congress
l.c.	lowercase
leg.	legal
legis.	legislation OR legislator
LF	low frequency
LIFO	last in, first out
LLC	limited license corporation
LLP	limited license partners
loc. cit.	in the passage cited (from Latin: *loco citato*)
long.	longitude
LPN	licensed practical nurse
LSAT	Law School Admission Test
LST	Local Standard Time
Lt.	lieutenant
Ltd.	Limited
m.	married
M.A.	master of arts
max.	maximum
MB	megabyte
M.C.	member of Congress OR master of ceremonies
M.D.	doctor of medicine (from Latin: *medicinae doctor*)
mdse.	merchandise
MF	medium frequency
mfg.	manufacturing
mgmt. or mgt.	management
mgr.	manager
MHz.	megahertz

min.	minute(s) OR minimum
misc.	miscellaneous
mo.	month
M.O.	mode of operation (Latin: *modus operandi*) OR money order
M.P.	military police OR Member of Parliament
mpg	miles per gallon
mph	miles per hour
Mr.	Mister (plural: Messrs.)
Mrs.	Mistress
Ms.	feminine title (first choice)
M.S.	master of science
ms.	manuscript
msg.	message
m.s.l.	mean sea level
MST	Mountain Standard Time
mtg.	meeting OR mortgage
N.	north
n/30	net in 30 days
NA	not available OR not applicable
narr.	narrator OR narrated by
NAS	National Academy of Science
natl.	national
NE	northeast
NLRB	National Labor Relations Board
No., Nos.	number, numbers
nt. wt.	net weight
numb.	numbered
NW	northwest
OAG	Official Airline Guide
obs.	obsolete
O.D.	Officer of the Day OR overdose
OED	The Oxford English Dictionary
OJT	on-the-job training
OK	okay
op. cit.	in the work cited (from Latin: *opere citato*)
opt.	optional
orig.	original
OS, OOS	out of stock
o/t	overtime
OTC	over the counter
p., pp.	page, pages

P&H	postage and handling		QT	on the quiet
P&I	principal and interest		qtd.	quoted
P&L or P/L	profit and loss (as in statement)		Q-T-D	quarter-to-date
			qtr.	quarter
P.A.	public address system OR power of attorney OR physician's assistant		qty.	quantity
			®	registered trademark
par.	paragraph		R&B	rhythm and blues
pass.	passive		R&D	research and development
PC	personal computer OR politically correct		R&R	rest and relaxation
			RAM	random access memory
pd.	paid		rbi	runs batted in
P/E	price/earnings ratio		Rd.	road
pers.	person		rec.	record OR recorded
Ph.D.	doctor of philosophy		recd.	received
PIN	personal identification number		reg.	registered OR regular
pkg.	package		rel.	relative OR released
pl.	plural		rept.	report OR reported by
Pl.	Place		resp.	respectively
P.M. or p.m.	afternoon (from Latin: *post meridiem*)		ret.	retired
			rev.	revised OR review
P.O.	purchase order OR post office (as in P.O. Box)		Rev.	reverend
			RF	radio frequency
P.O.E.	port of entry		R.F.D.	rural free delivery
pop.	population		RFP	request for proposal
POP	point of purchase		RFQ	request for quotation
POS	point of sale		Rh	Rhesus (blood factor)
poss.	possessive		RIF	reduction(s) in force
POV	point of view		RN	registered nurse
POW	prisoner of war		ROA	return on assets
ppd.	prepaid		ROE	return on equity
pr.	pair		ROI	return on investment
pref.	preface OR preface by		rpm	revolutions per minute
pres.	present		rpt.	reprint OR reprinted by
proc.	proceedings		RR	railroad
prod.	producer OR produced by		RSVP	respond, if you please (from French: *repondez s'il vous plait*)
Prof.	professor			
P.S.	postscript OR public school (with a number)		S.	south
			S&H	shipping and handling
PST	Pacific Standard Time		S&L	savings and loan
pt.	point OR part OR port OR pint		SASE	self-addressed stamped envelope
pub. (publ.)	publisher OR published by		SAT	Scholastic Aptitude Test
QA	quality assurance		SBA	Small Business Administration
Q&A	question and answer		s.c.	small caps
			SE	southeast

sec.	second OR secretary		UFO	unidentified flying object
sec. or sect.	section		UHF	ultra-high frequency
			UN	United Nations
SEC	Securities and Exchange Commission		UPC	universal product code
			URL	uniform resource locator
ser.	series		U.S.	United States
sess.	session		USA	United States of America OR United States Army
shtg.	shortage			
sic	this is the source		USAF	United States Air Force
sig.	signature		USCG	United States Coast Guard
sing.	singular		USDA	United States Department of Agriculture
SO	shipping order			
soc.	society		USMC	United States Marine Corps
SOP	standard office operating procedure		USN	United States Navy
			USS	United States ship
spec.	special		VA	Veterans Administration
specs.	specifications		VAT	value-added tax
Sq.	Square		VCR	video cassette recorder
Sr.	Senior		vers.	version
SSN	social security number		VHF	very high frequency
St.	street OR Saint		VLF	very low frequency
std.	standard		VIP	very important person
Ste.	suite		vol.	volume
stmt.	statement		V.P.	vice president
supp.	supplement		vs.	versus
Supt.	superintendent		W.	west
SUV	sport utility vehicle		w/	with
SW	southwest		w.f.	wrong font
TB	tuberculosis		WHO	World Health Organization
t.b.a. or TBA	to be announced		whsle.	wholesale
			w/o	without OR week of
t.b.d. or TBD	to be determined		w.o.p.	without pay
TD	touchdown		wt.	weight
ter., Ter.	territory, Terrace		YOB	year of birth
TM	trademark		yr.	year
Tp.	township		Y-T-D	year-to-date
treas.	treasurer OR treasury		ZIP or zip	zone improvement plan (U.S. Postal Service)
TV	television			
u.c.	upper case			

Writer's Tips:
Abbreviations used as shorthand in e-mail are
covered in our section on E-mail, page 72.

ACADEMIC STYLE

In general, business documents are written in a more casual style than academic papers and scholarly publications.

Rules

Although this style guide is not intended as one to be used in the preparation of academic or scholarly writing, it is worth mentioning several important distinctions:

1. Academic writing is much more formal than business writing. For this reason it is also less easily and less quickly read by business readers.
2. Consult the two organizations that produce noted and recommended style guides for the scholarly writer: the American Psychological Association (APA) and the Modern Language Association (MLA).
3. When producing scholarly papers or other academic writing, consult an authority about which style is required—and then *follow it*.

Examples and Explanations

1. **Academic writing is much more formal than business writing. For this reason it is also less easily and less quickly read by business readers.**

   Imagine a scale of writing style:

Informal	Formal

   What is your guess about where academic writing would fall in this scale, in comparison to most business memos? Business e-mails? Here are some points of interest for you on this scale:

Informal					Formal
Ad copy	Memos	Reports	Proposals	Academic	Legal Papers
	Newspapers	E-mail	Letters		

   When academic writing is called for, it is essential that you use the scholarly style that is much more formal than the business writing style recommended in this book. Do not fall into the trap of "writing like you read" that many business writers find themselves in. Many of the books and textbooks that professionals in today's workplace remember from their college and high school years were written in an academic style. And why would that be? Well, of course, most of the professors who write those textbooks are living in an academic environment—the jargon of scholarly writing is their native language.

   But take a moment and think about some of the most instructive books you've ever read. Were they easy to read or difficult? Were the sentences short or long? Was the vocabulary easily understood, made up mostly of more commonly used words? Or was it a heavy vocabulary, a vocabulary you might not have been totally confident of understanding?

   The reason that the best business writing is less formal is because your reader can understand it more quickly and clearly that way. If you look at our scale, you will see that the least formal style of all is advertising copy. Of course! Because that writer cares deeply that you do pay attention—even if you have little initial interest. Newspapers are written in a simple, casual style because the editors know that you are probably too busy to read them carefully. The information must be presented quickly and clearly.

   Albert Joseph, the author of some of the best books and training programs ever written about business writing, refers to use of academic style in the business world as a case of The Emperor's New Clothes. Someone with power, high up in the organization, uses an academic style in his or her writing because it's what he or she learned by osmosis through reading textbooks in college. The managers and employees who report to this academic writer then also use it because "it's the way writing is done here." And so on down through the entire organization.

Certainly, academic writing has its place. Just don't confuse yourself about where that place is—in academia.

2. **Consult the two organizations that produce noted and recommended style guides for the scholarly writer: the American Psychological Association (APA) and the Modern Language Association (MLA).**

If you do need an academic writing resource, choose either:

MLA Style Manual and Guide to Scholarly Publishing, Third Edition, Modern Language Association of America, 2008, New York.

OR:

Publication Manual of the American Psychological Association, Sixth Edition, American Psychological Association, 2009, New York

The MLA is traditionally used in the arts and humanities while the APA is used in the sciences. But check with the person who will be reading your paper, or the person who assigned you to write it, to make sure which style you are expected to follow.

3. **When producing scholarly papers or other academic writing, consult an authority about which style is required—and then** *follow it.*

This rule really applies to all kinds of writing: find out what style the reader wants you to use and then use that style. We could call this the "When in Rome do as the Romans do" Rule.

It is always better to check than to assume and then be wrong.

Once you have discovered what style is wanted, familiarize yourself with the requirements of that style by scanning through the appropriate style guide and any other documentation. Then, keep that guide available over the course of your writing so you can refer to it as needed.

If you are borrowing the guide, keep good notes as to the bibliographic information about it so you can specifically tell anyone who asks you about the reference material you used.

ADJECTIVES

An *adjective* is a word that adds more information about a noun or a pronoun. Adjectives can tell *how many* (*five* books), *what kind* (*large green* apples) or *which one* (*the oldest* chart). Adjectives (and adverbs) are referred to as **modifiers**.

Adjectives most often precede nouns, but they can also follow verbs of feeling (*feel, look, sound, taste, smell*) or state of being verbs (also known as linking verbs: like *be, are, become, was* and *were*).

a difficult project	(word)
a project of great difficulty	(phrase)
a project that is difficult	(clause)

◀ *An adjective can be a single word, a phrase or a clause*

Rules

1. Keep your adjectives as close as possible to the words they are meant to modify.
2. Use the most descriptive and specific adjectives available.
3. Use adjectives instead of adverbs after verbs that convey state of being or feeling.
4. Use the comparative and superlative -er and -est endings only on words that are one or two syllables long. Use *more* and *most* (or *less* and *least*) with all longer words and in any case where adding the -er or -est makes the word sound awkward.
5. When using organization names as adjectives, choose between the possessive style and the descriptive style. (The descriptive style is when the company name—usually considered a proper noun—is used as an adjective instead.) Once you have made your choice, stick with it for, at the minimum, the document. Ideally, make the choice and stick with it as your style forever. Unless, of course, the rules change in the future.

Business Writing

Examples and Explanations

1. **Keep your adjectives as close as possible to the words they are meant to modify.**

> The reports written by Jack and Susan were turned in Thursday. It's hard to believe how tedious they are, isn't it?

So what (or who) are so tedious? It's hard to tell because that adjective (tedious) has been moved away from the noun it was meant to modify. And in the second sentence, the pronoun *they* takes the place of which thing? The reports? Or Jack and Susan?

This would be better:

> On Thursday, Jack and Susan turned in their tedious reports. It's hard to believe their information could be so dull, isn't it?

2. **Use the most descriptive and specific adjectives available.**

Many writers get addicted to the same small repertoire of overused modifiers. Words like *great*, *wonderful*, *nice* … Or at work, how about the word *urgent*? Have you ever thought about how vague it is? Use the most specific and descriptive adjectives you can so that your reader gets your message clearly. As a writer, you know what you are trying to say. But please remember that your reader does not yet know—but needs to. Which is more clear: a great report or a clear, well thought out report?

Which sentence will get the work done sooner? ▶ Please complete this urgent report as soon as possible.

OR

Please complete this report by this Friday, July 20, at 2:00 in the afternoon. The client will be in to pick it up on his way to the airport that afternoon.

Notice that in the second sentence, the adjective *urgent* was replaced with a specific date and time. Then, to make the message even more clear, the author added the reason that it needs to be complete by then.

3. **Use adjectives instead of adverbs after verbs that convey state of being or feeling.**

> I feel sad. (adjective)   **NOT**   I feel sadly. (adverb)
>
> He looked angry. (adjective)   **NOT**   He looked angrily. (adverb)
>
> I feel good. (adjective)—(This sentence means I am in a good mood.)
>
> I feel well. (As an adjective the word *well* refers to physical health. As an adverb it refers to the quality of your physical sense of touch—a person who feels well, when the word *well* is used as an adverb, has a heightened sense of touch.)

The most common error in this vein is with the words bad and badly.

If you are in a rotten mood, say ▶ I feel bad.

If you have a diminished sense of touch, say ▶ I feel badly.

4. **Use the comparative and superlative -er and -est endings only on words that are one or two syllables long. Use *more* and *most* (or *less* and *least*) with all longer words and in any case where adding the -er or -est makes the word sound awkward.**

> Ed is smarter than Bob.
> This month's newsletter is clearer than last month's.

▲

When comparing between two items, add an -er ending to any one or two syllable adjective

When comparing two items, add the word more or less in front of any adjective longer than two syllables, or any shorter adjective that sounds awkward with the -er ending

> Neil is more productive than Grace on the phones.
>
> But Grace is more careful with what she says.
>
> Charlotte is less poetic in her descriptions but more proper in her style than Lou.
>
> (Do you see that the words *carefuller* and *properer* just don't work?)

In business writing, your first consideration needs to be your reader's ease of reading. This is the best rule to follow, and much easier than memorizing long lists of words that require -er endings as opposed to those that take the words *more*, *most*, *less* or *least* in front of them.

When comparing more than two items, the superlative form (-est, most or least) is made in the same way as the comparative

> Ed is smarter than Bob, but Mike is the smartest of the group.
>
> Charlotte is the least poetic person I know.
>
> Neil is more productive than Grace, but Stella is the most productive representative we have.
>
> (Can you see that the words *productiver* and *productivest* just wouldn't work?)

Note: Never use both an -er or -est ending and the word *more* or *most* in front: that would be a double comparison.

> **Don't use:** More smarter
>
> Most fastest

And a few common comparisons are irregular in their form:

Irregular comparisons		
Good	Better	Best
Bad	Worse	Worst
Far	Farther	Farthest
Little	Less	Least
Many, much	More	Most

5. **When using organization names as adjectives, choose between the possessive style and the descriptive style. (The descriptive style is when the company name—usually considered a proper noun—is used as an adjective instead.) Once you have made your choice, stick with it for, at the minimum, the document. Ideally, make the choice and stick with it as your style forever. Unless, of course, the rules change in the future.**

Of course, this rule is about consistency of style. It makes no difference whether you say:

Possessive style		Descriptive style
SkillPath's catalog	**OR**	the SkillPath catalog
Sony's music library	**OR**	the Sony music library

Once you make your choice, stick with it.

ADVERBS

Adverbs are modifiers that tell more about verbs, adjectives and other adverbs. They answer questions like *how*, *where* and *when* in a sentence.

Rules

To use adverbs correctly, follow these rules:

1. Keep your adverbs as close as possible to the words they are meant to modify.
2. Use the most descriptive and specific adverbs available.
3. In business writing, it is okay to split infinitives in order to guarantee clarity.
4. In business writing, it is acceptable to begin sentences with adverbs like *hopefully*, *truthfully* and *honestly* to tell something about the mood of the writer—even if that adverb does not modify the verb in the sentence.
5. Many adverbs end with the letters -ly. But so do a few adjectives, so be careful.
6. Do not use an adverb if the meaning is already understood in the verb.

Examples and Explanations

1. Keep your adverbs as close as possible to the words they are meant to modify.

This rule also applies to adverbial phrases and clauses, as well as to all adjectives. It is a matter of readability and clarity. Your reader is forming an image in his or her mind while reading, and by placing your modifiers as close as possible to the words they modify, that reader has an easier time of making a correct and complete picture the first time.

Do you see how the first sentence is both clearer and easier to read? ▶

> She moved quickly through the aisles of the grocery store as she desperately searched for her lost son.
>
> She moved through the aisles of the grocery store as she searched for her lost son quickly and desperately.

If you are concerned because you have been told in the past to avoid splitting an infinitive form of a verb with an adverb, please take a look at Rule #3.

2. Use the most descriptive and specific adverbs available.

If you remember that your number one goal as a writer is clarity, this rule becomes easy to follow. As the writer, you know what you are trying to say. It is your job to convey that specific message as clearly and precisely as possible.

Judge for yourself:
Which sentence paints a clearer picture? ▶

> She answered my questions well.
>
> She answered my questions accurately.

3. In business writing, it is okay to split infinitives in order to guarantee clarity.

You may remember an old rule from your elementary or middle school years regarding split infinitives: Don't split them. And if you are like most adults, even if you remember hearing that you shouldn't split them, you aren't really very clear about what one is to begin with.

Well, infinitive forms of verbs are the root forms of those verbs. In English, that always means the same thing.

An infinitive form of a verb is made by putting the word to in front of the verb. Some examples of infinitives: ▶

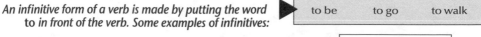

> to be   to go   to walk

The old advice dictated that you could not put an adverb in between the to and the verb ▶

> to *really* be
> to *boldly* go
> to *quickly* walk

This old rule is no longer valid. As a matter of fact, the best rule to follow now is Rule #1 in this section: Always keep your adverbs as close as possible to the words they modify.

And, sometimes, it's even an issue of sending the correct message as opposed to an incorrect one.

> She showed me how to *quickly* spot my errors.

In that sentence, the word *quickly* is splitting the infinite *to spot*. But if you move the word *quickly* somewhere else, you will damage the meaning of the sentence. If you move the word *quickly* to the beginning of the sentence, you change the meaning of the sentence.

Now, it is the showing that happens quickly, not the spotting ▶ She *quickly* showed me how to spot my errors.

And if you move it to the end of the sentence, you leave it up to the reader's imagination which word is being modified.

Some readers will think it is the showing, others will think it is the spotting ▶ She showed me how to spot my errors *quickly.*

Keep your writing simple: Split an occasional infinitive if it makes your writing clear and accurate.

Sometimes, though, splitting an infinitive just sounds awkward. Let your ear be your guide.

> Awkward: He wanted to deeply sleep because he was tired.
>
> Better: He wanted to sleep deeply because he was tired.

4. **In business writing, it is acceptable to begin sentences with adverbs like *hopefully*, *truthfully* and *honestly* to tell something about the mood of the writer—even if that adverb does not modify the verb in the sentence.**

Another rule that has fallen by the wayside is one that governs the use of certain adverbs at the beginning of your sentences. The old rule was that you couldn't use words like *hopefully* or *honestly* followed by a comma at the beginning of a sentence to convey a mood of the writer.

> *Honestly,* I have attended better meetings.
> *Hopefully,* Joe will speak next.
> *Truthfully,* Mark walked home from school—he didn't take the bus.

In each of these sentences, the word that begins that sentence is meant to tell about the writer's intent; it is not meant to describe more about the verb.

Traditionally, the function of an adverb in a sentence is to modify verbs, adjectives or other adverbs. In our more current usage, these introductory adverbs are permissible because your reader can easily understand your meaning.

5. **Many adverbs end with the letters -ly. But so do a few adjectives, so be careful.**

Many of us have been taught an easy way to find adverbs: They tend to end in -ly. And it is true—many adverbs do end in -ly. There are some that don't, though. And even more troublesome, there are some adjectives that do. Remember—the difference between adjectives and adverbs is that adjectives only modify nouns. Adverbs modify verbs, adjectives and other adverbs.

Adjectives like *friendly*, *costly* and *lonely* modify nouns:

> the friendly neighbor
> costly inventory
> lonely heart

Words like slow, fast, hard, soft, long and short can be used as adverbs without adding an -ly ending

▼

> They walk slow.

6. Do not use an adverb if the meaning is already understood in the verb.

In other words, avoid redundancy ▶
A family can gather—it doesn't need to gather together.
The team unites—it doesn't need to unite together.
The teacher can repeat her answer—but not repeat again her answer.

AGREEMENT

Subjects and verbs in your sentences must agree with each other in order for your writing to be understandable and coherent. The same is true of your pronouns and their antecedents (the words the pronouns are replacing).

Rules

1. In every sentence, use a verb that agrees with its subject in both person and number.
2. Most nouns are made plural by adding an -s or an -es to the ending of the noun. But verbs with an -s or -es ending are indicative of the third person singular (he, she or it).
3. Use plural verbs with a compound subject. But use a singular verb when the words *each*, *every*, *many a* or *many an* are a part of the subject or precede the subject, or when singular words that are compound subjects are joined by *or*, *either … or*, *neither … nor* or *not only … but also*.
4. If a compound subject consists of two or more plural words joined together with any words (whether connective words like *and* or separating words like *either … or*), use a plural verb. Also, if a compound subject contains both singular and plural words, put the plural word closer to the verb and then use a plural verb to match it.
5. When establishing agreement between subject and verb, ignore any phrases or clauses that have come between them.
6. The indefinite pronouns *each*, *every*, *either*, *neither*, *one*, *another* and *much* are always singular. The same is true for the compound pronouns *anybody*, *anyone*, *anything*, *everybody*, *everyone*, *everything*, *somebody*, *someone*, *something*, *nobody*, *nothing* and *no one*.
7. The indefinite pronouns *both*, *few*, *many*, *others* and *several* are always plural.
8. Collective nouns always take singular verbs.
9. Make a choice about whether you are going to use singular or plural verbs with organization names and then be consistent.
10. Make sure pronouns are the same in number, in gender and in person as the nouns they are replacing (their antecedents).
11. Use Rules #3 – 6, above, to determine whether you need a singular or plural pronoun in the case of compound antecedents.
12. Even when you are concerned about remaining nonsexist, make sure your pronouns and antecedents agree in number.

Examples and Explanations

1. **In every sentence, use a verb that agrees with its subject in both person and number.**

   Person refers to who the subject is: I? You? He? We? They? *Number* refers to whether the subject is singular or plural. It or they? I or we?

The new marker (it) writes (third person singular verb form) more clearly than the old one.
The new markers (they) write (plural verb form) more clearly than the old ones.
I appreciate (first person singular) your effort.
He appreciates (third person singular) your effort.

2. **Most nouns are made plural by adding an -s or an -es to the ending of the noun. But verbs with an -s or -es ending are indicative of the third person singular (he, she or it).**

   Here is the normal conjugation of a regular verb in English ▶
I run	We run
You run	You run
He, she, it or the dog runs	They or the dogs run

3. Use plural verbs with a compound subject. But use a singular verb when the words *each*, *every*, *many a* or *many an* are a part of the subject or precede the subject, or when singular words that are compound subjects are joined by *or, either … or, neither … nor* or *not only … but also.*

> Darla and Francisco work (plural verb) well together.
> Neither Darla nor Francisco works (singular verb) well alone.
> The catalogs and brochures cost (plural verb) 45 cents apiece.
> Each of the catalogs and brochures costs (singular verb) 45 cents.

4. If a compound subject consists of two or more plural words joined together with any words (whether connective words like *and* or separating words like *either … or*), use a plural verb. Also, if a compound subject contains both singular and plural words, put the plural word closer to the verb and then use a plural verb to match it.

> Our accountants and our customer service representatives are unhappy with the new benefit package.
> Neither our accountants nor our customer service representatives are happy with the new benefit package.
> Either the coffee or the donuts are going to keep our meeting participants awake.

5. When establishing agreement between subject and verb, ignore any phrases or clauses that have come between them.

> *Maria*, one of our most dedicated employees, is being promoted Friday.
> **NOT**: Maria, one of our most dedicated *employees*, are being promoted Friday.

6. The indefinite pronouns *each, every, either, neither, one, another* and *much* are always singular. The same is true for the compound pronouns *anybody, anyone, anything, everybody, everyone, everything, somebody, someone, something, nobody, nothing* and *no one.*

> Every dog has his day. (**NOT**: Every dog have his day.)
> One must go to the store Tuesday. (**NOT**: One must goes to the store Tuesday.)
> Everyone is thrilled with your results. (**NOT**: Everyone are thrilled …)

7. The indefinite pronouns *both, few, many, others* and *several* are always plural.

> Both managers agree.
> Others have gone before you.

8. Collective nouns always take singular verbs.

Collective nouns are singular in form but represent more than one member of the group. Examples are: group, team, majority and family.

> The group of union workers was unhappy with the results of our negotiation.
> Our family is pleased with our new house.

9. **Make a choice about whether you are going to use singular or plural verbs with organization names and then be consistent.**

Organization names may be treated as either singular or plural. Generally, we recommend using singular verbs with organization names unless the singular verb seems awkward, or you want to stress the individuals listed in the name. Either way, once you choose, be consistent.

> Ford Motor Company is introducing a new SUV.
>
> Boeing Aerospace competes well with Lockheed Martin.
>
> **OR**: Smith & Wesson has been manufacturing firearms for over a century.

10. **Make sure pronouns are the same in number, in gender and in person as the nouns they are replacing (their antecedents).**

> Jacob needs to know if you have approved his request for time off.
>
> The Sales Department and the Engineering Department agree that their time is too valuable for an excess of meetings.
>
> The committee has made its recommendation.

11. **Use Rules #3 – 6, above, to determine whether you need a singular or plural pronoun in the case of compound antecedents.**

> Neither Janet nor Sara will give up her office. (**NOT**: "their office." Only one has to give up an office.)
>
> Both Evan and George will move out of their offices this week. (**NOT**: "his office." Both are moving.)

12. **Even when you are concerned about remaining nonsexist, make sure your pronouns and antecedents agree in number.**

Everyone knows sexist writing is incorrect. But with third person singular pronouns it is sometimes difficult to avoid.

Here is a sexist sentence ▶ | Each worker needs to understand his job.

And here are ways to make it nonsexist ▶ | Each worker needs to understand his or her job.
Each worker needs to understand his/her job.

We would tell you that the use of a slash is not conversational, and therefore something you want to avoid. Think about it—do you speak in slashes? Can you imagine yourself saying: "Each worker needs to understand his slash her job?" So that one is definitely out.

As for the first alternative, with the word *or* in place of the slash—well, it's better, and more conversational. But is it your best option? We don't think so. Why not switch both the antecedent (each worker) and the pronoun to the plural? This will also mean switching the verb and the object to the plural.

We see this as the best option because it is the least obtrusive change ▶ | All workers need to understand their jobs.

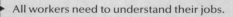

> *Writer's Tips:*
> *For more information on Nonsexist Language, see page 119.*

Your reader won't even notice it, while a reader could notice a constant stream of *he or she, him or her* phrases.

APPENDIXES

Appendixes (*appendices* is another correct spelling) are additions and supplements provided at the end of a main document. When writing to today's busy reader, it is a good idea to add detailed information that the reader may or may not be interested in seeing in an appendix rather than as a part of the document itself. This gives your reader the option of reading the details without the drawback of having to wade through them to read the rest of your main document.

Rules

1. Use appendixes to add any information that amplifies or supports your main document, but that your reader may or may not be interested in reading. Do not use appendixes for information that is crucial to the main document.

2. When adding an appendix, make sure to refer to it by both Appendix Number (or Letter) and Title in the body of the main document.

3. Number and title your appendixes clearly and logically.

Examples and Explanations

1. **Use appendixes to add any information that amplifies or supports your main document, but that your reader may or may not be interested in reading. Do not use appendixes for information that is crucial to the main document.**

   Appendixes are for extra information. All information needed to clearly understand the main document must be included in that main document. Information that amplifies or backs up or further illustrates the points in your main document can be put in appendixes.

   When you put extra information in appendixes, rather than in the main document, your readers will appreciate your thoughtfulness. Not only have you been thoughtful in keeping the main reading simple and unburdened, but you have also been thoughtful to those readers who are interested in studying the details.

   Do not use appendixes for the sole purpose of providing a larger document. Include only relevant information, charts, tables, photographs, case studies and the like.

2. **When adding an appendix, make sure to refer to it by both Appendix Number (or Letter) and Title in the body of the main document.**

   Every appendix found at the end of your document must have been referred to in the body of the document itself. For example:

   > See Appendix A (Contraindications of Bactofel Use Among T8 and Lower SCI Patients) for details of Dr. Anderson's recent research concerning the popular antispasmodic drug.

3. **Number and title your appendixes clearly and logically.**

   Choose letters (A, B, C) or numbers (1, 2, 3) or Roman numerals (I, II, III) and then be consistent within that document and all related documents.

   Give every appendix a title. When choosing a title for an appendix, keep it clear, short and specific. Capitalize the first word, the last word and all the important words in the middle of the title.

ARTICLES

The articles *a*, *an* and *the* are staples of the English language. And for most native speakers they present very few problems. For some non-native English speakers, though—especially native speakers of languages that have no articles—they can cause huge problems.

The words *a* and *an* are called indefinite articles because they do not fix the identity of the noun modified. The word *the* is the definite article because it points to something or someone specific.

Rules

1. Use the indefinite article *a* or *an* before singular nouns that represent items that can be counted.

2. Use the indefinite article *a* before nouns (or adjectives preceding nouns) that begin with the sound of a consonant. Use the indefinite article *an* before nouns (or adjectives preceding nouns) that begin with the sound of a vowel.

3. Use the definite article *the* before singular and plural countable nouns that you are pointing out to a reader. Also, use the definite article *the* in front of mass (uncountable) nouns.

4. Some common nouns and most proper nouns need no articles at all.

Examples and Explanations

1. Use the indefinite article *a* or *an* before singular nouns that represent items that can be counted.

a basket of flowers	a memo
an unhappy camper	an e-mail

2. Use the indefinite article *a* before nouns (or adjectives preceding nouns) that begin with the sound of a consonant. Use the indefinite article *an* before nouns (or adjectives preceding nouns) that begin with the sound of a vowel.

This rule also applies to acronyms and initials—use the article that makes sense in terms of how you pronounce the acronym or initials

a lasting impression	an old house
an impression	an IBM employee
a house	an FTC employee
an honest person	a CDOT employee

3. Use the definite article *the* before singular and plural countable nouns that you are pointing out to a reader. Also, use the definite article *the* in front of mass (uncountable) nouns.

the sales clerk who helped me (pointing out a single sales clerk)

the sales clerks (plural countable)

the water in an ocean (mass noun—water is uncountable)

the sand on Arroyo Beach (mass noun—sand is countable, technically— but who would want to?)

4. Some common nouns and most proper nouns need no articles at all.

Unfortunately, in the case of common nouns, most of the exceptions are idiomatic. That means that there are no specific rules to help a non-native English speaking writer figure out which words require an article and which words don't. Non-native English speakers are well served in having a reference guide especially for their needs.

Have you had dinner?
(**NOT**: Have you had a dinner?)

Hardly any proper nouns use articles—but again, the ones that do are determined mostly by idiom.

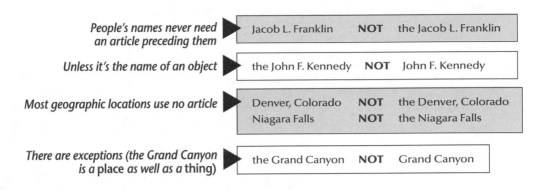

People's names never need an article preceding them	Jacob L. Franklin	**NOT**	the Jacob L. Franklin
Unless it's the name of an object	the John F. Kennedy	**NOT**	John F. Kennedy
Most geographic locations use no article	Denver, Colorado	**NOT**	the Denver, Colorado
	Niagara Falls	**NOT**	the Niagara Falls
There are exceptions (the Grand Canyon is a place as well as a thing)	the Grand Canyon	**NOT**	Grand Canyon

BAD NEWS

When it is necessary for you to deliver bad news in a letter, memo or e-mail, some of the general rules discussed elsewhere in this style guide must be modified.

While it is always a good idea in business writing to get to the point very quickly, in bad news letters we recommend that you write your first paragraph a little more gently. For example, can you find something positive to say or can you offer an alternative that might make the bad news more palatable?

Rules

Here are some guidelines:

1. When writing bad news, always use a courteous and positive tone.
2. Be tactful.
3. Avoid using the word *you* in a way that may be interpreted by your reader as aggressive.
4. Empathize with the reader.
5. Give reasons and suggest potential solutions, if possible.

Examples and Explanations

1. **When writing bad news, always use a courteous and positive tone.**

   Of course, this is no different from the advice you would follow for any document you write in the world of work. Always be polite, always be positive. Take a hint from child psychologists. They have suggested for many years that if parents want their children to stop slamming doors in the house and to be more quiet while the baby is asleep, the best way to ask is in the positive:

   > Jonathan, please be as quiet as you can while you close the door.
   > **AS OPPOSED TO**
   > Jonathan, don't slam the door.

   The same holds true for adults at work. All people respond better to positive, clear directions to *do* something, as opposed to negative, clear directions to *not* do something.

   > Lee, we expect our customer service reps to answer at least ten incoming calls per hour.
   > **AS OPPOSED TO**
   > Lee, you have to stop making so many personal calls and do your job instead.

   Some learning experts even claim that the human brain cancels out the negative words as it processes information. So instead of hearing:

   > Jonathan, don't slam the door.

   Jonathan would actually be hearing:

   > Jonathan, slam the door.

   (And if you have ever been a parent, you will agree that your experience offers ample proof of this theory.)

If you do this, you will gain a reputation as a person who cares about other people's feelings and about delivering the most accurate and clear message in the most positive and courteous way. A reputation you will be glad to have.

2. Be tactful.

Sometimes bad news is—well, bad. And it may seem like there is no tactful way to present it. But just imagine yourself needing to tell this bad news to your own grandmother, or to a small child. This usually helps even a jaded writer come up with something sensitive and displaying good judgment.

Which would you rather hear?

> The report you just turned in is the worst piece of writing I've seen in a decade!
>
> **OR**
>
> You must have been very busy this past week while you were writing this report. Your work is usually so much clearer and more powerful. I think you'll see that we need to make some changes. Is there anything I can do to help?

You may see that tact usually takes more words. Yes, it does. And sometimes when you are very angry or frustrated, it can feel very good—cathartic even—to write something tactlessly. But even if it is a release for you to write it, please be careful never to send something you have written in anger or frustration until you have calmed down and looked it over again.

It is always better to err on the side of tact. *Remember*, it is your reputation that is at stake.

Of course, just using Rule #3 below is going to help you and your reputation as a sensitive and clear writer blossom.

3. Avoid using the word *you* in a way that may be interpreted by your reader as aggressive.

Have you heard what happens when you point your finger at someone else? Three more fingers are pointing back at you.

And even if the other person is to blame for a problem or a difficulty, how will it help you to get that problem solved or the difficulty smoothed out by blaming someone else?

Focus on the solution, focus on what people can and have done right, not on what they have done wrong. This will help you develop positive relationships—and in those positive relationships you will have the power of influence.

This is the most positive use of the passive voice. Use it to spare people blame, shame and humiliation.

> **Instead of**:
> You made a mistake in this report.
>
> **How about**:
> A mistake was made in the report.

Writer's Tips:
For more information, see
Assertiveness in our Career
Success section, page 311.

When you spare people's feelings, they remember you warmly. And when your readers remember you warmly, you can count on their reading your next document. That's a valuable guarantee, isn't it?

4. Empathize with the reader.

Before writing any document containing bad news, put yourself in your reader's shoes for a few moments. How will it feel to receive this news? What kind of disappointment or anger might be felt? How would it be easier to hear this bad news; how would it be easier to read?

Work hard to start any document that contains bad news for your reader with a statement of empathy, support or appreciation.

Compare these two examples:

> Dear Stan,
>
> We have decided to move John Anderson into the open management position instead of you. While your tenure is longer, his future appears brighter.
>
> Thanks for your application, though.
>
> Sincerely,
>
> **WITH**
>
> Dear Stan,
>
> The choice the management selection committee had to make last week was the most difficult we remember in years. Mostly, that is because of your incredible qualifications and commitment to this organization's success over the years. We wish we had two management positions open instead of just one.
>
> We have decided to move John Anderson into this open spot. His proposal concerning future import/export strategies was something we couldn't ignore.
>
> We do hope that another position comes open soon, and that you will apply for it. Thank you for your dedication and your strong work ethic over the years.
>
> Sincerely,

It is true that the minute Stan reads the first sentence of this second, gentler letter he is probably pretty sure he is not the one who has gotten the promotion. But do you think he will be encouraged to apply again? More so than if he had received the more direct but less gentle first version?

5. **Give reasons and suggest potential solutions, if possible.**

If there are reasons that you can explain to your reader about why the news you are presenting needs to be bad, or if there are solutions or remedies the reader could use to change the bad, it is wise to present them.

It may be true that your reader does not agree with your reasoning or your suggestions, but at least you have offered them.

How much better would it be to offer Stan a solution to become more marketable the next time he applies? Compare the difference between even our very positive letter to Stan from Rule #4 (see above), and this letter:

> Dear Stan,
>
> The choice the management selection committee had to make last week was the most difficult we remember in years. Mostly, that is because of your incredible qualifications and commitment to this organization's success over the years. We wish we had two management positions open instead of just one.
>
> We have decided to move John Anderson into this open spot. His proposal concerning future import/export strategies was something we couldn't ignore. We encourage you to prepare a written proposal about an area you would like to explore and focus on once you move into management. This would certainly help you win the wholehearted recommendation of our entire committee for any management position that you'd be interested in moving into.
>
> We do hope that another position comes open soon, and that you will apply for it. Thank you for your dedication and your strong work ethic over the years.
>
> Sincerely,

You may be concerned that Stan will not see any of these letters as positive. You may be concerned that no matter what you say, he will feel bad that he lost out on a promotion to someone who hasn't even been around as long as he has. And it may be true. But that should not be your main concern as the author of the letter. Your main concern is to communicate clearly, kindly and as specifically as possible so that should Stan assume responsibility for doing better next time, he has the tools to do it.

BIBLIOGRAPHIES

In business writing, bibliographies are sometimes provided with reports and proposals, and less often with letters, memos and e-mail messages.

A bibliography provides your reader with a complete list of all reference materials used in the compilation of your document, along with all the information your reader would need to be able to access that original resource himself or herself. In some cases a bibliography could also list further reading that, while not used by the document's author, would still be interesting to the reader.

The advice presented in this section is geared to writers of business documents. Should you have the need to prepare a bibliography for an academic document or a document that has its own special needs, please consult a style guide appropriate to those special needs. These guidelines, however, will guarantee you a professional and credible looking bibliography for the world of work.

Rules

1. Choose a format for the main report, proposal, memo or letter and then use a matching format for the bibliography. If for some reason you are preparing a bibliography that is meant to be independent of any other document, choose a format for it that is appealing to the eye and logical in its presentation.

2. List all items in a bibliography alphabetically by the author's last name. If the entry has no author, list it alphabetically by title.

3. Invert the first name and last name of the author when presenting it in a bibliography so that the alphabetization you have done is more apparent.

4. Do not include page numbers in a bibliography unless the element you are citing is part of a larger work.

5. Record the correct information, in the correct order, for each type of media you have referenced.

Examples and Explanations

1. **Choose a format for the main report, proposal, memo or letter and then use a matching format for the bibliography. If for some reason you are preparing a bibliography that is meant to be independent of any other document, choose a format for it that is appealing to the eye and logical in its presentation.**

   The bibliography is usually the last section of a letter, memo, report or proposal. When the document that precedes it has been created in a certain style, it just makes sense that the bibliography appear in that same style.

   Your reader needs you to present your ideas as logically, as beautifully and as clearly as possible. And part of beauty to most readers is consistency.

2. **List all items in a bibliography alphabetically by the author's last name. If the entry has no author, list it alphabetically by title.**

   And if the title begins with the word *The* or *A*, ignore it and alphabetize based on the next word of the title. When the bibliography contains more than one work by the same author, replace the author's name with a long dash (six hyphens) in all the entries after the first. List that author's works alphabetically by title.

3. **Invert the first name and last name of the author when presenting it in a bibliography so that the alphabetization you have done is more apparent.**

   If a reference in your bibliography has more than one author, invert only the first one listed.

   > Poley, Michelle and Dusty Crocker

4. **Do not include page numbers in a bibliography unless the element you are citing is part of a larger work.**

   > Marshall, Louis, "Grammar Happiness," *Reader's Digest*, May 2000, pp. 145 – 152.

5. Record the correct information, in the correct order, for each type of media you have referenced.

Here's a chart to make it easy ▼

Books:

> Author(s), *Full Title, Volume Number, Edition Number*, Publisher, City of Publication, Date of Publication.
>
> Example: Forlini, Gary, *Grammar and Composition*, Prentice Hall, Englewood Cliffs, NJ, 1990.

Journal and Magazine Articles:

> Author(s), "Title of the Article," *Journal or Magazine Name*, Volume Number, Month or Quarter of Publication, Year of Publication, Page Numbers.
>
> Example: Goodhope, Stanley and Brigitte Houseman, "Where Have All the Teachers Gone?" *Education Review*, Volume 3, March 1998, pp. 101-123.

Electronic Media:

> Author, Title, Name of Publication or Web Page, Date of Publication, Web Address for Retrieval
>
> Example: Zinn, Howard, "The Rocker and the Teacher," Interview, March 1999, http://www.findarticles.com.

CDs, Videos, DVDs and CD-ROMs:

> Author, "Article Title," *Title of Work* (Type of Media), Publisher, Place of Publication, Year, Location of Quotation.
>
> Example: Abiera, Chris, *Assertive Communication Skills for Women* (Video), SkillPath Publications, Mission, KS, 1994, Tape 2.

There are many kinds of works you may find yourself quoting from or using as reference. When in doubt about what information to include in a bibliographic reference, keep it simple by asking yourself what information your reader would find useful in retrieving an original copy of that reference himself or herself.

BOLDFACE

Boldface is one of the best ways to highlight information in your printed documents.

Rules

There are two simple rules that will help you:

1. Boldface is the best way to highlight any material in a printed document that spreads past one printed line.

2. Do not use boldface in your e-mail unless you are certain that it will appear as boldface once the reader receives it.

Examples and Explanations

1. **Boldface is the best way to highlight any material in a printed document that spreads past one printed line.**

   Of underlining, italics, boldface and the use of all caps, boldface is the easiest to read of all the formatting changes that writers commonly use to emphasize their ideas.

   While any of these four methods can be useful for single words or very short phrases, once you ask your reader to sustain the reading process past a printed line, the other three have a tendency to be self-defeating.

   Both ALL CAPS and underlining are very difficult to read for sustained reading. This is a matter of how your brain works, and how you learned to read. When we learned to read as children, most of us learned by reading mostly lowercase letters. When you are faced with a whole paragraph of ALL CAPS today, it is like you are reading it in a foreign language. Because you didn't originally learn reading in ALL CAPS, your brain attempts to translate those capital letters into small letters while it is reading. This adds to your reader's workload and you run the risk of wearing out that reader.

Underlining is much the same way. Once the underlined passage stretches beyond one line, your brain becomes overwhelmed and attempts to filter out the underline so it can recognize the letters and words more readily. (Remember, when you learned how to read you most likely did not learn with underlines either.)

Words referred to as words are usually in italics. Letters referred to as letters are usually in italics as well.

> If I hear the word *yikes* one more time, I may scream.
>
> This time, I made sure every *i* was dotted and every *t* was crossed.

But boldface accomplishes all of your goals. The letters appear darker, so your reader emphasizes them in his or her mind without thinking. And, merely darkening the letters does not fundamentally change them, so your mind recognizes them much more quickly than it recognizes ALL CAPS, <u>underlines</u> or *italics*.

See for yourself. Compare the ease of reading of these four identical (at least content-wise) paragraphs:

> BUT BOLDFACE ACCOMPLISHES ALL OF YOUR GOALS. THE LETTERS APPEAR DARKER, SO YOUR READER EMPHASIZES THEM IN HIS OR HER MIND WITHOUT THINKING. AND, MERELY DARKENING THE LETTERS DOES NOT FUNDAMENTALLY CHANGE THEM, SO YOUR MIND RECOGNIZES THEM MUCH MORE QUICKLY THAN IT RECOGNIZES ALL CAPS, <u>UNDERLINES</u> OR *ITALICS*.
>
> <u>But boldface accomplishes all of your goals. The letters appear darker, so your reader emphasizes them in his or her mind without thinking. And, merely darkening the letters does not fundamentally change them, so your mind recognizes them much more quickly than it recognizes ALL CAPS, underlines or *italics*.</u>
>
> *But boldface accomplishes all of your goals. The letters appear darker, so your reader emphasizes them in his or her mind without thinking. And, merely darkening the letters does not fundamentally change them, so your mind recognizes them much more quickly than it recognizes ALL CAPS, <u>underlines</u> or italics.*
>
> **But boldface accomplishes all of your goals. The letters appear darker, so your reader emphasizes them in his or her mind without thinking. And, merely darkening the letters does not fundamentally change them, so your mind recognizes them much more quickly than it recognizes ALL CAPS, <u>underlines</u> or *italics*.**

2. **Do not use boldface in your e-mail unless you are certain that it will appear as boldface once the reader receives it.**

If you share e-mail servers with your reader, this is not a concern. But did you know that what one server recognizes as special formatting might not make it into the message as it appears on another e-mail server?

As an example, if both you and your reader are using AOL®, you can rest assured that if you boldface or underline or even color-code your message, your reader will see all of those formatting changes. But if you write that same e-mail in your AOL® program, then send it to someone not using AOL®, those formatting options may disappear. They could just show up as plain old typing.

The only formatting change that does translate from one e-mail program to another—guaranteed—is the use of ALL CAPS. But never send an entire e-mail message in ALL CAPS: that is interpreted by your reader as shouting. ALL CAPS work best for single words and for short phrases.

BUSINESS STYLE

Business style, as it applies to writing, refers to a clear, readable and conversational style. Business style takes your readers' needs into consideration. Especially, your readers' needs to get the point quickly, clearly and correctly.

Rules

Academic and formal styles have more rules governing them, and while they may sometimes be required, they are certainly less easy to read and understand, especially by busy readers.

1. Use a conversational tone in every business document you write so your reader more readily grasps and understands your message.
2. Follow conventional style rules and formatting strategies so that your reader quickly recognizes you as credible.
3. Proofread and edit every document for accuracy and clarity.

Examples and Explanations

1. **Use a conversational tone in every business document you write so your reader more readily grasps and understands your message.**

   When you use the kind of language in your writing that you would use in your conversation with your reader, you are using your easiest and clearest vocabulary. And generally, words that you easily understand will be more easily understood by your reader—at least more easily understood than words that you save for only writing.

   Which do you prefer? ▶ Pursuant to our recent telephone conversation, the utilization of the facility in question shall commence on the primary day of the calendar year.

   OR

   The building we spoke about today will open on January 1.

2. **Follow conventional style rules and formatting strategies so that your reader quickly recognizes you as credible.**

   Have you ever received a letter that began with a strange salutation (Greetings Earthlings!) or one that was formatted in a strange way—perhaps the paragraphs all appeared in the shape of holiday ornaments?

   Busy readers in the world of work do not react well to these kind of departures from convention. While in a holiday letter, ornament-shaped paragraphs could be cute, most would agree that in the business world they go beyond the pale.

   Make sure that you have used styles and formats that your reader has seen before. And make certain that you have been correct in your usage, as well.

   This style guide will be a helpful reference for you in accomplishing all these goals.

   Writer's Tips: This is an issue of readability, and you can find more information about it on page 7.

3. **Proofread and edit every document for accuracy and clarity.**

   Your reader is counting on you to make your point clearly and accurately. And you have only one chance to impress this reader with your credibility, authority and knowledge. Don't allow an error to get past you because that error could damage your reputation as a writer for a long, long time.

   At least, use your word processor's spell-checker. At best, offer your document to another person to proofread. Readers not as familiar with your intended message make excellent proofreaders and editors because they naturally have difficulty with the very same things in your writing that your reader would.

   Writer's Tips: Look up any questions you have by topic and check our formatting guides in our Model Documents section (beginning on page 208) to help you with conventional formatting techniques.

BUSINESS WRITING CLICHÉS

Business writing clichés are the tired and usually meaningless expressions that you and every other reader in the world of work have seen hundreds, if not thousands, of times.

Does this look familiar?

> Dear Sir/Madam,
> Enclosed please find as per our conversation the reference material previously mentioned.
> Please let me know as soon as possible if this information is as you expected.
> If you have any questions, please do not hesitate to contact us.
> Sincerely,

YAWN!

None of the phrases or sentences in that letter convey meaningful pictures, images, ideas or feelings to the reader—do they?

But the purpose of communicating is to do just that—to convey images, pictures, ideas and feelings clearly to a reader or a listener. Think of a favorite author. When you read that author, have you ever noticed that you forget that you are reading? Have you ever noticed that you are seeing the images that author is describing, not the words on the page?

Wouldn't it be great if that's what happened when your readers read your writing?

Business writing clichés bore your reader. When your reader becomes bored it is not likely that he or she will finish reading your letter, memo, report, proposal or e-mail. This is not good.

Think of clichés like you think of snow on your television screen. Have you ever been watching a favorite show when the picture turned into snow? How long will you sit and watch that snow waiting patiently for your cable company or satellite television company to get on the ball and fix it for you? Not long, right?

Your reader is the same way with cliché-laden writing. They don't stay tuned in.

Rule

There is really only one rule about business writing clichés:

Avoid using business writing clichés.

Example and Explanation

Very few people actually speak in clichés, so this is good advice. And it is the fastest way to become more conversational in your writing. To replace them, ask yourself, "How would I say this if I were speaking to my reader over lunch?"

Think about it: If you were meeting a reader over lunch to present him or her with your company's new brochure, how would you say:

> Enclosed please find the brochure you requested.

Wouldn't it come out more like:

> Here's the brochure you requested. Thanks for being so interested in our new product line.

Be especially careful about phrases that add no meaning to your sentences

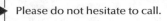

> Please do not hesitate to call.

There's nothing wrong with the more direct and simple:

> Please call me.

CAPITAL LETTERS

Capitalizing the first letter of a word gives that word special distinction and ensures that the reader will pay special attention to it. Capitalizing ALL the letters of a word is a fine way to highlight extremely short phrases, but is not recommended for sustained reading. (See pages 75 – 78 on Emphasis)

But be prepared: American grammar guides have disagreed among themselves for decades about what to capitalize and what not to capitalize. The rules given here will guarantee that your writing is quickly readable and very clear, but not overburdened with too many bizarre rules. Remember: Consistency and readability should be your watchwords, whatever choices you make about capitalization.

Rules

1. Capitalize the first letter of the first word of every sentence and every expression used as a sentence. Also, capitalize the first letter of the first word of any quotation that is itself a complete sentence.

2. Capitalize the first letter of the first word of each item in a bulleted list.

3. Capitalize the first letter of the first word of all salutations and complimentary closings in your letters.

4. Capitalize the first letter of every proper noun and every adjective made from a proper noun. Proper nouns are the specific names of people, places and things. The pronoun *I* is always capitalized.

5. Do not capitalize the first letter of common nouns. Common nouns are non-specific, more general ways of clarifying things.

6. Some common nouns, normally not capitalized, are capitalized when they are used as titles or as parts of a proper name.

7. Capitalize all titles of respect when they precede names.

8. Capitalize all job titles when they refer to specific individuals. And for a simple reason: You will never offend someone by capitalizing his or her title; you might offend him or her if you don't.

9. Capitalize all formal names of companies, organizations and government agencies the way they themselves capitalize them on their official letterhead or Web site.

10. Capitalize the names of departments in an organization when referring to a specific unit.

11. Capitalize all references to religion, deities and religious scriptures.

12. Capitalize the first word and all the important words in the titles of books, periodicals, reports, proposals, poems, stories, plays, paintings, songs, movies and other works of art or research.

13. Never send an e-mail message (or any written document) typed in ALL CAPS (all capital letters).

Examples and Explanations

1. **Capitalize the first letter of the first word of every sentence and every expression used as a sentence. Also, capitalize the first letter of the first word of any quotation that is itself a complete sentence.**

   > Write an e-mail about your meeting with John.
   > Would you please write an e-mail about your meeting with John?
   > Yes.
   > With a few conditions.
   > Mary said, "She amazed me with her aptitude for swimming."

2. **Capitalize the first letter of the first word of each item in a bulleted list.**

   There are five punctuation marks most adults are confused by:

   - Commas
   - Semicolons
   - Colons
   - Apostrophes
   - Quotation marks

Business Writing

46

3. Capitalize the first letter of the first word of salutations and complimentary closings in your letters.

Dear Max,	To all employees:
Yours truly,	Best regards,

4. Capitalize the first letter of every proper noun and every adjective made from a proper noun. Proper nouns are the specific names of people, places and things. The pronoun *I* is always capitalized.

Cleveland, Ohio	a Clevelander
Apple® computer	Wall Street
the Colorado Avalanche	The Producers
an Academy Award	Air Force One
Led Zeppelin	Burger King®
Sesame Street	the Stanley Cup
Bosnia	Bosnian
Emily Dickinson	Dickinsonian

Sometimes only one word of a proper noun is actually a specific name of a person, place or thing.

Irish wolfhound puppy	a Nobel-winning physicist
British currency	Microsoft® programs

5. Do not capitalize the first letter of common nouns. Common nouns are non-specific, more general ways of clarifying things.

city	person
computer company	financial hub
hockey team	award-winning musical
prestigious award	airplane
classic rock band	fast-food restaurant
popular children's program	sports trophy
country	native of a country
poet	like a poet

6. Some common nouns, normally not capitalized, are capitalized when they are used as titles or as parts of a proper name.

Common:	Proper:
street	45 Saratoga Street
company	the Anderson Company
professor	Professor Zerby

7. Capitalize all titles of respect when they precede names.

Ms. Luanne Helms	Dr. Stephanie Corso
Vice-President Mark Simonton	Governor Owens
Rabbi Stone	Undersheriff Kline

8. **Capitalize all job titles when they refer to specific individuals. And for a simple reason: You will never offend someone by capitalizing his or her title; you might offend him or her if you don't.**

> Luanne Helms is being considered for President of our company.
> Josh Stone, our family's Rabbi, is a good friend.
> Bill Owens has been a popular Governor.
> Mary is our Sales Manager.

However, do not capitalize prefixes like ex-, former, the late *or suffixes like* -elect *when they are used with titles*

> President-elect Helms
> ex-President Bush
> our former Rabbi, Josh Stone

9. **Capitalize all formal names of companies, organizations and government agencies the way they themselves capitalize them on their official letterhead or Web site.**

Ford Motor Company	Volunteers of America
the Social Security Administration	Federal Bureau of Investigation
Amazon.com	Cuyahoga County Public Library

10. **Capitalize the names of departments in an organization when referring to a specific unit.**

Again, this is a rule that grammar guides disagree about. If you feel strongly that you should not

> our Board of Directors   Ford's Advertising Department

capitalize department names, as long as you are consistent in your choice probably no one will complain. By the same token (you probably know what we are going to say here), you'll never offend someone by capitalizing his or her department name; you might offend them if you don't.

11. **Capitalize all references to religion, deities and religious scriptures.**

Obviously, follow this rule whether the religions and deities involved are ones you believe in or not.

God	the Bible	the Lord
Allah	the Koran	Buddha
the Father	the Talmud	Judaism
Catholic	Zeus	Apollo

The exception to remember concerns the words *god* and *goddess* when they are used in reference to ancient mythology.

Exception ▶ the Greek goddess Athena   the god Jupiter

The gods' and goddesses' names are capitalized but the words themselves are not.

12. **Capitalize the first word and all the important words in the titles of books, periodicals, reports, proposals, poems, stories, plays, paintings, songs, movies and other works of art or research.**

Here is the definition of "an important word:" All words four or more letters long as well as words shorter than four letters except for articles, short conjunctions and short prepositions.

Articles, short conjunctions and short prepositions are capitalized only when they are the first or last word in a title. Do not capitalize them if they are not actually part of the title.

> *The* Reader's Edge
> *A* Man to Come Home *To*
> *the* Physicians Desk Reference

When in doubt, you can probably guess what we will suggest: BE CONSISTENT.

13. **Never send an e-mail message (or any written document) typed in ALL CAPS (all capital letters).**

    If you have ever received one of these documents you know how annoying it is. When you write in ALL CAPS, especially in e-mail, your reader can't help thinking that you are yelling. Use conventional rules of capitalization in all written documents.

CITATIONS

Citations are the way you, as a writer, can identify the sources you are referring to or quoting within the text of your e-mail, letter, memo, report or proposal. They are not to be confused with footnotes (page 83), which are more formal and contain more specific information.

Another difference between citations and footnotes is that citations appear in the body of the text, while footnotes appear either on the bottom of each page or at the end of either the chapter or the document.

When using citations, a bibliography must accompany your document. This is where your reader will be able to find the full information about the resources you have cited.

One final note: The suggestions we make here are appropriate for the world of work—whether that work is technical or nontechnical. When you are called upon to prepare a document for a more formal audience or for any other special circumstance, please refer to an academic reference book for the specific styles that will be required.

Rules

1. Present the author's name and date of publication in parentheses immediately after any material that has been quoted or referred to in your document.

2. Always supply a complete bibliography at the end of your document that includes every reference you have referred to in your citations.

3. As always, be consistent.

Examples and Explanations

1. **Present the author's name and date of publication in parentheses immediately after any material that has been quoted or referred to in your document.**

    This parenthetical reference will appear before the final punctuation mark of the sentence that it refers to. No punctuation is needed between the author's name and date of publication.

    > The whole class was inspired when they read that Christopher Reeve believes he will walk again, given enough funding for research into spinal cord injuries and cures. They were especially moved by his statement, "When you're trapped in a dark room, you think: Where's the exit? You find the exit by remaining calm and slowly feeling your way in the dark until you reach the door" (Reeve 1998).

    If there is no author to refer to, use the title (or an abbreviated form of the title) and date instead. This will help your reader find the complete listing for this resource quickly in your bibliography.

    > Dr. Roger reported that the Dalai Lama "always comes into rooms giggling. I think it's the deep joy within him, no matter what he's faced" (*Spectrum* 2001).

2. **Always supply a complete bibliography at the end of your document that includes every reference you have referred to in your citations.**

    This gives your reader the source for your material.

3. **As always, be consistent.**

If you have chosen to use informal citations in a document you are preparing, don't switch to more formal footnotes halfway through. Make your mind up early on how you will present your information and then present it that way consistently.

When making your decision, realize that citations included in the body of your text do not appear to be as difficult as footnotes sprinkled throughout that document. But also realize that if you are aiming to impress your readers with your vast and detailed knowledge about something, footnotes can look more academic and therefore more impressive. All in all, it depends on your reader.

COMPLIMENTARY CLOSINGS

Complimentary closings are the phrases (or sometimes single words) used at the end of your letters before your signature.

Common complimentary closings ▶

Sincerely,	Regards,	Best regards,
Yours truly,	Cordially,	Thank you,

Complimentary closings are used only in letters and—if you like—e-mail. They are not used in printed memos, reports, proposals, press releases or any other business documents. In your letters and e-mails, however, they add a friendliness that will help you develop and build a positive rapport with your readers.

Rules

1. Find a complimentary closing (or several complimentary closings) that you feel comfortable with and use them in your letters and e-mails.
2. When using a complimentary closing longer than one word, capitalize only the first letter of the first word.
3. Use a comma after the complimentary closing.
4. Use a format for your letters and your e-mails that makes sense and then stick with it.

Examples and Explanations

1. **Find a complimentary closing (or several complimentary closings) that you feel comfortable with and use them in your letters and e-mails.**

   Many writers worry about using the most commonly used complimentary closing in America—the single word *Sincerely*. Their concern stems from their acknowledgment that they don't feel very sincere by the time they are writing it for the hundredth time in a day.

   Two thoughts:

   • If you truly dislike *Sincerely*, find something you like better! Make sure that whatever closing you choose is one you yourself have seen several times before—otherwise it may be seen as too offbeat or bizarre by your readers.

   • Do you know the etymology (origin) of the word *sincerely*? It might make you feel better about using it. The word has its origin in Latin. Apparently sculptors in ancient Rome had fallen into the habit of covering imperfections in their marble sculptures by rubbing melted wax into them before they were painted. When the Roman public caught on to this trick, they began demanding that those sculptors carve the words *sin cere* into the marble near their signatures. Those words, you see, mean "without wax."

2. **When using a complimentary closing longer than one word, capitalize only the first letter of the first word.**

   Unless, of course, there is some other reason for capitalizing those words.

   Exceptions: A religious person using a complimentary closing or a company executive using one that mentions the company name: ▶

May God bless you,
With my best wishes for Sysco's future,

3. **Use a comma after the complimentary closing.**

In very rare cases, you could use an exclamation point or a question mark instead. But be aware that anything but a comma will look strange to most of your readers.

Sincerely,	Yours truly,
Respectfully,	With hope for your speedy recovery,
Again, congratulations!	Will you call soon?

4. **Use a format for your letters and your e-mails that makes sense and then stick with it.**

Again, make sure you are using a style that your reader has seen before. This helps assure your reader that you know what you are doing and that you are a knowledgeable, credible person.

CONFUSED WORDS

Even writers who know better occasionally confuse like words and end up damaging the clarity of their message or ruining their credibility—and sometimes both.

Following are 50 of the most commonly confused word pairs (or triads) used in business writing, along with simple meanings and tips for keeping them straight:

a lot	many
	There's a lot of work today.
allot	to distribute by lot or in arbitrary shares
	Jack will allot a fair share of the work to each customer representative.
alot	a town in India

accept	to receive willingly
	I accept your offer.
except	to leave out
	I would like all of them except the large green one.

affect	(verb) to cause or influence
	We can affect employee morale with significant pay raises.
effect	(noun) a result
	The effect of significant pay raises was much-improved employee morale.

Special note: **Affect** can be used as a noun to refer to the mood of a person, but this is a usage normally reserved for mental health professionals. **Effect** is sometimes used as a verb but **we don't recommend it**. Instead of *We can effect a change*, we prefer the more straightforward *We can bring about a change*.

all together	together
	We are all together on our support for the new plan.
altogether	thoroughly, wholly
	Well, we like it because it is an altogether great plan.

allusion	reference
	The allusion he made was to an obscure passage from Shakespeare.
illusion	misleading image
	He is under the illusion that John cares what Shakespeare had to say about anything!
ante-	before
	ante-bellum (pre-Civil War)
anti-	against
	anti-war (against war)
appraise	to determine the value of
	The antique dealer recently appraised our oak table to be worth $12,500.
apprise	to notify
	Please keep me apprised as to your progress with the sale.
assure	to make certain (assure **someone**)
	I can assure you the delivery will arrive tomorrow.
ensure	to make certain (ensure **that**)
	I can ensure that the delivery will arrive tomorrow by bringing it to you myself.
insure	to give, take or procure insurance, as in policies
	Should I insure this package? It's worth $10,000.
beside	next to
	I will stand beside Jack in our company picture.
besides	in addition to
	There are several considerations besides his lack of education involved in my decision.
capital	money, seat of government (the city), uppercase letters
	She has the capital to invest.
	Denver is the capital of Colorado.
	Please never send an e-mail that has been typed in all capital letters.
Capitol	the building that houses government offices in a capital city (always use a capital letter when referring to a specific Capitol building)
	The Capitol in Denver has a golden dome.
complement	an addition to, something that completes
	Her bright paisley scarf is the perfect complement to an otherwise overly formal suit.
compliment	a flattering remark
	I complimented her on the choice she made.

consul	a diplomat
	Hakim has been our Deputy Consul in the Saudi embassy since May.
council	assembly
	The City Council has recently approved a budget for landscaping the city parks.
counsel	(verb) to advise, (noun) a lawyer, advice
	My supervisor offered to counsel me about my communication skills.
	My supervisor suggested I retain counsel because of the lawsuit that has been filed.
	My supervisor gave me some wise counsel in recommending that.
decent	respectable
	Everyone agrees Samantha is a decent person.
descent	the act of going lower
	They say a climber's descent of Mount Everest is as tricky as his or her ascent.
dissent	disagreement
	The only dissent I have heard to your plan is from Lou, who says there isn't enough money in the budget to make it work.
desert	arid piece of land
	Much of the western United States is made up of desert.
dessert	an after meal treat
	My favorite dessert is chocolate mousse macadamia nut pie.
eminent	renowned
	Janet LaMonica is one of the most eminent attorneys in Kansas City.
imminent	about to happen
	The restructuring of our firm is imminent—our CEO returned yesterday from the shareholders meeting.
envelop	to enclose or enfold
	Our manager has made it clear that we are to envelop the new hires with warmth and kindness.
envelope	a container for a letter
	I finished addressing those envelopes this afternoon.
farther	refers to distance
	The grocery store is farther from our office than the post office.
further	in addition to, refers to degree
	One further point I'd like to make: Therapeutic drawing could help your child.
fewer	refers to number, something that can be counted
	There are fewer coffee mugs in the cabinet today than there were yesterday.
less	refers to volume, something that can't be counted
	If you put less water in the coffee maker, the coffee will taste better.

Business Writing

holey	something containing holes
	Your old shirt is too holey to wear to work.
holy	sacred
	The high holy days of the Jewish year fall on different calendar dates each year.
wholly	completely
	We are wholly enthusiastic about your idea.
human	relating to a person
	His anger is a very human response.
humane	marked by compassion
	The humane treatment of laboratory animals is a big issue for PETA.
insoluble	undissolvable
	Oil is insoluble in water.
insolvable	cannot be solved
	The New York Times *crossword puzzle has always been insolvable to me.*
insolvent	bankrupt
	Upon further investigation, we discovered his firm was insolvent.
inter-	between, among
	Many interfaith marriages work well, as long as both husband and wife agree on issues ahead of time.
intra-	within
	Intrastate telecommunications are regulated less than those that cross state lines.
its	belonging to it (possessive)
	Our company is proud of its service record.
it's	it is
	It's a gorgeous day today!
its'	no such word

HINT: If you can remember that there is no such word as *its'*, then the only other thing you would need to remember is that *it's* is always *it is*. This makes *its* what you would use for anything else. Sometimes this is easier to remember than remembering possessives.

later	tardier, at a future time
	We can handle the details later—how about tomorrow?
latter	relating to the second one
	Do you want a copy of the former manual or the latter one?
lay, laid	to put down or set down, the past tense of to put down or set down
	Lay the report on my desk.
	I laid the report on your desk.
lie, lay	to recline, past tense of to recline
	Lie down before you fall down, Joe. You look terrible!
	He lay down this morning for an hour and he felt fine.

leased	rented
	Anderson and Company leased the new building for two years.
least	smallest
	The least of them is still stronger than the best of us—we need more practice.
lest	for fear that
	We should schedule more practices lest they beat us every game.
macro	large, prominent; also, a series of computer commands saved as a unit
	Jonathan executed the macro, which saved him 10 minutes.
micro	very small
	How few micromillimeters made the difference between the success and failure of your experiment?
median	middle point, a mathematical term
	The median home price in the Akron/Canton area has been rising steadily for the past four years.
medium	intermediate in size, quality, amount, etc.
	I would prefer a medium-sized yard—I just don't want to mow so much.
overdo	to do too much
	Mariette will probably overdo the preparations, but at least the party will go well.
overdue	late
	Al's project is now a week overdue. Have we heard from him?
parameter	an arbitrary constant or range
	The quality parameters we are working with allow us to achieve excellent results.
perimeter	boundary, outer limit
	The SWAT team established a perimeter and entered the building to find the perpetrators.
perpetrate	to bring about, to commit
	He perpetrated the crime with malice.
perpetuate	to cause something to last longer
	The manager has perpetuated the myth that his department produces the highest quality work.
personal	relating to a person, private
	Personal details are not required on our job applications.
personnel	employees in an organization
	Has anyone informed our personnel about the dress code?
populace	the members of a population, common people
	In general, the populace is content with the President's performance.
populous	densely populated
	The populous regions of the country generally have more museums.

portent	omen
	Black cats are usually considered to be portents of bad luck.
potent	powerful
	Some herbal supplements are quite potent—make sure to read the labels carefully.
precede	to go before
	Generally, the Pledge of Allegiance precedes the welcome song at their Rotary meeting.
proceed	to continue, to move along
	If you are through with your giggling, we will proceed with the discussion.
precedence	priority
	Which of these projects has precedence? We'll start it first.
precedents	acts or decision that serve as examples for later ones
	If we rule in this way we may be establishing some precedents that we will later regret.
preceding	going before
	The meeting preceding this one was far more effective.
proceeding	legal action, transaction
	The proceeding took less than an hour and my client lost everything.
principal	first, chief, sum of capital
	The principal reason your application was accepted was your education.
	The principals of our firm all drive luxury cars.
	The bank is concerned about the repayment of the interest and the principal on our loan.
principle	rule or value
	The principles I live by are written into my personal mission statement.
qualify	to modify, to exhibit a required degree of ability
	He qualified his statement with the words, "but only if management agrees."
	Do you think I qualify for early retirement?
quantify	to count, to determine the quantity of
	We asked our research department to quantify the results of their experiments.
recent	done not long ago
	The most recent update was written last week.
resent	to feel injured or angry at
	Molly has long resented Richard because of his promotion.
respectably	decently
	She handled the accounts we gave her quite respectably.
respectfully	with respect
	She always treats her customers respectfully—that's why they like her so much.
respectively	in the order given
	Now that we have described the three projects, would you please comment on them respectively.

stationary	stable, fixed
	The machine has remained in a stationary position since you called.
stationery	paper supplies, letterhead
	Your organization's stationery looks like it is of the highest quality.
statue	a sculpture
	Have you seen Michelangelo's statue of David?
stature	status
	Our Controller has considerable stature in the financial community here in town.
statute	law or rule
	Every year our Legislature ratifies statute after statute that no one ever hears about.
than	compared to
	I like ice cream more than I like cake.
then	at that time
	First we saw the movie, then we read the book.
their	possessive, belonging to them
	Have you seen their new house?
there	at that place
	There it is, at the end of the street.
they're	they are
	They're so excited they got it for under $200,000.
to	a preposition of direction
	Give your charts to Aimee and she will get them printed for everyone.
too	also
	Can she copy the report for everyone too?
two	the number
	Do you have an extra two copies?
vary	to change or deviate
	Have you thought about varying the assignments so no one person gets too bored?
very	exceedingly
	After all, those assignments can be very boring.
way	method
	The best way to handle this is to do it quickly and calmly.
weigh	to discover the weight of something, to think carefully, compare
	Weigh this box for FedEx® to see if it's under their limit.
	When making a decision, I hope you will carefully weigh the options we have discussed.
whey	liquid remaining after the coagulation of milk into cheese
	Little Miss Muffet sat on her tuffet eating her curds and whey.

weather	state of the atmosphere, climate
	The weather in Seattle is much better than people expect during the summer.
whether	if (usually used with *or not*)
	I will be attending the benefit whether or not you do.
your	possessive of you
	Did you remember to bring your coat?
you're	you are
	You're very lucky to have been invited to this meeting.

CONJUNCTIONS

A conjunction is a word that connects other words, phrases and clauses. Depending on which conjunction is used, the relationship between those words, phrases and clauses is established. There are three kinds of conjunctions:

Coordinating conjunctions: Connect words, phrases or clauses of equal rank. The coordinating conjunctions are *and, or, but* and *nor.*

Correlative conjunctions: Conjunctions that are made up of two parts, used in pairs. Examples of correlative conjunctions are: *both ... and, either ... or, neither ... nor, whether ... or not.*

Subordinating conjunctions: Conjunctions used to join a dependent clause to an independent one. Examples of subordinate conjunctions are: *since, though, provided that, before.*

Rules

1. Use the conjunction that most accurately conveys your exact meaning.
2. Do not use conjunctions where periods should have been used instead.
3. It is fine to occasionally begin a sentence with a conjunction.
4. Make sure to keep the construction parallel on either side of a conjunction.

Examples and Explanations

1. **Use the conjunction that most accurately conveys your exact meaning.**

   This, of course, is a matter of clarity. When you mean to combine more than one element, the word *and* is appropriate. When you want the reader to see a choice between two ideas, an *or* is appropriate. Carefully edit your writing to guarantee your conjunctions carry the meanings you intend.

2. **Do not use conjunctions where periods should have been used instead.**

   This is a rule that is meant to keep you from writing sentences that are too long, too rambling and, therefore, unclear.

It is fine to combine two short independent clauses in one sentence ▶ Business is getting better and I'm glad.

On the first day of May in the city closest to most committee members, our membership will meet to agree on the new rules governing how future meetings will be held and they will then attempt to agree on a restaurant at which they will eat a dinner paid for by the leadership of the committee. ◀ *But it is not okay to combine two long independent clauses— or worse yet, two long independent clauses plus some dependent clauses*

Too many ideas! At least, too many ideas in one sentence. Your reader is reading too quickly to be able to digest that much information without a breath (signified by your period, at the end of a reasonable sentence).

On May 1, in a convenient city, a membership meeting will be held. The purpose of this meeting is to agree on rules for our future meetings. Afterward, we will attempt to agree on a restaurant for dinner which the leadership will pay for.

We recommend certain sentence lengths in our section on Sentences (page 184), but the much more important rule is that a sentence should contain only *one major idea*. This is a rule unique to business writers, journalists and advertising copywriters.

You only have this one chance to communicate with your reader. Most business readers do not read something more than once just to clarify their understanding. They will sooner give up on the whole document and push it aside.

3. **It is fine to occasionally begin a sentence with a conjunction.**

This will help you keep your sentences relatively short and simple while at the same time maintaining a writing style that has a smooth flow for your reader.

Sometimes writers are concerned about this permission—it is so different from what they learned in elementary school. But as adults, our needs are different. We need to keep our readers interested. And we need them to accurately understand our message. That's clarity.

Did you notice the sentences in the last paragraph that began with conjunctions? Most readers don't—they just notice that the reading went quickly and easily and the meaning was clear.

If you still have doubts, check out the front page of *The Wall Street Journal*. Most days, there are as many as 5 – 10 sentences that begin with the words *and* or *but*.

4. **Make sure to keep the construction parallel on either side of a conjunction.**

Parallelism is the feature of writing that guarantees like ideas will be presented in like fashion. It makes any sentence or any paragraph much easier to read.

Compare these examples ▶ | **NOT:** Jack brought figs and Mary's dates were also delicious.
BUT: Jack brought figs and Mary brought dates. They were both delicious.

CONJUNCTIVE ADVERBS

A note about conjunctive adverbs …

Conjunctive adverbs are the words like *however, therefore, moreover, consequently, otherwise* and *nevertheless* that are sometimes used to connect two independent clauses and occasionally to begin a single independent clause presented as a sentence.

The question most writers encounter regards punctuation around conjunctive adverbs.

Rules

1. Always put a comma after a conjunctive adverb that begins a sentence or an independent clause.
2. Put either a semicolon or a period before a conjunctive adverb that follows an independent clause.

Examples and Explanations

1. **Always put a comma after a conjunctive adverb that begins a sentence or an independent clause.**

> Nevertheless, one shouldn't jump to conclusions.
>
> **OR**
>
> Your report is very thorough and quite detailed. However, I still need more information about last year's order history.

2. **Put either a semicolon or a period before a conjunctive adverb that follows an independent clause.**

> Your report is very thorough and quite detailed; however, I still need more information about last year's order history.

When deciding between using a semicolon or a period, consider that semicolons—if there are too many of them, or if the reading is otherwise difficult—can discourage your reader from going on. Also consider that when you give an idea its very own sentence, that idea is seen as more important by your reader.

CONSISTENCY

When you, as a writer, are consistent in the rules you follow and the styles you use, your reader has a much easier time reading and understanding your documents quickly. Your consistent style contributes to both readability and clarity.

Rules

1. Choose the grammar, punctuation and spelling rules that you are going to follow and then follow them all the time.
2. Choose a style that you use for your e-mails, your memos, your letters, your reports and your proposals and then stick with those styles.
3. And of course, be consistent in your use of a warm, positive style in your writing.

Examples and Explanations

1. **Choose the grammar, punctuation and spelling rules that you are going to follow and then follow them all the time.**

   Obviously, some grammar, punctuation and spelling rules are not open to argument. Those should be followed, period. As for the ones that are disagreed about (such as the ones we have highlighted throughout this style guide), make your choice and then stick with it.

   A common choice all writers face, for example, is whether to use serial commas or not. (See Commas, page 155.)

   > My brother enjoys pizza, spaghetti, kung pao chicken, and grilled hot dogs.
   > **OR**
   > My brother enjoys pizza, spaghetti, kung pao chicken and grilled hot dogs.

   They are both correct, but can mean two different things. The first means the items are all separate. The second can mean that the kung pao chicken and the grilled hot dogs are together. (I know, this sounds silly, but in another context, it makes perfect sense. Consider a will leaving an estate to three people: Bill, John and Erik. Written the first way, there's no question they each receive one third. Written the second way, Bill could claim he was to receive 50% of the estate.

   The same holds true for spelling choices. Do you spell the past tense of *cancel* with one "l" or two? *Canceled* or *cancelled* ? They are both correct, according to dictionaries. Make your choice and then follow it consistently.

2. **Choose a style that you use for your e-mails, your memos, your letters, your reports and your proposals and then stick with those styles.**

   This allows your reader to get comfortable with your formatting choices and the styles you use. Choose styles that are appealing to the eye. Especially in e-mail, be sensitive to your readers' need to see a break or two in your text so as not to feel overwhelmed.

   The same rule applies to letterhead and other stationery you use. Make sure it is of high quality and that it looks like it is all from the same family, using the same typefaces and colors.

3. **And of course, be consistent in your use of a warm, positive style in your writing.**

   There is never a good reason to be anything less than warm and positive in your writing. Develop a conversational style and use it in your business writing. Treat your readers and your potential readers with the same respect you would hope they would give you.

   When the message you are writing is negative or angry, make sure to let it wait for a few hours before you edit it and send it. Give yourself time to cool down. And remember—once a bell has been rung, you can't un-ring it.

CONTRACTIONS

Contractions are shortened forms of words in which an apostrophe takes the place of missing letters. While contractions should not be a part of very formal writing, they are welcomed by most readers in business writing.

Rules

1. Use simple contractions that your readers will easily recognize in your writing. Avoid using contractions that could be mistaken for possessives and contractions that look odd to your readers.

2. Be certain you are using the correct forms of the contractions that you use.

Examples and Explanations

1. **Use simple contractions that your readers will easily recognize in your writing. Avoid using contractions that could be mistaken for possessives and contractions that look odd to your readers.**

   Simple contractions are generally the ones that include a personal pronoun or the word **not**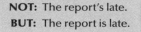

I'll	We're	They'll
He's	Don't	Couldn't

   The contractions you should avoid are the ones that consist of a common noun followed by an -'s.

   If you were speaking to someone, you would probably never say it without using the contraction. Unfortunately, though, many business readers are reading very quickly and sometimes with less than full attention. Any common noun (like report) followed by an -'s will look like a possessive. Your reader will end up confused because he or she is looking in vain to find something that report owns.

   > **NOT:** The report's late.
   > **BUT:** The report is late.

2. **Be certain you are using the correct forms of the contractions that you use.**

   One very commonly misused contraction is the contraction for *it is*. The correct form of that contraction is *it's*. Another commonly misspelled contraction is the one for *you all*, commonly used in the southern United States. The correct spelling is *y'all*, not *ya'all*. Always remember that the apostrophe is taking the place of missing letters and you won't make a mistake.

CONVERSATIONAL STYLE

In the world of business writing, we recommend that writers adopt a conversational style in their documents. This makes those documents easier to read for their readers and it also establishes those writers as warm human beings. Both of those considerations are valuable, especially in an over-communicated world. No reader reads every document he or she receives. If your reader has already learned that you are friendly, clear and readable, you are well on your way to having your future correspondence read.

Rules

1. Write the same way you speak, but make sure you are writing to your reader the way you would speak to that reader.

2. Realize that in writing you have a larger responsibility for correctness than you do in conversation.

3. When having trouble composing a document, imagine yourself giving the information to someone face to face or on the phone. How would you say it then?

Examples and Explanations

1. **Write the same way you speak, but make sure you are writing to your reader the way you would speak to that reader.**

   You use differing conversational styles when talking to the various people in your life, so be aware that you will need different conversational writing styles as well. Some people you naturally approach more casually, some you naturally approach more formally.

While it is true you would never say this to your boss over taco salads:

Example ▶ Pursuant to our earlier conversation, enclosed please find today's dessert selections. Please notify me at your earliest convenience regarding the decision you make pertaining to the aforementioned matter.

You probably shouldn't just poke her with the menu and grunt, either. Ask yourself, how would you ask your boss to share a dessert with you?

Example ▶ Here's the menu. Do you see anything you would like to have for dessert?

Using a conversational style helps you overcome a tendency toward business writing clichés.

2. **Realize that in writing you have a larger responsibility for correctness than you do in conversation.**

Meaning, go ahead and write the way you speak, but then proofread carefully. Many people you speak with let you get away with small grammar errors made in the heat of the conversation without even noticing, let alone mentioning them.

In writing, your errors are more permanent and more noticeable. People do notice. Make sure to be error-free.

3. **When having trouble composing a document, imagine yourself giving the information to someone face to face or on the phone. How would you say it then?**

This tip will help you write more quickly and overcome any writer's block you may normally experience. In fact, some writers carry small recording devices with them so they can say what they mean before sitting down at a computer to write. They say it saves them time.

CREATIVITY

For some writers, their biggest challenge lies in overcoming writer's block—getting the ideas they need to communicate to their readers into writing at all. Has it ever happened to you? You sit down at your computer and end up staring into a blank word processing file for minute after blank minute, maybe even lightly tapping your fingers on some of the keys of your keyboard, hoping for inspiration.

But nothing comes.

Many writers, perceiving themselves as too busy to spend extra time writing, set themselves up for this kind of writer's block by failing to **pre-write**.

Yet pre-writing, made up of four simple steps that will take very little time, is the key to always having easy access to the ideas you need to communicate in writing. Then, in a fifth step you will be easily able to write a first draft of your document.

The cognitive theory that supports a writer's need for pre-writing involves right brain/left brain theory. Cognitive psychologists tell us that the creative functions of a human's brain generally occur in the right hemisphere. Logical functions generally occur in the left hemisphere.

When you write, you use both creative and logical functions. Therefore, you are using both hemispheres of your brain. Unfortunately, it can be difficult when you attempt to rapidly switch between them over and over again. Many people end up "locked out" of one hemisphere or the other. And most of us in the business world find it much more likely to be locked out of our right, creative hemisphere than our left, logical hemisphere. This leads to writer's block.

The five steps to overcoming writer's block allow you to complete one creative function of writing before beginning a logical function. Then you complete that logical function before you move into the third step, another creative function—and so on. We are certain that if you give it a try you will be hooked forever.

Rules

1. Mind map your major ideas before ever opening a word processing file.

2. Profile your audience: What information from your mind map(s) is most important or useful to your readers?

3. Write the first draft of the first paragraph of your document.

4. Organize the rest of the information you want to include in your document in a logical manner.

5. Now, with your organizational scheme planned—and displayed in front of you—freewrite the rest of the document.

Examples and Explanations

1. **Mind map your major ideas before ever opening a word processing file.**

This is a job for the creative right hemisphere of your brain.

Mind mapping is a process originally used in teaching creative writing to high school and college students. It is similar to brainstorming, but the format might be new to you. Here's how it works:

In the center of a blank sheet of paper, write the key word of your topic. For example, if you are writing a job description you would probably write the words "My Job" or maybe the words of your job title, "Training Coordinator," in the center of the page.

Then, draw a circle around it.

Sit back for a moment and relax. Take a good breath, then lean back to the page and begin brainstorming everything you can think of about your job. When you think of an idea, draw a line from the center circle outward and then write the key word(s) of your idea there. Then, draw a circle around this new idea. Work your way around the circle, thinking of everything you can. In come cases you might even find that one of your new circles inspires more detail. In that case, draw your lines from that new circle. Like this:

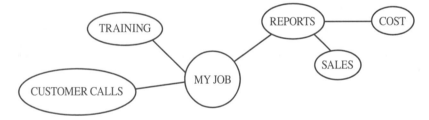

Always give yourself a time limit before beginning a mind map—no longer than five minutes for a single mind map. We realize that sometimes you may need more than one mind map to begin the process of writing a more complex letter, report or proposal—it's just that to mind map on a single mind map longer than five minutes is to risk frying your brain.

Mind mapping is a highly concentrated form of creativity. Have you ever gone into a creative zone for a little too long and ended up feeling like you were trapped in a mental Twilight Zone? It has happened to most of us. That's why the time limit.

When you have the need for more details, start with a general mind map. Let's say you are writing a report about the rules governing all punctuation marks. Your first mind map would look like this:

Then, you could separately mind map each subtopic that needed one. Sometimes you will need to do research to complete a mind map.

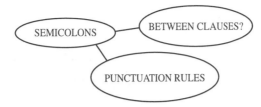

One other comment about mind mapping: The circles you are drawing help your brain stay in the right hemisphere, which is where your ideas are coming from. If, though, your brain is creating ideas so quickly that drawing circles around each of them slows you down, just draw the lines and write down your ideas. When you run out of those ideas, instead of staring into space, begin drawing the circles.

Your left brain can't draw a circle (except a zero at the bottom of a column of figures) to save its life. It is your right brain that enjoys drawing those circles. So if your left brain is thinking about how you have misspelled words, or how some of your ideas are worthless, the simple act of drawing the circles helps you move away from that critical, logical thinking—for now, at least. Move away from it long enough to be sure you have exhausted your creative ideas.

2. Profile your audience: What information from your mind map(s) is most important or useful to your readers?

This is a job for the logical and analytical left hemisphere of your brain.

Now that you have mind mapped most of the ideas you want to express, make sure to consider your readers' needs and interests. This way, you will be sure to get your readers' attention and be able to communicate what is most important to them early on.

If, when looking at your mind map, you have trouble determining what might be important to your reader, use the chart on page 8 (Readability) to help you determine the needs your readers have.

After you have identified the one or two most important points for your reader, give some thought to which of your ideas are most important to you, the ones you most want your reader to see.

These ideas will make up the first paragraph or two of whatever you are writing. You must include the things most important to your reader, of course, so your reader immediately notices that you are writing about things he or she is interested in. This keeps them reading. You need to include your important points also because whatever you include in the first paragraph and maybe even the second, your reader will most usually read. We can't make the same guarantee about the middle and end.

Here is an example of how you could mark a mind map:

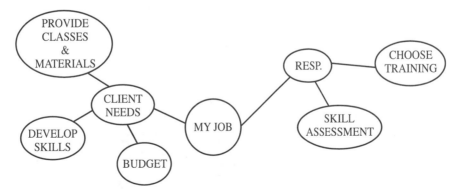

3. Write the first draft of the first paragraph of your document.

This task returns you to the right hemisphere of your brain. Any time you put your fingers on a keyboard or any time you pick up a pen and begin writing, the ideas you write are coming from the creative (right) hemisphere of your brain.

As you write this rough draft, do not be too concerned about how perfectly you spell or use grammar. Be concerned about getting your ideas down on the page in the most natural writing you can. Aim for correctness, but don't start debating with yourself about what's right and what's wrong. This is, after all, only a first draft.

But do your best to sum up your main ideas—both the ones you identified as important to the reader and the ones important to you. If necessary, you may make this two short paragraphs. But no more than that.

This is an exercise in getting to the point. It will also provide you with the focus you need to do the next two steps.

Here is an example of a rough draft of a paragraph you could write based on the MY JOB example we have been using up to this point

> As a Training Coordinator for ELS Corporation, my single most important responsibility is to provide the training classes and materials our employees need to do their jobs effectively and to further develop their skills. This involves monitoring the department's budget, conducting periodic skill assessments and choosing the best and most appropriate training we can afford at any given time.

Notice that this example makes reference to all three points the writer felt important to the reader (provide classes and materials to do jobs, develop skills and the department's budget). It also contains the two other points the writer felt were important (skill assessment and choosing best and most appropriate training).

4. Organize the rest of the information you want to include in your document in a logical manner.

Well, just the use of the word *logical* in this rule probably gives you an idea which side of your brain you'll be using. Of course, this step returns you to some analysis and organization—it's the left hemisphere that handles that.

You have already determined by this time what ideas are the most important in your document—you have even written a paragraph or two summing them up. Now it's time to outline the rest of what you will be presenting.

Don't worry about using formal outlining rules—there is no need for you to use Roman numerals, capital letters, Arabic numerals, small letters, small Roman numerals, etc. Whatever method helps you get (and stay) organized is fine.

Look at your mind map (or mind maps) and ask yourself which idea you want to present after your first paragraph, then which idea you'd like to present next and so on. You can either number those ideas on the mind map itself, or create a separate list.

When organizing your ideas, use any method that makes sense for your audience and your information. The most common method for organizing business writing is **in order of importance**. In journalism this method is referred to as **The Inverted Pyramid**.

Have you ever noticed that when you read a news story in a newspaper the first paragraph contains the most important information, the second paragraph contains the second most important information and so on? Do you ever scan the front page of your local newspaper? When you do, how often do you then turn to page 23A where those stories are continued? Most readers don't because they know there will be nothing there more important than what they have already read.

Your business readers find the same kind of assurance from you, their writer, comforting.

Have you ever noticed the habit some top executives have developed when handed a multi-page document? They often turn to the last page first. Why? Because they are looking for the bottom line. While it is fine to end a document with the bottom line, please make sure you have also begun it with the bottom line. Your reader should never need to hunt for it.

Another popular method of organizing some business documents (especially status reports) is **chronologically**. Make sure to note, however, that even chronological reports need to start with a bottom line. Maybe:

> This week our department accomplished five of its major objectives for the week, and we are leaving only one objective for next week.

Then you can continue with the chronological report.

> On Monday, ...

Or, a third method of organizing information is to work from **general to specific**. This is an especially good method for organizing reports. You start with the general topics and work your way down to the specific topics. With our punctuation report, for example, we could start with a general distinction: Some punctuation marks join ideas together, others separate ideas from each other. Then we could subcategorize specifically.

I. Punctuation marks that separate ideas
  A. Periods
  B. Question marks
  C. Exclamation points
  D. Semicolons (used as "small periods")
  E. Ellipses (at sentence ends)

II. Punctuation marks that join ideas
  A. Commas
  B. Colons
  C. Semicolons (used as "large commas")
  D. Dashes
  E. Parentheses
  F. Ellipses

Writer's Tips:
More information about
Organization can be
found on page 127.

Pro vs. con is an organizational style often used in sales writing. First, the writer presents all the pros of a particular idea, then that writer either directly or subtly refutes the cons and perceived cons.

But do you want to know the truth? You can use any organizational style you choose as long as you tell the reader what it is at the beginning. Perhaps you could write a report about punctuation called: *The Seven C's of Correct Punctuation*. Can't you imagine then that the whole report would be organized according to those seven C's?

▼ *Organizational methods*

Order of Importance	Reverse Chronological
Chronological	Numerical
General to Specific	Geographical
Pro vs. Con	

5. **Now, with your organizational scheme planned—and displayed in front of you—freewrite the rest of the document.**

Obviously, this is a creative right brain step.

The organizational scheme you created in Step Four serves now as a road map leading you smoothly on your way.

There are five guidelines for what we refer to as *freewriting*. And these guidelines will give you a good idea as to why it's called that!

- Write quickly (but stay legible).
- Don't read what you have just written. Most people start editing when they do that, and we are working to keep you in your *right* brain.
- If you run out of things to say, keep writing anyway. Write something like "I've run out of things to say right now, I've run out of things to say right now … " until you think of something else to say.
  THIS TIP ALONE WILL BANISH YOUR WRITER'S BLOCK FOREVER.
  Most people, when they run out of things to write stop writing. This gives their brains permission to stop thinking of ideas. It's as though a door to those ideas closes in their mind.
  On the other hand, when a writer keeps writing—even if the writing is nonsensical—the very act of writing holds that same door open. More ideas will come.
- Don't worry about grammar, punctuation, spelling or details of accuracy. You will edit and proofread for those later.
- Write for a set time—no longer than 20 minutes before taking at least a short break. Again, this process is a highly concentrated form of creativity and if you stick with it too long you could end up in that dreaded mental Twilight Zone.

To begin Step Five, write everything else you want to say about your first paragraph(s). Those are the ones you wrote in Step Three. Then, check your outline from Step Four. Write everything you have to say about the next idea, then the next, then the next, etc.

When you have finished, you will be ready to take a break, then begin Editing and Proofreading (pages 66 and 146).

Business Writing

EDITING

Editing is the process of making a document you have written clearer and more readable. It is easily as important (and sometimes even more important) than the writing of the first draft.

In this section we provide an editing checklist—a process you can rely on each and every time to guarantee that your documents are clear and readable. It begins with the larger pieces—overall content and tone first, followed by paragraphs, then sentences, then words. Ultimately, though, it ends with appearance.

Rules—Editor's Checklist

1. Content
- ☐ Is it accurate?
- ☐ Is it complete?

2. Tone
- ☐ Is it appropriate for the reader's needs?
- ☐ Will it help in accomplishing your goals?
- ☐ Is the bottom line stated early?
- ☐ Is it warm? Personal? Conversational? Positive?

3. Paragraphs
- ☐ Is each paragraph fewer than 10 lines long?
- ☐ Do the paragraphs vary in length?
- ☐ Is each paragraph devoted to only one major idea?
- ☐ Do the paragraphs flow coherently?
- ☐ Do the sentences in the paragraphs flow coherently?

4. Sentences
- ☐ Is the average number of words per sentence between 10 and 17?
- ☐ Are all sentences shorter than 32 words?
- ☐ Do the sentences vary in length?
- ☐ Do most sentences contain only one major idea?
- ☐ Have I avoided using too many passive voice sentences?

5. Words
- ☐ Have I avoided using unnecessarily large words? Obscure words? Overused words?
- ☐ Are most of the words short, common, clear and conversational?
- ☐ Does my vocabulary properly express my meaning?
- ☐ Will the reader be able to understand my message both intellectually and on a gut level?

6. The Reader's First Impression
- ☐ Is the stationery, paper or e-mail form attractive and clean?
- ☐ Is the reader addressed by name? Spelled properly? Correct title?
- ☐ Are the margins even?
- ☐ Is all tabbed material in line?
- ☐ Is the print dark and even?
- ☐ Is the font readable and professional?
- ☐ Is there enough white space to keep the reader interested and relaxed?

Examples and Explanations

1. Content

☐ **Is it accurate?** Before you edit anything in a written document to make it more stylistically appealing, you must ensure that what you have written is correct and factual. Double-check all dates, names and details before you even consider the rest of this checklist.

☐ **Is it complete?** Make sure that there is enough information provided so that even your reader—who is probably not as familiar with your topic as you are—can understand what you are saying easily and clearly. Don't be shy about providing the background or details your reader could find useful.

2. Tone

☐ **Is it appropriate for the reader's needs?** Most readers respond better to a warmer, less formal tone when they are sitting down to read their morning mail or e-mail. Help them find it easy to stick with your writing. Occasionally, however, you may find that a more formal tone can help convince a dubious reader of your expertise. This tends to be especially true when you are writing to people who tend to use a more formal tone in their own writing. Most often, though, aim for friendly. That's what over 95% of your readers will respond to best.

☐ **Will it help in accomplishing your goals?** By the way, what are your goals for this document? Have you clearly identified them? Did you clearly identify them before you started writing? (See Creativity, page 61.)

And no matter what your immediate goal is in any piece of writing (for example, explaining Process A to Sally or selling your boss on the idea of your weeklong vacation), you also have the goal of maintaining a positive relationship with your readers.

Most of the time a warm, personal tone will keep your reader in your camp. Even if that reader does not particularly like the actual message you need to communicate. Every once in a while, however, you may be writing to a reader who for one reason or another will respond more positively to you if approached in a different tone. Please always avoid using a negative or cold tone. But perhaps a formal tone could impress an occasional reader.

☐ **Is the bottom line stated early?** It must be or your reader will most likely stop reading before seeing it. Never forget that your reader is busy; too busy to read paragraph after paragraph without knowing your unifying thought. Make sure to put your most important information—or an overview of it—in the first and second paragraphs of whatever you write.

In the case of a document that conveys bad news, cushion your bad news in the first paragraph and then present it in the second.

☐ **Is it warm? Personal? Conversational? Positive?** Again, your reader will be more drawn to you and your message if it is stated in warm, personal, conversational and positive terms. Try checking your documents by asking these questions:

> - Can I read this aloud with a smile on my face? (Warmth)
>
> - Is it unique to the reader(s) I am addressing? (Personal)
>
> - Is it something I could have sent to anyone? (Impersonal)
>
> - Is it written in a style similar to the one I would use if I was having this conversation over lunch? (Conversational)
>
> - Have I avoided the words *can't, don't, won't, couldn't, wouldn't* and *shouldn't*? (Positive)
>
> - Have I coached toward the positive (*next time, please use a 12-point type*) instead of criticizing the negative (*don't use 14-point type*)?

3. Paragraphs

☐ **Is each paragraph fewer than 10 lines long?** Your busy reader will be overwhelmed by too much information compressed into too tight of a space. And the longer that reader must read before seeing white space (a rest!) in the distance, the less likely that reader will be able to make it. So even if there is no good reason content-wise to break a paragraph before ten printed lines, break it anyway. Your reader will appreciate it.

In e-mail, the advice is even less liberal. Your reader must be able to see at least one paragraph break in the window your e-mail has opened into. To be safe, consider eight printed lines the limit for e-mail. Some of your readers have very small windows that open in their e-mail programs!

☐ **Do paragraphs vary in length?** If all your paragraphs are the same length, that bores your reader too. Some longer paragraphs combined with some shorter paragraphs combined with an occasional very short paragraph keep your reader interested and rested.

☐ **Is each paragraph devoted to only one major idea?** Maybe not every paragraph you write needs a topic sentence, but every paragraph you write must be limited to one major idea, even if that major idea develops within the paragraph. Otherwise your reader becomes confused. It goes back to the way we were all taught reading in elementary school. We expected every sentence to have one main idea and every paragraph to be made up of a series of sentences that were united in the way they moved a major idea forward.

☐ **Do the paragraphs flow coherently?** The connections from one paragraph to the next need to be smooth. In fact, your reader should be reading so quickly that he or she doesn't even consciously notice them. Think about your favorite moments as a reader. Were you consciously aware of the mechanics involved in the writing? Or were you being carried by the ideas?

☐ **Do the sentences in the paragraphs flow coherently?** And of course the transitions between your sentences also need to be smooth and seamless.

> *Writer's Tips:*
> *More tips about how to accomplish a smooth flow between your paragraphs and your sentences can be found in the Transitions section on page 197.*

4. Sentences

☐ **Is the average number of words per sentence between 10 and 17?** Or 8 – 10 for more difficult or more technical writing? If you add together the number of words in each of the sentences of your document and then divide that total by the number of sentences those words were in, you will find the Average Number of Words Per Sentence of that document. Some of your sentences will be much shorter than 10 words, others will be much longer.

But to guarantee readability and clarity, writing and readability experts recommend the 10 – 17 number as your average.

Don't be surprised if most of your sentences are longer than 12 words. As a matter of fact, if you are the standard business writer, most of your sentences will probably be somewhere between 12 and 17 words long. But every once in a while a much shorter sentence provides great relief to your reader—as well as keeping your Average Number of Words Per Sentence low. And by the way, putting important information in a very short sentence, perhaps even a sentence that is itself a paragraph, is a great way to emphasize that information.

The recommended average gets lower for difficult or technical writing because the vocabulary the writer uses in that writing tends to be made up of much larger words than normal. Reducing the sentence length is a perfect way to compensate for heavier language.

Note: Most word processing software packages offer a "Readability Statistics" type of feature which will provide you with your average sentence length (as well as a great deal more information).

☐ **Are all sentences shorter than 32 words?** Never, ever write a sentence longer than 32 words. As a matter of fact, if you do write one this long, think twice. Every once in a while you might have a compelling reason, but consider 32 your top limit.

☐ **Do the sentences vary in length?** This will sound familiar, but it's still important. By varying the lengths of your sentences, you help your reader stay interested. If all your sentences are the same length, your reader may go into a trance. Have you ever gone into a trance while reading? You know—you read page after page but when you were finished you didn't even remember reading. Do everything you can to keep your reader from having that sad experience.

☐ **Do most sentences contain only one major idea?** This is the cardinal rule of sentence structure for business writing. Never put more than one major idea in the same sentence. Your reader is busy, reading quickly. When any reader reads quickly, that reader tends to find one major idea per sentence and then skim over the rest of that sentence to hurry to the next one.

Certainly, it is fine to include a subordinate (less important) idea along with the major idea. Just make sure that the less important one is punctuated to make it clear which idea is the important one.

☐ **Have I avoided using too many passive voice sentences?** Passive voice is neither correct nor incorrect, it's only a state a verb can possess. In the active voice, the actor (the subject) does something (the action) to some thing or someone (the object). In passive voice, some thing or someone (the object) has something done to it (the action) by someone (the actor).

> The dog buried the bone. (active voice)
>
> The bone was buried by the dog. (passive voice)

Passive voice is occasionally appropriate for a writer's needs. When the doer of an action is not as important as what happened:

> The research materials were placed in a petri dish stored at 22 degrees Centigrade for three weeks.

In that example, who cares that it was a scientist in the lab who placed those materials in the petri dish? What matters to the reader is that the materials were placed—for three weeks and at 22 degrees Centigrade.

Two other times it's appropriate to use passive voice are when you don't know who did the action and when you don't want to reveal who did the action.

Writer's Tips:
For more information about active and passive voice, see the Passive Voice section on page 134.

But this kind of writing—for most business writers—is the exception, not the rule. Generally, business writing is about subjects doing actions to, with or for objects. And that is the active voice.

> Jack contributed much good information at the meeting.
>
> Please deliver the new computers to the third floor.

5. Words

☐ **Have I avoided using unnecessarily large words? Obscure words? Overused words?** Ruthlessly edit yourself for the automatic writing most business writers (who, after all, are also business readers) have caught like a virus. Never use the words *utilization of* when a simple *using* can do the job. Never use a word like *facilitate* at all—that word has too many meanings. Instead, use *help* or *lead* or whatever other words clearly and accurately convey your meaning.

Also, watch your writing for words you tend to overuse. Again, these are likely words that you've over-*read*. You've come down with them like the flu. Finally, make sure that the words you use in your writing are not from some secret vocabulary you share only with yourself, your invisible twin and a couple of co-workers. Make sure the vocabulary in your writing passes the test of being conversational.

☐ **Are most of the words short, common, clear and conversational?** Never use a big word when a smaller one could be used instead. Never use an obscure word when a common one is available. Test the words you've used for clarity by asking yourself if your reader could possibly misunderstand. And if the answer is *Yes*, then keep editing. And finally—of course—make sure it is written as closely as possible to the way you would say it in conversation.

☐ **Does my vocabulary properly express my meaning?** If you have successfully edited for the two points above, you have probably taken care of this issue as well. Again, it goes to clarity. You can write beautiful words into beautiful sentences and paragraphs but if your reader misses the point, no one will call you a great writer.

☐ **Will the reader be able to understand my message both intellectually and on a gut level?** Advertising copywriters, who make their living by keeping their readers reading long enough to influence them into buying something, will tell you that most people buy from their emotions, not their intellects.

Maybe you are selling a product, maybe not. But all business writers are selling at least their own credibility and their organization's professional image. Work hard to ensure that your writing is logical—you will appeal to the intellect of your reader. But don't forget about your reader's heart. Make sure that your message is consistent, honest and positive. At the very least this will help your reader like you. If appropriate, remember to appeal to your reader's emotions in making your important points.

6. The Reader's First Impression

☐ **Is the stationery, paper or e-mail form attractive and clean?** Sad to say, but if you get this one wrong your reader probably won't even give himself or herself a chance to find out more. Your document will just end up in the garbage or deleted from your e-mail.

Make every document you write appealing to look at and your reader will read at least the first paragraph.

☐ **Is the reader addressed by name? Spelled properly? Correct title?** You have no doubt received much junk mail in your life. Have you ever noticed that when they can't even get your name right you don't even open the envelope? (Of course, sometimes even getting your name right isn't enough to encourage you to open something you know to be junk mail.)

When you get your reader's name wrong (Michele instead of Michelle, for example) you've got no hope. The same is true of using the reader's correct title. And that includes both a professional title and a courtesy title. The professional title is the one on a business card—Sales Manager, Marketing Director, Training Coordinator. A courtesy title is the one you put before a name: Mr., Ms., Mrs., Dr., Prof. (When you write to *Ms.* Pat McAulliffe when you are actually writing to a *Mr.* Pat McAulliffe you aren't going to make any friends in the McAulliffe household. It's just as bad to call Bonnie McAulliffe *Ms.* when she prefers *Mrs.,* if you know better.)

If necessary, make phone calls to clarify the correct names, spelling and titles of the people you write to. Or look them up in a directory.

☐ **Are the margins even?** On paper, the general rule about margins is two inches on the top and bottom of a page and one to two inches on each side—but make the ones on the side even with each other.

☐ **Is all tabbed material in line?** With the word processing software that most writers use now, there is no excuse if the tabbed material isn't in line. All like items must appear at the same tabbed locations. Make sure that your tabs make sense. In the process of writing, it is easy to confuse the levels of an outline. Double-check them in your editing.

A word about e-mail and tab settings: Realize that when you send documents through e-mail, some of your readers may get them with different (or no) formatting because of their own e-mail program. As a general rule, go lightly with tab settings in e-mail—unless you are sure your reader will get them as you have set them.

☐ **Is the print dark and even?** Yes, it's all about aesthetics. You think that's unfair, you say? That it should be about your content? Agreed. But it isn't. Face facts and make sure your writing looks as beautiful as it reads.

☐ **Is the font readable and professional?** One of the fun benefits of word processing software is the ease with which a writer can change typeface (font). In the world of work, using the more creative, less professional fonts can actually damage your credibility. Stick with a serif font most often—it is more readable than sans-serif. (Serifs are the little curlies and lines that appear on the ends and bottoms of the lines that make up the letters. Times New Roman, the default font used in Microsoft® Word, is a serif typeface. Arial is a sans-serif typeface.)

☐ **Is there enough white space to keep the reader interested and relaxed?** Have you used bulleted lists to make a series of points? They provide eye relief because of the white space surrounding those points. How about your paragraph lengths? None over ten printed lines, right? Have you inserted a one or two-line paragraph now and then in your longer documents to keep your reader interested? How about your e-mail? Can your reader see white space ahead the minute the first window opens?

Your use of white space shows consideration for your busy (and most likely tired) reader. Better, in fact, to spread your message over two pages with a lot of white space than one page that appears too compressed. Compressed = hard to read.

A few final notes:

- Use the correct editing symbols to show your changes.
- For several editors, use different colors (or use the track changes feature in your word processing software).
- Before you edit, make sure you have a list of agreed-upon editorial decisions so you can be consistent in your writing.

Editing symbols:

Delete

che̸ck   of̸fice   Mr̸.   edit̸ing

Add

ch__e__ck   o__f__ice   M__r__.   edit__i__ng

Transpose

chcek   ofiice   Mr.   edijtjing

Make lowercase

che̸ck   o̸ffice   M̸R.   Edi̸Ting

Make uppercase

≡ Skillpath   mr.   new York   buddha

Close up space

Skill Path   of fice   Mr .   edit ing

Add space

NewYork   officebuilding   Mr.Jones   BillyJoel

New paragraph

¶   The managers who attended last week's meeting were satisfied with Jack's report. Next week, we will discuss three new topics.

E-MAIL

Most business readers today will tell you that they receive more e-mail than they do regular mail (otherwise known as *snail mail*). The guidelines we recommend in this section come from the same philosophical base as the rest of the tips in this book: You need to be *clear*, *readable* and *correct* in order to communicate effectively with your readers. This philosophy, you will find, is even more essential when you are communicating electronically.

Rules

1. Make certain your reader prefers receiving your messages via e-mail as opposed to through regular mail or by fax. When you need to persuade your reader, consider a personal visit or a phone call instead of (or in addition to) an e-mail message.

2. Guard the reputation of your screen name with your life.

3. Use a clear and appealing subject line.

4. Get to the point within the opening screen.

5. Consider the potential limitations of your reader's software and/or hardware.

6. Use conventional style rules in the preparation of e-mail.

7. Don't be afraid to use generally accepted e-mail abbreviations and emoticons.

8. Never forget that there *is* a Big Brother.

9. Respect confidentiality and practice excellent netiquette.

10. Know your company's e-mail policy.

11. When forwarding an e-mail, remove all previous "forwards" before sending it.

Examples and Explanations

1. **Make certain your reader prefers receiving your messages via e-mail as opposed to through regular mail or by fax. And when you need to persuade your reader, consider a personal visit or a phone call instead of (or in addition to) an e-mail message.**

   The number of computer-literate and computer-comfortable people increases exponentially every month. But while it could be unfathomable to you that there is anyone left in the work world who isn't comfortable with e-mail, the fact is that there are—probably thousands. Make sure that your reader sees e-mail in a positive light before you make your decision to communicate to him or her with it.

   Also, realize that the easiest offer to turn down, the simplest no to say, comes in e-mail. Think about it: How easy is it for you to say no to an e-mail? Isn't it just as simple as pressing the Reply button, then typing the word no? N-O- Send. Easy! How difficult is it to say that same no to a human face, or a human voice on the other end of a telephone? Isn't it much more difficult?

   Keep this simple fact of human nature in mind: When you are asking for something you hope your reader says yes to, or when you are attempting to persuade that reader to believe or do something, make sure to initiate a more personal contact than only e-mail.

   It is a great idea, though, to follow up with an e-mail. "Thanks for your time on the phone this afternoon. Just to confirm our discussion, …" It will be a good reminder and provides a good paper trail memo for you, should you need one in the future.

2. **Guard the reputation of your screen name with your life.**

   Understand that your reader performs a quick preliminary sort on his or her incoming e-mail on a daily basis. We refer to that as triage—you know, like on those old M*A*S*H reruns. Triage is the sorting operation done by the doctors outside the hospital tent—who goes in first, who is too far gone to go in at all.

   You do the same thing to your incoming e-mail. Don't you? And so do your readers.

   Haven't you ever deleted an e-mail message unread just because you saw the screen name of the person who sent it to you? That person was someone who always sent you junk mail you resented getting?

If you, like most of us, have only one screen name at work: NEVER SEND JUNK MAIL. You can't afford the risk. Your reader could end up making a determination that most of what you send is junk and then most of your e-mail to that reader won't even be opened.

Also don't send too much e-mail to anyone. Even if every piece of e-mail you send is responsible, you could cause your reader to suffer from sheer overload. If you find yourself sending more than a couple e-mails daily to any one person, consider saving all the small messages for one larger one sent once per day. The exception to this, of course, is if you are having an in-the-moment discussion with a reader about a specific topic.

Finally, beware of the tendency many writers have of sending an e-mail too soon. Years ago, when the only way to send a letter or memo was on paper, a cool-down period was an automatic part of any writing process you undertook. If you changed your mind about sending something, you could usually pull it out of that day's mail pile that had not yet been forwarded to the post office. With e-mail, all you need to do is press the Send button and most likely it will be too late to change your mind. (Although some Internet Service Providers do have an option to unsend a message that has not yet been opened by your reader.)

Give yourself an hour to reconsider or rewrite your e-mail whenever possible. Choose to use the Send button later, rather than using the Send button now.

3. Use a clear and appealing subject line.

When we say *clear*, we mean you should use a subject line that sums up not just what your topic is, but also the bottom line of that topic, when possible.

> **Instead of**: Wednesday Phone Call
> **How about**: I Will Call You at 2 p.m. Wednesday

We also suggest, though, that if your message is negative or threatening, find a positive — or at least neutral — aspect of it to emphasize in the subject line.

> **NOT**: Your Abysmal Performance at Today's Meeting
> **BUT**: Today's Meeting — My Impressions

When replying or forwarding e-mail, consider putting your own subject line on it to reduce the number of Re: RE: re: RE: or FW: Fw: fw: notes that print out. These appear because a large number of people have already replied to or forwarded this particular message.

Another tip: The best subject lines have a maximum of 50 characters. You can use the subject line for the entire message, e.g., "Meeting on June 21, 3 p.m. in room M-327. End" The word "end" tells them the whole message is in the subject line — a great time saver. Alternatively, you can use "EOM" (end of message), "TA" (that's all) or "NM" (no more).

4. Get to the point within the opening screen.

Your reader probably gets a lot of e-mail. In fact, most readers report they get too much e-mail.

Help your reader read — and enjoy reading — yours: Get to the point before he or she ever has to lift a finger to scroll your message. You can start with a well-written subject line (remember, no longer than 50 characters). Continue your efforts to be clear and readable by summing up your bottom line within the first few sentences.

If you doubt the importance of this suggestion, consider your own e-mail reading habits. Do you scroll completely through each one? (Face it, if you are like most people you don't even open each one.)

5. Consider the potential limitations of your reader's software and/or hardware.

Depending on the e-mail system that you or your organization and your readers and their organizations use, it is possible that what you type may not appear in the same way on their screens as it does on yours.

Formatting options such as color-coding, boldface, underlining and italics do not always transfer from one ISP to another. For example, if you are writing to someone with an address @skillpath.com from your own address @aol.com, anything you have color-coded, boldfaced, underlined or italicized will appear only as plain text.

Certainly, when you share an @address with your reader, any formatting options you use will translate to them, as long as their computer is capable of displaying that option. (If your reader has a black and white monitor, your reader won't get a color-coded message no matter what address you write to!)

Business Writing

The same thing is true of connection speed limitations. If your reader has a slow connection to the Internet and you have a high-speed one, you could be tempted to send lots of links to interesting but electronically heavy Web pages. Unfortunately, it would take your reader way too long to get onto those pages—he or she would probably lose interest in your whole message before too long.

When you are uncertain about whether or not your reader will be able to see your special formatting, keep it simple. ALL CAPS will always work, but you must be careful to not overuse them. And certainly, never send an entire e-mail in ALL CAPS.

While we are aware that texting is increasing in popularity, *never* use the spelling you use in texting in your e-mail. When you send an e-mail, you never know where it will end up—maybe on the CEO's desk. And the CEO may not understand why you're spelling "before" with a letter and a number (B4). Stay conventional!

6. Use conventional style rules in the preparation of e-mail.

In the early days of e-mail the relatively few people who used it shared an extremely lax set of formatting rules. Back when it was just those few people, those lax rules were fine. They were almost a jargon in themselves.

Today, though, we live in a much different world. The majority of people at work in the U.S. use e-mail. Many people also use it at home. Because it has become such a popular medium and one so universally used, it is now vitally important that all of us who write it make sure to follow conventional rules.

For example, use conventional capitalization. How many times have you received an e-mail from someone who used ALL CAPS? Or maybe even worse, all small letters—no capital letters whatsoever. Those same people frequently forget about forming complete sentences, too, or using proper punctuation. Have you ever noticed that this overly lax style causes you, the reader, to have trouble understanding (and sometimes even reading) the message?

Use the same rules you would follow if the document you are sending in e-mail were printed out on paper. And remember: If your bottom line doesn't appear in the opening screen window, your reader might not be motivated enough to scroll down to find it. It is even more imperative in e-mail that you get to your point quickly.

7. Don't be afraid to use generally accepted e-mail abbreviations and emoticons.

There are a wealth of abbreviations and acronyms being used and understood every day by writers of e-mail. It is certainly fine to use the more popular ones, but only when you are sure your reader will understand them.

For example, when you receive an e-mail that contains some abbreviations, you can safely assume that writer to be able to understand those same abbreviations when you respond.

Emoticons are also acceptable in e-mail. They are the "faces" (and other symbols) made by typing various characters one after the other. But remember: Use emoticons *only* when you're sure the reader will "get" them. It's better to err on the side of formality and become more casual later than to be too casual and possibly put the reader off.

As always in writing, avoid the tendency to overdo it. You don't want your e-mail to look like a bowl of alphabet soup!

8. Never forget that there *is* a Big Brother.

The security and privacy of your e-mail (and everyone else's) is—at best—questionable. Be aware that some experts now agree that communication on paper is more secure than electronic communication.

In most e-mail systems there exists a potential for extra copies to be made and stored without the direct knowledge of the original writer. To say nothing about the privacy issues that come up when the message you write privately to one individual is purposely forwarded to others, whether you approve or not.

In general, the best rule to follow is a rule of discretion. Unless you are absolutely certain of the security in the system you are using, never write anything in an e-mail that you wouldn't proudly shout from the mountaintops yourself.

Also, be careful about what you forward. Respect the privacy of others as diligently as you defend your own and you will go a long way in establishing yourself as a trustworthy and credible communicator.

9. Respect confidentiality and practice excellent netiquette.

This one is simple. Never read an e-mail unless it has been addressed to you, whether originally or as a copy. Never forward someone else's e-mail without their agreement or without their knowledge, whether that knowledge is implicit or explicit.

Don't rant, gossip or backbite in e-mail. Write your e-mail with a smile on your face, and make sure that it can be read in a positive tone. (As you know, e-mail has a reputation for sometimes being too curt and too abrupt.)

Of course, this rule is actually a more specific way of illustrating Rule #2. Guard the reputation of your screen name (and yourself) with your life.

10. Know your company's e-mail policy.

Most organizations do have a policy about e-mail. This policy will tell you who owns the e-mail and whether your boss has access to yours. It will also tell you whether there are filters on your e-mail and whether copies of e-mail are routinely forwarded to people you might not be aware of. There are a large number of issues involved when you write e-mail in the workplace.

If there isn't a written policy on file in your organization, don't assume that your organization doesn't have a policy. Only you can judge, but we recommend that you limit your personal e-mailing any time you are at work. And never send an e-mail at work that you wouldn't be proud to have read by your supervisor or your supervisor's supervisor … just in case.

11. When forwarding an e-mail, remove all previous "forwards" before sending it.

It's important to remove all previous addresses the e-mail has been forwarded to—it's a confidentiality issue. It will also shorten the length of the e-mail.

EMPHASIS

Emphasis is what a business or technical writer uses to control the reader's attention level—it guides the reader to pay attention to one thing more than another.

Make it easy for your reader to quickly see, understand and digest the information you present. There are two main ways of showing emphasis in your writing: formatting for emphasis and writing for emphasis.

> *Writer's Tips:*
> *This is the kind of readability*
> *advice you will find important in*
> *your business writing. For more*
> *about Readability, see page 7.*

Formatting for emphasis involves the way your document looks, before your reader even begins reading it. Writing for emphasis covers the mechanics of how you structure your information so the most important ideas are readily apparent.

Rules

1. Highlight your most important ideas with white space. Bulleted lists, single line paragraphs, headings and margins are all methods you can use to get more white space around your important ideas.

2. Use an easy-to-read typeface.

3. Keep your most important ideas at the beginning of your document.

4. Use graphics every time they would help your reader understand your message more quickly, as long as the graphics are appropriate in the particular document.

5. Use boldface type or color to emphasize your most important ideas. If what you wish to emphasize is shorter than a printed line, ALL CAPS or underlining could also be used.

6. Use specific subject lines.

7. Put only one major idea in each sentence. When you must place a less important idea in that sentence, make it clear with punctuation or syntax which idea is most important.

8. Repeat your most important ideas and consider using them as a summary in the last paragraph of your document.

Examples and Explanations

1. **Highlight your most important ideas with white space. Bulleted lists, single line paragraphs, headings and margins are all methods you can use to get more white space around your important ideas.**

   Hands down, your single best option for highlighting information in a printed document is with white space. It is the white space that gets your reader's attention—not the printed words.

   When you have a list of items, present them as a bulleted list. Introduce the list with a colon, then indent each item in the list, lining them up one underneath another. If the bulleted items are longer than a few words, consider skipping a line between each one to make the reading even easier.

   Always use plentiful margins on the tops, bottoms and sides of your printed pages. They reduce the cluttered appearance that could scare a reader away. And especially in e-mail, never produce a paragraph that takes up a whole window in your reader's e-mail program.

   Many business writers have received some bad advice somewhere along the line. Have you? Have you ever been told to keep your memos and letters to one page whenever possible? And have you ever reduced the size of the margins to accomplish that? Or how about the font—have you ever reduced the size of the font? Or maybe you changed a bulleted list into a long rambling paragraph, just to save those precious few lines that would allow you to "keep it to one page."

   Think about your own business reading habits: What would you pick out of your morning mail first? One crowded page, overloaded with tiny little letters? Or a two-page document that looked easy and open because of the plentiful amount of white space? You know the answer.

   If your concern is that your reader may well read the first page, but then be resistant to turning that page to the second one, try this: keep the sentence flowing onto the next page. Your reader will turn the page without even noticing.

2. **Use an easy-to-read typeface.**

   Generally, serif typefaces are easier to read than sans-serif ones. A serif typeface is one that includes the little feet on the bottoms of the letters, and the little curlies at the ends of the lines that make up a particular letter. Sans-serif typefaces do not have the little feet or the little curlies.

   > Times New Roman, the default typeface in Microsoft® Word, is a serif typeface.
   >
   > Courier, the old typeface used by typewriters, is a serif typeface.
   >
   > Arial, the default typeface in many e-mail programs, is a sans-serif typeface.

   Reading experts tell us that (at least on paper) most of us are more accustomed to reading a serif typeface, therefore it goes more quickly and easily for us. (Think about it—most of us originally learned how to read with serif type. Do you remember? See Dick. See Jane. See Spot. Do those sentences look familiar?)

   Also, whether they are serif typefaces or not, avoid using anything that is too offbeat, cutesy or hard to read.

   > *Edwardian Script looks very elegant on an invitation, but could you imagine reading an entire memo that looked like this?*
   >
   > The same thing goes for any font that appears as handwriting. The people who read your business documents just aren't expecting them to look like this, so they will be slowed down.
   >
   > And finally, everyone understands that SOME of the correspondence you get sounds as though it COULD have been written in this Curlz Font. But ...

   Keep it simple.

3. **Keep your most important ideas at the beginning of your document.**

Communication experts tell us that there is a law governing how well people remember what they see, hear or read. It's called the Law of Primacy and Recency. People tend to remember best what they see, hear or read first and last.

If you have read this style guide for longer than 20 minutes you probably have already learned that ALL business writing should begin with the bottom line of your document. Your most important idea or a summary of the important ideas you will cover belongs in your first paragraph. This way, even if your reader quits reading before reaching the end of the document you can rely—with certainty—on the fact that he or she read the most important material.

Also, putting your most important information up front helps your reader understand the rest of the document as well. It helps that reader organize his or her own thinking while reading what you have to say.

There is also an almost subliminal advantage to putting your most important information on the top of the page. The "top" has always been the place for the best, or the most important.

4. **Use graphics every time they would help your reader understand your message more quickly, as long as the graphics are appropriate in the particular document.**

If a chart, table, photograph or map would illustrate a point you are making, then by all means include it. Learning theory tells us that if you can show someone something you want them to learn they always understand it more quickly than they would have if you had only told them.

Certainly, writing is the process of telling. Including graphics will get your point across twice as quickly and three times as clearly.

Occasionally, of course, graphics are not appropriate. For example, if you need to send a very quick message, the time it takes to build a graphic in your e-mail program could be counterproductive. Or, in a very formal letter, it may be inappropriate for your reader to suddenly come across a chart.

Use your best judgment, but remember that people learn and understand best when they both hear and see your information. Your writing is what they hear—your graphics provide the picture.

5. **Use boldface type or color to emphasize your most important ideas. If what you wish to emphasize is shorter than a printed line, ALL CAPS or underlining could also be used.**

Boldface is your best choice for emphasizing more than just a few words of any text. Because it is darker than the normal typeface, those words will get your reader's increased attention. Because boldface letters look just like non-boldfaced letters, your reader isn't slowed down in the reading.

Underlining and ALL CAPS, while okay for short blasts of information (no more than six or seven words), become difficult to read over a longer period. You see, your reader's brain has to subtract the underline in order to recognize the letter. And while your reader never consciously realizes this process is going on, it does contribute to an overall sense of tiredness if it goes on long enough.

Plus, none of us learned how to read with only ALL CAPS. And as you know, many letters are totally different in form as capital letters than they are as small letters. So for your busy reader, reading ALL CAPS line after line is somewhat akin to reading a foreign language—it is very tiring for the brain to translate all of those words.

Color is also a powerful way to emphasize information in a standard, mostly black on white, document. Be sure you are using colors that are powerful and, when you are communicating via e-mail, make sure your reader will be able to see the colors you are sending.

Actually, the same thing is true of boldface and underlining in e-mail. If you do not share the same e-mail program with your reader it is possible (in some cases it's even likely) that your reader won't get those formatting changes. In e-mail, the only change you can make to the text that is guaranteed to translate across all e-mail programs and servers is ALL CAPS. But be careful. Don't overdo them.

6. Use specific subject lines.

This advice is especially important in your e-mail communication. Your reader will determine whether or not to even open your e-mail with two tests:

- Does your screen name have credibility? (Or are you known to be the sender of pointless or useless mail?)
- Does your subject line indicate that your e-mail is interesting or important?
  (Or is it a never-ending series of FW: FW: FW: FW: FW:?)

Sum up your most important idea in your subject line ▶

> Quarterly Profits Up 25%
> **instead of**
> Quarterly Profit Announcement

7. Put only one major idea in each sentence. When you must place a less important idea in that sentence, make it clear with punctuation or syntax which idea is most important.

This is the cardinal rule of sentence structure for business writers: Never put more than one major idea in the same sentence. Your readers are reading too quickly for it. They will miss at least one of those ideas and perhaps both (*please* tell us you don't have more than two).

It is fine to put supporting or subordinate ideas in a sentence with that major idea. Just be sure that your punctuation or syntax (the order of the words in the sentence) makes it clear which idea is the major one.

> I can't reach Conner again until Monday, but he was definitely interested in our last offer.
> Conner was definitely interested in our last offer, but I can't reach him again until Monday.

Generally, your more important information should come first

Do you see the subtle difference in emphasis between those two sentences?

Exception

> On Monday, Conner will call us to accept our last offer.

What is the major idea in this example? That Conner will accept the offer? Or that he will call on Monday? Certainly, both are useful but the real news is that he is accepting the offer. By the way, he will do it by phone on Monday.

8. Repeat your most important ideas and consider using them as a summary in the last paragraph of your document.

In a longer document (over two pages), summarize frequently. Recap your most important points so that your reader stays with you. Also, consider adding a summary paragraph at the end of a longer document.

In shorter documents (two pages or less), this tip is usually not necessary. The document itself is short enough for your reader to re-read what he or she chooses to.

EXECUTIVE SUMMARIES

Executive Summaries are found at the very beginning of many business reports and some business memos and letters. They summarize the most important information to be found in the whole document.

Rules

1. Always use an Executive Summary, whether or not you label it as such.
2. When your Executive Summary contains more than one bottom line idea, use visual formatting techniques to make them clear.
3. When the bottom line is bad news, cushion the blow briefly before presenting it.

Examples and Explanations

1. **Always use an Executive Summary, whether or not you label it as such.**

   Every document you write needs a statement of its bottom line point or points, as close to the beginning of the whole document as possible. This is an Executive Summary, whether or not you actually label it as such with a heading.

   In a short letter, this bottom line statement would appear in the first paragraph (but without the heading **Executive Summary**). In a longer, more formal business memo or e-mail, this bottom line statement would be in the first paragraph, perhaps even after the heading.

   In a major report or proposal, check the formatting requirements for that report or proposal and follow them. In most cases, an Executive Summary will be expected near the beginning.

2. **When your Executive Summary contains more than one bottom line idea, use visual formatting techniques to make them clear.**

   In a longer memo or report it is likely that your bottom line covers more than one point. When this happens, use a bulleted list to list the main points of your Executive Summary—again, whether or not you actually label this section with the heading **Executive Summary**.

3. **When the bottom line is bad news, cushion the blow briefly before presenting it.**

   Sometimes, even when an Executive Summary is required by formatting guidelines you are following, the bottom line is unpleasant. When it is, cushion the blow before presenting the bottom line. One easy way to do this is to give them the information in a way that leads them to the conclusion.

   If, for example, the bottom line message of a document you must prepare is that six months of research produced no tangible result, mention that the scientists doing that research were diligent and missed no opportunity for success.

   Or if the bottom line message of a memo you must send to your employees is that layoffs are certain within the next month, mention that the organization is going to do everything it can to aid anyone who needs it in finding another position. Also tell them what fine employees they are. Tell them about the economic conditions that make this news necessary.

   What responsible writers work hard to avoid is being too abrupt with a negative message. You never know when you will need the trust of these readers again, so it is best to stay as positive as possible no matter what the circumstances. Plus, your overall reputation as a writer and as a communicator will improve, adding to your professional credibility.

FAXES

Faxes (that word is short for the longer *facsimiles*) are used often in business communication. They are faster than conventional mail and more concrete than e-mail. When a sheet of paper or a hard copy of a signature is required and required *quickly*, most writers elect to send a fax. And no one can argue about the speed of a fax.

The concerns that can arise, though, need to be considered. Many fax copies look—frankly—terrible. And while your reader may appreciate the speed with which the information reached his or her office, that reader might have second thoughts about your professional image because the fax machine that received your document doesn't print well.

This sounds ludicrous to many people. But examine your own reactions when you receive a fax that looks sloppy or unclear just because of the quality of the fax machine. Of course, no one would *consciously* hold this against the writer. But how about *unconsciously*?

Another concern about faxes is the same concern we have about e-mail. It is possible to send a fax very quickly. Therefore, you might regret sending a fax. It is possible to wish that you could get it back. Of course, you cannot.

Rules

The guidelines below should help you send the most professional and clear faxes you can.

1. Make sure your reader wants to receive your message via fax before sending it.
2. Include a cover sheet that is both clear and easily received. Also, do your best to ensure that all pages you fax will be easily understandable once they have been transmitted.
3. Include a list of the documents being faxed on the cover sheet.
4. Include a notation on the bottom of a letter that it was sent by fax. If appropriate, also include the fax number the document was transmitted to.
5. Don't over-fax.

Examples and Explanations

1. **Make sure your reader wants to receive your message via fax before sending it.**

   In other words, don't fall into the trap of sending mail via fax for the sole reason that faxes are your preferred way of receiving mail. Consult the recipient of that mail to discover his or her preferred way of receiving it.

2. **Include a cover sheet that is both clear and easily received. Also, do your best to ensure that all pages you fax will be easily understandable once they have been transmitted.**

*Never send a fax without a cover sheet that clearly
identifies at least these important items*

▼

• Date	• Your reader's contact information (phone, fax & e-mail)
• Who you are	• A subject line
• Your organization	• The number of pages included in the fax
• Your contact information (address, phone, fax & e-mail)	• A short but warm note
• Your reader	• If appropriate, a list of the items being faxed
• Your reader's department and organization	• Your signature

Also, make sure that you are using a cover sheet that translates well into black and white—preferably a cover sheet that is presented in a black and white medium itself. While it is true that some of your readers use color faxes, you will most likely not know ahead of time which ones do and which ones don't. Better safe than sorry.

3. Include a list of the documents being faxed on the cover sheet.

Always mention the item(s) you are faxing on your cover sheet. If you are sending just one document, a simple mention of what that document is in the note you have written on the cover sheet should be enough.

However, when you are sending several items, you will make it easier for your reader to quickly discover what is included by presenting the list as a bulleted list, including the number of pages per item.

For example, in our model fax cover sheet, we could have listed the items being sent separately

▼

Included in this fax are:

- Contract for Cover Art Production, dated 9-29-2003 (signed)   2 pgs.
- Contract for Color Palette—Style guide pages (dated 9-29-2003) (signed)   2 pgs.
- Copy, Proposed Art A-3 (with notes)   1 pg.
- Copy, Proposed Palette C-5 (with notes)   1 pg.

Notice that this presentation makes the information much more accessible to your reader. In some cases, though, if you are aiming for a very casual and warm style, it could be overkill. Use your best judgment and always put the reader's needs above your own.

4. Include a notation on the bottom of a letter that it was sent by fax. If appropriate, also include the fax number the document was transmitted to.

Underneath the signature block, where you would make note of any CCs or Enclosures, type the words **By fax**.

If you think it could matter later, also include the fax number the document was sent to.

This notation will help anyone who consults your file (or files on the receiving end once the document has been received) in case a question arises about when it was sent, how it was sent or where it was sent. (Yes, files are usually kept for just this purpose: Cover Your Backside.)

By fax to (222) 111-3333

5. Don't over-fax.

Faxes, if you receive too many, no longer appear urgent. This is the same for all kinds of mail and correspondence you regularly send and receive.

Never send a fax when it isn't necessary.

Of course, never send a letter that isn't necessary—or an e-mail either. If you find yourself returning to your fax machine hour after hour to send some new urgent communication to a reader, consider pooling the information that accumulates over a few hours and sending just a couple faxes per day to that reader. This way, you still get to communicate but the reader still gets the benefit of seeing your fax as urgent.

FAX COVER SHEET

Date: September 29, 2010

SkillPath

FAX NUMBER
(913) 362-4264

PHONE NUMBER
(913) 362-3900

To: Laura Smith
Marketing Director
Rambo and Krause Creative Arts
Fax #: (913) 444-7545
Phone #: (913) 444-5553

From: Susan Poley
Editor
SkillPath Publications

Subject: Cover Art Approval—SkillPath Style Guide
Number of pages (including cover sheet): 7

Notes:

Dear Laura,

Thanks for your patience with us as we considered the options you presented to us for the SPSG cover—you put a lot of good work into all of them.

Bill and I have decided on Art A-3 with the color palette you suggest for C-5. Included in this fax are the contracts with our signatures attesting to these choices, as well as copies of both A-3 and C-5 with the relevant notes.

Please call me sometime this afternoon to let me know you have received this fax and to clarify any questions you may have.

Susan

SkillPath Inc. • 6900 Squibb Road • Mission, KS 66202
director@email.com

▲

An example of a cover sheet that works

FOOTNOTES

Footnotes have two important uses in business and technical writing. First, they are the most accepted method for citing the references you have used in the preparation of your own documents. Second, they are an easily accessible way to provide extra information not essential to the document, but perhaps interesting to some readers. Technically, footnotes are the references that appear on the bottom of a page and endnotes are the notes that are assembled in a section at the end of a document. Other than the location and the semantics, there is no difference in how the writer would present them. However, as a general rule, we recommend footnotes over endnotes. Most readers find it easier to reference the additional information page by page rather than turning to the end of the document.

Footnotes and endnotes are especially common in more formal documents. In less formal documents, the same information that would be provided in a footnote or endnote could just as easily be provided as a *textnote*, within the document itself. These textnotes can be provided within parentheses or as part of a sentence referring to the information.

When your document does require footnotes or endnotes, it is vitally important that you get them right. This is one of those picky little details that your reader will probably notice—but only if you do them incorrectly. Don't give any of your readers an excuse to doubt your expertise or credibility.

Rules

1. Use a consecutive superscript numeral immediately after the information that was culled from the reference you intend to footnote and the matching superscript numeral immediately before the footnote itself. Provide the matching footnote on the bottom of that page or in a section containing all the endnotes at the end of the document.

2. When using footnotes or endnotes to give source information, include all bibliographic information plus the specific page numbers of the reference in the footnote or endnote. When you are using more than one footnote or endnote referring to the exact same reference, it is permissible to use only the author's name and the page numbers appropriate to the new material.

3. When using footnotes (or endnotes—which we don't recommend) to provide supplementary information to your text, follow all conventional rules of writing.

4. No matter what, make sure your footnotes, endnotes and textnotes are clear and easily traceable to your main sources.

Examples and Explanations

1. **Use a consecutive superscript numeral immediately after the information that was culled from the reference you intend to footnote and the matching superscript numeral immediately before the footnote itself. Provide the matching footnote on the bottom of that page or in a section containing all the endnotes at the end of the document.**

Traditionally, footnotes and endnotes are numbered. The first one in a document is numbered with a superscript 1, the second a superscript 2 and so on. If there is only one footnote to be made in your document, you could use an asterisk instead of a numeral. But once you see that you need more than one footnote or endnote, asterisks no longer work. They are too difficult to follow sequentially. Stick with numbers.

It is easier for the writer to supply all the notes together as endnotes, on a separate page or in a separate section at the end of a document. And if the only thing that's being listed in those notes is source information for various references you used in the preparation of your document, your reader probably doesn't mind.

But consider this: if you are putting extra information into your footnotes, keeping them removed from the very page where that extra information could be interesting to your reader doesn't serve that reader.

Always, always, ALWAYS make your writing choices with your reader's needs foremost in your mind.

The good news is that now, with word processing software, the placement of footnotes isn't as difficult as it used to be. There is a command (usually found on the insert menu) that handles the spacing needs for you. Check your program's Help files if you have specific questions.

Business Writing

2. When using footnotes or endnotes to give source information, include all bibliographic information plus the specific page numbers of the reference in the footnote or endnote. When you are using more than one footnote or endnote referring to the exact same reference, it is permissible to use only the author's name and the page numbers appropriate to the new material.

And use the correct format. In the case of a book, that would be: Author, Title, Publisher, Date, City, Page number(s).

> [1] Ayn Rand, *Atlas Shrugged*, Plume, 1957, New York, page 633.

The second time you refer to the same reference in a footnote, you can use less information in your footnote. Just make sure you have given enough to make certain your reader will be clear. If the only reference in your bibliography written by Rand is *Atlas Shrugged*, the next time you refer to that book, you could get away with using just the author's name and the new page number(s).

> [2] Ayn Rand, pages 875 – 876.

If, however, you have more than one book by Ayn Rand in your bibliography, use both the author's name and the title of the particular book, as well as the pertinent page numbers.

> [3] Ayn Rand, *Atlas Shrugged*, page 765.

3. When using footnotes (or endnotes—which we don't recommend) to provide supplementary information to your text, follow all conventional rules of writing.

In other words, use well written, complete sentences in any footnotes you provide to supply extra or optional information. Avoid the tendency to provide just the words you think to be relevant. Remember—your reader is a better reader when your writing is conversational.

4. No matter what, make sure your footnotes, endnotes and textnotes are clear and easily traceable to your main sources.

Your readers will, after all, occasionally actually use your footnotes, endnotes and textnotes to locate more information. So make sure that the information you have placed in them is correct, understandable and accurate.

You are using footnotes, endnotes and textnotes for the very same reason you are writing in the first place: to send a clear, readable and correct message.

GRAMMAR ERRORS

Much of this style guide covers basic rules of English grammar, punctuation, spelling and style. This section is devoted to the most common (and the most embarrassing) grammar errors even educated business writers fall prey to. There are ten of them.

The Ten Most Embarrassing Grammar Errors Business Writers Make	
Error #1: The Nonsexist Error	Error #6: The S Error
Error #2: The Dangling Error	Error #7: The Who/Whom Error
Error #3: The That (vs. Who) Error	Error #8: The Syntax Error
Error #4: The Other That (vs. Which) Error	Error #9: The Jargon Error
Error #5: The Reflexive Error	Error #10: The Collective Error

Many grammar errors made by adults are just careless errors: double negatives, wrong verb tenses, pronouns that disagree with their antecedents … They are wrong, and to most readers they look wrong. But those readers generally understand the intended message.

When a writer mistakenly writes "I can't barely see the sky," it is doubtful that any reader would actually do the math of two negatives canceling each other out and becoming a positive. That reader will instead assume that:

The writer can hardly see the sky.

AND

The writer is a careless or uneducated person.

We would suggest that the second assumption is much worse than the reader getting the wrong meaning. You see, now, you've ruined your credibility.

In other words, your grammar, spelling and punctuation errors don't interfere with your meaning as much as they interfere with your reputation. And of course, to be successful as a business or technical writer, your reputation had better be impeccable.

In this vein, here are the ten most common grammar errors that even educated writers sometimes make, and not just out of carelessness.

Some of them, your readers may not even notice. Or more accurately, some of them, SOME of your readers may not notice. But why take the chance?

The Ten Most Embarrassing Grammar Errors Business Writers Make— And How to Avoid Them

Error #1: The Nonsexist Error

Let's get it out of the way first. Of course, our intentions with nonsexist English have always been honorable. It is only our constructions that have been cumbersome, if not downright grammatically incorrect.

How would you make this sentence nonsexist? ▶ Each student is responsible for his own work.

The most obvious choice would be to change it to ▶ Each student is responsible for *his or her* own work.

For one sentence, it's a choice you can live with. But what if there had been a whole paragraph of sentences that would need the "his or her" change. That would be cumbersome, and with its weight, it would draw attention to itself as style instead of as meaning.

That's when a common (but well-meaning) grammar error comes in ▶ Each student is responsible for *their* own work.

Many of us have heard that the most invisible way to make writing nonsexist is to change the offending third person singular pronoun into a plural one. Great idea! But you can't suspend the rules of pronouns agreeing with their antecedents.

Making the sentence plural does work—but only if you make the whole sentence plural ▶  *All students* are responsible for *their* own work.

Other nonsexist options also exist. In some cases, it is possible to leave out the third person singular pronoun altogether:

> **NOT:** A writer must be persistent and industrious before he becomes rich.
>
> **BUT:** A writer must be persistent and industrious *before becoming* rich.

In still fewer cases, it is possible to switch the whole sentence to the second person:

> **NOT:** An employee of our company can be proud of his contribution to our success.
>
> **BUT:** As an employee of our company, you can be proud of your contribution to our success.

Nonsexist language is also a consideration when using words that themselves could be interpreted by your reader as sexist. This is why we now call mailmen *letter carriers* and stewardesses *flight attendants*. But what about manhole covers? Believe it or not, many utility workers have informed us that their departments now call them *utility lids* or *utility covers*, just to be sure no one could ever sue them. "Well, the reason they didn't hire me is because I am a woman and they have 'manhole covers' so they didn't think I was qualified to work there ..." Scary, isn't it?

Error #2: The Dangling Error

Do you remember hearing about a grammatical error called a dangling participle? Actually, the dangling variety of grammar error is much larger than just with participles—it is an error that regularly occurs with all manner of modifiers.

First, some definitions:

- A *modifier* is any word, phrase or clause that is used to describe or limit other words.

- A *dangling modifier* is a modifier that is misplaced in the sentence, so that it does not seem to relate to the word(s) it is intended to describe or limit. In the worst cases, it is actually so misplaced it appears to describe a word other than the one the writer intended.

- A *dangling participle* is a modifier—usually placed at the beginning of a sentence—that contains an -ing verb (present participle) or -ed verb (past participle) without a reference to the doer of that verb immediately after. Like this:

> While reviewing the statistics, many contradictions appeared.

Who reviewed those statistics? One good test for a dangling modifier is to make sure that every introductory phrase or clause followed by a comma is actually describing (or limiting) the first main word after the comma.

The preferred solution ▶ While reviewing the statistics, Dr. Beckett noticed many contradictions.

Or, if you don't know (or don't want to say) who did that review:

The generic solution ▶ Many contradictions appeared while reviewing the statistics.

Another problem with modifiers is that sometimes a writer misplaces modifiers—look at how embarrassing this one could be for the police department in question:

> Before that arrest, the Kinky Korner had been viewed mainly as a shop dealing in novelties to police.

What one word does the word *police* need to appear closer to, in order to clarify the meaning here (we hope)?

The solution ▶ Before that arrest, the police viewed the Kinky Korner mainly as a shop dealing in novelties.

Much clearer, right?

Error #3: The That (vs. Who) Error

That and *who* are often used as pronouns.

> The company that works hard is the company that succeeds.

The *that* is correct both times, because it is serving as a pronoun for a thing (taking the place of the noun *company*). Here is one that is not correct. Can you tell why?

Wrong ▶ The employees that work hard are the employees that succeed.

Of course: Employees are people and therefore the appropriate pronoun to replace them with is *who*.

Correct ▶ The employees who work hard are the employees who succeed.

Error #4: The Other That (vs. Which) Error

Here is an example of a grammar rule that will help you build up the necessary muscle to tackle the who/whom rule. This one is about *restrictive* vs. *nonrestrictive* phrases and clauses.

Here are some definitions:

- **Restrictive** means that the information being added to the sentence with the phrase or clause in question is *essential* to the correct and clear meaning of that sentence.

- **Nonrestrictive**, as you have probably already guessed, means that the information is *not essential* (although it may be interesting or expansive) to the correct and clear meaning of that sentence.

> **RESTRICTIVE:**   The meeting room that is upstairs needs new chairs.
> **NONRESTRICTIVE:**   The meeting room, which is upstairs, needs new chairs.

What is the difference in meaning between those two sentences? The only difference in their construction is the "that" vs. the "which"—or is it? Notice that the "which" clause is enclosed in commas. Do you remember what those commas mean to the reader? (Our Comma section begins on page 155.)

Those commas give the reader "permission" to lift the words enclosed between them out of the sentence temporarily to see what the "root" or main sentence is. So in the second example, the main sentence is:

> The meeting room needs new chairs.

And oh, by the way, it is upstairs. What is the difference in meaning when the "that is upstairs" is part of the main sentence? Well, maybe there's more than one meeting room. Only the one that is upstairs needs new chairs. The one in the basement got new chairs just yesterday, and the one on the main floor got new chairs last week.

Error #5: The Reflexive Error

You've probably seen this done and it irritates you.

> If you have any questions, give Dennis or myself a call.

Name the one person who can call *myself:*

  A. Dennis   B. Dennis, if he has a split personality   C. I   D. Both A & C

The correct answer is *C:* only *I* can call myself. Dennis cannot call *myself*. But he can call *himself*.

The corrected sentence ▶ If you have any questions, call Dennis or me.

Reflexive pronouns all end with -self or -selves. (Myself, yourself, himself, herself, itself, ourselves, themselves.)

Think of the word *reflexive* as coming from the same root as the word *reflect*, and using reflexive pronouns correctly becomes simple. The only time it is correct to use a reflexive pronoun is when the subject of a sentence is doing an action that reflects that same subject. It's like looking at a reflection in a mirror.

> If you have any questions, I can answer them myself.

> *Writer's Tips:*
> *For more on reflexive*
> *pronouns, see page 141.*

Error #6: The S Error

To be specific, we should probably refer to this as the "To Apostrophe or Not To Apostrophe Error." We all know that to make a plural of a singular word, the general rule is to add an *s* to the word:

We also all know that there are more exceptions to the rules of making plurals than there are to any other spelling rule in American English.

one dog	two dogs
one writer	three writers

Here, let's deal only with the possessive problem. If one manager owns a computer, add "apostrophe *s*" to manager:

> manager's computer

If two managers each own a computer, then just "add an apostrophe"—sound familiar?

> managers' computers

But what happens when it is a child who owns a computer?

> child's computer

More than one child?

Who each own a computer?

This is where most people become confused. The confusion lies in the rule we repeat to ourselves about more than one manager owning more than one computer: "Just add an apostrophe." Obviously, the rule fails here. And actually, the reason it does is because it was never really the rule to begin with.

So forget it. You need to forget the phrase: "Just add an apostrophe."

Here is the rule that always works: To make a possessive, add an apostrophe *s* unless the word already ends in *s*, then add just an apostrophe.

This is so important, and the true key to so many correct possessives in your future, it bears repeating. To make a possessive, add an apostrophe *s* unless the word already ends in *s*, then add just an apostrophe.

The plural of *child* is *children*. According to the rule above, how do you make it possessive? Add apostrophe *s* (because it does not already end in *s*).

The solution 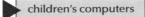 children's computers

A question many people now ask is, "Well, what about words or names that end in *s*?" It's a good question, and frankly, grammar guides disagree.

We recommend: Pronounce the apostrophe *s* in speaking, but do not write it.

This way you get the best of both worlds. It doesn't look awkward and it doesn't sound awkward.

So, in writing ▶ Ross' hat   *In speaking* ▶ Ross's hat

Error #7: The Who/Whom Error

Let's cover the grammar rule first. The word *who* is a subject pronoun. The word *whom* is an object pronoun.

This would be enlightening if we just knew what that really meant in practical usage.

Who and *whom* make for a great example of why native speakers of any language usually know more than they think they do about its grammar. So when you are at the end of a sentence like:

> Take these banana bran blintzes over to (he/him).

You would just know to use a *him*. It never dawns on you that you have to use the object pronoun because the person is receiving the blintzes, not delivering them. You've just heard it and read it so many times, you know it by instinct today.

The reason that "him" is the one who gets those blintzes is because "him" is the object pronoun, and that object pronoun is the one you need for the reason explained above—he isn't delivering the blintzes, he is receiving them.

Now, let's say you didn't hear the end of the chef's command, so you need to ask:

> You want me to take these banana bran blintzes over to (who/whom)?

Do you see why whom is correct? If so, you have a tool that will work 99.9% of the time.

Here is a handy chart ▶

SUBJECT	OBJECT
he	him
who	whom

If you just don't have time to diagram the sentence (does anyone do that anymore?) to find out whether you are looking for a subject pronoun or an object pronoun, just use the substitution method: Temporarily put the word *he* or *him* in the spot. Which one works? If it is *he*, use *who*; if it is *him*, use *whom*.

> You want me to take these banana bran blintzes over to (him or whom)?

See? It's actually very simple.

Error #8: The Syntax Error

Syntax is the word we use to refer to the order of words in a sentence. Proper syntax happens when the words are in the most predictable and understandable order available.

The most frequent problem with syntax is something we have already covered: misplaced and dangling modifiers (Error #2). There are other considerations:

Subjects and their verbs should be as near to each other as possible. Conjunctions and transitional words or phrases should be used to keep the idea moving in the right direction. Then again, maybe some of those conjunctions and transitions deserve more attention.

Have you ever written a sentence that you couldn't easily follow? Perhaps the solution is to make two (or sometimes three or four) shorter and clearer sentences. Think about it—if you are the author and you don't get it, do you suppose your readers will? You know what you are trying to say—they don't. It can be very confusing for them.

So here it is—a writing rule that is so critical to your reader's understanding of your writing that it should be a grammar rule: Keep most sentences short and simple in construction.

By short, most writing experts agree that you limit most sentences to no more than 32 words, and that the average number of words per sentence is 10 – 17. (See Editing, pages 66 – 71.)

An even more important consideration for credible and persuasive business writers (and those who want to be) is that second suggestion: Keep most sentences simple in construction.

Don't put more than one major idea in many of your sentences. Business writers whose readers are busy can't afford it. Long sentences with ideas piled upon each other like so many pancakes wear out your readers. What do you suppose happens when your reader gets worn out?

A. The reader stops reading.

B. The reader reads someone else's writing instead.

C. The reader makes a mental note of your e-mail screen name and deletes all future communication from you unread.

D. If you write a lot, the reader considers setting up a special e-mail rule that will delete it without waiting to be told.

E. Perhaps *all of the above*.

You can't afford it. Impress your readers with the ideas you have, not with how many of them you can put between two periods.

Error #9: The Jargon Error

Jargon is defined as the specialized language the members of any subculture (ethnic, professional, regional, etc.) understand and use to mean the same thing.

We all speak a lot of jargon. Most people have jargon they take for granted at their jobs; in their homes; in their cities, states and countries; and with their friends.

Most people speak some technology jargon. Do you? Have you *poked* someone today? Where do you store your *cookies*? Have you ever *surfed* the Web? These words and phrases have a definite meaning that all computer and Internet users share. But have you ever asked a friend or co-worker about their cookies? What did you get? Probably a blank stare.

Here is the rule to follow about jargon: Use jargon only when you are willing to bet your life (and it will be your business writing life) that your reader understands it as you intend them to.

Business Writing

Error #10: The Collective Error

Collective nouns take singular verbs. They just don't always look like they do.

> The committee of accountants was startled by the sudden crash.

Many less careful writers notice that this sentence doesn't sound right, so they change it:

> The committee of accountants were startled by the sudden crash.

Yet this is wrong. *Committee* is the subject of the sentence. It is a collective noun (meaning a committee does have more than one member but there is just one committee). Because we are writing about just one committee, the verb must be singular: *was*.

But, do your readers know that? Or is it possible they would think you have made an error—even when you went to the trouble of following the rule about collective nouns always taking singular verbs? Well, here's a better idea: When you write a sentence that sounds awkward to you, rewrite it so it is no longer awkward. (But don't break grammar rules in doing so.)

Solution ▶ All the accountants on the committee were startled by the sudden crash.

Your writing style should never call attention to itself, except as it serves your meaning. It is doubtful that your readers have an opened copy of any grammar guide in their laps as they read your writing, just to double-check. Most readers use only one rule to judge your correctness: Does it sound right?

Grammar is an invisible means to your desired end. What is your desired end? I would hope it is the understanding, respect and acceptance of your reader. While we don't want to be overly formal or stuffy, we must remember that we are the professionals here. We are the ones who know what we are trying to communicate. We are the ones who know what we need our readers to be persuaded of by the time they have finished reading. If we don't do it right, who will? If we won't make the better but more humane usage of our shared language a priority, who will?

GRAMMAR RULES YOU CAN IGNORE

Truth be told, the world you are writing in today as a business or technical writer is much different from the world you wrote in as a younger student. In fact, you can break any of these eight rules and your reader will usually thank you for the effort.

This style guide is intended to tell our readers the options available, then to make recommendations about usage depending on the purpose of your writing. In these eight examples, we recommend you err on the side of readability. These outdated rules actually inhibit your reader's ability to understand. That's why you shouldn't follow them.

Here are the "Eight Rules You Learned in Junior High That Now You Can (Usually) Ignore!" Do they sound familiar?

Rules

1. Never end a sentence with a preposition.
2. Never begin a sentence with a conjunction.
3. Never use the word *hopefully* at the beginning of a sentence.
4. Never split an infinitive.
5. Avoid using contractions in your "formal" writing (including all letters).
6. Avoid using the personal pronouns *I* and *me* when referring to yourself in letters.
7. Do not re-use words. (Think of new ones instead, so your reader does not become bored.)
8. Always put a comma after the year when using a date in a sentence.

Examples and Explanations

Let's deal with them one at a time to learn where these rules came from to begin with (in most cases) and why your writing is more clear and professional without them.

1. **Never end a sentence with a preposition.**

   Never? Not even when it makes more sense to?

   Take a look at that last sentence. How would you need to rewrite it to keep it from ending in a preposition? Well, there's, "Not even when it makes more sense to end a sentence with a preposition?" Too wordy. Or how about, "Not even when to do it makes more sense?" This is better than the wordy option, but still not as clear and straightforward as the original "Not even when it makes more sense to."

   Have you ever caught yourself breaking this rule? Did you then try to fix it? Didn't you end up with one of the weirdest sentences you'd ever written?

   "What are you using that computer for?" becomes "For what are you using that computer?" Which one is more conversational? Which one is less awkward? Which one is easier on the eyes of the reader?

   This old rule could have its origin in the hearts of well-meaning kindergarten and first grade teachers. Have you ever heard a child that age talk? Many times they add unnecessary prepositions to the ends of their sentences (usually questions):

   > Where are my toys at?
   > What do I need to clean my room for?
   > So that's where my teddy bear is at!

   Notice that in these three examples, the sentences work perfectly if you just drop the last word:

   The easy solution ▶
   > Where are my toys?
   > Why do I need to clean my room?
   > So that's where my teddy bear is!

   Such is not the case with our more adult examples of:

   > Not even when it makes more sense to.
   > What are you using that computer for?

   Simply dropping the preposition doesn't work ▼

   > Not even when it makes more sense?
   > *(Leaving open the question, "Making more sense to what?")*
   > **OR**
   > What are you using that computer?
   > *(Which makes NO sense at all)*

   > *Writer's Tips:*
   > *For more information on prepositions, see page 139.*

   Never forget: As a writer, your first goal is to make sure your reader clearly understands the message you are intending to send with your written words. When your sentences sound awkward to you, just think how awkward they must sound to your reader who is relying on them to discover your intended meaning!

   By the way, if you are feeling shaky about what a preposition is, here is the definition:

   Prepositions are words that connect or relate nouns and pronouns to words and phrases before and after them. Most of us needed to memorize a list of them in our younger years. Does this one sound familiar?

   Examples: of, in, by, at, down, from, between, on, near, over, across, against

   In business writing, it is okay to end a sentence with a preposition. Certainly, don't go out of your way to do it and don't do it just to add unnecessary words to the ends of your sentences.

2. Never begin a sentence with a conjunction.

Conjunctions connect words, phrases and clauses while telling the relationship between them. (If this sounds eerily familiar, you are not crazy. You just read a similar definition about prepositions.)

Many of you probably remember being told that you aren't allowed to start sentences with conjunctions. Or at the very least, you were told you can't begin sentences with *and*, *but* or *because*. Some of you may have asked, "Why not?" The answer was usually: "Because we said so!"

The theory that motivated those well-meaning teachers was probably this: How can you use a conjunction when there is nothing to connect? Their thought was that because a sentence had just ended, so had a complete idea.

Today we see things differently. When your choice is between using a single long sentence with many ideas or using several shorter, simpler sentences, you must go with the shorter simpler sentences. But you'll need a conjunction to connect them. With a beginning conjunction included, your reader not only gets the benefit of separate sentences (easier to read and understand) but also the benefit of a smooth flow between those sentences.

Your reader does not have the time or energy to meditate upon your words. If you make it difficult, that reader will most likely just push your writing aside, thinking "I'll come back to this later." But later rarely comes.

Honestly, think about your own reading habits. Don't you do the same thing?

Start looking for sentences that begin with conjunctions in the reading you do. Certainly you will find them in journalism, even in the most formal newspaper in America, *The Wall Street Journal*. Look at the front page. On any given day, carefully read each sentence, looking for the words *And* and *But* at the beginnings of them. Circle them when you find them. How many did you end up with? (Many days there are over 10.)

How about the reading you do for pleasure? With most authors, you can open their books to just about any page and find an example of a sentence beginning with a conjunction.

In other sections of this book, we have mentioned what we call the cardinal rule of sentence structure: Never put more than one major idea in the same sentence.

Because your reader is busy and maybe even tired, your reader can only be depended upon to truly understand one major idea per sentence. Think about the way you were taught to read. Wasn't it: "Read from the capital letter to the period for the major idea"? It wasn't for the major ideas, plural—just for the one. When your readers, who are busy and reading quickly, find that first major idea, they mentally skip over the rest of that sentence to find the beginning of the next one.

Now that you have permission to begin some sentences with conjunctions like *and*, *but*, *or*, *because*, *however* and *therefore* you can make sure your reader gets both of these great benefits:

1. A smooth flow to the reading

   <u>AND</u>

2. A clear understanding of all the points you had hoped to make

3. Never use the word *hopefully* at the beginning of a sentence.

What part of speech is the word *hopefully*? (The parts of speech are: noun, verb, pronoun, preposition, conjunction, adjective, adverb and interjection.)

Did you say "adverb"? It certainly looks like an adverb, what with that "-ly" ending.

Sometimes it is used correctly as an adverb ▶ | Joe spoke hopefully of seeing his sister again. |

Adverbs modify verbs (or adjectives or adverbs). In this case, *hopefully* modifies the verb *spoke*. Joe had a hopeful tone in his voice as he spoke of seeing his sister again.

What about this one, though ▶ | Hopefully, Joe will speak next. |

What is the word *hopefully* modifying in this sentence? Is it describing Joe's tone of voice? No. Here, it is describing the mental state of the writer. The writer hopes that Joe will speak next. Actually, up until just a few years ago, it was grammatically incorrect—for the reason that an adverb must describe (modify) a word that is in the sentence. But guess what? Grammar nitpickers kept correcting us, and we kept doing it anyway. Eventually, we did it so much that even noted communicators started to do it. And that's when the grammar guides change.

Here is what the newest edition of the *Gregg Reference Manual* (one of the most conservative style guides we know) has to say today:

"Although the subject of much controversy, the use of *hopefully* at the beginning of a sentence is no different from the use of *obviously*, *certainly*, *fortunately*, *thankfully*, *actually*, *apparently*, and similar words functioning as independent comments. These adverbs express the writer's attitude toward what he or she is about to say; as such they modify the meaning of the sentence as a whole rather than a particular word." (*Gregg Reference Manual*, Tenth Edition, William A. Sabin, McGraw Hill, New York, 2005, p. 328.)

4. Never split an infinitive.

This advice is probably familiar to you. Do you remember (or were you ever told) what an infinitive is?

An *infinitive* is simply the verb with the word *to* in front of it. The infinitive forms of the verbs trust, love and go:

> to trust   to love   to go

Split infinitives

▼

> to blindly trust
> to passionately love
> to boldly go

A split infinitive, then, happens when you put an adverb in between the *to* and the verb.

Yes, even Captain James T. Kirk of the Starship Enterprise split infinitives! (Remember? "To boldly go where no man has gone before …") Often, it makes the sentence less awkward. Other times, it actually prevents miscommunication.

> He showed me how to quickly access the chat room.

For example, how would you change the above sentence to "un-split" the infinitive?

> He quickly showed me how to access the chat room.

Doesn't that change the meaning of the sentence? Before, it was the accessing that was happening quickly; now it is being quickly shown.

Even worse, though, would be:

> He showed me how to access the chat room quickly.

The problem with this last example is that the reader can't be sure which happened quickly because the adverb is not right next to either verb. To make it worse, most readers would never even notice that they didn't know. They would assume that the quickly goes wherever they subconsciously put it when they read the sentence the first time. Worst of all, the writer may not notice the error either! This is a great example of how difficult it can be to proofread something you are very familiar with. The writer knows what he or she intended and therefore reads the sentence with the proper inflection—without even thinking twice.

Here is a better rule to follow about all modifiers: Make sure to keep modifying words as close as possible to the words they modify.

Never forget that the first goal of a successful business or technical writer must be to communicate his or her message clearly to the reader. If occasionally you need to sacrifice an un-split infinitive for the greater good of clarity, so be it.

5. Avoid using contractions in your "formal" writing, including all letters.

Certainly, when you are writing on the more formal end of the writing style continuum (See Readability, page 7), it's important to avoid using contractions. But in letters, even in business letters, it would be overly formal to avoid all contractions. You are aiming for a conversational tone.

What would your conversation sound like without any contractions? ▶ "Hey, it is great to see you again! How have you been? How is your wife? How is your son? How is your daughter? How is your job going? Are you not getting annoyed listening to me avoid contractions?"

Commonly used contractions like *I'm, I'll, how's, aren't, can't, you're* and *don't* are easy to read and easy to understand. They are the correct choice for conversational writing.

Contractions that are less frequently used and contractions that look too much like something else should be avoided.

Awkward ▶ The dog's running down the street.

This is not easy to read because dog's (meaning "dog is") is not the first usage most readers will think of when they see a common noun (dog) followed by an apostrophe and an *s*. Most readers would read that the first time and become confused, looking for something the dog owns in the sentence.

This old rule also deals with the important philosophical question: How formal should my writing be? Have you already been convinced of the answer? In most cases, you should write in a conversational style because it is the easiest style for your reader to understand.

6. Avoid using the personal pronouns *I* and *me* when referring to yourself in business letters.

This is a holdover from the old and out-of-date rules many of us were taught governing business writing. It is also the rule that brought about all those strange constructions like "the undersigned remains" and "If we can be of any further assistance please do not hesitate to contact us. We can be reached at 555-1234, ext. 23."

How many people are sitting at that phone, ext. 23? When you are referring to just yourself, the correct pronouns are the singular ones *I* and *me*. When you are referring to yourself plus others, then use *we* or *us*.

The fear was that you would appear egotistical if you mentioned yourself. Certainly, your message and your reader should always be in the forefront of anything you write. But going out of your way to hide yourself will only result in an awkwardly worded piece of writing—and a less warm rapport with your reader.

7. Do not re-use words.

This comes from your elementary school education. "Class, I'd like you to write a report about this workbook; but remember, call it a workbook the first time and then think of something else to call it so your reader doesn't get bored."

What else could you call a workbook? A book, pamphlet, resource, reference material, notebook, brochure, thing— or the old standby: it.

So let's say you are writing an e-mail about that workbook, and you follow the old rule:

> This workbook details the history of the English language as we know it today. Furthermore, the pamphlet also gives some interesting advice about how to use the resource to gain more insight into the origin of grammar rules used today. If you would like a copy of the notebook, call the 800 number listed below and request their reference material. They have assured us they will send the brochure within two weeks and you will have it within three weeks.

What? If you were reading that article, and if you called that 800 number to order "it," wouldn't you be surprised if you only got one thing in the envelope? "Hey," you'd say, "where's the pamphlet, and the resource, and the brochure and the reference material? All I got was a workbook!"

For clarity's sake, once you name something a workbook, call it a workbook forever. Occasionally, you can use the pronoun "it" instead, but only if it is entirely clear what the "it" refers to. Remember the main purpose of writing: your reader's clear understanding of your intended message!

8. Always put a comma after the year when using a date in a sentence.

Some ultra-conservative grammar guides still advise you follow this rule. *Use two commas to set off the year when it follows the month and the day.*

They go on to give examples like this ▶ The November 2, 2003, edition of *Newsweek* …

The more conversational advice is to avoid the comma after the year (unless it is necessary for some other reason) because the absence of the comma does not affect—except in a positive way—the meaning or clarity of the sentence.

You wouldn't write ▶ The newest, edition of *Newsweek* …

Of course not—that would be incorrect because you are separating a noun from its adjective. Well, isn't the date of the issue also an adjective? This is an example of a rule that is truly okay either way these days.

DISCLAIMER—
The Difference Between Proofreading and Editing

Editing and proofreading are not the same thing. Editing is the process where you verify the document is accurate, clear, coherent, complete, concise, considerate, consistent and effective. You may do some re-writing while editing. Proofreading is verifying that the capitalization, grammar, numbers, paragraphing, punctuation, sentence structure, spelling and usage, as well as style and format are correct.

The eight changes recommended in the previous section are **editing** changes. They have a huge potential to make your written message clearer to your reader. When you are writing on the conversational or journalistic end of the writing style continuum, you will be well served to use them. They are, however, not appropriate in formal writing. If you have any doubt about the style your reader will be expecting, you need to do more research and find out. If you're not sure, err on the side of formality. Remember: your credibility is at stake.

One Weird Grammar Rule No One Cares About Anymore (at Least, not Much)

The subjunctive mood   Have you ever heard of it? For most of us, a more appropriate question is probably: Have you ever heard that a verb always has a mood? The mood of the verb refers to the manner of the action. There are three moods: indicative, imperative and subjunctive.

Most people don't care, especially about the subjunctive mood.

Most sentences you write and read are in the indicative mood, which is used to state a fact or ask a question. The imperative mood gives a command or makes a request. The subjunctive mood is more complex (which is probably why no one cares anymore).

Two examples of subjunctive verbs being used ▶ "The shareholders demand that their voices be heard."
"If the senator were to be re-elected, I would resign."

Most likely you would use the proper form in the first statement without even knowing what it is called. In the second sentence, though, would you use the *were*? Or are you like more and more writers today? Many writers would use a *was* and not look back. Nor would they even be aware there was anything to look back at.

This raises the question: Could an otherwise educated person read the sentence "If the senator were to be re-elected, I would resign" and actually believe that the writer made a mistake? The answer: yes. It happens every day. Most readers today are unaware of the subjunctive mood and its proper usage. So what should you do?

There are two subjunctive sentences that everyone still knows to be correct, whether they know why or not ▶ If I were you …
AND
I wish I were an Oscar Mayer wiener.

No one would ever dream of saying or writing, "If I was you." And no one would ever say or write "I wish I was an Oscar Mayer wiener." We have heard them, read them, said them and sung them so many times the subjunctive way, we know them.

The best choice is to use the subjunctive mood for those two sentences and to try to write your way out of it for other situations. If you can't write your way out of it, use your conscience as your guide—which way will make more sense to your particular reader(s)?

The following sentence is correct according to the subjunctive rules:

> If Michelle were an expert in quantum physics, she would know this answer.

But speaking as a normal adult reader now, be honest: Did that sound right to you as you read it to yourself? How could you avoid it?

> It doesn't look like Michelle is an expert in quantum physics; otherwise, she would know this answer.

One possible solution

It takes more words, but in this case, it's worth it to avoid the no-win situation of doing it correctly but having readers think you are wrong.

Look for the rules about subjunctive mood to change or totally disappear—soon. They are already showing the signs of being highly endangered!

HEADERS AND FOOTERS

Headers and footers are the top and bottom margins of pages, as laid out by word processing programs. They are the places you can put page numbers and other identifying information to help guide your readers through a multi-page document.

Rules

1. Become familiar with your word processing software package's rules and conventions for using headers and footers.

2. Always use page numbers for any document longer than a single page. And never put a page number on the first page of a formal letter.

3. For a more formal presentation, also include the recipient's name, the subject and/or the date of the correspondence in your header or footer.

Explanations and Examples

1. **Become familiar with your word processing software package's rules and conventions for using headers and footers.**

   They can be found in the Help files of whatever program you run. Usually, you are able to set the header and footer for all pages of an entire document. The program itself takes care of sequencing the page numbers forward.

2. **Always use page numbers for any document longer than a single page. And never put a page number on the first page of a formal letter.**

   Numbering your pages just makes your document so much easier to follow. Your word processing software will allow you to put those page numbers on the top (header) or bottom (footer) of any page. You will also have the flexibility to place them on the right, left or in the center of the page.

   When your document is a letter appearing on letterhead, you do not need a page number on that first page. Also, when preparing reports or proposals, your page numbers should begin with the first page after the title page. The title page has no page number.

3. **For a more formal presentation, also include the recipient's name, the subject and/or the date of the correspondence in your header or footer.**

In your more formal letters, reports, articles or proposals, consider adding the recipient's name, the subject and/or the date to your headers or footers.

For example

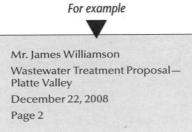

Mr. James Williamson
Wastewater Treatment Proposal—
Platte Valley
December 22, 2008
Page 2

HEADINGS

Headings are the "headlines" that a business writer includes in a document to help readers in three important ways:

1. Headings help readers quickly find which sections of a document they are most interested in reading.

2. Headings break a document up into more manageable looking pieces and help readers avoid feeling overwhelmed.

3. Headings sum up the most important information contained in a document, making the document easier to scan. Even the busiest reader gets at least the headline information by reading the headings.

While headings are not essential in one- or two-page documents, there is no law that states you can't use them. And certainly, any document containing more than two pages should have headings to reduce the reader's reading workload. The same holds true for any e-mail message longer than a couple of screens.

Rules

1. Use headings as headlines stating the most important concepts in that section throughout any document longer than two printed pages or two screens of an e-mail.

2. Write headings that provide the conclusion of each section whenever possible.

3. In a longer or more complex document, use varying levels of headings to help the reader see the differences between main sections and subsections. Stick with a stylistic format that clearly shows which headings belong with each level. Use your original outline (or mind map, see pages 117 – 119) as guideposts in determining these headings.

4. Keep your headings parallel in their structure within each sublevel.

Explanations and Examples

1. **Use headings as headlines stating the most important concepts in that section throughout any document longer than two printed pages or two screens of an e-mail.**

   These headings allow your busy readers to pick and choose the sections that they need to read and help them see the summary point of the sections they choose to skip. Also, headings help break up the document and make it look easier to understand.

2. **Write headings that provide the conclusion of each section whenever possible.**

   In your more traditional or formal reports and proposals it is likely your headings are pre-determined. They will be words such as *Introduction*, *Findings*, *Recommendations*, etc. When you have the ability to write headings specific to your content, make them clear, concise and conclusion oriented.

   Heading examples ▶

   Wastewater Study to be Completed by January 31, 2009
   NOT
   Wastewater Study Deadline

   Conclusions Center Around Cost Reduction and Quality Specifications
   NOT
   Conclusions

3. **In a longer or more complex document, use varying levels of headings to help the reader see the differences between main sections and subsections. Stick with a stylistic format that clearly shows which headings belong with each level. Use your original outline (or mind map, see pages 117 – 119) as guideposts in determining these headings.**

In most of your e-mails, letters and memos you will probably only need one level of headings. But in your longer or more detailed documents it could be helpful to use a technique for organizing your information more like an outline.

Decide upon a formatting code you will use. For example, perhaps your main headings would be **ALL CAPS, BOLDFACED AND UNDERLINED**. Perhaps the next level down could be **Boldface with Initial Caps and Underlined**. The third level could be **Boldface, Initial Caps with No Underline.** The fourth level could be No Boldface, Initial Caps, Underlined.

You should also make use of tab positions to indicate your various subcategory levels, and consider using font size variations. Do not use differing typefaces, though. While it is okay to use varying fonts of Times New Roman—**boldfaced** and *italic*, for example—to mix some Times New Roman and some `Courier just confuses your reader.`

SPINAL VERTEBRAE

    <u>Cervical</u>

       Function

           <u>Breathing</u>

           <u>Head and Neck Movement</u>

           <u>Shoulders and Arms</u>

           <u>Hands—Dexterity</u>

◄ *An example of tab use and font variations*

Word processing packages have heading settings that can be changed to whatever you want. They can also be set to automatically change heading levels according to what you want. See the Help files of your word processing program for how to use this feature.

4. **Keep your headings parallel in their structure within each sublevel.**

Parallelism is a quality of your writing that helps your reader read more quickly and with greater understanding. It means that all like items are structured in a like way.

Perhaps your biggest headings are single words or very short phrases. That means that all of your biggest headings should be single words or very short phrases. It does not mean that your subheadings need to be, though. Perhaps they could be short statements. And the sub-subheadings could be single words. Just make sure that *within one level*, your headings and subheadings are consistent with each other.

Writer's Tips:
For more information on
Parallelism, see pages 132 – 134.

COFFEE

<u>**Recent Trends Among Major Importers Have Changed the Industry**</u>

    Environmental Concerns

    Local Economic Development

    Shipping Policies

<u>**We Can Survive—and Thrive—in This New Reality**</u>

    Marketing Support

    Customer Confidence

    Product Quality

An example of correct parallelism in headings

HUMOR

The more formal your business document, the less humor you will include in it. By the same token, the more conversational and less formal your document, the more likely it is that some appropriate humor could be included.

Remember your three main goals as a writer: clarity, readability and credibility. Certainly, any humor you use must be tasteful and appropriate for your reading audience. Given that the humor is both tasteful and appropriate, it can add greatly to the readability of your document and the rapport (which contributes to credibility) you build with your reader.

Rules

1. Never use humor in your most formal documents.
2. Consider using humor when you are writing an e-mail, a memo or a less formal letter or report.
3. Never use humor that is at anyone else's expense.
4. Be extremely sensitive to cultural differences when using humor in business writing. Never attempt to use humor in international writing.

Explanations and Examples

1. **Never use humor in your most formal documents.**

   It just isn't appropriate in formal proposals, formal reports or formal business letters.

2. **Consider using humor when you are writing an e-mail, a memo or a less formal letter or report.**

   But ask yourself: Will it serve my main purpose? Will the humor that I inject make me more readable and more credible in my reader's view? Or will it make me less?

3. **Never use humor that is at anyone else's expense.**

   You just don't know who will get a forwarded copy of your e-mail or a photocopy of your letter. Make sure the humor you use can offend no one. You, after all, are a business writer. It is your responsibility to maintain relationships that are as positive as possible with everyone you come in contact with as a professional. This will help guarantee that people will be able—and willing—to support you in the future.

4. **Be extremely sensitive to cultural differences when using humor in business writing. Never attempt to use humor in international writing.**

   Make sure you understand your audience's sensibilities and remind yourself often that not everyone has the same sense of humor that you do. When you are live, face to face with someone, it is easy to gauge their response to your humor and to adjust your approach in a split second if you are seen as inappropriate. This is not possible in writing.

   The best advice? When in doubt, leave humor out.

INDEXES

Indexes are a convenient way for readers to access particular subjects within lengthy documents. Although they are rarely required, the responsible business writer considers using them, especially in very long or complex documents.

Indexes alphabetically list the subjects in a document, along with the page numbers where those subjects are mentioned. In general, they appear at the end of the document. In the case of on-line documentation, the index is generally found on its own Web page.

Rules

1. Prepare an index by first identifying the subjects that an interested reader could want quick access to, then cataloging them in alphabetical order and documenting all appropriate page numbers.

2. Use an index when your document is very long or highly technical or complex.

3. Use the index your reader will find most helpful.

4. Proofread your index carefully.

Explanations and Examples

1. **Prepare an index by first identifying the subjects that an interested reader could want quick access to, then cataloging them in alphabetical order and documenting all appropriate page numbers.**

   Most word processing software packages contain an indexing feature. To find out if yours does, check the Help files. If it does have an indexing feature, use the Help files instructions to learn how to use it. If your word processor does not contain an indexing feature, you can use a spreadsheet or a database program or index cards written by hand to compile an effective index.

   If you're using a spreadsheet program, make sure you have column headings for subject and page number. If you are using a database program, build a database with fields for subject and page number. If using index cards, include those pieces of information on each card—one card per mention of the subject. Then, when the entire document has been indexed in one of these ways, alphabetically arrange the database by subject or alphabetize the cards (separating them into further subtopics if necessary) and type the index into a word processor for printing.

2. **Use an index when your document is very long or highly technical or complex.**

   Remember that if the document is very long, the busiest readers will rarely have time to read it. An index helps those readers quickly find the information most important to them.

   In the case of highly technical or otherwise complex documents, an index helps a reader who may be overburdened by the weight of the content to find (or to find again) information that he or she needs to understand—or understand better.

3. **Use the index your reader will find most helpful.**

   If you know that your reader needs quick reference to lots of small details, your index will probably be more detailed than if you know your reader just needs general access to broader topics.

   Don't forget about the needs of future readers, as well as the readers to whom you are writing the document today. If your document will be around for a while, realize that perhaps some future reader may need a more detailed index than your present reader does.

   Above all, don't overdo it. An overly ambitious index can intimidate your reader just as much as a document with too many pages, too many long sentences and too many big words. It is important that your reader feels that your document will be easy to digest—that helps it to be "readable." Use an index appropriate to your readers' needs.

   One technique for getting the best of both worlds is to make use of cross-referencing in your index. This way you won't have too many index entries, but you will be able to redirect your reader to other topics closely related to the one they have accessed.

4. **Proofread your index carefully.**

   Maybe even twice. Your reader appreciates the trouble you have taken to produce this index. Don't ruin that great reputation by having citations that don't match the reality of your document. Even if your word processor has indexed the document for you, re-check all page numbers for accuracy.

INSTRUCTIONS

All business writing needs to be clear. And instruction writing is the textbook picture of why making sure your writing is clear can be so very frustrating.

Instructions and procedures are generally being written by someone who knows how to do the task very well. But they are being written to someone who may have no background information at all about that task.

Therefore, the expert—the writer—has to both clearly write his or her expertise, but at the very same time forget much of what he or she knows to test the instructions. The writer must ask, "Would I understand this if I were the one who had to follow these instructions for the very first time?" This is easily done by following the instructions, and doing *only* what the instructions say to do. You will quickly find any errors in the instructions.

Rules

1. Outline all instructions and procedures in detail before you begin writing.

2. Use visual formatting strategies and a consecutive numbering system to help your reader correctly follow any instructions or procedures you write.

3. Make sure you identify who is supposed to do each item in the instructions. (Avoid the passive voice.)

4. Write in the imperative tone, not the indicative tone, and use future verb tense.

5. Include only one activity or action in each line of instruction.

6. Clearly indicate page numbers (and how many pages are a part of the document) and dates on all pages of instructions and procedures.

7. Provide troubleshooting and contingency information as a part of your written instructions and procedures whenever possible.

8. Always provide a written copy of any instructions or procedures but go through those instructions with your reader either face to face or on the phone.

Explanations and Examples

1. **Outline all instructions and procedures in detail before you begin writing.**

   All business writing is made more clear in the pre-writing phase. In the case of instruction writers, though, pre-writing is more than just nice to do. It is essential.

   As the writer, you must make sure that every detail has been explained and placed in the proper sequence. This is a much easier task when using index cards or a written outline than it is when you are trying to store it all in your head as you write.

   > *Writer's Tips:*
   > *See our Creativity section*
   > *on pages 61 – 65 for more*
   > *information on pre-writing.*

   Take the time to outline. Consider using index cards so you can put them in order quickly and re-order them just as quickly if the need arises. It is also easier to add items in between other items when the original outline has been done on index cards. While your written document will still need a good edit, the work involved will be much less because you have taken the time to organize yourself in advance.

2. **Use visual formatting strategies and a consecutive numbering system to help your reader correctly follow any instructions or procedures you write.**

   Make your instructions and procedures easy to read by organizing them in a visually clear and appealing way. Number the steps involved in any procedure, and use decimals and indented instructions to indicate sub-steps.

   Also, use lots of white space. In the case of instructions—and especially difficult instructions—you are much better off with multiple open, airy looking pages created by skipping lines and using appropriate indents than you are with one crowded page of non-stop information.

3. Make sure you identify who is supposed to do each item in the instructions. (Avoid the passive voice.)

A common mistake by many instruction writers is to leave out the "by whom."

> In written instructions, the passive voice should be avoided.

Okay, the passive voice should be avoided. But by whom? This sentence doesn't make it clear. The writer has assumed that the reader (the person who will eventually use these instructions) knows that the "whom" is indeed himself or herself.

But when writing instructions, writers should never assume that their readers know anything. This doesn't mean to say that most readers of instructions aren't intelligent, well-meaning people. It's just that they may see things differently from the way you do. Spell out every detail in your instructions and be sure that you always include who will be doing each of those details.

> Writers should always avoid using the passive voice in their instructions.

4. Write in the imperative tone, not the indicative tone, and use future verb tense.

Writing that is in the imperative tone gives your reader a clear instruction. *Press the Enter key.* Writing that is in the indicative tone is longer and not as urgent. *The user should press the Enter key.*

Using future verb tense tells the reader what is going to happen. *The Font dialog box will open.* This keeps the reader from any nasty surprises.

5. Include only one activity or action in each line of instruction.

This is the same advice we have given you about sentence structure and clarity. To keep things clear for readers who could be busy or preoccupied, it is essential you stick with only one major idea per sentence.

The same is true in instruction writing: Include only one instruction per bullet point. This keeps your readers focused

One action per sentence

▼

> 1. Open paper supply Drawer A on the front of the photocopier.
> 2. Place 200 sheets of copy paper in Tray A of the photocopier.
> 3. Gently close Drawer A.
>
> **NOT**
>
> Open Drawer A on the front of the photocopier and place 200 sheets of copy paper in it before closing it gently.

and allows them to get through Step One before they have to consider Step Two. It keeps them mentally organized and more able to pinpoint their trouble spots should some arise.

6. Clearly indicate page numbers (and how many pages are a part of the document) and dates on all pages of instructions and procedures.

Indicate the page number on each page (even if there is only one page) and the total page count of the document.

> Page 1 of 1   Page 3 of 7

Also, include the date of the instructions on each page. This will help your reader replace older instructions with newer ones.

7. **Provide troubleshooting and contingency information as a part of your written instructions and procedures whenever possible.**

   Have you ever noticed that the best driving directions you have ever received from a friend also included how to tell you had gone too far? "If you get to Maple Street, you've gone too far. Turn around and come back one block."

   The same is true for any kind of instructions or procedures you are communicating professionally.

   Whenever possible, include contingency statements ▶ | If the paper tray does not easily slide back into its spot, reach in behind it to see if there is some paper jammed there.
   OR
   You will know that this step has been properly completed if the indicator light in the upper left corner of the main panel turns green.

8. **Always provide a written copy of any instructions or procedures but go through those instructions with your reader either face to face or on the phone.**

   This is simple communication theory. It is imperative that all people who need to follow your instructions receive a written copy of those instructions. This written copy makes it possible for them to refer back if they have a question or potential misunderstanding.

   It has long been known that the most effective way to teach someone to do something new is to first tell them how to do it. Next, show them how to do it. And finally, have them show you how to do it.

   Different people learn best in different ways. A majority of us tend to be visual learners. We learn best by seeing something done. Others of us, though, are auditory learners. Auditory learners learn best by hearing how to do something. And finally, there is a kinesthetic group—they learn best by doing it themselves.

   Often, a face-to-face visit to your reader is impossible. But if you, the writer of a set of instructions, have the ability to make a face-to-face visit, or even a phone call—you must. Your instructions will automatically become clearer to your reader.

   Then—of course—follow up in writing.

INTERNATIONAL WRITING

When writing to readers whose native language is not English, careful business writers go out of their way to be both clear and credible. The guidelines in this section focus on using a slightly more formal style than we recommend for your general business writing. The reason for this is easy to understand: Most people from other countries who speak or read English have learned their English from British sources, not American ones. British English is more formal than American English.

Our theory? Better safe than sorry.

Rules
1. When writing to readers in a particular foreign country, become as familiar as you can with the cultural differences between you. Then, use what you know to write for your readers' needs.
2. When in doubt about cultural expectations, err on the side of being too respectful and too formal rather than taking the risk of being seen as disrespectful or inappropriately informal.
3. Use correct units of measure, correct format for dates and correct denominations for currency.
4. Be vigilant about sentence length (short) and word choice (best known) in your writing.
5. Avoid idioms, jargon, brand names and nonspecific geographical designations. Use language that a reader anywhere can clearly understand.
6. Avoid humor and sarcasm.
7. Check with your reader, when possible, to make sure you have been clear.
8. If possible, use courtesy spelling.
9. Determine the appropriate salutation and complimentary close for the country.
10. When sending anything that has been translated, include an English version as well.

Explanations and Examples

1. **When writing to readers in a particular foreign country, become as familiar as you can with the cultural differences between you. Then, use what you know to write for your readers' needs.**

When an American writer in the United States writes to a Japanese reader in Japan, there are particular cultural differences that the U.S. writer needs to be aware of. Mostly they have to do with the level of formality that reader is expecting and the sense of seriousness with which he or she sees the business world.

When you are writing to people from other countries, and you know what countries you're dealing with, do some research so you know what those readers will be expecting from you. How do they define respect? How important is respect to them? Is humor appropriate? What units of measure are used in that country? How is the currency referred to? Are expectations about the roles of men and women different from what you may assume? How about age differences? Do they matter? How?

These are the kinds of questions that will help you develop a positive rapport with any reader—no matter where that reader lives or what that reader sees as "normal." And it is never too much trouble to do what you can to develop a positive rapport.

A more difficult circumstance arises when you are writing to many different readers in many different countries. Especially when you are sending one e-mail or letter to all of them. In those cases, follow the rest of the guidelines listed here and in most cases you will be perceived as both a clear and a readable writer.

2. **When in doubt about cultural expectations, err on the side of being too respectful and too formal rather than taking the risk of being seen as disrespectful or inappropriately informal.**

Because most non-native English speakers and English readers are more accustomed to British style, they are more comfortable with a formal and respectful style. Most likely, it's what they learned.

For example, it is a good idea to avoid the use of contractions like *I'm* and *don't*. Use *I am* and *do not* instead. Also, it is better to be less casual than this book would normally recommend for your business writing. Treat your reader with utmost respect. Even if you overdo it, you will be more easily forgiven than if you treat your reader too casually. Some foreign readers will see your lack of formality as disrespect.

As a general rule, avoid bending grammar rules in any writing that is being sent internationally (page 90). In America, your American readers generally bend those rules as often as you do. In a British-based language, those rules still stand.

3. **Use correct units of measure, correct format for dates and correct denominations for currency.**

Remember that hardly any other country but the U.S. refers to measurements in feet, inches, pounds or miles (avoirdupois—to have weight). Most of the rest of the world uses metric measurements. (Interestingly enough, it was the U.S. that convinced Canada to change to them back in the 1960s. We had told them we were about to change. When we changed our minds, Canada went forward with the change to metric.)

Become familiar with the units of measurement your readers will understand. To ensure clarity, provide both metric and avoirdupois. The same holds true for how you format your dates. To be safe, never use just numbers with dashes or slashes between them to signify a date internationally. In many European countries, for example, 6/7/07 would mean July 6, 2007—not June 7, 2007. Always spell out the months and you will avoid confusion.

Currency can also be quite different. If you are quoting any dollar amounts, see if you can find the equivalent in whatever currency your reader is more familiar with. Again, to ensure clarity, provide the amount in both currencies. It is true that if you are discussing a business deal, it is likely that you have already communicated with your reader and decided what currency you are going to be communicating in. But as always when writing internationally: Better safe than sorry.

4. **Be vigilant about sentence length (short) and word choice (best known) in your writing.**

It is always best to use shorter sentences rather than longer ones and well-known words rather than obscure ones.

In international writing this becomes even more important. Most likely your reader is already struggling—at least a little bit—because he or she is reading something in a non-native language. For many readers, that means they are mentally translating every sentence of yours into their own language to understand it more clearly.

If you use the first word that comes to your mind to describe something, you can be reasonably confident that it is the most commonly used word to describe that thing. However, double-check to make sure you're not using slang, which your reader most likely will not be familiar with.

By the same token, make sure that your sentences are short enough for your reader to understand the first time through. This may mean some sentences need to be even shorter than ones you would send without question to another native speaker of American English. As always, of course, never put more than one major idea in the same sentence. And that is good advice, no matter who you are writing to.

5. Avoid idioms, jargon, brand names and nonspecific geographical designations. Use language that a reader anywhere can clearly understand.

You just can't be sure you will be understood by a reader from a different culture.

Have you ever spoken to someone who has learned English for the first time as an adult? They have some interesting questions! Like why does one stand *in* line but *on* a bus. Why is a car parked *in* a driveway but that same car drives *on* a road. These are some of our simplest examples of American English idioms.

An *idiom* is a phrase that we have used for so long, we all understand it. But it follows no particular rule that a non-native speaker could follow.

The same holds true for jargon. In short, never use a word or phrase in international writing that you wouldn't be willing to bank your retirement on—remember that your final test is: Will they understand me clearly?

Brand names can also be a problem. Do you think that all nations have Parkay? Do you think everyone worldwide knows what the NFL is? Do you know that not everyone around the globe agrees on what the game of football is?

Finally, beware of non-specific geographic terms like the Northwest. In the U.S., the Northwest is generally agreed to be made up of the states of Washington, Oregon and Idaho. People who live on another continent may not know of or understand that geography.

6. Avoid humor and sarcasm.

Cultural mores are different from place to place, and what's funny in one culture may be cruel in another. Of course, that doesn't make anyone right or someone else wrong. We are all just different.

Better safe than sorry. Avoid humor when writing internationally. And always avoid sarcasm, no matter whom you are writing to or where they live.

7. Check with your reader, when possible, to make sure you have been clear.

When you are beginning a writing relationship with someone from a foreign country, consider checking with that reader about the styles and conventions he or she would prefer you use.

And once you have written a document, and it has been read, check it again. Did your reader understand it accurately? If you are going to be writing again to this reader, it is better to know up front how effective you have been. It will help you make any necessary adjustments to become more clear and more readable next time.

8. If possible, use courtesy spelling.

British English spells many words differently than American English. The two most common of these differences is adding a *u* to some words that have an - or ending and using an *s* instead of a *z*.

American English	British English
color	colour
humor	humour
honor	honour
organize	organise
sympathize	sympathise

9. Determine the appropriate salutation and complimentary close for the country.

In British English, a typical salutation is the same as ours. However, the first name is rarely used in the salutation of a business letter.

The complimentary close, on the other hand, is more formal in British English. When the recipient of the letter is unknown, the standard closing is "Faithfully yours" or "Yours faithfully." Once the writer knows the reader, it changes to what American writers use regularly: "Sincerely yours" or "Yours sincerely."

10. When sending anything that has been translated, include an English version as well.

Even the most experienced of translators will, from time to time, make a mistake. To ensure nothing embarrassing happens, always include an English copy of the letter with the translated copy.

ITALICS

Italics are the slanted type fonts used in publishing and word processing to indicate that a word, phrase or sentence should receive special emphasis or attention. Before word processing software allowed most writers to use italics at will, underlining was the accepted substitute.

Most commonly, italics are used for titles of books, magazines and other complete works. They are also used to indicate foreign words being used in English text and to show that a word is being referred to as a word instead of as its meaning.

Rules

1. Use italics to indicate the title of any complete work published or produced as a separate item.

2. Italicize foreign words, phrases, sentences or abbreviations used in standard English writing.

3. Italicize words referred to as words, and letters or numbers referred to as letters or numbers.

4. Italicize the word being defined when presenting a definition, whether in a sentence or in a list.

5. When using italics for phrases or sentences, also italicize the punctuation. Do not italicize the words that merely connect the words being emphasized. Also, do not italicize the possessive or plural endings added on to words being emphasized.

Explanations and Examples

1. Use italics to indicate the title of any complete work published or produced as a separate item.

This includes books, magazines, journals, newspapers, movies, plays, individual video cassettes, CDs, DVDs, long musical pieces, paintings, sculptures and yes—even the individual names of ships, trains or airplanes.

> Two of my favorite books were written by Ayn Rand: *Atlas Shrugged* and *The Fountainhead.*
>
> Have you seen the latest issues of *Time* and *Newsweek*?
>
> The movies *Apocalypse Now* and *The Deer Hunter* treat the subject of America's involvement in Vietnam very differently.
>
> Captain Kirk may have been the captain of the *USS Enterprise*—but do you think he could have commanded an aircraft carrier like the *Roosevelt*?

If there is concern that the italics might not make it through e-mail, titles of complete works could be typed in all capital letters. But be consistent. Also, in case you are curious, the titles of articles from complete works (such as magazine articles) are placed in quotation marks. This is because they are excerpted from the complete work (and magazine).

2. Italicize foreign words, phrases, sentences or abbreviations used in standard English writing.

But you do not need to italicize words, phrases, sentences or abbreviations that have been accepted as regular parts of the English language through common usage.

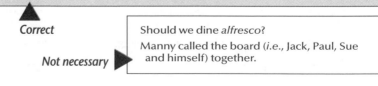

> Jacques, recently transferred from our Montreal office, must have forgotten where he was temporarily when he asked, *Quelle heure est-il*?
>
> So exactly what is *la vida loca*?

Correct

Not necessary

> Should we dine *alfresco*?
>
> Manny called the board (*i.e.*, Jack, Paul, Sue and himself) together.

3. **Italicize words referred to as words, and letters or numbers referred to as letters or numbers.**

When using words, letters or numbers as themselves, italicize the words, letters or numbers.

> Does she know her *ABC*s yet?
>
> After they have counted off, please take the *1*s and *2*s to Conference Room B. I will keep the *3*s and *4*s here.

4. **Italicize the word being defined when presenting a definition, whether in a sentence or in a list.**

> The label *grunge* refers to a style of music that has also influenced the dress and attitudes of those who listen to it.
>
> The sociological term *ethnocentric* describes any culture or people who assume that their own culture is more "right" in the way it lives than another culture.
>
> Most people have heard of *split infinitives* before—they just don't know what they are. Here's an easy definition: In English, the *infinitive* form of a verb always begins with the word *to*. A *split infinitive* occurs when a word comes between that *to* and the rest of the verb. For example, *to* truly *care*.

5. **When using italics for phrases or sentences, also italicize the punctuation. Do not italicize the words that merely connect the words being emphasized. Also, do not italicize the possessive or plural endings added on to words being emphasized.**

These guidelines make the reading job easier. Which, of course, contributes to readability—one of our three main objectives.

> The four French words *belle, beau, grande* and *petite* all have gender. That's a strange concept to a native English speaker.
>
> This writer has used too many *therefore*s and too few *period*s in his writing!

JARGON

Jargon is the specialized language shared by any subculture. There is generational jargon, cultural jargon, ethnic jargon, jargon determined by geography, jargon from various interests and jargon from various professions and areas of expertise.

When the writer and his or her readers speak and understand the same jargon, it can serve as an excellent shortcut that actually contributes to both clarity and readability. When the writer and reader do not share that understanding, jargon inhibits the communication.

Sometimes, a writer assumes his or her readers know more than they actually do. That's how a computer consultant failed to communicate the correct way to make a copy of a CD onto the hard drive to his customer. He told his customer to *make a copy* of the CD. A few minutes later, the customer returned with a photocopy of that CD and asked, "What next?"

A medical doctor with an expertise in spinal cord injuries will know what an *SCI C6 complete* is—but do you? (Spinal cord injury, at the sixth cervical vertebrae with no sensation below that.)

Rules

Here are the two rules that will help you communicate with absolute clarity and credibility while protecting you from possible embarrassments.

1. Use jargon in your writing only when you know your readers will understand it the way you intend. There are two other options: Provide a glossary or provide a parenthetical definition the first time you use a questionable piece of jargon.

2. Be especially sensitive to the needs of your foreign readers. They are probably struggling enough translating your English into the language they are more comfortable reading and understanding. Avoid using any language that would increase their mental workload or be unclear—including jargon.

Explanations and Examples

1. **Use jargon in your writing only when you know your readers will understand it the way you intend. There are two other options: Provide a glossary or provide a parenthetical definition the first time you use a questionable piece of jargon.**

When you are considering whether or not your readers will understand the jargon you use, also consider future readers. Will your jargon survive the time it spends in a file somewhere? Do you remember when all teenagers were using the word *groovy*? Have you heard it lately?

Also, consider checking with a co-worker, editor or friend before sending any document that contains undefined jargon.

If you are using much jargon, but it is truly the most clear way to communicate the ideas you are expressing, add a glossary at the end of the document that defines each questionable word. Also, make reference to that glossary early in your document so your readers know it is there.

In less formal writing, it would also be acceptable to simply place an informal definition of the word you believe might not be clearly understood in parentheses immediately after the word is used in text for the first time. Once you have provided the definition once, it is not necessary to provide it again, no matter how many times you use the word of jargon again.

2. **Be especially sensitive to the needs of your foreign readers. They are probably struggling enough translating your English into the language they are more comfortable reading and understanding. Avoid using any language that would increase their mental workload or be unclear—including jargon.**

As always, clarity, readability and credibility are your only goals as a writer. When you are writing to readers who may already be overworked just trying to understand your normal writing, adding too many frills is counterproductive. Keep it simple.

JOURNALISM

The rules for writing that are used in journalism are very similar to the rules used throughout this book to illustrate excellent business writing. And the reason should be apparent: The only readers out there who have less time and less energy to devote to reading than the people reading at work are the people reading on the way to work. Hardly anyone would tell you they read a newspaper carefully. And the editors know that.

Have you ever noticed how short the sentences are in most news stories? Have you ever noticed that there isn't a lot of punctuation—other than periods—in most news articles? (The sentences don't often get long enough for anything more complex than a few commas to separate items in a series.)

Journalists are taught to put their very most important ideas in the first paragraphs of their articles. WHO, WHAT, WHEN, WHERE, WHY and HOW—journalists are told to answer those questions as clearly and simply as they can.

Rules

If you find yourself needing to write for publication in a newspaper or even a popular magazine, here are some tips that will help you stay clear, readable and credible.

1. Honor the Inverted Pyramid method of organizing your ideas.

2. Keep your sentences short and simple.

3. Consider outlining ahead of time by asking the questions: Who? What? When? Where? Why? How?

4. Always include a short cover letter when submitting any article, letter, press release or other material to a newspaper or magazine.

5. Use *The Associated Press Stylebook and Briefing on Media Law* as your style guide whenever you have a grammar, punctuation or word usage question in your journalistic writing.

Explanations and Examples

1. **Honor the Inverted Pyramid method of organizing your ideas.**

   Always start with your single most important or clarifying piece of information in the first paragraph. Then, follow with your next most important piece of information, then the next most important. And so on.

2. **Keep your sentences short and simple.**

   The easiest way to follow this rule? Make sure you have only one major idea in each sentence. The readers of newspaper and magazine articles have even less time to devote to their reading than do the readers of business memos and e-mails.

3. **Consider outlining ahead of time by asking the questions: Who? What? When? Where? Why? How?**

   Outlining will keep you so organized in your quest for clarity you will find that the extra time you spend doing it is well worth the investment. By the way, you will also find it easier to use fewer words when you have outlined ahead of time.

4. **Always include a short cover letter when submitting any article, letter, press release or other material to a newspaper or magazine.**

   Editors are people, after all. Send a courteous note that includes a very brief overview of the writing you hope to have published and a very brief biography of the author (that's most likely you). Include contact information so someone from the publication can quickly get in touch with you if there are any last minute questions that need an answer from you.

   Of course, if you are hoping to pitch a major story or article, look into the journals of the professional writing community to get the tips you need for preparing a formal proposal.

5. **Use *The Associated Press Stylebook and Briefing on Media Law* as your style guide whenever you have a grammar, punctuation or word usage question in your journalistic writing.**

   The Associated Press Stylebook and Briefing on Media Law (Norm Goldstein, Associated Press) is considered the Bible of people who write for the public. The Associated Press are the keepers of the standard for journalistic writing.

   The book contains glossaries of words and how to use them correctly. You will also find an extremely concise grammar and punctuation guide. An up-to-date briefing on media law is also included. If you plan on writing many press releases, articles for newspapers or magazines or just lots of letters to the editor, it would be a good addition to your reference library.

Business Writing

> *Writer's Tip:*
> *For more information*
> *on writing press releases,*
> *please see page 145.*

KNOWING YOUR READER

You must know at least enough about your reader or your reader's needs to write a subject line, title or first paragraph that will grab that reader. Remember, you are in competition with every other person who sent your reader mail today. It is doubtful that your reader will read all of it—let's make sure he or she at least reads yours.

Here, again, are the questions to ask yourself about your reader and your reader's environment. The more of them you can answer, the more likely you will be well prepared to grab that reader.

WHO?	Job title, department, responsibilities
	Length of time with company
	Educational background, specialty
	Personal: Age, gender, attitudes, hobbies
WHAT?	What does the reader already know about the subject?
	What else does the reader need to know?
	What will the reader do about this message (decide, delegate, transmit, do)?
	What's in it for the reader? Benefits? Risks?
	What else does the reader want to know?
WHEN?	When will the reader read this message?
	How much time will the reader spend on it?
	When does the reader have to act?
WHERE?	Where in the company hierarchy is this reader located?
	Where is most of the reader's work done?
	Where else in the company does the reader have to go for approval to act?
	Where else in the company could the communication go?
HOW?	How interested is the reader in this message?
	How will the reader feel about this message?
	How will the reader's job, workload or life be affected by this message?
WHY?	Why am I writing?
	Why should the reader respond?

Note: Considering the "how" and "why" questions will save your reader frustration.

LETTERS

Business writing style has been covered quite thoroughly in this style guide. You can find our tips in many sections: Clarity, Readability, Correctness, Business Writing Philosophy and Business Style to name just a few.

This section does not attempt to reiterate all that has been presented elsewhere. Nor does it attempt to provide you the formatting techniques and definitions you can find in Letters—Formatting. Of course, the model documents provided on pages 208 – 271 speak for themselves.

This section means to inspire you. To remind you that letters were once noble—and they can be again, in your hands. People like to get mail. They just don't like to get boring mail, pointless mail, wordy mail or unnecessary mail. If you truly want to impress someone, a well-written, friendly and clear letter typed on a beautiful piece of stationery with a warm handwritten note on the bottom might just be the trick. Think about it. Do you like to get letters like that?

Rules

1. Use the most beautiful letterhead or stationery you can find. But keep it tasteful and appropriate for your profession and your message.

2. Use a conversational style in your writing. Don't be more casual than you would be if you were having lunch with your reader.

3. Don't be afraid to write by hand occasionally—especially the warmer notes you have to send. You can either send an entirely handwritten note or letter or you can add a handwritten note to the end of a typed letter.

4. E-mail is often practical and sometimes even fun. But an occasional letter, in an envelope with postage, sends the message that you care enough to spend real time on your reader.

5. Make the envelope as beautiful or memorable as the letter itself.

Explanations and Examples

1. **Use the most beautiful letterhead or stationery you can find. But keep it tasteful and appropriate for your profession and your message.**

   Obviously, if you are the owner of a funeral parlor you don't want to use a letterhead that would be seen as frivolous. The same is probably true if you are a banker keeping thousands of dollars safe for your investors.

   Your letterhead or stationery serves you in two important ways. First, it is your reader's first contact with you. He or she will make judgments about whether you have good taste or are willing to invest in the best—and more—based on the appearance of your letter as it comes out of the envelope.

   Second, your letterhead or stationery will also help your reader identify you quickly. Once you find something you like, something that fits you and your message, you should stick with it. It's said that Jacqueline Kennedy Onassis always used the same color of blue stationery—forever. You would know you were receiving something from her just seeing that color in your pile of mail.

   Of course, in order to make a good impression with that letterhead or stationery it would be good that your readers enjoy your letters.

2. **Use a conversational style in your writing. Don't be more casual than you would be if you were having lunch with your reader.**

   Write the way you speak, but make sure you are writing to this reader the way you would speak to this reader over a taco salad at lunch.

3. **Don't be afraid to write by hand occasionally—especially the warmer notes you have to send. You can either send an entirely handwritten note or letter or you can add a handwritten note to the end of a typed letter.**

   Handwritten notes get a lot more attention from your business reader than typed ones do—because they are so rare in the mail pile at work.

   Make sure, of course, that your handwriting is legible. And in the case of handwritten notes on the bottoms of typed letters, make sure you aren't adding something vitally important that hasn't yet been mentioned. That would make you look forgetful.

   Readability experts have often said that if your reader reads nothing else, he or she will read a handwritten note on a typed page.

4. **E-mail is often practical and sometimes even fun. But an occasional letter, in an envelope with postage, sends the message that you care enough to spend real time on your reader.**

   This is the reason that everyone needs some snail mail in his or her life at least occasionally. It makes an impression. While in some environments and some professions (like the computer industry) you will most often communicate electronically, people do like to get mail occasionally. Especially when it is friendly and memorable.

5. **Make the envelope as beautiful or memorable as the letter itself.**

Again—it gets your reader's positive attention. Always try to match the envelope with the stationery.

Avoid sending important mail for bulk rate. Avoid using a printing program that makes your envelope look too impersonal. Your reader will decide whether or not to open this envelope based on how it looks and, in many cases, by how much it cost to send it.

For your most important letters consider using an express mail service—complete with special "priority" packaging. Even if the letter didn't need to be there that quickly, it will certainly make a splash when it arrives. Depending upon your message, the splash alone could be worth the extra effort and expense.

LISTS

Lists, especially bulleted lists, are an excellent way of communicating more than one piece of information to a busy reader.

Rules

1. Use a bulleted list to display any series of items that you want to bring to your reader's attention. This list can be introduced by either a sentence ending with a period or an anticipatory expression that ends with a colon.

2. Use dashes, hyphens, numbers, letters, bullets or any consistent symbol you choose to mark each item in the bulleted list. But reserve numbers for items that are truly being presented in a logical order.

3. When listing items inside a sentence, use a colon to announce the list.

4. When a colon is used to announce a list and the list is then presented as the remainder of the same sentence, do not capitalize after the colon unless what comes after the colon can stand alone as a complete sentence.

5. When a colon or a period is used to announce items presented in a bulleted list, always capitalize the first letter of each item that is itself a complete sentence.

6. When a colon is used to announce items presented in a bulleted list, and the items themselves are not complete sentences, it is up to the writer whether to capitalize or not. But be consistent. (Be aware that capital letters will look better and will get more reader attention.)

> *Writer's Tips:*
> *Many of the guidelines suggested in this section can also be found in our section on Colons, pages 153 – 155.*

7. When some of the items in a bulleted list are complete sentences and some of them aren't, rewrite the list so that they are all one or the other. (It is usually easier on the writer to make them all complete sentences.) This is called *Parallelism*, an important component of clear, readable writing. (See pages 132 – 134.)

Explanations and Examples

1. **Use a bulleted list to display any series of items that you want to bring to your reader's attention. This list can be introduced by either a sentence ending with a period or an anticipatory expression that ends with a colon.**

   Because a bulleted list comes with so much white space, it commands your reader's attention. Remember—it isn't the words on your page that get your reader's attention—it's the white frame around those words that draws the reader's eye.

2. **Use dashes, hyphens, numbers, letters, bullets or any consistent symbol you choose to mark each item in the bulleted list. But reserve numbers for items that are truly being presented in a logical order.**

   If the items in your list are equal and non-sequential, use anything but numbers to list them. Numbers imply order or steps, so they should be reserved for lists that do have an order.

> The successful candidate for this position will have the following qualities:
> - Excellent keyboarding skills
> - Current Microsoft® Word experience
> - Five years of experience in the transportation industry
> - Excellent references

> The first three steps of the new process are relatively simple:
> 1. Empty Container A.
> 2. Add 12 ounces of water to Container B.
> 3. Switch the toggle switch to ON.

3. When listing items inside a sentence, use a colon to announce the list.

> Five local celebrities attended the opening of the museum's new Impressionists Wing: Clark Duncan, John Evans, Mark and Maggie Overton and Cindy LaRue.

4. When a colon is used to announce a list and the list is then presented as the remainder of the same sentence, do not capitalize after the colon unless what comes after the colon can stand alone as a complete sentence.

> The dress is available in five colors: red, green, blue, black and purple.
>
> The dress is available in five colors: Red, green, blue, black and purple have been our best sellers for over a year.

5. When a colon or a period is used to announce items presented in a bulleted list, always capitalize the first letter of each item that is itself a complete sentence.

> The dress is available in three colors:
> • Red is our top seller.
> • Green is the most popular with teenagers.
> • Black is our most formal color.

6. When a colon is used to announce items presented in a bulleted list, and the items themselves are not complete sentences, it is up to the writer whether to capitalize or not. But be consistent. (Be aware that capital letters will look better and will get more reader attention.)

> The dress is available in three colors: **OR**   The dress is available in three colors:
> • red   • Red
> • green   • Green
> • black   • Black

Which one do you think looks better? It's up to you.

7. When some of the items in a bulleted list are complete sentences and some of them aren't, rewrite the list so that they are all one or the other. (It is usually easier on the writer to make them all complete sentences.) This is called *Parallelism*, an important component of clear, readable writing. (See pages 132 – 134.)

Awkward list

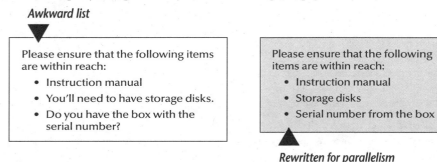

> Please ensure that the following items are within reach:
> • Instruction manual
> • You'll need to have storage disks.
> • Do you have the box with the serial number?

> Please ensure that the following items are within reach:
> • Instruction manual
> • Storage disks
> • Serial number from the box

Rewritten for parallelism

Punctuation in a Bulleted List

When using bulleted lists, many people wonder about the correct punctuation between the items. Obviously, when a list appears in its own sentence or paragraph, the use of commas or semicolons to separate the items is essential.

When the items are already separated by a hard return and a bullet of some kind, the use of commas and semicolons is redundant—they are unnecessary. The return and the bullet are enough.

This is one of the reasons bulleted lists are recommended to business writers. They present sometimes complex information in the most readable format available. Your reader can actually see the separation of ideas. (In the case of very formal writing or legal writing, it is best to check with a specialized grammar guide about requirements for punctuation.)

Items in bulleted lists that are complete sentences themselves require periods (or perhaps question marks or exclamation points) at the end.

Items that are not complete sentences by themselves do not require any punctuation.

Do not put a period after the last item in a bulleted list for the sole reason that it is the last item. No punctuation is needed to end a bulleted list (unless that last item is a complete sentence itself, of course, in which case it will have terminal punctuation).

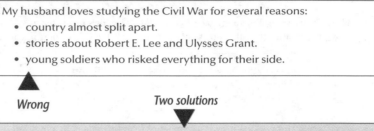

My husband loves studying the Civil War for several reasons:
- country almost split apart.
- stories about Robert E. Lee and Ulysses Grant.
- young soldiers who risked everything for their side.

Wrong   *Two solutions*

My husband loves studying the Civil War for several reasons:
- country almost split apart
- stories about Robert E. Lee and Ulysses Grant
- young soldiers who risked everything for their side

OR

My husband loves studying the Civil War for several reasons:
- He thinks it is fascinating that the country almost split apart.
- He enjoys the stories about Robert E. Lee and Ulysses Grant.
- He admires the young soldiers who risked everything for their side.

MATHEMATICAL NOTATIONS

Before using mathematical notations in the text of a business letter, memo, report, proposal or e-mail, check with the receiver of your document to see if he or she expects you to use a particular style. As you might imagine, grammar and style guides disagree among themselves about some of the guidelines we recommend here.

In most cases, though, for your standard correspondence and reports, here are the guidelines that will help your reader quickly and clearly understand them.

Rules

1. Except for the shortest of mathematical expressions or equations, use a separate line of type for each expression or equation.
2. Should it be necessary to continue an equation or expression onto a second line, always divide *before* the equal sign or sign of operation (+, -, x, /).
3. In mathematical expressions, parentheses go inside brackets. Brackets go inside braces. And braces go inside larger parentheses.
4. Be consistent in your use of all mathematical symbols and notations.

Explanations and Examples

1. **Except for the shortest of mathematical expressions or equations, use a separate line of type for each expression or equation.**

   When presenting mathematical formulas or equations, display them on a separate line, centered on the page and preceded and followed by a blank line. This helps your reader more quickly and easily understand them.

   Even when your audience is mathematically or technically expert, seeing a mathematical formula in the middle of a written document can be startling in at least a small way because math looks like a different language. Framing it in this way with white space prepares the reader to switch languages, so to speak.

2. **Should it be necessary to continue an equation or expression onto a second line, always divide *before* the equal sign or sign of operation (+, -, x, /).**

Even better, don't divide any mathematical expressions onto more than one line if at all possible. But if it is necessary, the convention used by most everyone is to divide displayed expressions before the equal sign or sign of operation. This is the syntax of math.

3. **In mathematical expressions, parentheses go inside brackets. Brackets go inside braces. And braces go inside larger parentheses.**

4. **Be consistent in your use of all mathematical symbols and notations.**

No matter what style book you choose to follow, make sure that once you have committed to using any rules or conventions regarding mathematical notations you stick with those rules or conventions consistently. This includes everything from the symbols you use (for example, in division—do you use a slash / or a dividing sign ÷) to the format in which you present the equations and formulas themselves.

Mathematical syntax

▼

Parentheses are the first level of separation

$$4(a+b) = 16(d-c)$$

Brackets are the second level of separation

$$13[4(a+b) - 3(c+d)] = 230$$

Braces are the third level of separation

$$\{4+3[4(a+b) - 3(c+d)]\} - 8(e+f) = xy(a+b)$$

Larger parentheses can serve as a fourth level of separation

$$(\{4+3[4(a+b) - 3(c+d)]\} - 8(e+f)) - xy(a+b)$$

MEMOS

Memos in the business world have much in common with the newer (and more commonly used) written form: e-mail. But several important differences remain. Because memos appear on paper, it is imperative that they be beautiful to behold. Readers are easily turned off by an unattractive written presentation.

Plus, once your reader does start reading your memo, it becomes crucial that you have followed the rules discussed throughout this style guide to communicate clearly, correctly and in a readable fashion. The guidelines listed here will not surprise you if you have studied the rest of this guide, but it is useful to assemble them in this one place.

Rules

1. As you may remember from our section at the beginning of this book on Readability (pages 7 – 10), your number one goal is to KEEP THE READER READING. Make sure your memo is visually appealing with plenty of white space, a readable typeface, short paragraphs, visually organized ideas and dark clear print on a clean page.

2. Your number two goal as the writer of a memo is to be clear. Follow the rules of clarity (pages 2 – 7) throughout your memo.

3. Use a subject line that sums up the bottom line of the memo.

4. Start with your most important idea or a summary of important ideas in the first paragraph.

5. Keep your words as simple as possible and your sentences as short as practical.

6. Try to keep your memo to a single page. But (and this is a monster-sized *but*) better to make your memo two *readable* pages than one tightly packed *unreadable* page.

7. Use a small amount of handwriting on the memo to make it more personal.

8. Don't over-memo people. Also, be politically savvy about sending CCs and BCCs.

9. Never forget the interoffice memo's place on the workplace food chain. While it may be a great way to cover your tracks, it is not your best way to persuade or befriend your reader.

Explanations and Examples

1. As you may remember from our section at the beginning of this book on Readability (pages 7 – 10), your number one goal is to KEEP THE READER READING. Make sure your memo is visually appealing with plenty of white space, a readable typeface, short paragraphs, visually organized ideas and dark clear print on a clean page.

   Put yourself in your reader's position. Would YOU pick up the memo you are about to send and eagerly begin reading it? Does it look professional but clear? Is there enough white space to make the reading look easy? Is the typeface a familiar, readable one? Have you put the most important idea in the first paragraph? Does the subject line accurately sum up your main idea in an appealing way?

2. Your number two goal as the writer of a memo is to be clear. Follow the rules of clarity (pages 2 – 7) throughout your memo.

   Never forget that the only reason you write is to clearly communicate to someone or to a group of someones. Be sure that you have written in such a straightforward and clear way that your reader can't possibly be confused about your message.

3. Use a subject line that sums up the bottom line of the memo.

   Avoid a subject line that just states the subject. Actually make your point in the subject line if at all possible. This saves your reader valuable time—time that he or she will be grateful to you for.

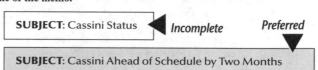

   SUBJECT: Cassini Status ◀ *Incomplete* *Preferred*

   SUBJECT: Cassini Ahead of Schedule by Two Months

4. Start with your most important idea or a summary of important ideas in the first paragraph.

   We aren't necessarily claiming it is true, but consider that the first paragraph of your memo might be the ONLY paragraph of that memo that your reader reads. And even if it isn't, putting your overview up front will help the reader more quickly and accurately understand any elaboration you have made later in the memo.

5. Keep your words as simple as possible and your sentences as short as practical.

   Again, this is standard business writing advice. Never use a $50 word when a $5 word can do the job. Never include more than one major idea in the same sentence, if at all possible. Unnecessarily large words and complex sentences slow your readers down. Readers who have been slowed down often stop reading altogether.

6. Try to keep your memo to a single page. But (and this is a monster-sized *but*) better to make your memo two *readable* pages than one tightly packed *unreadable* page.

   By now, you have probably absorbed one of the main principles of this style guide: Intelligent use of white space makes your words more appealing to most readers. Unfortunately, some writers have become so paranoid about writing letters and memos longer than one page they have actually made some very bad choices.

   Have you ever made the typeface smaller in a memo just so it would print out to one page instead of two? Have you ever narrowed the margins? Or have you ever removed the bulleted lists and replaced them with crowded, long paragraphs laden with semicolons?

   These are not good choices. They make the memo harder to read, not easier. And this discourages your reader.

   Certainly, don't be redundant and don't be wordy just for the sake of looking like you know a lot. Most people, by now, have figured out that the more varied ways you say the same thing, the less you actually know about that thing. But when you do need more than a page, take it. Remember your number one goal—the real one.

   READABILITY.

7. **Use a small amount of handwriting on the memo to make it more personal.**

   Handwriting gets your reader's attention. Certainly, sign your own initials next to your printed name on the FROM line.

   Handwritten notes can be placed in an upper corner or at the bottom of the printed memo. They not only attract your reader's eye, they also make you look like a living, breathing human being—which always helps when you are trying to communicate or persuade.

8. **Don't over-memo people. Also, be politically savvy about sending CCs and BCCs.**

   Most people acknowledge that they get too much mail. If you get a reputation as a writer who sends too much, you may also end up with readers who throw your memos away before even reading the first paragraph. Write only when you have something valuable to communicate. If you find yourself sending too many memos to a particular person, try keeping a file on your desk of items you need to communicate to that individual and combine them into a daily or weekly memo instead. You could even give it a title like "Daily Status Report—8-23-10" to help the reader identify it immediately in a large pile of mail.

   Regarding CCs and BCCs, be sensitive to the potential paranoia of your readers. It is appropriate to note on a memo the other people, departments or organizations that are receiving a copy of that memo. But will your readers be frightened by a CC line that references a boss? And are you indeed using that CC line as a way to intimidate your reader? And, while we're asking the tougher questions: Where do you stand on blind CCs? Do you believe they are ethical? Do you use them?

   We don't intend here to offer an opinion for you—we just intend to give you a moment to think about it. Once you make up your own mind, be sure you are consistent in the way you use both CCs and BCCs.

9. **Never forget the interoffice memo's place on the workplace food chain. While it may be a great way to cover your tracks, it is not your best way to persuade or befriend your reader.**

   A written document in a file, whether in your computer in the form of stored e-mail or as a copy of a written memo in a file folder, can be invaluable in proving a case you need to prove down the line. Remember, though, the persuasive power you have as the author of a memo or an e-mail may not be great.

   Your single best way to communicate—if persuasion and/or rapport are your goals—is to make a face-to-face visit. Your second best option is a phone call. Third, a fax. Fourth, a written letter delivered through an express delivery service like FedEx®. Fifth, a written letter mailed in the conventional way. Sixth, a memo sent in an interoffice envelope. Seventh, an e-mail.

   If your goals include both persuasion and a need to cover yourself, consider taking a memo with you to your face-to-face visit. You can present it as you leave with a comment such as, "Oh, by the way—I've summed up all the points I mentioned in this memo in case you want it for your file."

MIND MAPPING

Mind mapping is a process originally used in teaching creative writing to high school and college students. It is similar to brainstorming, but the format might be new to you. Its purpose is to allow a writer to think of as many ideas as possible in as short a time frame as possible. Then, because of its format, those items can be quickly organized for presentation in a written document.

Rules

1. In the center of a blank sheet of paper, write the key word of your topic. Then, draw a circle around it.

2. Begin brainstorming everything you can think of about your job. When you think of an idea, draw a line from the center circle outward and write the key words of your idea there. Then, draw a circle around this new idea.

3. Give yourself a time limit of no more than five minutes before beginning a mind map. Of course, if your ideas are flowing freely, just keep mind mapping.

4. When you have the need for more details, start with a general mind map. Then, mind map each of the subtopics separately that you wish to from that first mind map.

5. Mind mapping can also be used to take notes or to record minutes from a meeting.

Explanations and Examples

1. **In the center of a blank sheet of paper, write the key word of your topic. Then, draw a circle around it.**

   If, for example, you are writing a job description you would probably write the words "MY JOB" or maybe your job title, "TRAINING COORDINATOR," in the center of the page. Then, draw a circle around it.

   Sit back for a moment and relax. Take a good breath, then …

2. **Begin brainstorming everything you can think of about your job. When you think of an idea, draw a line from the center circle outward and write the key words of your idea there. Then, draw a circle around this new idea.**

   Work your way around the circle, thinking of everything you can. In come cases you might even find that one of your new circles inspires more detail. In that case, draw your lines from that new circle. Like this:

   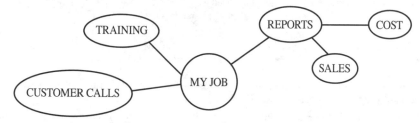

3. **Give yourself a time limit of no more than five minutes before beginning a mind map. Of course, if your ideas are flowing freely, just keep mind mapping.**

   We realize that sometimes you may need more than one mind map to begin the process of writing a more complex letter, report or proposal—it's just that to mind map on a single mind map longer than five minutes is to risk frying your brain.

   Mind mapping is a highly concentrated form of creativity. Have you ever gone into a creative zone for a little too long and ended up feeling like you were trapped in a mental Twilight Zone? It has happened to most of us. That's why the time limit. Remember, though, if your ideas are flowing freely, keep on mind mapping.

4. **When you have the need for more details, start with a general mind map. Then, mind map each of the subtopics separately that you wish to from that first mind map.**

   Let's say you are writing a report about the rules governing all punctuation marks. Your first mind map would look like this:

   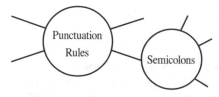

   Then, you could separately mind map each subtopic that needed one. Sometimes, as a matter of fact, you will need to do research to complete a mind map.

   One other comment about mind mapping: The circles you are drawing help your brain stay in the right hemisphere, which is where your ideas are coming from. If, though, your brain is creating ideas so quickly that drawing circles around each of them slows you down, just draw the lines and write down your ideas. When you run out of those ideas, instead of staring into space, begin drawing the circles.

   Your left brain can't draw a circle (except a zero at the bottom of a column of figures) to save its life. It is your right brain that enjoys drawing those circles. So if your left brain is thinking about how you have misspelled words, or how some of your ideas aren't worth much, the simple act of drawing the circles helps you move away from that critical, logical thinking—for now, at least. Move away from it long enough to be sure you have exhausted your creative ideas.

5. Mind mapping also can be used to take notes or to record minutes from a meeting.

The process of mind mapping forces you to write down the important key words and allows you to avoid the filler words. This makes your notetaking quicker and more reliable. Here is an example of a mind map from a management meeting. Notice how easy it would be to prepare a written memo of the minutes from this meeting.

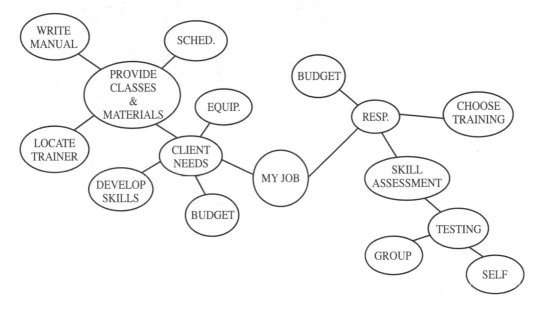

NONSEXIST LANGUAGE

Using nonsexist language is more than mere political correctness—it is also the law. Many state and federal laws and regulations exist to protect the rights of all Americans, regardless of gender. Should they be violated, these laws provide for penalties that are applicable to both individuals and their organizations.

It is simple enough to stay on the right side of these laws, though—and to guarantee your credibility with all readers. Of course, our intentions with nonsexist English have always been honorable. It is only our constructions that have been cumbersome, if not downright grammatically incorrect.

Here is a sexist sentence ▶ Each student is responsible for his own work.

Here is a way to make it nonsexist ▶ Each student is responsible for his or her own work.

For one sentence, it's a choice you can live with. But what if there had been a whole paragraph of sentences that would need the "his or her" change. That would be cumbersome, and with its weight, it would draw attention to itself as style instead of as meaning. That's when a common (but well-meaning) grammar error comes in to play:

Each student is responsible for their own work.

Many of us have heard that the most invisible way to make writing nonsexist is to change the offending third person singular pronoun into a plural one. Great idea! But you can't suspend the rules of pronouns agreeing with their antecedents. Making the sentence plural does work—but only if you make the whole sentence plural.

This is the best option because it is the least obtrusive change ▶ All students are responsible for their own work.

Other nonsexist options also exist. In some cases, it is possible to leave out the third person singular pronoun altogether.

> A writer must be persistent and industrious before he becomes rich.
> **BECOMES**
> A writer must be persistent and industrious before becoming rich.

In still fewer cases, it is possible to switch the whole sentence to the second person.

> An employee of our company can be proud of his contribution to our success.
> **BECOMES**
> As an employee of our company, you can be proud of your contribution to our success.

Nonsexist language is also a consideration when using words that themselves could be interpreted by your reader as sexist. This is why we now call mailmen *letter carriers* and stewardesses *flight attendants*. But what about manhole covers? Believe it or not, many utility workers have informed us that their departments now call them *utility lids* or *utility covers*, just to be sure no one could ever sue them. "Well, the reason they didn't hire me is because I am a woman and they have 'manhole covers' so they didn't think I was qualified to work there …" Scary, isn't it?

Here are the guidelines that will make your life—and your corporate attorney's life—easier:

Rules

1. Avoid using gender-specific nouns. Replace them with gender neutral ones.

2. When possible, switch sentences to the plural to avoid the need for a singular pronoun meant to represent either a man or a woman.

3. Sometimes, you can totally eliminate the pronoun. Be creative, but make sure the original meaning of your sentence stays intact.

4. When all else fails, use the more awkward he or she OR he/she construction. Do not use s/he and do not make a statement at the beginning of the document forgiving yourself for whatever poor nonsexist choice you make.

Examples and Explanations

1. **Avoid using gender-specific nouns. Replace them with gender neutral ones.**

   And be creative if you need to be. But avoid the truly offbeat.

   Here is a sample list of words that are not appropriate and some reasonable substitutes:

Avoid:	Use:
Mankind	People
Businessmen	Business executives, business people
Congressmen	Representatives, members of Congress
Mailmen	Letter carriers
Workmen	Workers, employees
Policemen	Police, police officers
Salesmen	Sales force, salespeople, sales representatives
Man-hours	Working hours
Stewardess	Flight attendant
Man (used generically)	One, person
Manhole cover	Utility lid

Some would say that sensitivity to using words that are gender specific has gone too far. Maybe that's true, maybe it isn't. But why not take the tack of being better safe than sorry? Why risk offending your reader (not to mention possibly breaking a civil rights law)?

2. **When possible, switch sentences to the plural to avoid the need for a singular pronoun meant to represent either a man or a woman.**

   Most often, this issue arises when the writer has used a singular indefinite pronoun like *each, every* or *some.*

   In this example, it is relatively simple to change the sentence to the plural to avoid the issue.

   > Each employee should monitor his telephone usage.
   > **BECOMES**
   > All employees should monitor their telephone usage.

   This construction avoids the need to use the clumsier but nonsexist he/she. Not every sentence can survive this simple change, but if you apply it to the ones that you can, you reduce the collective overload of too many sentences with the clunkier and harder to read he/she.

3. **Sometimes, you can totally eliminate the pronoun. Be creative, but make sure the original meaning of your sentence stays intact.**

   > To become truly successful, a musician must make sure he practices every day.
   > **BECOMES**
   > To become truly successful, a musician must make a habit of practicing every day.

4. **When all else fails, use the more awkward he or she OR he/she construction. Do not use s/he and do not make a statement at the beginning of the document forgiving yourself for whatever poor nonsexist choice you make.**

   When it is not possible to make the sentence plural or to avoid using the pronoun altogether, use either the words *he or she* or *he/she*. Because slashes are not particularly conversational, we suggest you use the first option. If you have used your other options wherever possible, you probably won't have too many of these in your document.

NOUNS

Nouns are the parts of speech we use to name people, places and things. There are two kinds of nouns: common nouns and proper nouns. Common nouns are the general names of people, places and things—including ideas and emotions (man, woman, city, village, pen, paper, anger). Proper nouns are the names of specific people (Mother Theresa, Martin Luther King, Jr.), places (New York City, Amsterdam) and things (the Eiffel Tower, the *Conflict Management Skills for Women* seminar).

While most adults know in general how to use nouns correctly, there are some fine points where even the most experienced writers and speakers can make errors. While we briefly go over the basics, these finer points are the areas we address most specifically in this section. For more basic advice about using nouns, we recommend a middle school grammar text—the simpler the better.

Rules
1. Capitalize all proper nouns. Do not capitalize common nouns.
2. Once you have named something with a noun, use that same noun (or a pronoun like *he, she* or *it*) to name it later.
3. Use singular verbs with collective nouns.
4. Spell any compound nouns consistently throughout a document. Check a dictionary to be sure when in doubt.

122

Examples and Explanations

1. **Capitalize all proper nouns. Do not capitalize common nouns.**

Proper nouns are the names of specific people, places and things. The important words of a proper noun are always capitalized. (Important words are usually considered to be all the words except articles and prepositions.)

the State of Oregon	Thomas Anderson
Leonardo da Vinci	the Chrysler Building
Australia	Buddha
Marja McCallum	the Declaration of Independence

Common nouns are the general, non-specific names of people, places and things—including ideas and emotions. Do not capitalize common nouns.

the state	the computer programmer
a painter	a building in a city
a country	a spiritual leader
an author	a founding document of our country
happiness	capitalism

2. **Once you have named something with a noun, use that same noun (or a pronoun like *he*, *she* or *it*) to name it later.**

Many writers were taught as children to avoid using the same words over again. Elementary school teachers were heavily invested in improving our vocabularies. But in today's busier, more hectic world your reader will actually understand you more clearly and more quickly if you re-use the same words when you intend the same meaning.

Here's an example ▶

> Dear Jane,
>
> Thanks for your inquiry about our new *workbook*. This *publication* has been revised in the past year and should meet the needs you and your students have for *learning materials*.
>
> If you would like more copies of our *booklet*, please let us know. You can call our customer service department to request *them* anytime.
>
> Once again, thanks for your interest in our *curriculum practice books*.
>
> Sincerely,
>
> The Department of Creative but Unclear Writing

Can you imagine Jane opening up the package that accompanies this letter? All that it contains is a workbook. Do you think she might wonder where the rest of the things the author mentions are? At any rate, finding synonyms every time the workbook is mentioned makes for awkward and potentially unclear writing.

Business Writing

How does this sound instead? ▶

> Dear Jane,
>
> Thanks for your inquiry about our new *workbook*, which has been revised in the past year. We think it will meet the needs you and your students have for *learning materials*.
>
> If you would like more copies of this *workbook*, please let us know. You can call our customer service department to request *them* anytime.
>
> Once again, thanks for your interest in our new *workbooks*.
>
> Sincerely,
>
> The Department of Clear Writing

You have used one synonym instead of three, plus the pronoun *them*. And the letter is both clear and readable.

3. Use singular verbs with collective nouns.

Collective nouns are nouns that refer to some kind of group. But the collective nouns themselves are singular.

Here are some examples ▶

a family	the committee
a group	a band

Yes, a family, by definition, has more than one member. But when using the collective noun *family* you are referring to only one family, therefore the word is singular.

Using plural verbs with singular collective nouns is a common error among even careful business writers.

Note: British writing uses plural verbs with collective nouns, e.g., *The Government are in session this week.*

Check this sentence ▶

> The group of accountants verify our financial statements.

In this sentence, the subject is actually *group*. *Group* is a singular noun, even though it refers to a group of more than one accountant. Therefore, the correct verb for the sentence would be the singular *verifies*.

Solution ▶

> The group of accountants verifies our financial statements.

Some would say that this sentence sounds awkward, even though it is correct. In that case, perhaps an even better solution would be to re-word the sentence to make it both clear and readable.

How about ▶

> All the accountants in the group verify our financial statements.

Remember your main writing goals: clarity, readability and correctness. Keeping these in mind will help you write the best sentences possible.

4. Spell any compound nouns consistently throughout a document. Check a dictionary to be sure when in doubt.

Many nouns we use are compound nouns. Compound nouns are two nouns put together to form another noun.

Here are some examples ▶

Chairwoman	land owner
homeowner	congressman
overhaul	classroom
cure-all	father-in-law

Some compound nouns are spelled as separate words, some are hyphenated and others are spelled as one word. In a few cases, dictionaries themselves tell you that there is more than one correct way of spelling the compound word. (*Homeowner* and *home owner* are both considered correct.)

When unsure about the correct spelling of *any* word, look up the correct spelling in a dictionary or use your word processor's spell-checking software. When there is more than one correct spelling listed, make a choice and then apply it consistently—to the word in question and all like words. For example, if you are using *homeowners* as one word, use *landowner* as one word also.

NUMBERS

The rules for using numbers in business writing can vary depending on the style guide you use. This guide will recommend the clearest and most readable alternatives available because it is our view that numbers are no different than words: Your goal in using them is to communicate clearly and easily.

Rules

1. Spell out all single digit numbers (0 – 9) as words. Present all other numbers as numerals.

   Exceptions:

   a. When you use more than one number in a sentence and at least one of them is larger than a single digit (10 or above). Then, use numerals for all the numbers in the sentence.

   b. When one or more of the numbers is the first word of the sentence. Always spell out a number at the beginning of a sentence.

   c. If the number is so large that spelling it out makes for awkward reading. In that case, re-word the sentence to avoid beginning it with a number.

2. Always use numerals to represent ages, weights, measurements, percentages, time, dates, years and amounts of money.

3. When using a date following a month, do not add an ordinal *-nd* or *-th* (even though you would pronounce the number as though that ending were there).

4. Use a numeral in front of a word for very large round numbers.

5. Use numerals for any number that includes a fraction.

6. In large numbers, use commas to separate the digits into groups of threes counting from right to left.

7. Form plurals of numerals by adding a lowercase *s* to the end of the numeral.

8. Consider using government style when writing numbers into formal documents, contracts or other binding agreements.

9. Above all, be consistent.

Examples and Explanations

1. **Spell out all single digit numbers (0 – 9) as words. Present all other numbers as numerals.**

   Most every style guide agrees with this basic rule. When referring to one single digit number in a sentence, spell out the word for the number.

   > Our department has requisitioned seven new computers.
   > My co-worker has taken eight sick days this month.

   a. **When you use more than one number in a sentence and at least one of them is larger than a single digit (10 or above). Then, use numerals for all the numbers in the sentence.**

   This exception is about consistency, of course. When using more than one number in a sentence, always use the same form for each number. And because numerals are easier to read than the words representing larger numbers, always favor numerals when you are making this choice.

   > **Incorrect:** My neighbor has three dogs and 23 cats.
   > **Correct:** My neighbor has 3 dogs and 23 cats.

b. When one or more of the numbers is the first word of the sentence. Always spell out a number at the beginning of a sentence.

This exception is about readability. One of the subconscious cues to your reader that a new sentence has begun is the capital letter at the beginning of the word that begins that sentence. Obviously, if a numeral begins a sentence the reader is denied that capital letter. Therefore, if a sentence you write begins with a numeral, always spell out that numeral as a word—it helps the reader read more quickly.

> **Incorrect:** 23 cats live in the house next door to me.
>
> **Correct:** Twenty-three cats live in the house next door to me.

c. If the number is so large that spelling it out makes for awkward reading. In that case, re-word the sentence to avoid beginning it with a number.

This exception is about your ability to apply common sense to help your reader easily read your writing. Obviously, very large and complex numbers make difficult reading when presented as words.

> **Incorrect:** Four hundred thirteen cats live in the house next door to me.
>
> **Correct:** A lot of cats live in the house next door to me.
>
> **Or:** Before I moved out, 413 cats lived in the house next door to me.

2. Always use numerals to represent ages, weights, measurements, percentages, time, dates, years and amounts of money.

Your readers expect numerals in these places. Spelling out the words would actually slow them down in comprehension and reading.

> Mary Beth turns 40 next Tuesday—there will be a party during our morning break.
>
> Please store the 5 lb. boxes across the storeroom from the 8 lb. boxes.
>
> The office space is roughly 50 ft. x 100 ft.
>
> Only 3% of our workforce has reported an incident in the past year.
>
> The meeting will begin at 10:15.
>
> Americans will always remember September 11, 2001.
>
> The supplies alone will cost us $1,987.65.

3. When using a date following a month, do not add an ordinal -nd or -th (even though you would pronounce the number as though that ending were there).

When using a date without the month, or when using a date before the month, do add the ending to the number.

> **Incorrect:** September 23rd was a good day to have our fall meeting.
>
> **Correct:** September 23 was a good day to have our fall meeting.
>
> **Incorrect:** The 23 of September was a good day to have our fall meeting.
>
> **Correct:** The 23rd of September was a good day to have our fall meeting.

4. Use a numeral in front of a word for very large round numbers.

When referring to a certain number of millions, billions or other very large round numbers, use a numeral for the number of millions or billions followed by the word.

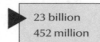

> 23 billion
> 452 million

5. Use numerals for any number that includes a fraction.

Fractions are easier to read in numerals, therefore the whole number should be presented in numerals.

> **Incorrect:** Nine and 1/2
> **Correct:** 9 1/2

6. In large numbers, use commas to separate the digits into groups of threes counting from right to left.

You probably didn't need to be reminded of this. It is the rule that governs how we make thousands (525,600), millions (4,930,355) and billions (99,000,000,000).

7. Form plurals of numerals by adding a lowercase *s* to the end of the numeral.

No apostrophe is needed.

> The CEO is always talking about how great the 60s were.
> Please make separate piles of 10s, 20s and 50s.

8. Consider using government style when writing numbers into formal documents, contracts or other binding agreements.

Government style for writing numbers is when you present them both ways, once as a numeral, once as the written word. The second is placed in parentheses. Either order is correct, although the one we present first is more common:

> Our order was for 12 (twelve) reams of paper, 30 (thirty) boxes of pens and 45 (forty-five) Canon BC-20 printer cartridges.
> Please provide fifteen (15) examples of the writing you did in your last position.

In effect, every time you write a check at the grocery store you use government style. You put the numerals in the space to the right of the name of your payee, then on the line below you write that same amount out in words.

The reason this is effective in some business writing is for the same reason it is effective in check writing. The second presentation of the number is your reader's (or the bank's) second chance to accurately understand the number.

9. Above all, BE CONSISTENT.

Consistency, as always, helps your reader for three reasons: First, your message is clearer because your reader doesn't need to struggle to determine if there are different meanings intended every time you change your mind about a stylistic point. If you use the word *three* to refer to the number of computers your department needs in one sentence and the numeral *3* to refer to those same computers in another, your reader might have to think twice.

Second, your message is far more readable. Without even realizing it, most readers learn (and come to expect) your style as they read. When you stay consistent within that style, your writing can be read much more quickly and easily. When you change style mid-document, the reader will have to slow down to re-learn or to make sense of the inconsistency.

Finally, your writing will appear more correct to the reader. As we mentioned in our opening section about Correctness (page 11), many times style guides disagree with each other about the correct form to use in a particular situation. As long as you choose a form that works for you and then apply it consistently, your reader will assume that you know what you are doing, especially in cases where he or she knows that there is disagreement.

What that means is that you certainly can't get away with looking correct just because you consistently misspell the word *the* as *teh* (everyone knows you're wrong — there is no dictionary to back you up). But the choices you make about how to present numbers or how to use commas are open to some discussion. There is disagreement among style guides. Use the reference of your choice, make your decision and then apply it consistently.

ORGANIZING YOUR WRITING

Most business writing is organized in order of importance. This principle has been mentioned many times throughout this style guide. As you no doubt are aware by now, your reader is probably too busy to wait too long to find your most important ideas. Plus, by beginning with the important material you give your reader a good idea of what to expect in the rest of the document. This helps him or her make a decision as to how much of that document needs to be read.

This section will give you directions for using this most popular organizing format, as well as several others.

Rules

1. Organize most reports, memos, letters and e-mail messages in order of importance.
2. Consider other organizing techniques for special situations.

Explanations and Examples

1. **Organize most reports, memos, letters and e-mail messages in order of importance.**

   Begin most documents with a summary statement that either tells the reader your document's most important idea or gives the reader an overview of the multiple important ideas you are about to cover.

   Fully explain your most important idea in your first paragraph(s), then move on to your second most important idea and so on. This organizing technique, you may remember, is called the Inverted Pyramid. It is the same format used by most journalists when writing news stories.

2. **Consider other organizing techniques for special situations.**

   The main organizing techniques used by business writers are:

   - Order of Importance
   - Chronological
   - General to Specific
   - Pro vs. Con
   - Reverse Chronological
   - Numerical
   - Geographical

   > *Writer's Tips:*
   > *More information about*
   > *Organization can be found*
   > *on pages 64 – 65.*

   We have already covered order of importance. Now we will address the other six methods.

   Chronological

   Chronological order is another popular method of organizing some business documents (especially status reports). Make sure to note, however, that even chronological reports need to start with a bottom line.

   Maybe ▶ This week our department accomplished five of its major objectives for the week, leaving only one objective for next week.

   Then you can continue with the chronological report ▶ On Monday, …

   In a chronologically organized report, the first thing that happened comes first, the second thing that happened comes second and so on.

   General to specific

   A third method of organizing information is to work from general to specific. This is an especially good method for organizing some reports. You start with the general topics and work your way down to the specific topics.

Pro vs. con

This organizational style is often used in sales writing. First, the writer presents all the pros of a particular idea, then that writer either directly or subtly refutes the cons and perceived cons.

> As you know, our monkey wrenches have been the top selling small tool for the past 25 years. This year, to make them even more desirable, we have added a line of left-handed tools. Not only can you get our monkey wrenches nickel-plated but they are also available with a stainless steel finish. Many of our customers tell us they are still using the first one they bought from us, even 20 years ago. (*Those are all the pros.*) Now isn't that kind of reliability and flexibility worth the extra investment? (*Now the writer is refuting the perceived con of expense.*)

Reverse chronological

This, of course, is just like chronological order except it is the most recent event that comes first, then the next most recent, etc. The last item covered would be the first one that happened.

Numerical

Anytime you write a step-by-step process of how to do something, you are writing in numerical order. This is also why we recommend that you do not use numbers for listed items unless the items actually do fall into a necessary order. When your reader sees things presented numerically, he assumes that Item Number One must come before Item Number Two.

Geographical

Sometimes it is appropriate to order a document in terms of geography or location. Obviously, if you were writing a report about the various offices of your company around the country you might order them by location.

The truth is, you can use any organizational style you choose as long as you tell the reader what it is at the beginning. Perhaps you could write a report about punctuation called *The Seven C's of Correct Punctuation*. By telling your reader so soon—in the title—what your method of organization is, you have allowed that reader to figuratively put seven little hooks in his or her brain to hang your seven ideas on. This is much easier for that reader than trying to figure out that there are seven of these tips in your document, and that they all begin with C just by reading the document. Always provide an overview of your organizational style up front if you are using a style that is not standard.

OUTLINES

Business and technical writers use outlines to organize material before the final document is written. Outlines allow those writers to check their logic and clarity, especially when writing more complicated material. An outline can also be used as a part of a document itself or as a titling system throughout a longer or more complex document that a reader may need to cross-reference.

Rules

1. Use both a logical numbering system and visual formatting strategies to distinguish among the levels of an outline.

2. Use outlines when your reader might need to cross-reference from one part of your document to another.

3. While it is desirable that each sublevel of an outline has more than one point, do not add nonessential items to an outline just to make sure that you are giving more than one point per sublevel.

4. If at all possible, avoid using an outline with more than five levels of subordination.

Explanations and Examples

1. **Use both a logical numbering system and visual formatting strategies to distinguish among the levels of an outline.**

The most common numbering systems for outlining are Traditional and Decimal. A traditional outline uses both numbers and letters, including Roman numerals:

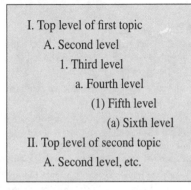

```
I. Top level of first topic
   A. Second level
      1. Third level
         a. Fourth level
            (1) Fifth level
               (a) Sixth level
II. Top level of second topic
   A. Second level, etc.
```

One of the benefits of using a traditional outline is that most readers are familiar with it. Another benefit is that it can expand at any point and at any time. If you think of a fourth level point after the report has been prepared, you can just add the next lowercase letter and reprint the document.

On the other hand, a decimal outline is also expandable at any point. And because we will never run out of numbers (theoretically, we can run out of alphabetic characters—there are only 26 of them unless you double the letters) it can expand even more infinitely than a traditional one.

```
1. Top level of first idea
   1.1  Second level
      1.1.1  Third level
         1.1.1.1  Fourth level
            1.1.1.1.1  Fifth level
2. Top level of second idea
   2.1  Second level
   2.2  Another second level
      2.2.1  Third level
```

A benefit of using the decimal method for outlining is that once the reader gets accustomed to it, it is even easier to follow than the traditional method. In the technical and scientific communities, it is the preferred method for outlining.

Notice that each lower level is also indented several spaces from the one above it whether alphabetic or numeric. This visual formatting strategy helps the reader—again—see very quickly the relationships between the ideas in the outline.

Other formatting strategies that can be helpful in outlines are boldfacing, underlining, italicizing and the use of ALL CAPS. Just be certain that you use the same strategy consistently per outline level. If you have boldfaced all the second level outline points under the first top level idea, be sure to boldface all the second level outline points throughout the outline. Remember, ALL CAPS are hard to read.

2. **Use outlines when your reader might need to cross-reference from one part of your document to another.**

   The numbering system that an outline provides makes it easy for your reader to find what he or she is looking for.

3. **While it is desirable that each sublevel of an outline has more than one point, do not add nonessential items to an outline just to make sure that you are giving more than one point per sublevel.**

   Perhaps you remember a rule from grade school that if you are putting together an outline, each sublevel needs more than one point. The reasoning was:

   How could there be an A with no B?

   Well, in business writing, our main goals are clarity, readability and correctness. Clarity demands that only essential information be included in any document. Never make something up later to add to an outline for the sake of form and tell yourself that it is necessary for the clarity of that outline.

   As far as readability concerns go, your reader would rather read *less*, not *more*. So there is no need for those extra points.

   Finally, in business writing outlines you can best achieve correctness by adhering to the visual formatting strategies and the numbering system you have chosen for your outline and forget about adding unnecessary fluff.

4. **If at all possible, avoid using an outline with more than five levels of subordination.**

   Give some thought to the needs of your poor reader's brain! It is hard to keep more than four or five ideas in mind at the same time for most adults. This isn't a disability—it's a reality. When you find yourself getting into more than five levels of subordination in an outline, consider breaking the document itself into more than one document to keep your message clear to your reader.

PARAGRAPHS

Paragraphs are the collections of sentences we use to organize our ideas into logical pieces that make up the body of a document. In general, a paragraph contains a major idea and then the support or background for that idea. Here are the guidelines business writers should keep in mind for paragraphs.

Rules

1. Limit paragraphs to a single major idea or topic.
2. Limit all paragraphs to a length of ten printed lines. In e-mail, limit paragraph lengths to eight printed lines.
3. Vary the length of your paragraphs and the length of the sentences in those paragraphs.
4. Include an opening sentence that accurately reflects the content of the paragraphs.
5. Organize the ideas in your paragraphs logically.
6. Use an occasional one line paragraph to renew your reader's interest.
7. Indenting the first line of your paragraphs makes them more readable for most readers.

Explanations and Examples

1. **Limit paragraphs to a single major idea or topic.**

   Your reader digests your document the same way you digest a meal—in bites, not the whole meal at once. Consider your paragraphs to be the bites. Make sure that each paragraph has a single purpose—to communicate and elaborate on one main idea or topic.

   Note: When the subject cannot fit into one paragraph, it is sometimes necessary to have more than one paragraph for the subject.

2. **Limit all paragraphs to a length of ten printed lines. In e-mail, limit paragraph lengths to eight printed lines.**

   This is a rule that you won't find in an academic style guide. In academia the paragraphs can be as long as it takes the author to develop a point—sometimes pages! In business writing, we are concerned about your reader's first impression. How does the reader react when he or she looks at the page, or looks at the computer screen for the first time? When busy readers see long unbroken paragraphs, they tend to get discouraged and often decide to put the document aside until "later." (Of course, "later" rarely comes.)

So even if you have no good reason to break a paragraph content-wise after ten lines (or eight in e-mail), break the paragraph anyway. Your reader will appreciate it!

3. **Vary the length of your paragraphs and the length of the sentences in those paragraphs.**

Again, this advice will keep your reader from becoming bored. Have you ever looked at a document that appeared to be made up of all seven line paragraphs? It looks very dull. And documents that look dull tend to get pushed aside by your reader. Vary your paragraph lengths, and also vary the sentence lengths inside those paragraphs.

You don't want to sound like a first grade reader ▶
See Dick. See Jane. See Spot. See Dick run. See Jane run. See Spot run.
John attended the meeting yesterday. He said it was very interesting. They talked about the new sales initiative. There were good donuts. It ended an hour before lunch.

Instead, write so that some of your sentences are longer, others are medium-length and a few are very short. It keeps your reader interested. ▶
John attended the meeting yesterday, which he said was very interesting. They discussed many interesting points about the new sales initiative, and also covered some of the material he had missed from last week. Plus, he said the donuts were great.

See? It's much more interesting to read, don't you think?

4. **Include an opening sentence that accurately reflects the content of the paragraphs.**

This would be what you may remember as the *topic sentence* from elementary school. Notice that our advice to use one in most sentences is consistent with our advice about organizing your writing: Start every document (in this case, start every *paragraph*) with the most important idea of that document (or paragraph).

An opening sentence that gives the reader a preview of what will be coming helps that reader to stay mentally organized and therefore helps that reader to understand your message both quickly and clearly.

Sometimes, a paragraph will be a continuation of an idea you have already stated in an earlier paragraph. In this case, a new topic sentence is not needed. In other cases, it may be more interesting to your reader to have a question posed or to be presented with a quote or a statistic that leads into the information your paragraph contains. But make sure that no matter how you begin a paragraph, your reader knows where you are heading in it by the end of its first sentence.

Autumn is a beautiful and sentimental time of year for me here in New England. The air is crisp and cool, but the skies are often sunny. The leaves turn their incredible variety of colors and I can still smell the ones that are burning in piles in all the backyards down our street—even though I haven't lived in that house for 30 years, and the city no longer allows open fires, even for leaf burning.

How would that paragraph have read without its opening sentence? Yes, it would still make some sense, but the reader wouldn't have been looking for both beauty and sentiment from the beginning, therefore he or she might have been caught off guard. Or worse—not noticed it at all.

5. **Organize the ideas in your paragraphs logically.**

Again, organizing your ideas in order of importance is always a good choice. But in some paragraphs, the purpose of your sentences is to further explain or develop the central idea you stated at the beginning. Sometimes this can be done by offering proof, other times it is done by telling a story. Stories are usually told in *chronological* order.

Just remember to keep it simple. Certainly, keeping it simple makes you much easier to understand, but it also helps you as the writer. Focus on a conversational style and when you are in doubt about how to put a paragraph together, imagine yourself having lunch with a friend and telling that friend the story of what it is you are attempting to write. Your sentences often come more easily this way.

And paragraph breaks? Well, those would be when you feel the urge to take a bite of your lunch mid-conversation.

> **Writer's Tips:**
> *As a matter of fact, all the organizing options presented in the section Organizing Your Writing on pages 127 – 128 can be used to help you organize your paragraphs.*

6. Use an occasional one line paragraph to renew your reader's interest.

Especially in longer documents or lengthy e-mails, your readers' interest can wane just because of the work they are doing to keep reading. An occasional one line paragraph is like a refreshing vacation in a tropical paradise. All that white space around it provides readers with something to look forward to as they make their way down the page, closer and closer to that small break.

One line paragraphs are also an effective way to convey very important information that could otherwise be overlooked, especially by tired, stressed or overworked readers.

7. Indenting the first line of your paragraphs makes them more readable for most readers.

Over the past years the block style for letters and memos has become very popular, practically convention. In the block style, every line begins flush left—all the way to the left-hand margin.

While this style does have a very clean appearance, it is also what most readers have come to expect. And to expect again and again and again …

Using the modified block style, where the date and signature block start at the center of the line and the first line of each paragraph is indented by several spaces, sets you apart in a reader's pile of incoming mail. You will look friendlier and more conversational. It is also easier for your reader to keep track cognitively of where he or she is in the document should a distraction come up during the reading.

This becomes especially important in e-mail, where most readers are tired of reading before they ever double-click on your subject line.

PARALLELISM

When writing, ideas that are alike should be presented in ways that are alike so that your reader easily perceives the existing similarities. This principle is referred to as *parallelism*.

An example of a non-parallel sentence ▶ We need to hire a new sales rep who will be able to build relationships with our existing customers, have the writing skills needed to win over the Marketing Director and consistent selling of new accounts is also important.

Each idea is presented in a different form ▶ build relationships
have the writing skills
consistent selling of new accounts

Here is the same sentence, made parallel ▶ We need to hire a new sales rep who will be able to build relationships with our existing customers, write well enough to win over the Marketing Director and sell new accounts consistently.

Rules

1. Present words and phrases being used in like ways within the same sentence in a similar form.
2. Make sure that items in a list are parallel in their construction.

Explanations and Examples

1. **Present words and phrases being used in like ways within the same sentence in a similar form.**

   Correct: The report should include an introduction, a discussion and a conclusion.

   Not: The report should include an introduction, discussion and a conclusion.

   Correct: The latest manual clearly states that *whoever* applies the coating must also be the one *who* places the sheets in the processing solution.

   Not as good: The latest manual clearly states that whoever applies the coating must also place the sheets in the processing solution.

2. **Make sure that items in a list are parallel in their construction.**

   Whether the listed items are presented in a bulleted format or within a paragraph, each item in the list must be equal to the others in style and form.

   Correct: The meeting was attended by most supervisors and all directors: Stanley Goodhope, Sales Director; Marjorie Simpson, Inside Sales Supervisor; Jerrold Harris, Outside Sales Supervisor; Felicity Morgenstern, Finance Director; Bryan Rivera, Human Resources Director; Shelley Matsachuska, Training Supervisor; Lydia Herrera, Payroll Supervisor; and Gaelen O'Rourke, Administrative Director.

   Not as good: The meeting was attended by most supervisors and all directors: Stanley Goodhope, Sales Director; Marjorie Simpson; Jerrold Harris, Outside Sales Supervisor; Felicity Morgenstern; Bryan Rivera, Human Resources Director; Shelley Matsachuska, Training Supervisor; Lydia Herrera; and Gaelen O'Rourke, Administrative Director.

   Notice that the list reads more easily when all attendees have been listed using the same format (Name, Job Title.)

   The same holds true for bulleted lists. Notice how much easier it is to follow the first example below than the second one.

   Correct: There are seven steps involved in the writing process:
   1. Prepare a mind map of all the ideas you have pertaining to your topic.
   2. Choose the most important idea and write your opening paragraph based upon it.
   3. Organize the rest of your ideas by numbering them in the mind map.
   4. Freewrite the rest of your document by writing about the rest of your numbered ideas.
   5. Get away from this first draft for at least a few minutes.
   6. Edit the document by checking for clarity and readability.
   7. Proofread the document for correctness.

Notice that in this example each bulleted item begins with a verb and each bulleted item is structured as a complete sentence. Here is an example of the same list when the bulleted items have NOT been constructed in a parallel way:

Incorrect: There are seven steps involved in the writing process:

1. Prepare a mind map of all the ideas you have pertaining to your topic.
2. The most important idea should be the first paragraph.
3. Organize the rest of your ideas by numbering them in the mind map.
4. Freewriting
5. Get away from this first draft for at least a few minutes.
6. Edit the document by checking for clarity and readability.
7. Correctness through proofreading

When the rules of parallelism are not followed, not only does the reading slow down, but the meaning becomes less clear. As far as bulleted lists go, one of the most common questions business writers have is what to do about punctuating the items in a list if some of them are sentences and some of them aren't. The answer is to be found in the principle of parallelism: Rewrite the list so that all the items are structured in the same way—they all need to be complete sentences or they all need to be phrases.

PASSIVE VOICE

Passive voice is a quality that a verb could possess. If you use a grammar checking program as part of your word processing software package, you are probably accustomed to being warned that you are using the passive voice. There are two things you need to know about that:

1) Passive voice is not *wrong*, it just could be less clear than active voice.

2) Your grammar checking software could be mistaken to begin with.

Perhaps an explanation of exactly what passive voice is would be appropriate here. There are two main kinds of verbs that we use in the English language: linking verbs and action verbs.

Linking verbs are verbs that convey a state of being: for example, all of the forms of *to be* and verbs such as *look*, *seem*, *appear*, *become* and *grow*.

Linking verbs ▶

I *am* an author. (form of *to be*)
I *have been* an employee of this company for 20 years. (form of *to be*)
I *feel* sick. (verb referring to a state of being)
I *feel* angry. (verb referring to an emotional state)

Action verbs
▼

I *drove* to work in my new Camaro today.
She *sharpened* all the pencils last night.
The evidence of wrongdoing *has been destroyed.*

An action verb is a verb that conveys action that has taken place or will take place.

The subject is doing the action
▼

I (subject) drove (action verb)
She (subject) sharpened (action verb, active voice)

In all three of the sentences above, action has occurred—driving, sharpening and destroying. Notice the different structures of the sentences, though. The first two sentences are written in the active voice.

The third sentence is written in the passive voice.

The subject is having an action done to it ▶ The evidence (subject) has been destroyed (action verb, passive voice)

Notice that in the passive voice sentence, we do not know who or what has destroyed the evidence. This, as a matter of fact, is the main reason business writers should usually avoid using passive voice constructions: Sometimes important information is left out of sentences by accident. Other times, the important information is being left out on purpose. Here are the guidelines we recommend concerning passive voice:

Rules

1. Favor active voice verbs in most writing situations.

2. Use the passive voice when the receiver of the action or the result of the action is more important to the reader than the doer of the action.

3. BEWARE: Overuse of the passive voice could lead the reader to think that the writer is purposely withholding information.

4. Make passive voice sentences into active voice sentences by asking the question, "By whom?"

Explanations and Examples

1. **Favor active voice verbs in most writing situations.**

   Not only are active voice verbs more clear, they are more predictable in reading for your reader. Most sentences are written in the active voice. It is easy for your reader to build an image in his or her mind while reading.

   Presented in active voice
   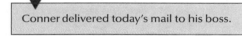
   Conner delivered today's mail to his boss.

   As you read that sentence, you could build the image easily. First you see Conner, then you see him delivering something, then you see that it is mail—to his boss.

   Presented in the passive voice ▶ The boss's mail was delivered to him today by Conner.

   Your first image is of the boss's mail. Then you see that it is being delivered, but as of yet the delivery person is faceless. OH! Look, it's Conner! Certainly, this sentence is understandable—but at what cost? Wouldn't it have just been easier to present it the first way?

2. **Use the passive voice when the receiver of the action or the result of the action is more important to the reader than the doer of the action.**

   Most scientific reports are written in the passive voice for this reason. If they weren't, the subject of every sentence would probably be *I*.

   Passive:
   The three chemical solutions were placed in three separate beakers. After the solutions had each been boiled for 90 seconds, samples were taken and placed on separate slides. The slides were then analyzed with an electron microscope to determine if the hypothesized changes had taken place.

   Active:
   This researcher placed the three chemical solutions in three separate beakers. Then, after boiling each solution for 90 seconds, this researcher took samples and placed them on separate slides. Then this researcher analyzed the slides with an electron microscope to determine if the hypothesized changes had taken place.

   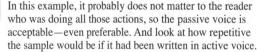
   In this example, it probably does not matter to the reader who was doing all those actions, so the passive voice is acceptable—even preferable. And look at how repetitive the sample would be if it had been written in active voice.

3. **BEWARE: Overuse of the passive voice could lead the reader to think that the writer is purposely withholding information.**

And of course, passive voice is a great way to do just that—purposely withhold information that could be damaging to the author or to the author's interests. Unfortunately, most business readers today have had passive voice used on them for this reason so many times they have developed quite a sensitivity to it.

Would you get resentful if a government agency wrote you a letter explaining that you would not be receiving an amount of money that you were expecting and used this passive voice sentence?

> Mistakes have been made in the processing of your refund.

Most readers (and taxpayers) would suspect that the doer of the mistake had been protected purposely by the author of this sentence. Would you?

So double-check your motives every time you choose a passive voice sentence. Make sure that you will remain credible to your reader.

4. **Make passive voice sentences into active voice sentences by asking the question, "By whom?"**

This is also the advice for finding whether or not your grammar checking software has been accurate in labeling a particular sentence of yours as passive. Most grammar checkers are programmed to find helping verbs (forms of the verb *to be*) to indicate that a sentence could be passive. And (thankfully), no matter how sophisticated your word processor may be, it simply can't read your documents for *understanding*. All it can do is let you know that there *could be* a problem. It is always up to the writer, to the user of the software, to double-check himself or herself.

When your grammar checking software flags a sentence as passive, read the sentence to yourself and ask the question, "By whom?" If there is an answer to that question (whether that answer is included in the sentence or not), then your grammar checker was correct and indeed you have a passive sentence. If the question "By whom?" is nonsensical in relation to the sentence, then most likely you are just dealing with a sentence that is using forms of the verb *to be* for some other reason (most likely to change tense).

Once you do find a passive voice sentence that would be easier on your reader as an active voice one, it is simple enough to change it. Answer the question "By whom?" and make that answer the subject of the new, active voice sentence.

> **Passive sentence:** The project was completed on April 12.
>
> **Ask:** By whom?
>
> **Answer (and realize that you might have to do some checking to find this answer):** By Celia
>
> **New, active voice sentence:** Celia completed the project on April 12.

PLURALS

Your best guide to forming plurals of nouns you are uncertain of is a good and recent dictionary. (We recommend on-line dictionaries, of which there are several.) There are some guidelines, though, that could help you to learn the tricks that will help you overcome many business writers' most common errors.

Please also check the next section on Possessives for more information about adding *-s* to the ends of words. Many times, busy writers confuse their need for plurals and their need for possessives.

Rules

1. Most words are made plural by adding *-s* or *-es* to the end of the word (regular plurals).

2. Many plurals, however, are not regular.

3. The best way to be sure you are correctly spelling irregular plurals is to check them in a dictionary.

Explanations and Examples

1. **Most words are made plural by adding *-s* or *-es* to the end of the word (regular plurals).**

    These would be considered the *regular* plurals.

2. **Many plurals, however, are not regular.**

    The words that are not made plural in this predictable way could be made plural in any number of irregular ways.

Singular	Plural
employee	employees
office	offices
report	reports
project	projects
fax	faxes
lunch	lunches

Sometimes the whole word changes ▶

I	we
he	they

Other times, the spelling of a part of the word changes ▶

knife	knives
crisis	crises
child	children

3. **The best way to be sure you are correctly spelling irregular plurals is to check them in a dictionary.**

    Any good dictionary (and certainly any on-line dictionary) will show you the preferred spellings of the word you look up as well as the words that are made from that word. If you were looking for the correct plural of the word *appendix*, for example, all you would need to do is look up the word *appendix*. Toward the end of the listing of the word's origin and meanings, you would see the abbreviation *pl.* And following this abbreviation, you would find the preferred spelling (and sometimes spellings) of the word *appendix*. (Most dictionaries today do list both *appendixes* and *appendices* as correct plural spellings. In general the one that is listed in a dictionary first is the one considered to be more preferable.)

POSSESSIVES

The rules for making a possessive are much simpler than most writers would believe. As a matter of fact, there are only two rules.

Rules

1. To make a possessive, add an apostrophe *s* to the word unless the word being made possessive already ends in an *s*. In that case, just add an apostrophe.

2. When making a word both plural and possessive, make the word plural first. Then, follow the rule above to make it possessive.

Explanations and Examples

The reason that the simplicity of the first rule might be unbelievable to you is because so many writers have become confused in the forming of plural possessives over the years. Let's delve into this rule just a little more deeply.

1. **To make a possessive, add an apostrophe *s* to the word unless the word being made possessive already ends in an *s*. In that case, just add an apostrophe.**

    Most possessives are made by simply adding an apostrophe *s*.

employee	employee's review
project	project's deadline
copier	copier's paper supply
program	program's glitches

When a word already ends with an *s*, your reader will be able to read the possessive more quickly with just an apostrophe. The reason? Well, look for yourself:

boss' desk	**NOT**	boss's desk
Lars' review	**NOT**	Lars's review

Some style guides suggest that you should add an apostrophe and an *s* to all words that are being made possessive, even if they do end with an *s*. These style guides would have you write *boss's desk* and *Lars's review*. Most readers report that adding the extra *s* makes the word look so strange it would slow them down in the reading. And the apostrophe—even without the *s*—makes the possessive meaning clear.

Because this is a style guide focused on business writing, we absolutely recommend that writers leave off the *s* in this case. We are concerned with readability.

2. **When making a word both plural and possessive, make the word plural first. Then, follow the rule above to make it possessive.**

We all know that to make a plural of a singular word, the general rule is to add an *s* to the word:

one dog	two dogs
one writer	three writers

We also all know that there are probably more exceptions to the rules of making plurals than there are to any other spelling rule in American English.

Here, let's deal with the plural possessive problem.

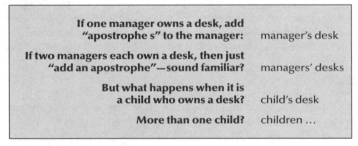

If one manager owns a desk, add "apostrophe s" to the manager:	manager's desk
If two managers each own a desk, then just "add an apostrophe"—sound familiar?	managers' desks
But what happens when it is a child who owns a desk?	child's desk
More than one child?	children ...

This is where most people become confused. The confusion lies in the rule we repeat to ourselves about more than one manager owning more than one desk: "Just add an apostrophe." Obviously, the rule fails here. And actually, the reason it does is because it was never really the rule to begin with.

So forget it. We mean it. You need to forget that phrase: "Just add an apostrophe."

Here is the rule that always works ▶ To make a possessive, **add an apostrophe *s* unless the word already ends in *s*, then add just an apostrophe**.

This is so important, and the true key to so many correct possessives in your future, it bears repeating. To make a possessive, add an apostrophe *s* unless the word already ends in *s*, then add just an apostrophe.

Children. According to the rule above, how do you make it possessive? Add apostrophe *s* (because it does not already end in *s*).

 children's desks

A question many people now ask is, "Well, what about words or names that end in *s*?" It's a good question, and frankly, grammar guides disagree.

Business Writing

We recommend: Pronounce the apostrophe *s* in speaking, but do not write it.

So, in writing ▶ Ross' hat   **In speaking** ▶ Ross's hat

This way you get the best of both worlds. It doesn't look awkward and it doesn't sound awkward.

PREPOSITIONS

Prepositions are words that relate the nouns or pronouns following them to the other words in a sentence. The choice of preposition affects the way the other words in the sentence relate to each other. The chart below contains a list of the most frequently used prepositions:

Most Frequently Used Prepositions

about	beside	into	through
above	besides	like	to
across	between	near	toward
after	beyond	of	under
against	but	off	underneath
along	by	on	until
among	down	onto	up
around	during	opposite	upon
at	except	out	with
before	for	outside	within
behind	from	over	without
below	in	past	
beneath	inside	since	

Some prepositions are compound, meaning they consist of more than one word:

Frequently Used Compound Prepositions

according to	in front of
ahead of	in place of
apart from	in spite of
aside from	instead of
as of	in view of
because of	next to
by means of	on account of
in addition to	on top of
in back of	out of

Prepositions must always be followed by a noun or pronoun. *Prepositional phrases* are the groups of words beginning with the preposition and ending with the noun or pronoun. Many prepositional phrases also contain other words as well.

Example ▶

> under the broken red shelf
> under (*preposition*) the broken red (*modifiers*) shelf (*noun*)

Rules

In business writing, the rules for using prepositions are clear and easy.

1. Always use the preposition that most accurately communicates your message.
2. Avoid using prepositions that are unnecessary to your intended meaning.
3. It is permissible to end sentences with prepositions—if it makes the sentences clear.

Explanations and Examples

1. **Always use the preposition that most accurately communicates your message.**

   Should the technician place his completed report *in* the box, *next to* the box, *under* the box or *on top of* the box? As the writer, it is your responsibility to be as specific and as accurate as possible.

2. **Avoid using prepositions that are unnecessary to your intended meaning.**

   The overuse of unnecessary prepositions is a symptom of wordiness. Notice in these examples that the sentences make perfect sense even without the preposition in parentheses.

   > All (of) the doctors agreed on my diagnosis.
   > The meeting will start (at) about noon.
   > We all agree he should get up off (of) his chair and help us.

3. **It is permissible to end sentences with prepositions—if it makes the sentences clear.**

   This guideline is also covered in our section about grammar errors that are no longer considered errors. (See pages 90 – 96.)

   Business writing is not as formal as the writing most of us were taught in schools. Your reader needs to understand a message quickly and clearly. That's why clarity and readability must remain our primary focus.

   > **Have you ever written a sentence that accidentally ended with a preposition? Did you then attempt to rewrite the sentence? Did you end up with a weird and awkward-sounding sentence like this?**
   >
   > Once you have completed your report, Salma is the one to give it to.
   >
   > **OOPS! Okay, let's re-word it:**
   >
   > Once you have completed your report, Salma is the one to whom you should give it.
   >
   > **Of course, you could have rewritten it as:**
   >
   > Once you have completed your report, please give it to Salma.
   >
   > **But do you see the problem? What happens when there isn't such a desirable (and creative) option available?**
   >
   > Where did these disks come from?
   >
   > **That would have to change to:**
   >
   > From where did these disks come?

   It's understandable, but awkward. You are better off just letting the original sentence stand with its preposition at the end.

PRONOUNS

Pronouns are words that take the place of nouns or groups of words acting as nouns. They should be used when it would not make sense to repeat the noun *and* it is clear which noun the pronoun is replacing. Pronouns can take the place of nouns within the same sentence or in an earlier sentence.

Pronouns are closely related to the nouns they replace. Those nouns are referred to as *antecedents*. Most antecedents come before their pronouns.

The most common pronouns writers use are *personal pronouns*. Personal pronouns can refer to three categories of nouns: (1) a person speaking, (2) a person being spoken to or (3) the person, place or thing being spoken about.

Personal Pronouns Chart

	Singular	Plural
First Person	I, me, my, mine	we, us, our, ours
Second Person	you, your, yours	you, your, yours
Third Person	he, him, his she, her, hers it, its	they, them, their, theirs

First person pronouns are used by the person or people speaking or writing to refer to himself, herself or themselves.

> ▶ I will notify you as soon as I have received my shipment.

Second person pronouns are used when the speaker or writer is speaking or writing directly to another person. Second person pronouns use the same form for both singular (one listener or reader) or plural (multiple listeners or readers).

> ▶ You will notify me when you have received your shipment, won't you?

Writer's Tips:
This is why switching the entire offending sentence to the plural to avoid sexist language is a good piece of advice. See pages 119 – 121.

Third person pronouns have more forms than first and second person pronouns do. There are masculine pronouns, feminine pronouns and neuter pronouns. In the plural forms, there are no gender distinctions.

> ▶ Nancy will notify us when she receives her shipment.

There are also indefinite pronouns, demonstrative pronouns, interrogative pronouns, relative pronouns and reflexive pronouns.

Indefinite pronouns refer to people, places or things—often without specifying which ones.

Indefinite Pronouns

<u>Singular</u>			<u>Plural</u>	<u>Both</u>
another	everyone	nothing	both	all
anybody	everything	one	few	any
anyone	little	other	many	more
anything	much	somebody	others	most
each	neither	someone	several	none
either	nobody	something	some	
everybody	no one			

Indefinite Pronouns ▶ *Someone* should handle this call soon.
Both of them talked to Mr. Greene about his order.

Demonstrative pronouns point out specific people, places or things. There are four demonstrative pronouns: *this*, *that*, *these* and *those*. A demonstrative pronoun can come before or after its antecedent.

Demonstrative Pronouns ▶ *These* donuts are delicious.
Of all the reference guides we have, *this* one is the clearest.

Interrogative pronouns are used to begin questions. There are five interrogative pronouns: *what*, *which*, *who*, *whom* and *whose*. Usually, interrogative pronouns do not have antecedents. Their "antecedents" would tend to be the answers to the questions they ask, if you think about it.

Interrogative Pronouns ▶ *What* did he tell us yesterday?
Who left the coffee pot on?

Relative pronouns begin subordinate clauses and connect them to other ideas in the same sentences. There are five relative pronouns: *that*, *which*, *who*, *whom* and *whose*.

Relative Pronouns ▶ The small project *that* he took on last week has turned into a monster.
She is the one *whose* office is next to Jack's.

Reflexive pronouns refer (or reflect) back to a previously stated noun or pronoun. They can be used either reflexively or intensively.

Reflexive Pronouns ▶ Sally went to the store to buy herself a blouse. (Used reflexively)
Sally herself went to the store to buy a blouse. (Used intensively)

Rules

Here are the rules to remember in business writing regarding pronouns of all different kinds.

1. It is acceptable (even desirable) to use personal pronouns in business writing—no matter what you may remember being told.

2. Make sure your pronouns agree with their antecedents in number, gender, case and function.

3. Use reflexive pronouns only when they are truly reflecting back onto the subject of the sentence.

4. Make sure that your pronouns agree in number with the verbs you use with them.

5. Avoid overusing pronouns and using pronouns that aren't clear.

Explanations and Examples

1. **It is acceptable (even desirable) to use personal pronouns in business writing—no matter what you may remember being told.**

   Many adults in today's workforce remember being told never to use personal pronouns in business letters or memos—to especially avoid the use of the words *I* and *me*. Yet if we agree on a conversational tone in your writing, the use of personal pronouns is automatic.

   Certainly, be careful about using too many references to yourself (I, me, mine, my) in any document. Your reader could think that you are an egotist! But using personal pronouns as you naturally would in a conversation is perfectly acceptable.

Just a note: Should you find yourself needing to edit some of the mentions of yourself out of a document, there is an easy way to do it. Just ask yourself, "How would this sentence need to be changed if the first word was *You* or *Your*?"

> I would like to take this opportunity to express my sincere wish that our conference will be attended by you.

Now—how could you re-word that so you don't use any first person pronouns and the first word is *You* or *Your*?

> You are invited to attend a conference that has been planned with your needs in mind.

2. Make sure your pronouns agree with their antecedents in number, gender, case and function.

This sometimes takes careful editing. Most writers are aware of the common pitfall of using a singular antecedent with a plural third person pronoun just to avoid a sexist construction.

> Each employee is responsible for their own work.

The correct sentence would read either:

> All employees are responsible for their own work.
> **OR**
> Each employee is responsible for his or her own work.

Especially in longer sentences, where pronouns can become separated from their antecedents by great distances, the careful writer must be vigilant to make sure that they still agree.

Another common error made concerning agreement of pronoun and antecedent concerns which form of a pronoun to use after a linking verb: Should one say *This is me* or *This is I*?

Technically, it is the *I* that would be correct. But it would sound terrible! To say nothing about how it would look in a written document. Your best option in cases like these is to rewrite the sentence and find a less awkward way of expressing your idea.

> **Correct (but weird):** The engineer who thought of it was he.
> **Better:** He was the engineer who thought of it.

Use subjective case pronouns (*I, he, she, we, they, who*) when the pronoun is the subject of a verb or when the pronoun is being used after a linking verb. Use objective case pronouns (*me, him, her, us, them, whom*) when the pronoun is the object of a verb or the object of a preposition.

> Jason and I (*subject*) thought of the plan.
> The plan was thought of by Jason and me (*object of preposition*).
> Jason told me (*object of the verb*) about the plan.

Be aware that this same rule applies to the interrogative pronouns *who* and *whom*. If you find yourself having difficulty, just temporarily substitute either *he* or *him* for the interrogative pronoun. This will help you determine whether you need a subjective pronoun (*he* and *who* are subjective) or an objective one (*him* and *whom* are objective).

3. Use reflexive pronouns only when they are truly reflecting back onto the subject of the sentence.

The reflexive pronouns *myself, yourself, himself, herself, itself, ourselves* and *themselves* should only be used when the subject of the sentence they are being used in is the same person or thing that is being referred to in the pronoun.

The word *reflexive* derives from the same root word as the word *reflect*. This makes it easy to remember what reflexive pronouns do. They reflect back.

> Janelle said she would handle the call herself.
>
> Did you hear yourselves?
>
> I would rather pick up the documents myself.
>
> **But NOT:** Please deliver the documents to Randy and myself.

> Please deliver the documents to Randy and me.

The subject of the sentence is an understood *You. You, please deliver the documents* ... Do you see that *You* does not reflect back on *myself*? The correct pronoun for the end of that sentence is *me*.

Remember, too, that reflexive pronouns can be used intensively—to strengthen the reference back to the noun or pronoun. For example: *I called for the appointment myself* (reflexive). *I myself called for the appointment* (intensive).

4. **Make sure that your pronouns agree in number with the verbs you use with them.**

This is especially tricky when using indefinite pronouns. Some indefinite pronouns *seem* to be plural when they are indeed singular.

> Everybody (*singular*) loves (*singular*) Raymond.
>
> Anyone (*singular*) near the beach was (*singular*) probably exposed to the contaminants found in the water.

5. **Avoid overusing pronouns and using pronouns that aren't clear.**

Pronouns can be a great convenience and can help your reader be more comfortable with your document. But there is a danger. It is tempting to rely too much on pronouns and to therefore lose the clarity of your message. When you find yourself using a pronoun for which the antecedent appeared paragraphs ago, it is time to mention the antecedent specifically again.

Also, be careful that there isn't more than one potential antecedent.

Example ▶ **Confusing:** Mike and John have both had their complaints about the weekly staff meeting, but this week he had a really great idea.

Better: Mike and John have both had their complaints about the weekly staff meeting, but this week Mike had a really great idea.

And finally, when using a sentence such as, "This is so great!" make sure that your reader will know for sure what it is that impressed you.

You would be better off with ▶ This month's financial report is so great!

PRESS RELEASES

Writing a press release has specific guidelines and requirements that other writing doesn't have. A press release is used for two main reasons: to inform the public of special events and to influence public opinion.

Rules

1. Write the press release so the editor will use it.
2. Write it from an outsider's perspective.
3. Avoid big words, acronyms and abbreviations.
4. Make sure everything is accurate; proofread and edit it carefully.
5. Keep your press release to one page.
6. Double-space the press release and use one-inch margins.
7. End the press release correctly.
8. Provide your contact information.
9. Fax or e-mail the press release to the appropriate person.
10. Clearly state when you want the document released.

Explanations and Examples

1. **Write the press release so the editor will use it.**

   If the editor won't print what you've written or read it on the air, the important information or announcement you want publicized will not be publicized.

   In order for your press release to be used, it must be newsworthy, timely and of interest to the audience. Make sure that at least two of these three criteria are met before submitting your press release.

2. **Write it from an outsider's perspective.**

   A press release is public relations for your organization. Therefore, it is important that you write it from an outsider's perspective. For example, instead of writing "We're pleased to announce that Gina Fagnoli has been promoted to Director of Operations at Soteria Consulting," write "Soteria Consulting is pleased to announce that Gina Fagnoli has been promoted to Director of Operations." To write it the first way gives the impression that the publication the press release is appearing in is pleased about Gina's promotion.

3. **Avoid big words, acronyms and abbreviations.**

   The average reader reads at an 8th grade level—using big words will not convey your message correctly. Also, acronyms and abbreviations don't communicate to your reader, unless your reader is familiar with them.

4. **Make sure everything is accurate; proofread and edit it carefully.**

   Over time, you will develop a relationship with the editors you send press releases to. Make the relationship better by developing the reputation of always providing accurate press releases that are well-edited and proofread.

   It is your responsibility to ensure the accuracy of the information you submit. It is also your job to make sure you've written the release with the verbiage you want and thoroughly checked it for typos. If there is a typo, the editor of the publication will either not print the press release or print it with the typo.

5. **Keep your press release to one page.**

   Keeping your press release to one page will help you focus your message and eliminate unnecessary words. However, if you must write more than one page, remember to use the Inverted Pyramid method of organization—the most important information first, the next most important, etc.

   If the editor allots your press release two column inches and it takes three and a half, your wonderful writing will be cut off at two inches. The editor will not rewrite it to include important information at the end of the release. If it is to be read on the air and they have allotted 15 seconds for it, the reader will stop at 15 seconds—no matter where they are in the press release.

6. Double-space the press release and use one-inch margins.

Double-spacing makes the press release easier to read and one-inch margins are what a majority of editors want to see.

7. End the press release correctly.

Professional news writers use these symbols to end their submissions to AP or UPI. Use one of them to make your press release look professional:

###	000	—xxx—	—30

8. Provide your contact information.

While the editor may never use it, it is better for you to provide your contact information than to have the editor need and not have it.

9. Fax or e-mail the press release to the appropriate person.

If you do not know the appropriate editor's name, call and get it. Submitted articles and press releases that come into a publication's office addressed simply to *Editor* are often shoved aside and never looked at.

If you cannot get the correct name, address it to their specific title, for example, *Business Editor* (for a print media) or to *Assignment Editor* or *News Director* for air media (radio or TV).

10. Clearly state when you want the document released.

If you do not tell the editor when you want your press release printed or read, he or she will release it whenever they have the space or time to do so. Specify a date using one of the following formats:

FOR RELEASE   FOR RELEASE AFTER
(date)   (date)

OR

FOR IMMEDIATE RELEASE

> *Writer's Tips:*
> *For additional information*
> *on Journalistic Writing,*
> *see page 108.*

PROOFREADING

Proofreading is the process by which a previously written document is double-checked for accuracy and correctness. And in fact, at the beginning of this style guide you will find a treatise on how important correctness is, and how to proofread accurately (pages 11 – 13).

In this section, we will provide you with a process—complete with chart—you can use reliably every time you proofread.

Proofreading Chart

I. If you are not the author, read the document for meaning before making any changes to it.

   A. To understand its intent (so you avoid changing that intent)

   B. To find the things you don't understand (and ask the author to explain)

     1. Poor handwriting

     2. Over your head

     3. Nonsense

II. If you are the author, separate yourself from what you just wrote before attempting to proofread it.

   A. Take a break.

   B. Print it out in a larger font size.

   C. Use your software program's spell-checker and—perhaps—grammar checker. But take them with a grain of salt. (In other words, proofread anyway.)

   D. Read aloud.

   E. Read with a different light source (incandescent instead of fluorescent).

   F. Read in a different place.

III. If there is an original, proofread against it—preferably, with a proofreading partner.

IV. Proofread line by line, using a ruler or a blank sheet of paper to guide you down the page.

V. Check the trouble spots. Visually scan or use the Find command in your word processor to double-check around:

     1. Commas—are they necessary?

     2. Periods—does the next word begin a sentence? Is it capitalized?

     3. Capital letters—are they correct? Consistent? Are the letters after them mistakenly capitalized?

     4. Underlining, boldface, italics—are they toggled on and off correctly?

     5. Quotation marks—are both of them there, opening and closing?

     6. Apostrophes—are the possessives correctly spelled?

     7. Numbers—are they accurate? Are the rules applied consistently?

     8. Headings—are all words spelled correctly? Do they make sense? Is the visual formatting consistent throughout the document?

     9. Any other of your personal trouble spots—do you have a tendency to mistype *form* as *from*? Perhaps you should use the Find command to check them all.

VI. Read the entire document through a final time for meaning and any last errors.

And finally, there are several other considerations every thoughtful proofreader should be aware of.

Rules

1. Throw away your red pen.
2. Explain your corrections to the writer.
3. Mention the positives you find too.
4. When in doubt, look it up in a reference guide.

Explanations and Examples

1. Throw away your red pen.

Most writers are pre-conditioned to fear red ink. It started back in elementary school and continued through middle school, high school, college and even through post-graduate education for many of us. Red ink was the tool most of our teachers used throughout the years to let us know that we weren't making the mark.

Now, when you proofread others—and even when you proofread yourself—you may find resistance when you mark the errors and changes in red.

Certainly, you do need a color other than black or blue: business readers are so accustomed to seeing black and blue ink in business writing that they may not notice the changes you have made if you use those colors. But just as certainly, there must be another color that could work for you just as well.

We recommend green ink for proofreading. Green is a "GO" color, not a "STOP" color. Yet it stands out from the black type on the white page, so the writer will be sure to notice it. Give it a try and see if everyone doesn't start feeling better about the changes—even yourself!

2. Explain your corrections to the writer.

Maybe you won't have time to explain all of your corrections to a writer, but do keep the line of communication open by encouraging dialogue. Perhaps you could say, "I changed your word *facilitate* to *help* because of some advice I read in the style guide we use—did you know that in business writing the advice is to use smaller more common words every time possible? I guess the theory is that readers are overworked to begin with and that if we ask them to think too hard to determine meanings they may give up on the reading before they get to the end of the document."

Sometimes a simple explanation like this can save the writer from developing hurt feelings and possible resentment.

3. Mention the positives you find too.

This is advice you should follow no matter whose writing you are proofreading. Most writers dread being proofread because of the blow to their egos—even though they know it is for the best. If you begin mentioning some of the positive qualities in anyone's writing (including your own), that writer will come to dread you and your proofreading less and less. And of course, the more open any writer is to the corrections and suggestions that proofreading brings, the more likely the document will be as good as it can be.

4. When in doubt, look it up in a reference guide.

Whether you need a dictionary, a specialized reference about the topic or perhaps this Style Guide, don't be shy about admitting you don't know everything. In proofreading the most important thing for any proofreader to know is that he or she doesn't know everything. Think about it—if you never needed to look anything up in a reference, that would mean you had all that information available in your own head. Doesn't it take up a lot of space? Space that you could be using in a more productive way?

Psychologists tell us that humans don't use even a majority of their brain space, that we haven't learned how to access more than a small portion of what we have available. If we are already working with limited space, why on earth would we want to waste space on trivial details of grammar (that could change tomorrow)? Keep a good set of reference materials handy.

PUNCTUATION

Introduction

There are two main purposes of punctuation in writing:

1. To join ideas together in a meaningful way.
2. To separate ideas from each other.

All of the punctuation marks covered in this section are used at least occasionally by most writers in their daily work. But many of those writers have been confused because of the vast number and variety among the rules they have been taught.

This style guide presents the punctuation rules most commonly accepted in the world of work to advance the clarity, readability and correctness of everything you write.

At the end of this section we have presented a separate list of rules about spacing around these punctuation marks.

When in doubt, remember that the purpose of punctuation is to make your message clear to your reader. If a particular punctuation mark helps your reader better understand your message, keep it in. If that punctuation mark could confuse your reader and make your message more difficult to understand, take it out.

APOSTROPHES

Apostrophes have four main uses: to form possessives, to indicate quotes within quotes, to make contractions and to form plurals of single letters. The most troublesome use for most business writers is the one involving possessives, especially plural possessives. It's actually very simple if we take it step by step.

Rules

1. Use an apostrophe followed by an *s* to make the possessive of any singular noun unless the noun being made possessive already ends with an *s*. In that case, just add an apostrophe.
2. The same general rule applies to the making of plural possessives. In other words, whether a word is plural or not has no effect on where the apostrophe would go. If the word ends in *s*, just add an apostrophe. If the word does not end in *s*, add an apostrophe then an *s*.
3. Use an apostrophe to make a plural only when making a plural of a single letter.
4. Use an apostrophe as a replacement for the missing letters in a contraction.
5. Use apostrophes to indicate that material already found within quotation marks is a quote itself (commonly called quotes within quotes).

Examples and Explanations

1. **Use an apostrophe followed by an *s* to make the possessive of any singular noun unless the noun being made possessive already ends with an *s*. In that case, just add an apostrophe.**

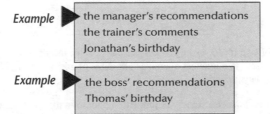

Example ▶ the manager's recommendations
the trainer's comments
Jonathan's birthday

Example ▶ the boss' recommendations
Thomas' birthday

YOUR CALL: Some grammar guides tell you to add the *s* even if the word being made possessive ends in an *s*. Although we encourage you to avoid adding that *s*, as long as you make a choice that you apply consistently—either way is okay. (We believe that the extra *s* looks strange to your reader, therefore slowing that reader down. This would violate one of our foundational principles: READABILITY.)

2. The same general rule applies to the making of plural possessives. In other words, whether a word is plural or not has no effect on where the apostrophe would go. If the word ends in *s*, just add an apostrophe. If the word does not end in *s*, add an apostrophe then an *s*.

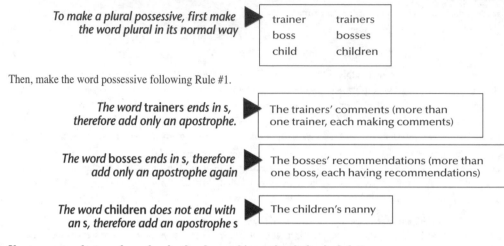

To make a plural possessive, first make the word plural in its normal way

trainer	trainers
boss	bosses
child	children

Then, make the word possessive following Rule #1.

*The word **trainers** ends in s, therefore add only an apostrophe.*

The trainers' comments (more than one trainer, each making comments)

*The word **bosses** ends in s, therefore add only an apostrophe again*

The bosses' recommendations (more than one boss, each having recommendations)

*The word **children** does not end with an s, therefore add an apostrophe s*

The children's nanny

3. **Use an apostrophe to make a plural only when making a plural of a single letter.**

   Without the apostrophe, the single letter plus an *s* could be confused for a word by a busy reader.

   The Oakland A's are a popular baseball team.
   My daughter got four B's and two A's on her report card.

   Note: Without an apostrophe, notice what happens to the baseball team from Oakland. They become the As. And for consistency's sake, we then apply the rule to all single letters (B's, C's, D's, etc.).

4. **Use an apostrophe as a replacement for the missing letters in a contraction.**

   Please note that in business writing the use of easily understood contractions is allowed—even encouraged. They can speed up the reading for your busy reader.

I will	I'll
Cannot	Can't
We are	We're

   Just two warnings: First, do not overuse negative words, whether they are contractions or not (for example: can't, don't, won't, shouldn't, couldn't, wouldn't).

   Second, avoid using contractions that look like something else—most notably, plurals: That sentence is intended to mean *The meeting is going well.*

   The meeting's going well.

   But there is too much danger of your reader trying to find something that the meeting owns because most of the time an apostrophe *s* indicates a possessive. (It is true that when speaking, most people would say *The meeting's going well.* The danger of confusion exists only in writing.)

5. **Use apostrophes to indicate that material already found within quotation marks is a quote itself (commonly called quotes within quotes).**

   "Mary," she asked me, "Is it true that Jack's proposal includes the phrase, 'to be completed by March 31 or subject to penalty'?"

   "She claims the photocopier 'blew up' when she added the toner," Mark explained.

BRACKETS

For most business writers, brackets are used only rarely. Technical writers use them more often, especially in mathematical or scientific notations.

Rules

1. Use brackets to clarify or provide comment about another writer's work.

2. Use the Latin word *sic* in brackets immediately after another writer's error that you have left intact.

3. Use brackets to set off parenthetical items that fall inside other parenthetical expressions.

Explanations and Examples

1. Use brackets to clarify or provide comment about another writer's work.

> The document states: "Insurance Provider [Coastal Medical Affiliates in this case] is responsible for expenses of rehabilitative therapy only until the point patient progress in recovery remains quantifiable."

2. Use the Latin word *sic* in brackets immediately after another writer's error that you have left intact.

When the word *sic* appears in brackets, it indicates a misspelling, an incorrect use of grammar or a misstatement within a sentence.

> The Governor then said, "Aid to dependent children are [*sic*] increasing."

3. Use brackets to set off parenthetical items that fall inside other parenthetical expressions.

> Erik Weihenmayer's ascent of Mount Everest in May of 2001 has been covered by most of the major news organizations and magazines. (*Time* [June 18, 2001] even presented it as a cover story.)

Readability and Brackets

When you have written yourself into a situation that calls for many sets of brackets, consider rewriting to avoid them. Brackets add to the collective workload of your reader. Never forget that your reader is busy and sometimes discouraged by punctuation and other symbols they do not see frequently.

For example, the sentences above about Erik Weihenmayer's ascent of Mount Everest could just have easily been written (and more easily read) without brackets:

> Erik Weihenmayer's ascent of Mount Everest in May of 2001 has been covered by most of the major news organizations and magazines. (The June 18, 2001 issue of *Time* even presented it as a cover story.)

BULLETED LISTS

When using bulleted lists, many people wonder about the correct punctuation between the items. Obviously, when a list appears in its own sentence or paragraph, the use of commas or semicolons to separate the items is essential.

But when the items are already separated by a hard return and a bullet of some kind, the use of commas and semicolons is redundant—they are unnecessary. The return and the bullet are enough.

This is one of the reasons bulleted lists are recommended to business writers. They present information that is sometimes complex in the most readable format available.

Rules

1. Items in bulleted lists that are complete sentences themselves require periods (or perhaps question marks or exclamation points) at the end.

2. Items that are not complete sentences by themselves do not require any punctuation.

3. Do not put a period after the last item in a bulleted list for the sole reason that it is the last item.

4. When some of the items in a bulleted list are complete sentences and some aren't, re-word the list so they are all one or the other.

Note: In the case of very formal writing or legal writing, it is best to check with a specialized grammar guide about requirements for punctuation.

Explanations and Examples

1. **Items in bulleted lists that are complete sentences themselves require periods (or perhaps question marks or exclamation points) at the end.**

   > My husband loves studying the Civil War for several reasons:
   > - He thinks it is fascinating that the country almost split apart.
   > - He enjoys the stories about Robert E. Lee and Ulysses Grant.
   > - He admires the young soldiers who risked everything for their side.

2. **Items that are not complete sentences by themselves do not require any punctuation.**

   > My husband loves studying the Civil War for several reasons:
   > - Country almost split apart
   > - Stories about Robert E. Lee and Ulysses Grant
   > - Young soldiers who risked everything for their side

3. **Do not put a period after the last item in a bulleted list for the sole reason that it is the last item.**

   No punctuation is needed to end a bulleted list (unless that last item is a complete sentence itself, of course, in which case it will have terminal punctuation).

   > **NOT:** My husband loves studying the Civil War for several reasons:
   > - Country almost split apart.
   > - Stories about Robert E. Lee and Ulysses Grant.
   > - Young soldiers who risked everything for their side.

4. **When some of the items in a bulleted list are complete sentences and some aren't, re-word the list so they are all one or the other.**

   > **INCORRECT:** My husband loves studying the Civil War for several reasons:
   > - He thinks it is fascinating that the country almost split apart.
   > - Stories about Robert E. Lee and Ulysses Grant
   > - Young soldiers who risked everything for their side
   >
   > **CORRECT:** My husband loves studying the Civil War for several reasons:
   > - He thinks it is fascinating that the country almost split apart.
   > - He enjoys the stories about Robert E. Lee and Ulysses Grant.
   > - He admires the young soldiers who risked everything for their side.

COLONS

The major use of colons by most business writers is to introduce lists of items. This section will present several other minor uses, as well as the rules of capitalization and punctuation for presenting items in bulleted lists.

Rules

1. Use a colon to announce a list of items, whether the list appears as a part of the sentence or as a bulleted list.

2. Use a colon between two independent clauses when the second one illustrates or defines the first.

3. In business correspondence, use colons after words like *Attention*, *Regarding* and *cc*.

4. Use a colon to separate the hours and minutes of a time expressed in numerals.

5. Use a colon to represent the word *to* in a ratio.

6. Use a colon to separate the title and the subtitle of a book.

7. Use a colon after the salutation in a business letter.

Explanations and Examples

1. **Use a colon to announce a list of items, whether the list appears as a part of the sentence or as a bulleted list.**

   The sentence or clause that comes before the listed items is referred to as the *anticipatory expression*.

   > Five local celebrities attended the opening of the museum's new Impressionists Wing: Clark Duncan, John Evans, Mark and Maggie Overton and Cindy LaRue.
   >
   > The successful candidate for this position will have the following qualities:
   > - Excellent keyboarding skills
   > - Current Microsoft® Word experience
   > - Five years in the transportation industry
   > - Excellent references

2. **Use a colon between two independent clauses when the second one illustrates or defines the first.**

   > We have a new rule in our office: no food is allowed at employees' desks.
   >
   > Our boss says we can no longer keep food at our desks: You can guess how thrilled we all are about that.

3. **In business correspondence, use colons after words such as *Attention*, *Regarding* and *cc*.**

   > Attention: Customer Service Department
   > RE: Year-end Tax Summary for SS# 123-45-6789
   > cc: Mr. Jay Smithers

4. **Use a colon to separate the hours and minutes of a time expressed in numerals.**

   > 10:00   3:15   7:45

5. **Use a colon to represent the word *to* in a ratio.**

   > Her odds are better than 2:1.

6. **Use a colon to separate the title and the subtitle of a book.**

   > *Productivity Power: 250 Great Ideas for Being More Productive*

7. Use a colon after the salutation in a business letter.

> Dear Mr. Sylindo:
>
> Dear Ms. Evans:
>
> Dear Dr. Butler:

CAPITALIZATION AFTER A COLON

Rules

1. When a colon is used to announce a list and the list is then presented as the remainder of the same sentence, do not capitalize after the colon unless what comes after the colon can stand alone as a complete sentence, is a proper name, needs special emphasis or introduces speech.

2. When a colon is used to announce items presented in a bulleted list, always capitalize the first letter of each item that is itself a complete sentence.

3. When a colon is used to announce items presented in a bulleted list, and the items themselves are not complete sentences, it is up to the writer whether to capitalize or not. Be consistent. (Be aware that capital letters will look better and will get more reader attention.)

Explanations and Examples

1. **When a colon is used to announce a list and the list is then presented as the remainder of the same sentence, do not capitalize after the colon unless what comes after the colon can stand alone as a complete sentence, is a proper name, needs special emphasis or introduces speech.**

> The dress is available in five colors: red, green, blue, black and purple.
>
> The dress is available in five colors: Red, green, blue, black and purple have been our best sellers for over a year.

> I was very excited about what Mrs. Jones has done for me: She took care of all my bookkeeping. In addition, she took on over half of the administrative tasks.

> The committee took on an interesting group: Ivor Davis is the first of a number of distinguished scientists.

> Let me say this: If this organization is going to succeed, we will need every person to be completely committed to our cause.

> Lincoln, in his Gettysburg Address said: " ... And this government of the people, by the people, and for the people shall not perish from the earth."

2. **When a colon is used to announce items presented in a bulleted list, always capitalize the first letter of each item that is itself a complete sentence.**

> The dress is available in five colors:
> - Red is our top seller.
> - Green is the most popular with teenagers.
> - Blue is our classic color.
> - Black is our most formal color.
> - Purple has become popular most recently.

3. **When a colon is used to announce items presented in a bulleted list, and the items themselves are not complete sentences, it is up to the writer whether to capitalize or not. But be consistent. (Be aware that capital letters will look better and will get more reader attention.)**

| The dress is available in five colors:
- red
- green
- blue
- black
- purple | **OR** | The dress is available in five colors:
- Red
- Green
- Blue
- Black
- Purple |

COMMAS—WHEN TO USE THEM

Commas are the single most commonly misunderstood and misused of all punctuation marks.

Since clarity, readability and correctness are your three main goals as a business writer, let's make it simple. Commas have only two functions:

1. They separate ideas, or
2. They set off ideas

Rules

1. Use commas to separate three or more items in a series. These items could be single words, phrases or even clauses.
2. Use a comma to separate two independent clauses joined in a sentence with a conjunction like *and*, *but* or *or*.
3. Use commas to separate two or more adjectives that describe the same noun. (Remember to follow your own rule about serial commas consistently.)
4. Use a comma after introductory words, phrases or clauses that begin a sentence but come before the main independent clause of that sentence.
5. Use commas to set off words, phrases or clauses that interrupt the flow of the main independent clause.
6. Use commas to clarify meaning if the sentence could be hard to understand because the word order is not traditional or there are words missing.
7. Use a comma after the salutation in social business letters.
8. Use commas to separate numerals into thousands.
9. Decide which comma rules you are going to follow, and follow them consistently.
10. Always remember: The purpose of writing, especially business writing, is to be understood, both clearly and quickly.

Explanations and Examples

1. **Use commas to separate three or more items in a series. These items could be single words, phrases or even clauses.**

> Jake, Marty, Bill and I met over breakfast this morning to discuss our next step.
> That new software package contains too many applications, too few tutorials and no sample documents at all.
> The alarm went off at 8:00, the fire department arrived at 8:12, and the fire was out by 10:30.

YOU CHOOSE—The serial comma is the comma that some writers use before the *and* in a series. In our examples above, the first two sentences do not contain one. The last sentence does.

This is a choice that is up to you. Even ten years ago, grammar guides disagreed about the serial comma. Some said you had to use one, others said you should never use one. Today, most grammar and style guides agree that either way is okay. But, they mean different things. In the legal world, adding that comma before "and" indicates they are three entirely separate entities: The heirs to the estate were Nord, Jon, and Erik. (This is clearly three people.) However, if it had been written "The heirs to the estate were Marie, Jon and Ed," the estate could be divided in halves—one half to Marie and one half to Jon and Ed, or it could be divided into thirds.

Business Writing

We recommend you consider your main business writing goals: clarity, readability and consistency. Then, make your best decision.

In our opinion, the first two sentences do not need a serial comma for clarity or readability. And as you can probably tell from our style throughout this book, it is not our choice to use them. Therefore, there is no need to use them in our first two examples to satisfy a need for consistency.

We think the third sentence does need the serial comma because it is made up of three clauses. And clauses are by nature independent. They can stand separately as sentences. As you will soon see in Rule #2, below, it is most always a good idea to separate independent clauses with commas.

2. **Use a comma to separate two independent clauses joined in a sentence with a conjunction like** *and*, *but* **or** *or*.

> The phone calls had already been made, and then Ms. Robinson decided it would be better not to alert our customers about the price increase.
>
> So far your travel expenses look reasonable, but I need to check last month's air expenses to be sure.

> Business is great and I'm glad.
> I love hockey and my husband prefers football.

UNLESS: The clauses are so short and clear no reader could make a mistake in understanding your meaning:

3. **Use commas to separate two or more adjectives that describe the same noun. (Remember to follow your own rule about serial commas consistently.)**

> David is *tall*, *dark* and *handsome*.
> Our *well-written*, *carefully proofread* proposal is finally ready for FedEx®.

UNLESS: The words are so short and clear without commas they would not help with the clarity or readability of your sentence.

> The large green truck ...
> The older easier version of that program ...

4. **Use a comma after introductory words, phrases or clauses that begin a sentence but come before the main independent clause of that sentence.**

> *Hey*, I know what I'm doing here.
> *On the first Thursday of the last month of each quarter*, Jack will present our sales results to the board.
> *After the meeting is adjourned*, Barbara and Andrea will call us with details.

YOU CHOOSE—Some writers prefer to leave the comma out after especially short and clear introductory words or phrases. This is fine, as long as you are certain your reader will understand the sentence.

> On Tuesday Jack will present our sales results to the board.
> After eating breakfast she drove herself to work.

> You are with us, *right*?
> The board has finally agreed to pay those bonuses they've been promising, *thank goodness*.

By the same token, use a comma before an added expression at the end of a sentence's main independent clause.

And of course, use a pair of commas when interjecting words into the middle of the main independent clause.

> The announcement, *if you can believe it*, said that we would all be getting bonuses this December.
> The facts, *however*, don't back up her account.

5. **Use commas to set off words, phrases or clauses that interrupt the flow of the main independent clause.**

Extra information ▶ Mary, *who spent an hour on the highway this morning*, was angry when she got here.
Janet, *our Sales Director*, will call you tomorrow.

In both of those sentences, the added information is nonessential to the meaning of the main independent clause. It is extra information—nice to know, but not the main idea.

▶ Mary was angry when she got here. Oh, by the way, she had just spent an hour on the highway this morning.
Janet will call you this morning. By the way, she is our Sales Director.

6. **Use commas to clarify meaning if the sentence could be hard to understand because the word order is not traditional or there are words missing.**

You can think of this as the Yoda Rule. Do you remember how everything Yoda, the Jedi Master in the *Star Wars* movies, said was reversed?

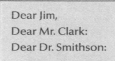

Even non-Jedi masters have found this comma handy:

Half the balance is due now. The other half, upon delivery.

7. **Use a comma after the salutation in social business letters.**

8. **Use commas to separate numerals into thousands.**

Dear Jim,
Dear Mr. Clark:
Dear Dr. Smithson:

23,000,000	(23 million)
4,700	(four thousand, seven hundred)

9. **Decide which comma rules you are going to follow, and follow them consistently.**

The writers who send you things to read don't always follow the same rules you do, but you can usually understand their meaning. This is because most readers quickly get a sense of the writer's style and adapt their reading to it. For example, when you get a document from someone who uses serial commas—even if you don't—you quickly figure out what is happening and have no trouble understanding the meaning.

The same will happen among your readers. They will notice your style, and as long as you are consistent in that style, they will understand your meaning.

10. **Always remember: The purpose of writing, especially business writing, is to be understood, both clearly and quickly.**

Too many nonessential commas actually get in the way of your reader's ability to understand. Imagine that every reader has a comma meter in his or her brain. Different people's comma meters are set at different numbers. Maybe one person can easily read 50 commas, but another can only easily read 25 before tiring out. Remember: Most business readers are hoping to read (and understand) quickly.

Never use a comma that doesn't help your reader understand your meaning.

COMMAS—WHEN NOT TO USE THEM

Rules

1. Never separate a subject from its verb.

2. Never separate a verb from its object.

3. Never separate a noun from an adjective or a prepositional phrase that describes it.

4. Do not separate the two words of a compound subject, predicate or object with commas.

5. Do not put a comma after a year in a sentence unless you are putting it there for some other reason.

Writer's Tips:
Many more commas are
required in academic writing.
For a fuller explanation,
see pages 26 – 27.

Explanations and Examples

1. **Never separate a subject from its verb.**

2. **Never separate a verb from its object.**

> John talked to me.
> **NOT:** John, talked to me.

> Makai sold more extended warranties than any other sales clerk last quarter.
> **NOT:** Makai sold, more extended warranties than any other sales clerk last quarter.

3. **Never separate a noun from an adjective or a prepositional phrase that describes it.**

> The last version of this software was easier to use.
> **NOT:** The last, version of this software was easier to use.
> **NOT:** The last version, of this software was easier to use.

4. **Do not separate the two words of a compound subject, predicate or object with commas.**

> Jerry's wife and Sally's husband are joining us for lunch.
> **NOT:** Jerry's wife, and Sally's husband are joining us for lunch.
>
> Sharon drove to the store and bought more coffee filters for the office coffee station.
> **NOT:** Sharon drove to the store, and bought more coffee filters for the office coffee station.
>
> Rick sold the computers and the printers for one low price.
> **NOT:** Rick sold the computers, and the printers for one low price.

5. **Do not put a comma after a year in a sentence unless you are putting it there for some other reason.**

In this case, you are using the commas to set off the useful but nonessential information of the date the meeting was held.

> The March 19, 2003 report states …
> **NOT:** The March 19, 2003, report states …
> (You are separating a noun from its adjective when you use that comma.)

But, this one is correct ▶ The meeting, held on March 19, 2004, was fascinating.

YOU CHOOSE—Many people ask if they need to put commas after introductory conjunctions that introduce independent clauses.

For example ▶

> But, he's always been like that.
> **OR**
> But he's always been like that.
>
> Expenses for the month of May are
>   outrageous, and, I think I know why.
> **OR**
> Expenses for the month of May are
>   outrageous, and I think I know why.

Usually we would recommend that you avoid using the extra comma. But if you want to add extra emphasis to the idea that follows the conjunction, the extra comma can help you do it. Just beware of comma overload. Remember that it is helpful to imagine your readers have comma meters in their heads, and they are counting every one you use against their ability to easily read your document.

And Finally, a Note About Two Imperfect Rules: Have you ever heard either of these comma rules?

1. Use a comma any time you would pause in speech.

2. When in doubt, leave it out.

Neither rule works consistently. Look for a good balance. It is true that when you are using commas to set words off, sometimes you can tell where the commas should go by speaking the sentence and noticing where you put the emphasis.

It is also true that you should avoid using unnecessary commas. Remember the comma meter.

Our advice? Do your best to apply these simple and coherent rules as consistently as possible.

DASHES

Dashes add emphasis to your writing. They are more casual than semicolons and colons, and they bring more attention than commas and parentheses.

Rules:

1. Use a dash instead of a comma to add more emphasis to nonessential information that has interrupted the flow of a sentence.

2. Use a dash instead of a semicolon to make a more casual break between two complete thoughts (independent clauses).

3. Use a dash to interrupt your own thought in writing.

4. Use dashes instead of parentheses when you want to amplify rather than diminish the information inside them.

5. Use dashes to set off single words or phrases that are being defined.

6. Use a dash when attributing quoted material.

Explanations and Examples

1. Use a dash instead of a comma to add more emphasis to nonessential information that has interrupted the flow of a sentence.

With dashes ▶ Mary—who spent an hour on the highway this morning—was angry when she got here.

How it is read

Mary—WHO SPENT AN HOUR ON THE HIGHWAY THIS MORNING—was angry when she got here.

This is the same sentence that we used back on page 157 to illustrate that commas should be used to set off nonessential information that has interrupted the flow of thought between the subject and the verb in a sentence.

The dashes put more emphasis on whatever is enclosed within them. In this way they are the opposite of parentheses. Let's try the same sentence, using parentheses instead of dashes or commas.

With parentheses ▶ Mary (who spent an hour on the highway this morning) was angry when she got here.

How it is read

MARY (who spent an hour on the highway this morning) WAS ANGRY WHEN SHE GOT HERE.

With commas, everything is read with the same amount of emphasis.

With commas ▶ Mary, who spent an hour on the highway this morning, was angry when she got here.

2. Use a dash instead of a semicolon to make a more casual break between two complete thoughts (independent clauses).

I say it here—it comes out there.

3. Use a dash to interrupt your own thought in writing ...

Another idea Margot presented—and I think we would be well served listening to her, she has a lot of experience with this process—was to run a beta test first.

... even if you don't have a new thought after the interruption.

If only she'd listened to me—

4. Use dashes instead of parentheses when you want to amplify rather than diminish the information inside them.

Roger—who hasn't played for half a year—can't get his guitar tuned.
Send an e-mail to Steiner and Hart—Mark Addison is our contact there—about our meeting.

5. **Use dashes to set off single words or phrases that are being defined.**

> Incendiary—capable of starting fires—devices can be dangerous ...
>
> Within the cancellation period—within no more than 30 days from final purchase approval

6. **Use a dash when attributing quoted material.**

> I have a dream.
> — Martin Luther King, Jr.
> Ask not what your country can do for you;
> ask what you can do for your country.
> — John F. Kennedy

Typing the Dash

Because most computer keyboards do not have a key representing a dash, the most common way of typing one is to type two hyphens with no space between them: "--". Alternatively, many software packages create a dash when you type a space, a hyphen and a space. As soon as you start to type the next word, the hyphen elongates into a dash.

YOU CHOOSE—As to whether or not to put spaces before and after the dash, grammar guides have disagreed.

Here's a case where you can see the difference:

> Roger — who hasn't played in half a year — can't get his guitar tuned.
> Roger—who hasn't played in half a year—can't get his guitar tuned.

EM DASHES AND EN DASHES

In the professional typesetter's world, there is more than just one dash. "En" dashes are the length of a capital *N*. "Em" dashes are the length of a capital *M*.

In publishing, en dashes are used to say *up to and including* when used in expressions like these:

> The most important information can be found on pages 45 – 65.
> Our normal office hours are 7:00 a.m. – 8:00 p.m. CST.

Em dashes are used for the purposes we have covered in our rules in this section. They are the ones that you can type by placing two hyphens next to each other.

ELLIPSES

Rules:

1. Use an ellipsis to indicate a missing word or words in a quotation.
2. Use an ellipsis at the end of a sentence to indicate a trailing off.
3. In advertising, ellipses can be used to connect several loosely related phrases.
4. Also, in advertising, an ellipsis is used to imply something will continue.

Explanations and Examples

1. **Use an ellipsis to indicate a missing word or words in a quotation.**

   "Freedom is not a gift received from a State or a leader but a possession to be won every day by the effort of each and the union of all." – Albert Camus

   "Freedom is not a gift ... but a possession to be won every day by the effort of each and the union of all."
   – Albert Camus

2. Use an ellipsis at the end of a sentence to indicate a trailing off.

> It seemed like a good idea …

3. In advertising, ellipses can be used to connect several loosely related phrases.

> Come one, come all … no reservations needed … free tickets to dinner … the first 150 will receive a special gift.

4. Also, in advertising, an ellipsis is used to imply something will continue.

> Take advantage of this offer and you will receive benefit after benefit …

EXCLAMATION POINTS

Exclamation points add strong emotion to the ends of sentences. While it is fine to use them sparingly, overusing them makes you look like you have lost control.

Rules:

1. Use an exclamation point after a sentence, a condensed sentence or even a question to show strong emotions like shock, delight, joy, disbelief, horror or frustration.

2. Use an exclamation point, enclosed in parentheses, immediately after a word you want to emphasize in some way.

Explanations and Examples

1. **Use an exclamation point after a sentence, a condensed sentence or even a question to show strong emotions like shock, delight, joy, disbelief, horror or frustration.**

2. **Use an exclamation point, enclosed in parentheses, immediately after a word you want to emphasize in some way.**

> You found my necklace! Thank you!
> You must be kidding!
> What on earth were you thinking!
> Congratulations!

> We just got confirmation that all employees with more than six months ' employment will be receiving new BMWs(!) as their company cars.
> They think we should be able to finish the project by next Monday(!).

Remember: Overusing exclamation points will damage your credibility; in e-mail you can come across as very sarcastic. For milder emotions, use more conventional punctuation. Also, when the emotion you are conveying is negative, the use of exclamation points can be seen as negative by your reader.

> No, I don't believe you.
> (**NOT:** No! I don't believe you!)
> Why bother?
> (**NOT:** Why bother!)

HYPHENS

Hyphens are used to separate the parts of words (or groups of words acting as a single word) from each other. Hyphens are shorter than dashes and should not be confused with them.

Rules

1. Use a hyphen to divide a word that has become too long for a line so it can be continued on the next line. When dividing words, be certain you are dividing the word into its syllables conventionally. (You can check a dictionary for this information.)

2. Use a hyphen to separate two parts of a word that would be mispronounced by your reader on the first reading without the hyphen.

3. Use a hyphen to clarify the meaning of a word that could otherwise be misunderstood.

4. Use hyphens to separate the individual words of a compound word. (In earlier days, this rule was limited to compound adjectives. But today, because clarity and readability are your two primary goals, the rule has stretched to help you.)

5. Use a hyphen to indicate a suspension between the first and second parts of a hyphenated compound.

Explanations and Examples

1. **Use a hyphen to divide a word that has become too long for a line so it can be continued on the next line. When dividing words, be certain you are dividing the word into its syllables conventionally. (You can check a dictionary for this information.)**

   Readability Bonus: Most proportional fonts make it easy to avoid hyphenating at the ends of lines. Many readability experts suggest that hyphenation makes the reading more difficult. Interestingly, the exception is at the end of a first page of a multi-page document.

   Guidelines for dividing words:

   - Hyphenate after the second syllable.
   - Do not hyphenate the last word in the first line of a paragraph.
   - Do not hyphenate the last word in more than two subsequent lines.
   - Do not divide the last word on a page.

2. **Use a hyphen to separate two parts of a word that would be mispronounced by your reader on the first reading without the hyphen.**

reentry	**OR**	re-entry
coop	**OR**	co-op

3. **Use a hyphen to clarify the meaning of a word that could otherwise be misunderstood.**

recover (get better)	**OR**	re-cover (cover again)
remark (comment)	**OR**	re-mark (mark again)

4. **Use hyphens to separate the individual words of a compound word. (In earlier days, this rule was limited to compound adjectives. But today, because clarity and readability are your two primary goals, the rule has stretched to help you.)**

   state-of-the-art technology
   man-on-the-street interview
   a follow-up report
   just a follow-up

   Note: When in doubt about whether and how to hyphenate words, you can always check a current or on-line dictionary. But be aware that dictionaries often disagree with each other and even more often apply no consistent rule. We would suggest you apply the five rules offered in this section so your reader will appreciate your consistent style.

5. **Use a hyphen to indicate a suspension between the first and second parts of a hyphenated compound.**

   We looked at mid- to full-sized cars.
   He felt like he had moved from low- to middle-income.

PARENTHESES

Parentheses are used to set off nonessential information or to tell readers that what is enclosed in them is extra or explanatory information. Consider them to be the opposite of dashes, which are usually used to emphasize material.

Rules

1. Use parentheses around material that explains or illustrates the main idea of a sentence. This material could be a single word, a phrase, a sentence, a page number, a date—there really is no limit to what the material in the parentheses can be.

2. When ending a sentence with a parenthetical expression, the period (or question mark or exclamation point) comes after the closing parenthesis. No other punctuation is required when using parentheses unless there is a special reason for it.

3. When a parenthetical expression is a complete sentence itself, make sure the previous sentence has ended with its own punctuation mark. Then, use a capital letter to begin the new sentence inside the parentheses and a period, question mark or exclamation point before the closing parenthesis to end it.

4. Use parentheses to set off the numerals or letters used to enumerate longer items within a sentence.

5. When a parenthetical expression falls inside another parenthetical expression, the inside expression is placed in brackets.

Explanations and Examples

1. **Use parentheses around material that explains or illustrates the main idea of a sentence. This material could be a single word, a phrase, a sentence, a page number, a date—there really is no limit to what the material in the parentheses can be.**

   > He sent her a dozen of her favorite flowers (yellow roses).
   >
   > The restaurant we've been going to for lunch all year (they have the best cheeseburgers and fries in town) is closing next week.
   >
   > The meeting will be held at 10 a.m. this Friday (June 15).
   >
   > She was born in Cleveland (Ohio).

2. **When ending a sentence with a parenthetical expression, the period (or question mark or exclamation point) comes after the closing parenthesis. No other punctuation is required when using parentheses unless there is a special reason for it.**

   > The new display cases arrived in three colors (black, white and tan).
   >
   > **NOT:** The new display cases arrived in three colors, (black, white and tan).
   >
   > **BUT:** The company that shipped us these spools of cable, Martin Fiberoptic Solutions (from San Jose), requested we call them once they had been delivered.

   Note: The comma after the parenthetical expression here is necessary because it is the closing comma of a set surrounding a nonessential phrase. (See Rule #5 in Commas, page 157.)

3. **When a parenthetical expression is a complete sentence itself, make sure the previous sentence has ended with its own punctuation mark. Then, use a capital letter to begin the new sentence inside the parentheses and a period, question mark or exclamation point before the closing parenthesis to end it.**

   > The new display cases arrived in three colors. (The company says black, white and tan are their most popular so they sent 50 of each.)

4. **Use parentheses to set off the numerals or letters used to enumerate longer items within a sentence.**

> Please bring the following items to your interview with our human resources department Monday: (1) the completed employment application, (2) three written personal references and (3) a portfolio of your past three years of published commercial art.

5. **When a parenthetical expression falls inside another parenthetical expression, the inside expression is placed in brackets.**

> Some members of our finance committee (Chris [McDonald] and Gloria) voted with the Chairman, but most (Mark, Marie, Chris [Herrera] and Jackson) did not.

PERIODS

There are three possible punctuation marks that can end a sentence: periods, question marks and exclamation points. Of these, the period is the most commonly used.

Periods are also used at the end of abbreviations and as decimal points in mathematical notations.

Rules:

1. Use a period at the end of a statement or command.
2. Use a period at the end of a condensed statement that is meant as a complete sentence or command.
3. Use a period at the end of a question that is meant to be rhetorical or polite.
4. When using a word processor with proportional spacing, type one space after a period that is used to end a sentence, a condensed statement or a polite or rhetorical question. When using a typewriter, type two spaces after the period that ends a sentence.
5. Use periods to end most abbreviations (see pages 14 – 25).
6. Use periods to represent decimal points in mathematical expressions or when referring to dollars and cents in numerals.
7. Use a period after a heading typed at the beginning of a paragraph.
8. Use periods after numbers or letters used in an outline format or a bulleted list.
9. Use three periods for an ellipsis (see page 161).

Explanations and Examples

1. **Use a period at the end of a statement or command.**

> The project notes taken by Patrice yesterday have been very helpful to us.
> Stan, please talk to Jack about his expenses before our next meeting.
> Raymond Kennedy has asked if his family can attend the company picnic.

2. **Use a period at the end of a condensed statement that is meant as a complete sentence or command.**

3. **Use a period at the end of a question that is meant to be rhetorical or polite.**

> Yes.
> No.
> Perhaps.
> To summarize.

> Will you please let me know if anything changes.
> If Mary asks, could you please help her with the report.

Note: If you think your reader could be offended by a perception of your question being presumptuous, use a question mark instead of a period to end a rhetorical or polite question.

4. **When using a word processor with proportional spacing, type one space after a period that is used to end a sentence, a condensed statement or a polite or rhetorical question. When using a typewriter, type two spaces after the period that ends a sentence.**

   YOU CHOOSE—Some grammar authorities suggest that you always type two spaces after a terminal period because some proportional typefaces don't allow enough space to make it clear that a sentence has ended. Whichever appears most readable to you is the style to adopt consistently.

5. **Use periods to end most abbreviations (see pages 14 – 25).**

6. **Use periods to represent decimal points in mathematical expressions or when referring to dollars and cents in numerals.**

   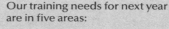
   > 67.9 percent of our employees
   > My daughter raised $560.25 selling magazines door-to-door.

7. **Use a period after a heading typed at the beginning of a paragraph.**

   > **Comments**.
   > Most of the attendees had very helpful comments after our presentation. Frank Hampton thought we should add another week for analysis of the final data, and after some discussion he has convinced us. Martha Stevenson mentioned that the plant closes for the week of July 4th for retooling, so we need to factor that downtime into our final schedule.

8. **Use periods after numbers or letters used in an outline format or a bulleted list.**

   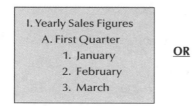

   > I. Yearly Sales Figures
   >   A. First Quarter
   >   1. January
   >   2. February
   >   3. March

   OR

   > Our training needs for next year are in five areas:
   >   A. Communication skills
   >   B. Organizational skills
   >   C. Priority management
   >   D. Word processing skills
   >   E. Database management

9. **Use three periods for an ellipsis (see page 161).**

QUESTION MARKS

Question marks tell your reader that a sentence asking a question has ended.

Rules:

1. Use a question mark at the end of a sentence that is a question.

2. Use a question mark at the end of a condensed statement that is intended as a question.

3. Use a question mark after a question, even if you are not expecting a reply.

4. Use a question mark, enclosed in parentheses, to express uncertainty about something you have written. But, be warned: Your credibility shrinks every time you are inaccurate or nonspecific. It is much better advice to do the needed checking or research before you write.

Explanations and Examples

1. Use a question mark at the end of a sentence that is a question.

> Are you ready for work?
> Have you seen Mark lately?

Note: Even if a question is presented in the form of a declarative sentence, use a question mark at the end if you are needing an answer.

> Mary is attending tomorrow?
> You want me to update the files now?

2. Use a question mark at the end of a condensed statement that is intended as a question.

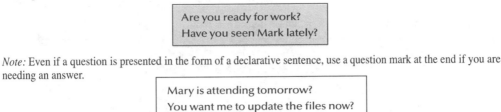

> Who?   What?   When?

3. Use a question mark after a question, even if you are not expecting a reply.

> She says she'll take them up on the extra week of vacation. Who wouldn't?
> Can you believe what he said?

4. Use a question mark, enclosed in parentheses, to express uncertainty about something you have written. But, be warned: Your credibility shrinks every time you are inaccurate or nonspecific. It is much better advice to do the needed checking or research before you write.

> The merger is planned to go through on June 23 (?).
> Sara, Amber and Heather (?) are attending the meeting for us this morning.

QUOTATION MARKS

In business writing, quotation marks have three functions. Their most common use is to indicate that your written words were spoken or written by someone else. Their other uses are to highlight words that should get special attention for some reason and to enclose the titles of certain works.

While most experienced writers know instinctively when to use most quotation marks, punctuating around those quotation marks can give even a seasoned author a migraine. We will clear up the confusion here.

Rules

1. Use quotation marks to set off words that have been directly quoted from someone, whether you are quoting something said or something written.

2. Do not use quotation marks to set off internal dialog or thoughts.

3. Put quotation marks only around material that is quoted exactly.

4. Use quotation marks around any words or phrases that you have coined, words or phrases that are considered to be jargon by your readers, or words or phrases that you are using as labels, not as words.

5. Use quotation marks to enclose the title of anything that is only a part of a complete work. This would include sections of a report, articles in a magazine or journal, song titles from a complete CD, titles of separate sessions of a conference and the like.

6. If you need to use quotation marks inside quotation marks, use apostrophes for the internal quotation marks.

Explanations and Examples

1. Use quotation marks to set off words that have been directly quoted from someone, whether you are quoting something said or something written.

> "Yikes!" Mary said. "When did that happen?"
> The third paragraph of their shareholder report is the most interesting. It says: "While fourth quarter inventories remained high, the promise of increased demand in Asia over the course of the next six months guarantees we will be in normal ranges sooner rather than later."

2. Do not use quotation marks to set off internal dialog or thoughts.

▶ So then I asked myself, what did you do that for?

Maybe I should have said something different—like Yes, sir.

3. Put quotation marks only around material that is quoted exactly.

Mark called the members of the press corps "savages."

NOT: Mark called the "members of the press corps savages."

BUT: Mark said, "The members of the press corps are a bunch of savages."

(*Note:* IF that is indeed what Mark said.)

4. Use quotation marks around any words or phrases that you have coined, words or phrases that are considered to be jargon by your readers, or words or phrases that you are using as labels, not as words.

Harold refers to the older computers in our office as "paperweights."

Are you sure Martha understands that when we say "RAM" we're not talking about an animal that likes to butt things with its head?

Park your car in the spot that says "Sahara Parking Only" when you come to pick up your dinner.

5. Use quotation marks to enclose the title of anything that is only a part of a complete work. This would include sections of a report, articles in a magazine or journal, song titles from a complete CD, titles of separate sessions of a conference and the like.

His "Executive Summary" and "Final Recommendations" sections contain the best information.

Did you read "What I Know for Sure" in the October magazine?

Should we play Jackson Browne's or Eddie Vedder's version of "I am a Patriot" with the slide show at this year's Fourth of July picnic?

6. If you need to use quotation marks inside quotation marks, use apostrophes for the internal quotation marks.

On page 3 of their proposal, it says: "Failure to comply with the specifications itemized in the 'Needs' section will result in immediate termination of the contract."

Punctuation with Quotation Marks

In American business English, the rule for punctuating around quotation marks is actually quite clear cut. It has three main components:

a. Periods and commas always go outside opening and inside closing quotation marks.

Edward said, "Lunch is being served upstairs on the terrace."

"Seating is available," the maitre'd told us. "But not for your cell phones."

Even when it looks strange ▶ Back in the 1960s people used words like "uptight," "cool" and "groovy."

b. Colons and semicolons always go outside both opening and closing quotation marks.

> Remember to include the following under "Books to Have at Your Desk":
> - An up-to-date dictionary
> - A thesaurus
> - The *SkillPath Business Communication Style Guide*

c. All other punctuation marks go where they belong—meaning, if they are part of the quote they would stay inside the quotation mark, if they aren't they would go outside the quotation mark.

> Then Mike asked me, "How can you approve that vacation request?"
> Can you believe that she said, "Yes, take your vacation next week"?

In the first example the author is quoting Mike asking the stated question. So the question mark goes inside the question.

In the second example the writer is the one with the question. The quoted statement is not a question, the writer is asking a question about it. So because the question is the writer's, the question mark goes outside the quoted statement. In this second example, notice that the quote itself has no terminal punctuation of its own.

> "Yes, take your vacation next week"

You don't need two punctuation marks to end a sentence when one of them is a period that is easily assumed by your reader.

A Strange but Helpful Historical Anecdote

In British English, there is still precedent for putting periods outside closing quotation marks—as was traditionally done years and years ago. What changed it all? Lead type. Before there were computers to produce typeset documents, printers actually used small pieces of lead type that they laid into trays (backwards) to make a form which they would then mount onto a printing press which then inked and stamped that form onto paper.

So imagine lead type. Very small lead type. The pieces that were periods and commas were the smallest pieces of lead type of all. They were placed on the bottom of the line. The pieces of lead type that were quotation marks were larger, but they were pushed to the top of the line.

So imagine how that set together in a printer's tray  LETTERS".

Do you see how far away the quotation mark is from the period? The periods (and also the commas) often fell off the printers' trays when they were set like this.

In England, it's not easy to just change a rule of punctuation because the lead type is falling off of the printers' trays. But in America, years and years ago, typesetters started stuffing those periods and commas inside the closing quotation marks and not one citizen became outraged enough to complain. That became the new rule.

Now, of course, computers don't care where you put the commas, periods and quotation marks, right? So will the rule shift back now?

The answer is: Maybe, but not yet.

SEMICOLONS

To many writers (and their readers), semicolons are the single most puzzling punctuation mark. Actually, the rules governing them are quite clear cut.

Semicolons are used in two different circumstances:

1. As super-size commas. (Rules 1 and 2)
2. As half-size periods. (Rules 3 and 4)

But no matter how clear semicolons become for you by reading this section, please remember they probably will still scare your readers. Just think: What documents contain more semicolons than any others? That's right—legal documents. And most people feel threatened when they are sent legal papers to read. So use semicolons sparingly.

Rules

1. Use semicolons instead of commas when you list items in a sentence and one or more of those items already contains commas (a complex list).
2. Use semicolons to separate phrases and clauses that are being listed in a paragraph if they are longer or if at least one of them contains commas. Do not use semicolons to separate longer phrases or clauses that are presented in a bulleted list (see page 112).
3. Use a semicolon instead of a period between two independent clauses that are very closely related in content.
4. Use semicolons with transitional expressions.

Explanations and Examples

1. **Use semicolons instead of commas when you list items in a sentence and one or more of those items already contains commas (a complex list).**

> The flags were red, green and blue; white, gold and black; and fuchsia, turquoise and yellow.
>
> The following officers attended the meeting June 12: Stan Goodhope, Chairman; Marjorie Blankenship, President; Jeremy Lawson, Vice President; Louann Ramirez, Treasurer; and Sally Jackson, Secretary.

Notice, as in both of the preceding examples, that a final semicolon is always used before the *and* that introduces the last item. Because a semicolon is so much stronger than a comma, this final semicolon is essential to maintain equal emphasis among the items being listed.

Without the final semicolon, it would be as though the last two items together have equal importance or weight to each of the preceding items alone.

Example ▶ I leave my entire estate to be equally divided among: Marshall Ackerman, my son; Amanda Ackerman, my daughter; Lawrence Ackerman, my step-son and Elena Ackerman, my current wife.

Compare that to ▶ I leave my entire estate to be equally divided among: Marshall Ackerman, my son; Amanda Ackerman, my daughter; Lawrence Ackerman, my step-son; and Elena Ackerman, my current wife.

The only difference between these two sentences is a semicolon between the words *step-son* and *Elena*. Do you see how that semicolon changed their fortunes? Without that semicolon, Marshall and Amanda have an argument to a court that their father intended them to receive one-third each and intended Lawrence and Elena to split the other third. With the semicolon, Marshall, Amanda, Lawrence and Elena are entitled to separate equal quarters.

2. **Use semicolons to separate phrases and clauses that are being listed in a paragraph if they are longer or if at least one of them contains commas. Do not use semicolons to separate longer phrases or clauses that are presented in a bulleted list (see page 112).**

> Mark taught me the best process for making great coffee: First, use only freshly roasted beans; second, grind them to the correct texture; third, fill the filter half-way to the top with the ground coffee; fourth, pour eight cups of spring water into the pot; fifth, turn the coffee machine on; and sixth, enjoy great coffee.

3. **Use a semicolon instead of a period between two independent clauses that are very closely related in content.**

This causes your reader to pause for a shorter time than if you had used a period between them (making them separate sentences). But it provides more emphasis than if you had used a comma.

In this example, notice that Larry and Monica have equal emphasis
> Larry started his new position yesterday; Monica started hers last week.

If the writer had used a period instead, the sentences could sound choppy
> Larry started his new position yesterday. Monica started hers last week.

By the same token, if the writer has used a comma (or no punctuation) between the two clauses, see how the emphasis changes:

> Larry started his new position yesterday, and Monica started hers last week.
>
> **OR**
>
> Larry started his new position yesterday and Monica started hers last week.

In both of these examples, notice that Larry received more of the reader's attention than Monica.

The reason for this is to be found in simple reading theory. Most people, when taught to read as children, were taught to read from a capital letter (the beginning of a sentence) to a period (the end of a sentence) for *the main idea* of that sentence. Once the reader reads: *Larry started his new position yesterday*, that reader instinctively recognizes that he or she has gotten the main idea. Most busy readers tend to fast-forward over the rest of the words in that sentence on the way to a period—even if there is a comma present. Only a semicolon or a period will make that reader stop and look for another major idea.

Here is another example of a well-used semicolon, in a quote from Oscar Wilde
> I spent the whole morning putting in a comma; I spent the whole afternoon taking it out again.

Notice that in that sentence the semicolon adds to the humor and irony of the thought.

4. **Use semicolons with transitional expressions.**

YOU CHOOSE—Older grammar rules dictated that when you used a word like *however* to connect two independent clauses, you were always supposed to put a semicolon before the transitional word and a comma after it.

> Your report is very thorough and quite detailed; however, I still need more statistics about last year's travel expenses.

Today we would suggest that this rule is much less concrete. In many cases, we would even recommend turning the compound sentence into two separate sentences by placing a period before the transitional word.

> Your report is very thorough and quite detailed. However, I still need more statistics about last year's travel expenses.

As far as a comma after the transitional word, it depends on the reading.

Many times the transitional word is introducing contrary information to the information expressed in the first clause (as in our example above). Words like *however, nevertheless, besides* and even the much simpler *but* indicate that what comes next is different from what came first. A comma would be necessary with those words.

At other times, though, the transitional word is providing a smoother flow of ideas. The word *and* is an example of a transitional word that probably would not need a comma.

Decide for yourself by how much of a pause you intend your reader to "hear" in your sentence while reading.

SLASHES

Formally called the diagonal, a *slash* is used in business writing to indicate more than one alternative. It is also used in some abbreviations and mathematical notations.

Rules

1. A slash can be used to express alternatives or more than one part of something.
2. A slash can be used to indicate a fraction.
3. In nonsexist writing, slashes have been used to separate the two third person singular pronouns he/she and him/her.

Explanations and Examples

1. **A slash can be used to express alternatives or more than one part of something.**

> The window/aisle choice is always tough for me to make.
> Bring coats and/or raingear.
> Many newer cars come with CD/MP3 players.

2. **A slash can be used to indicate a fraction.** Over 2/3 of our sales team has already achieved the end-of-quarter goal.

3. **In nonsexist writing, slashes have been used to separate the two third person singular pronouns he/she and him/her.**

   While this is not incorrect, we suggest other alternatives to achieve a more readable nonsexist document. (See Nonsexist Language, page 119.)

SPACING

Period	No space:	Before a period
		After a decimal point
		After a period when another punctuation mark follows the period (for example, a closing quotation mark or parenthesis)
	One space:	After the period ending an abbreviation midsentence
	One or two spaces (your call):	After a period following a number or letter in an enumeration
		After a period at the end of a sentence, depending upon the readability of the font being used

Question Mark or **Exclamation Point**

	No space:	Before the mark
		After the mark, when immediately followed by another punctuation mark (for example a closing quotation mark or parenthesis)
	One space:	After a question mark or exclamation point in the middle of a sentence
	One or two spaces (your call):	At the end of a sentence, depending upon the readability of the font being used

Comma

	No space:	Before the comma
		After the comma within a number
	One space:	After the comma (unless it's immediately before a closing quotation mark)

Semicolon

	No space:	Before the semicolon
	One space:	After the semicolon

Colon

	No space:	Before the colon
		Before OR after the colon in time (1:35 p.m.)
	One or two spaces (your call):	After the colon within a sentence
		After notations such as the attention and subject lines

Dash

	No space:	Between the two hyphens that represent a dash
	One space:	Before and after dashes used midsentence
	Two spaces:	After a sentence that breaks off abruptly with a dash

Hyphen

	No space:	Before or after a hyphen, unless it's being used at a line's end to continue a word to the next line

Parentheses and **Brackets**

• **Opening**	No space:	After the parenthesis or bracket
	One space:	Before, when parenthetical material falls midsentence
	One or two spaces (your call):	Before, when the parenthetical material begins a new sentence
• **Closing**	No space:	Before the parenthesis or bracket
		After, if another punctuation mark immediately follows
	One space:	After, when parenthetical material falls midsentence
	One or two spaces (your call):	After, when the parenthetical material is a sentence in itself

Quotation Mark

• **Opening**	No space:	After the quotation mark
		Before the quotation mark, when preceded by an opening parenthesis
	One space:	Before the quotation mark, when quotation appears midsentence
	One or two spaces (your call):	Before the quotation mark, when quotation begins a new sentence
• **Closing**	No space:	Before
		After the quotation mark, when another punctuation mark immediately follows

One space:	After the quotation mark, when quotation appears midsentence
One or two spaces (your call):	After the quotation mark, when end of quotation is also end of a sentence

Apostrophe	No space:	Before the apostrophe, whether within a word or at the end of a word
		After the apostrophe, when another punctuation mark follows immediately
	One space:	After, at the end of a word in a sentence
	As single quotation marks:	Follow the same spacing rules as for quotation marks

Ellipses	No space:	Before the ellipsis or after each period in an ellipsis (unless the font you are using makes them look too close to each other)
		Before, when an opening quotation mark or parenthesis precedes the ellipsis
		After the ellipsis when a closing quotation mark or parenthesis follows the ellipsis
	One or two spaces (your call):	After ellipses that begin a sentence or fragment after another sentence has ended

Slash	No space:	Before or after a slash

REFERENCE TOOLS

Every writer needs easy access to the reference tools he or she needs to stay accurate, correct and clear.

Rules

Make sure that you have access to:

1. A large recently published dictionary
2. A style guide that is in tune with the kind of writing you do
3. An easy-to-understand reference guide for your word processing software
4. A collection of model documents from your own organization
5. Optional items: thesaurus, detailed grammar guide

Explanations and Examples

1. **Have access to a large recently published dictionary.**

   Your dictionary should either weigh more than three pounds OR be available any time you need it on-line.

   Our preference is for on-line dictionaries. There are many good ones you can find using a search engine.

   If it is not possible for you to go on-line at will, then you will need a good current dictionary. The more recently it has been published or updated, the more helpful it will be to you. The spellings, meanings and correct usage of words do change in American English—rather quickly.

   There are two basic types of dictionaries—prescriptive and descriptive. A prescriptive dictionary "prescribes" how the language is to be used. A descriptive dictionary "describes" how the language is used.

   Your dictionary should be large enough to include the correct spellings of the words that are made from the word that has been looked up. Another great feature to have is (at least) short notes covering word origins and the correct spellings of abbreviations and plurals related to the word.

2. **Have access to a style guide that is in tune with the kind of writing you do.**

   For most readers, that will be this style guide, because it covers the rules and styles that should be used by most business writers. It is also highly appropriate for technical and scientific writers in the world of work.

3. **Have access to an easy-to-understand reference guide for your word processing software.**

   In most cases, this will not be the manual that was published by the programmers who created the software. In general, most computer users find that other references are much more clear and easy to understand. Find the one (or maybe two) that you find easiest to use and understand and stick with it (or them).

4. **Have access to a collection of model documents from your own organization.**

   This guide includes formats for the most common business documents you will write (pages 208 – 271). But nothing beats your own collection of letters, memos, reports, proposals and e-mail messages that have proven effective in your own environment. Start your collection today and use it to answer questions you may have about style, format and consistency.

5. **Optional items to consider:**

   a. Thesaurus: If you find yourself at a loss for words too often, a thesaurus provides synonyms for words you might be overusing. A thesaurus is also a great reference tool for truly poor spellers. When you don't have any idea about how to spell *hors d'oeuvre*, a dictionary won't be much help. How would you even know to start in the *H*'s?

      But with a thesaurus handy, you could look up the word *appetizer* and easily find what you are looking for: the correct spelling of *hors d'oeuvre*.

   b. A very detailed grammar guide: If you are occasionally required to write in an academic or formal style, a guide like the *Gregg Reference Manual* can be an invaluable resource. It includes every grammar rule that is being enforced by anyone in America on the day it was published. For example, in the Tenth Edition (copyright 2005) there are 33 pages of comma rules. For most business writers, we would consider that excessive. But if you need that information, you know where to find it. Remember: It's great to have the security, but it isn't going to be your best first reference. Can you imagine how much work it is to find one particular rule among 33 pages?

REPORTS

Writers in today's workplace are called upon to produce a variety of reports. In general, most writers find themselves needing to write at least simple reports—perhaps a status report memo or a summary of a visit with a client. But many members of the business world, and certainly members of the technical and scientific communities, are also called upon to write some longer, more formal reports.

This section is devoted to the general advice business and technical writers should follow when writing in a report format.

Rules

1. Determine who will be reading your report and tailor your writing to his, her or their needs.

2. Follow any existing guidelines or report requirements you have been given to the letter.

3. Use topic headings, bullets, numbers and lists to organize your material. Be consistent in how you treat each sublevel of information.

4. Begin every report with an executive summary or overview statement.

5. Write a cover letter or memo with every formal report.

6. As in all your business writing, be direct, clear and specific. Back up any claims or assertions with facts, figures and other available proof.

7. Be honest.

8. As always, be concise and to the point.

9. Avoid putting anything unnecessary in your report.

10. Be judicious in your use of footnotes.

11. Don't lapse into a cold and impersonal writing style.

> *Writer's Tips:*
> The formatting tips for simple business reports, formal business reports and scientific and technical reports can be found in the Model Business Documents section of this book, pages 208 – 271.

Explanations and Examples

1. Determine who will be reading your report and tailor your writing to his, her or their needs.

If you have been using this guide for much at all up to this point, this advice will not surprise you. Positioning your message to your readers' needs is one of our consistent themes. It helps your reader get into your document, stick with your document and know you care. Do some research before you write (see page 110, Knowing Your Reader).

2. Follow any existing guidelines or report requirements you have been given to the letter.

A style guide such as this one is helpful for you when you have not been presented with directions from your readers or their representatives. But even if your reader is asking you to format your report in a manner you think is incorrect, do it anyway. Meet your readers' needs and it is a hundred times as likely your reader will meet yours.

3. Use topic headings, bullets, numbers and lists to organize your material. Be consistent in how you treat each sublevel of information.

Visual formatting strategies like headings, subheadings, boldface, italics, underlines and indents all help your reader get through your report more quickly. But double-check for consistency. As an example, are all your second level headings both boldfaced and underlined? As another example, have you indented all fourth level subheadings 10 spaces?

4. Begin every report with an executive summary or overview statement.

Your reader needs to know your bottom line right up front. Remember, business readers are busy. They often don't have the time to wade through a document to find your most important points.

The only exception to this point *could* be found in the arena of scientific report writing. Some highly analytical readers prefer to build up to the conclusion the writer reached in the same manner that writer did: step-by-step. But don't leave out this important section unless you know for certain you are dealing with one of those readers. Better safe than sorry.

5. Write a cover letter or memo with every formal report.

Use the cover letter explain the purpose of the report, what response you expect or hope for and when you expect to hear from the reader (or when you will contact him or her). Make this letter friendly and conversational—it's a great opportunity to build rapport.

6. As in all your business writing, be direct, clear and specific. Back up any claims or assertions with facts, figures and other available proof.

There's usually no other way to influence a reader to agree with you. Offer sufficient proof for all statements you want your reader to believe. In a case where you know your reader is in disagreement with you before you even start, do not rest until you have found at least three proofs or examples that support your side.

7. Be honest.

Be honest about all risks or costs associated with the content you are reporting on. Being straightforward helps build trust and credibility. And should the worst thing happen, you will not be blamed—well, you will have already made them aware of the risks. You can always point out that they were stated up front. If there are critics positioned against you, pointing out the risks up front helps you undercut their arguments.

8. As always, be concise and to the point.

Use short paragraphs, concise sentences and familiar words. Avoid jargon and gobbledygook.

The best way to guarantee a concise report is to spend as much time as possible *editing* that report. Build sufficient editing time into your timetable. As you write what you know, it is common to be wordy. Once you have put it aside for a few days, the wordiness can easily be cut away by your more relaxed and sharper mind.

9. Avoid putting anything unnecessary in your report.

Visual proof is great, but too much proof could get tedious. While visual aids like charts, tables and graphs can be amazingly helpful, too many of them can overwhelm your reader. Be moderate in all things report-related. Say what needs to be said and show what needs to be shown. But then: stop.

10. **Be judicious in your use of footnotes.**

Footnotes are for information that is nonessential to the main report but that could be interesting to the reader. *Never* bury important information in one. And be gentle with your readers. Too many footnotes can scare people. (In some cases, of course, too many footnotes can impress people—let's hope you aren't dealing with too many readers like that.)

Many report writers are now putting their footnotes in an appendix at the end of the report, usually called "endnotes."

11. **Don't lapse into a cold and impersonal writing style.**

Most reports are written in a cold and impersonal style. It may be your subconscious tendency to write as you have been written to. Edit carefully to switch passive voice sentences to active voice, to simplify overly complex sentences and to avoid meaningless jargon or clichés. Your reader needs you to be a living, breathing, warm human being. Even if you are a report writer.

RESEARCH

It wasn't so long ago that in order to do research, a writer needed a trip to a library or corporate resource center. Now, of course, the fastest way to do research and the way to have access to the most comprehensive collection of sources is to use the Internet.

Surprisingly, some of the best tips for accessing the very most appropriate and current reference information haven't changed that much.

Rules

1. Shop until you find the Internet search engines that work best for you.

2. Build your own file of commonly used Web sites.

3. If you are having trouble finding what you need, ask a reference librarian.

4. Keep excellent notes—especially about the bibliographic information that will allow you or your reader to find the same source again should you, he or she need to.

5. Give proper credit to all sources you have used in the preparation of any document.

Explanations and Examples

1. **Shop until you find the Internet search engines that work best for you.**

If you use a commercial Internet provider (like AOL®, MSN® or EarthLink®), you have no doubt noticed that a search engine is included as an easy link. And while these search engines are usually very good, you may find one you like better if you look. Actually, you can do a search for search engines!

You can also get a good idea of what search engines are currently popular by checking a list of most popular Web sites.

2. **Build your own file of commonly used Web sites.**

Depending on your Web browser, these may be called Bookmarks or Favorites. You can file the URLs (Web site addresses) for your favorite Web sites simply by clicking on the appropriate icon or menu item. All on-line service providers and Web browsers have some variation of this procedure available—find out how to store URLs in the program you use.

Once you have a collection of commonly used Web pages, organize them in a way that makes sense to you. Perhaps some of your commonly used pages are related to one topic and some are related to another. You could divide them into those two categories. Plus you probably have some sources like dictionaries that you can use for all purposes. There could be a third category for those pages.

3. **If you are having trouble finding what you need, ask a reference librarian.**

Believe it or not, they will even help you over the phone. Most reference librarians are highly trained in making their way around the Internet themselves these days, so they can be valuable resources for you while you use your work or home computer to do research.

4. **Keep excellent notes—especially about the bibliographic information that will allow you or your reader to find the same source again should you, he or she need to.**

Most of the time when you print directly from Web pages, the complete URL (Web address) will print on each page as well. Make sure before you leave the site! When making notes from books, journals, magazines or any other sources, make sure that you have accurately recorded all names, titles, dates, editions and volume numbers.

Also, consider keeping a master list of all the references you are using in a particular document. This makes it both easier to access the information and easier to prepare a bibliography if you need one. (See pages 40 – 41 for more information about Bibliographies.)

When quoting directly from a source, be sure to use quotation marks in your notes so that you don't accidentally plagiarize that author when preparing your own document. (It is easy to forget that you didn't just paraphrase what you read.)

5. **Give proper credit to all sources you have used in the preparation of any document.**

It is the only ethical thing to do. And in most cases, your readers will be impressed that you went to the trouble of looking things up for them.

SALUTATIONS

Salutations are the greetings used at the beginning of all letters and some e-mail. They welcome the reader into your document and could be the make it or break it point for that reader's decision to keep reading—or not.

While most everything else about business letters is covered together under the headings *Letters* (pages 110 – 112) and *Formats for Letters* (pages 216 – 237), salutations are so important we felt this separate section to be necessary.

If you make a good impression with your reader as early as the salutation, you can rest assured that reader will read at least most of the rest of your letter. If you make a poor impression early on, you may waste your time writing the rest of the letter.

Rules

1. Always use the reader's name and correct title in the salutation.
2. When addressing women, use *Ms.* unless the woman has told you she prefers something else (*Mrs.* or *Miss* or *Dr.*).
3. When you would call the person by first name in a phone call, use the first name in the salutation. When you would call them Mr., Ms. or Dr. on the phone, use that in the salutation.
4. Use commas when using the first name in the salutation; otherwise, use a colon.
5. Know (and use) the correct forms of address for special situations.
6. Use salutations in e-mail when you have a need to appear more friendly and less rushed.
7. It is okay to use a salutation without the word *Dear* if you think the word *Dear* would be awkward for you.

Explanations and Examples

1. **Always use the reader's name and correct title in the salutation.**

If you don't know the reader's name, make a phone call to find out. If you can't make a phone call, do the necessary research any way you can. When you address readers by their names, they will read the first paragraph of your letter. If you don't address them by name, we can't make that guarantee.

Of course, verify the person's title, gender and spelling of their name, even if it's a common one. For example, does he spell his name "Steven" or "Stephen"?

If for some reason you cannot find the name, gender or correct title of the reader:

a. *If you don't know the gender, but do know the name*—use the reader's first and last name with no title in front.

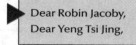

Dear Robin Jacoby,
Dear Yeng Tsi Jing,

b. *If you don't know the name at all*—use the most accurate descriptive title you can think of. This is the tip you may have to use when you are sending copies of the same letter to many different people and you need one general salutation for all of them.

> Dear Voter:
> Dear Parent:
> Dear Union Member:

c. *If you don't know the name and can find no unifying descriptive title*—never use *Dear Sir* unless you are certain you are writing to a man. *Dear Sir or Madam* can work but in e-mail it can appear too formal. The same holds true for *Gentlemen* and *Ladies and Gentlemen*. Perhaps this would be a good time to consider the American Management Style of letter formatting.

d. *The American Management Style*—everything about the format of this letter is the same as a normal business letter except for the salutation.

Instead of a salutation, the American Management format calls for a subject line

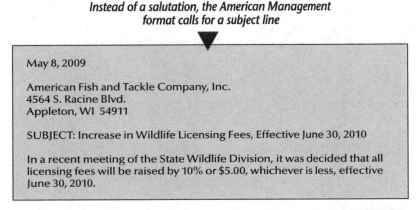

May 8, 2009

American Fish and Tackle Company, Inc.
4564 S. Racine Blvd.
Appleton, WI 54911

SUBJECT: Increase in Wildlife Licensing Fees, Effective June 30, 2010

In a recent meeting of the State Wildlife Division, it was decided that all licensing fees will be raised by 10% or $5.00, whichever is less, effective June 30, 2010.

2. **When addressing women, use *Ms*. unless the woman has told you she prefers something else (*Mrs.* or *Miss* or *Dr.*).**

Make sure you are using the correct titles for the readers you address. When you call a Dr. a Mr. or a Ms., that could be insulting to him or her. When writing to women, *Ms.* is the preferred title unless the reader has told you differently.

3. **When you would call the person by first name in a phone call, use the first name in the salutation. When you would call them Mr., Ms. or Dr. on the phone, use that in the salutation.**

Another method for determining how to address your reader in the salutation is to determine how you plan on signing the letter. Will you hand write just your first name above your printed name and title? If so, that's a good sign the relationship is warm enough for you to address the reader by first name as well. If, on the other hand, you will be more likely to sign both your first and last name above your printed name and title, that can be taken as a sign that you should address that reader with a title (Mr., Ms., Dr.) and last name. When in doubt, always err on the side of formality. It is easier to become more casual than to become more formal.

4. **Use commas when using the first name in the salutation; otherwise, use a colon.**

Commas are more casual, more conversational and more friendly than colons. Your reader will feel more welcomed into your letter with a comma after the salutation. And when you are using salutations in e-mail, always use a comma after the salutation. E-mail, by its very nature, is casual and friendly. A colon looks standoffish and formal. Save colons after your salutations for your formal writing.

5. Know (and use) the correct forms of address for special situations.

Salutations for Special Situations	
To Two People:	Dear Mr. Lawrence and Ms. Appleby:
	Dear Mr. Lawrence and Mr. Greenburgh:
	Dear Ms. Appleby and Ms. Berlin:
	Dear Ms. Berlin and Mr. Greenburgh:
	Note: The person in the salutation with the most power or the bigger title should be addressed first. If they are equal in rank, put them in alphabetical order.
To Several People:	Dear Mr. Lawrence, Ms. Appleby and Mr. Greenburgh:
Married Couple with Same Surname:	Dear Mr. and Mrs. Lawrence:
Married Couple with Same Surname, Husband has Special Title:	Dear Dr. and Mrs. Dermish:
Married Couple with Same Surname, Wife has Special Title:	Dear Dr. and Mr. Riveras:
Married Couple with Same Surname, Both have Special Title:	Dear Drs. Abramson: Dear Professor and Dr. Abramson:
Married or Unmarried Couple with Different Surnames:	Dear Mr. Grayson and Ms. Pietras:
Married Couple with Hyphenated Surname:	Dear Mr. and Mrs. Kellogg-Hakim:

6. Use salutations in e-mail when you have a need to appear more friendly and less rushed.

This may be more often than you would think. As people read their e-mail, they are often feeling pressured and rushed. To take the time to write the word *Dear*, followed by the name of your reader shows that you do care about having a warm relationship with that reader.

When you use a salutation in e-mail, remember to use a complimentary closing and to sign your name at the bottom as well.

7. It is okay to use a salutation without the word *Dear* if you think the word *Dear* would be awkward for you.

Better advice, of course, would be to use it anyway. The word *Dear* is expected by most readers as the first word of a salutation. But if you just don't think it is appropriate in your case, you can simply drop it and use only the name:

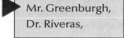

Mr. Greenburgh,
Dr. Riveras,

If you drop the *Dear*, we encourage you to always use a comma instead of a colon after the salutation—a colon would be way too abrupt in this case.

SENTENCES—Structure

Does the title of this section frighten you? Are you concerned that finally the moment has come that as an adult you are going to be asked to step up to a chalkboard and diagram a sentence? Do you remember diagramming sentences as a child?

Well, do not fear. There will be no sentence diagramming. It is easy enough to learn the basics of proper sentence structure without it. In fact, we will even present some of the special problems many business writers encounter in this area—and how to solve them—all without the need to diagram even one sentence.

When you understand the function of each word in a sentence you can guarantee that you will write that sentence correctly. There are three main functions that most of the words in a sentence will fill most of the time: **Subjects**, **Verbs** and **Objects**.

Rules

1. Every sentence must contain a subject and a verb.
2. Every sentence must express a complete thought.
3. A group of words that includes both a subject and a verb but that does not contain a complete thought needs a complement to complete the thought.
4. Be careful to place only one major idea in each sentence.
5. Structure most sentences so that they are written in the active voice, as opposed to the passive voice.

Explanations and Examples

1. **Every sentence must contain a subject and a verb.**

   The subject of a sentence is the word or group of words that tells *Who* or *What*, usually before the verb. The verb in a sentence tells what the subject does, what is done to the subject or what the condition of the subject is.

   > The photocopier (*subject*) broke (*verb*).
   > Joe (*subject*) fixed (*verb*) the photocopier.
   > Martha and Jack (*subject*) handled (*verb*) the account well.

   Occasionally the subject could be understood, not stated. This happens in *imperative* sentences—the type of sentences that give orders or directions.

   Imperative sentences ▶
   > Stop! (*The subject* You *is understood.*)
   > Listen to what I am saying. (*The subject* You *is understood.*)

   In questions, it is likely that the subject will appear *after* the verb, or between two words that together make up the verb.

   Questioning sentences ▶
   > Has (*verb*) anyone (*subject*) fixed (*verb*) the photocopier?
   > Where is (*verb*) Joe (*subject*)?

2. **Every sentence must express a complete thought.**

   Any group of words that contains a subject and a verb expresses a complete thought if it can stand alone and make sense.

   Here is an example of an incomplete thought masquerading as a complete sentence ▶
   > The fax machine in our office.

   The reader is left with questions: What about the fax machine in their office?

   Here is the same sentence, completed with a verb ▶
   > The fax machine in our office never stops.

   Now the sentence makes sense—it conveys a complete thought.

Here is another example of an incomplete thought, this one a little harder for some to recognize because it does contain both a subject and a verb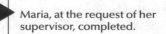

> Maria, at the request of her supervisor, completed.

In this case, the subject (Maria) did the verb (completed). But we don't know what it was that she completed. This sentence is missing a needed object.

3. **A group of words that includes both a subject and a verb but that does not contain a complete thought needs a complement to complete the thought.**

A *complement* is a word or group of words that completes the meaning of a subject and verb. There are three types of complements: direct objects, indirect objects and subject complements.

Direct Objects: A *direct object* is a noun or pronoun that receives the action of a transitive verb. A verb is transitive if it needs the receiver of its action to be named in order to complete the thought of a sentence. Generally, a direct object can be found by asking *Whom?* or *What?* after an action verb.

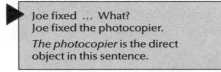

> Joe fixed ... What?
> Joe fixed the photocopier.
>
> *The photocopier* is the direct object in this sentence.

Indirect Objects: An *indirect object* is a noun or pronoun that names the person or thing that something is being done for. Generally, an indirect object can be found by asking the questions *To or for whom?* or *To or for what?*

Look at this sentence

> The supervisor (*subject*) told (*verb*) the employees (*indirect object*) the bad news (*direct object*).

In this sentence, *the employees* is the answer to the question *To whom did the supervisor tell the bad news?*

Here is another example

> Trent (*subject*) gave (*verb*) each participant (*indirect object*) a new workbook (*direct object*).

In this second example, *each participant* is the answer to the question *To whom did Trent give a new workbook?*

Notice that either of these example sentences could have been worded using prepositional phrases instead of the indirect objects

> The supervisor told the bad news to the employees.
> Trent gave a new workbook to each participant.

In that case, the prepositional phrases are not considered indirect objects. Indirect objects never follow the prepositions *to* or *for* in a sentence. Prepositional phrases in sentences like this are considered *adverbial phrases*. They are telling more about the verb in each sentence.

More Grammar Information Than You Need

SUBJECT COMPLEMENTS: Both direct objects and indirect objects are complements used with action verbs. Subject complements are complements used with linking verbs. Linking verbs are verbs that connect nouns or pronouns at the beginning of a sentence with a word or words at or near the end of that sentence. The subject complement is a noun, pronoun or adjective that follows the linking verb and tells something about the subject. These subject complements are sometimes called *predicate nouns, predicate pronouns* and *predicate adjectives*.

Predicate nouns and predicate pronouns follow the linking verb in a sentence and rename or further identify the subject of the sentence.

Josh and Marcia (*subject*) are (*linking verb*) the supervisors (*predicate noun*)
of our two most profitable sales teams.

This (*subject*) is (*linking verb*) it (*predicate pronoun*).

Predicate adjectives follow linking verbs and describe the subject of the sentence.

The meeting (*subject*) was (*linking verb*) helpful (*predicate adjective*).

The new director (*subject*) seems (*linking verb*) easygoing (*predicate adjective*).

---

4. Be careful to place only one major idea in each sentence.

Again, this tip goes to the readability of a sentence, especially when a hurried or busy reader is reading it. While it is fine to include a subordinate (less important) clause or idea within your main sentence, it is your responsibility as a business writer to make sure that your reader can clearly isolate the most important thought in that sentence, and isolate it quickly.

> Neil and Tim, who have worked together in this organization for the past ten years, have always been role models for the less motivated—and lately it seems that the less motivated population has been growing—among the customer service staff, despite their rather unfortunate habit of being practical jokesters, especially where management is concerned.

> Neil and Tim have always been role models for the less motivated among the customer service staff.

What? That first sentence contains way too many ideas. And while a careful reader could eventually figure it out, no reader should be asked to! What is the main idea of the sentence?

All of that other information, while it may be interesting, is just extra information. If one of those extra ideas is important enough to warrant a subordinate place in the sentence, then so be it. But there just isn't room for all of them.

5. Structure most sentences so that they are written in the active voice, as opposed to the passive voice.

Passive and active voice are covered more fully in another section of this guide (pages 134 – 136). But here, it is important to remind you that most readers expect to read a sentence that starts with a subject that then does something toward an object. If you remember, in the passive voice, that order is not followed.

In the passive voice, a subject receives the action of the verb that was acted upon by an object. Passive voice is harder to read for this reason—it slows the reader down and runs the risk of making your message unclear.

SENTENCES—Style

Sentences are the way we communicate our thoughts. A group of sentences together make a paragraph, an e-mail message or even a comprehensive report. The easiest definition of a sentence is that it almost always has at least one subject, one verb and that it contains at least one complete thought.

In middle school grammar books, there is an emphasis on encouraging young writers to put more ideas in each sentence, to make their sentences longer and more complex.

In a business writing guide, the advice is much different. Most of the time, adults writing in the world of work need shorter, simpler sentences.

A short sentence is one that doesn't contain too many words. A simple sentence is one that doesn't contain too many ideas.

If you remember, short simple sentences help your busy (and potentially tired) reader keep reading. They improve the *readability* of your document.

There are four kinds of sentences. Here is a chart that quickly illustrates them:

The Four Types of Sentences

Demonstrative sentences are the sentences writers use most often to state facts and opinions.
> The pharmaceutical research team completed its study of antispasmodics last Friday.
> The finish could be applied at any temperature between 60 and 90 degrees Fahrenheit.
> Rudi is the best supervisor I've ever had.

Interrogative sentences are used to ask questions.
> When will the study be finished?
> How many reviews still need to be completed?
> Where will we ever find the budget?

Imperative sentences are used to give directions or issue commands.
> Christine, please answer the customers' questions as directly as you can.
> Hurry!
> Please go outside to smoke, and only during your appointed breaks.

Exclamatory sentences are used to show surprise, shock or strong emotion. While it is okay to occasionally use an exclamatory sentence, don't use too many in your business writing. It will damage your credibility.
> Jerry Humphreys just got promoted to a directorship!
> Marcia won the lottery last night!
> Please stop gossiping about each other!

Rules

1. Keep the average sentence length in most documents between 10 and 17 words. If you are writing technical, scientific or complex material keep the average sentence length between 8 and 12 words.
2. Work hard to avoid writing any sentence longer than 30 words.
3. Never put more than one major idea in the same sentence.
4. Make your sentences as clear and direct as possible.
5. Within reason, use a variety of sentence lengths and structures to keep your reader from becoming bored.
6. Use all four types of sentences to make your document more interesting to the reader.

Explanations and Examples

1. **Keep the average sentence length in most documents between 10 and 17 words. If you are writing technical, scientific or complex material keep the average sentence length between 8 and 12 words.**

   Count all the words that are in the sentences of a given document. Then divide that total by the number of sentences those words appear in. In this way you will arrive at the figure that represents the average number of words per sentence for that document. Most word processing programs have a built-in feature that will do this automatically once it's turned on. This measurement is a key component of most readability indexes. It tells much about the ease (or lack of ease) your reader faces when reading your document.

   An average sentence length of 10 – 17 words, where most of the words are standard vocabulary, generally indicates a reading grade level of 8th or 9th grade. An 8th grader would have no trouble understanding your document, in other words—as long as that 8th grader understood the concepts you were writing about.

   This doesn't mean that we should assume most of our business readers have only 8th grade educations. It means that if an 8th grader can read something, it certainly isn't going to overtax an engineer with advanced degrees.

   Good business writers always strive to impress their readers with the quality of their ideas—not the size of their sentences. In fact, the easier the document is to read, the more your reader will recognize the quality of your ideas.

   By the same token, if you are using a heavier vocabulary, your readers will need a break sooner so your sentences should be slightly shorter. And of course, no matter what kind of vocabulary you use, we don't mean to suggest that all sentences be 8, 9, 10, 11 or 12 words long. That would be truly dull writing! Some of your sentences may have more than 20 words in them. Others could have just a single word. The concept is that when you count them and average them, or have your word processing software do this for you, your ideal average should be somewhere between 10 – 17 (8 – 12 for technical).

2. **Work hard to avoid writing any sentence longer than 30 words.**

   Your readers will thank you. In general, once your reader gets to about 30 words, he or she loses the ability to comprehend the information. When you find longer sentences (most grammar checking software programs are good at this), find a way to split those sentences into two or three separate ones.

   There may be a few exceptions. For example, you may be listing, in a sentence, the names of all the people who attended a meeting and there are 20 people. The commas or semicolons you use to separate those names from each other help compensate for having so many words in one sentence.

3. **Never put more than one major idea in the same sentence.**

   Your reader is probably reading too quickly to fully comprehend more than one major idea per sentence. It goes back to the way we were taught to read: from a capital letter to a period for the main idea of the sentence. If there turns out to be more than one main idea in that sentence, the reader has likely stopped looking for it.

   Certainly, you will want to put some dependent or subordinate ideas in sentences that already contain a main idea. Just make sure the main idea is clear and apparent.

   Too many main ideas ▶ Jake and Toby presented the new communication program to the sales department that just the week before had been restructured—at the cost of three full-time employees.

   That sentence contains three main ideas: (1) Jake and Toby presented the new communications skills program to the sales department; (2) The sales department had been restructured the week before; and (3) The restructuring led to the layoffs of three full-time employees. Wouldn't it have been more clear to present that much important information in separate sentences?

   Solution ▶ Jake and Toby presented the new communication program to the sales department. That's the department that just the week before had been restructured. I hear they lost three full-time employees.

   If some of the extra information was less important, it could have been put in a subordinate phrase or clause:

   Jake and Toby presented the new communications program to the sales department whose manager provided coffee and pastries for everyone.

   The coffee and pastries are a nice touch, but not important enough for their own sentence.

4. Make your sentences as clear and direct as possible.

If you word your sentences in a conversational way, you will probably meet this requirement automatically.

If you remember to limit your sentences to only one major idea, you will be clear and direct.

The same is true about sentence length—if you keep your sentences within the bounds of an ideal average length of 10 – 17 words, you won't be able to avoid directness and clarity.

5. Within reason, use a variety of sentence lengths and structures to keep your reader from becoming bored.

Some sentences should be very short, others longer and a few up to 28 – 30 words. Most of your sentences should be structured in traditional American English syntax: Subject – Verb – Object. But occasionally, an inverted sentence or a complex sentence could keep the reader interested—or at least keep the reader from slipping into a hypnotic trance!

6. Use all four types of sentences to make your document more interesting to the reader.

By varying the types of sentences within your paragraph, you add interest to the paragraph. The reader will be more likely to read it.

SIGNS AND SYMBOLS

Many writers use signs and symbols to communicate with their readers more quickly and clearly. In fact, most readers have now come to expect symbols such as $ and % instead of the words *dollars* and *percent*.

Rules

There are just a couple of rules to be aware of when using signs and symbols in your writing.

1. Make sure your reader understands the signs and symbols you use.

2. When you need to use specialized symbols, learn where to find them in your word processing program or choose a font that includes the symbols you need.

Explanations and Examples

1. **Make sure your reader understands the signs and symbols you use.**

    Many signs and symbols—like the basic symbols used in math (+, -, x, =, ˜) are self-explanatory. Readers have been using them for years. The same holds true for the symbols used with money ($ and ¢) and the percentage sign (%).

    Other symbols, though, could be less clear to a reader who might not have the background the writer does. When using signs and symbols that might be unfamiliar, always spell them out at the first use and provide the sign or symbol in parentheses. This will teach the reader what that sign or symbol means. From that point on in the document, the sign or symbol will suffice.

    > *Spell out unclear signs or symbols* ▶ The alpha (A) and the omega (Ω)
    >
    > Throughout our experiment, hydrogen (H) and helium (He) were found in abnormal levels throughout the test area.

    In the past, business writers were advised to avoid using symbols, to spell the words out instead. The key words in that sentence are *in the past*. Your readers are busy and they are literate. Everyone knows what $ and % mean, so it speeds up comprehension to use them.

    In your very formal documents, of course, spell the symbols out as words. But for most letters, most memos, most reports and all e-mail—use the symbols!

2. **When you need to use specialized symbols, learn where to find them in your word processing program or choose a font that includes the symbols you need.**

For example, the most commonly used typeface in the Microsoft® Word program, Times New Roman, does not include a traditional division sign. You must use the "Insert Symbol" function to find one. Check the Help files in your word processor to learn how to add special characters.

Also, be aware that different fonts contain different symbols—no matter what your keyboard may look like. Experiment to find a comfortable fit for yourself and the kind of symbols you need to use in your writing.

SPELL-CHECKING

Perhaps you have noticed how convenient yet imperfect your computer program's spell-checker is. Here are the rules for getting the most from yours, without getting burned by its limitations:

Rules

1. Spell-check every document you produce on your computer.

2. Then, make sure the document is also proofread by a person—preferably, a person other than you.

3. Add the words you need to your computer's dictionary, but be careful!

4. Add the specialized dictionaries you need to your spell-checker.

5. And finally, spell-check *after* you write, not *while* you write.

Explanations and Examples

1. **Spell-check every document you produce on your computer.**

It's not perfect, but what a quick and simple way to catch some of your most embarrassing mistakes and typos. Words like *teh* instead of *the* and *Corproation* instead of *Corporation* can quickly tell your reader that you aren't careful enough to trust. It's true, there are many readers who judge your intelligence and reliability based on spelling or grammar errors.

Make it your rule: If it's in a word processing file, spell-check it. Better safe than sorry.

2. **Then, make sure the document is also proofread by a person—preferably, a person other than you.**

As you type your brain is making a mental picture of what it meant to type. That's right—what it *meant* to type. When you reread that typing, your brain superimposes the image it created with the image you created. That's why you miss even some of your most pronounced typos. Your brain, literally, didn't see them while proofreading. It's best to have someone else proofread for you. Even if that new reader doesn't know as clearly as you do what it is you're writing about, that new reader does have the advantage of being able to see what's really there on the page.

If, for one reason or another, you must proofread your own writing, use the tips in our Proofreading section (page 146). Seriously consider reading your writing backwards, word for word, as a special hedge against misspellings.

3. **Add the words you need to your computer's dictionary, but be careful!**

   Your word processor's dictionary will not match up with your writing vocabulary without some help from you. The names of people you commonly write to or about will be missing, as well as some of your jargon, technical language or regional vocabulary. Go ahead and add those words to your spell-checker's dictionary when you are prompted to, but before you click "Add to Dictionary" do yourself a favor: Make sure you're right!

4. **Add the specialized dictionaries you need to your spell-checker.**

   There are specialized add-on dictionaries for many professional specialties (like engineering, medical and legal) as well as for foreign languages. Make sure to get the ones that you need—they'll save you the time of adding those words yourself and the potential embarrassment of adding them incorrectly.

5. **And finally, spell-check *after* you write, not *while* you write.**

   Most of us have enough trouble overcoming writer's block without some computer program correcting us as we write. (See Creativity on pages 61 – 65.) Set your word processor to leave your errors alone as you write. But do remember to spell-check everything after it's written.

SPELLING

Do you believe you could be a better speller? If you speak and write English, the answer is probably yes. The spelling rules we follow are not consistent, and because our language has derived from a wide variety of sources we cannot count on the rules that work for one word to work for all words.

Basically, English is a combination of a Germanic language (Anglo-Saxon) and a Romance language (French). In 1066, the Battle of Hastings was the culminating battle of the Norman Invasion of England. The Normans had been living in France, the Anglo-Saxons were living in England. The Normans came to England and beat the Anglo-Saxons. Then they moved in. The Anglo-Saxons became the peasants and the Normans became the ruling class. Each group kept its own language—at least for a while. As time passed and the people mingled and lived together, the roots of the English we speak and write today were planted.

For years people have tried to determine what makes a good speller. There was an old theory that those of us who learned how to read via phonics lessons are better spellers than those of us who learned by sight reading.

It's an interesting theory but not accurate. True, phonics helps in the spelling of words that are spelled like they sound. But only sight reading strategies will help you with words like *hors d'oeuvre*.

Another theory postulates that those of us who are left-brain dominant (likely to be more logical than creative) are better spellers than those of us who are right-brain dominant (likely to be more creative than logical). This theory doesn't pan out either.

The fact is this: English is a tough language to spell in. The rules don't always work and the exceptions to the rules are often too numerous to list. Your best bet to become a better speller is to become a better speller of the words that consistently give you trouble. Learn your trouble list.

Rules

Here are the only rational tips you'll need for becoming a better speller:

1. Learn only one spelling rule.
2. Use your word processor's spell-checker.
3. Use a dictionary or a thesaurus to find correct spellings of words.
4. Write the word ten times, saying it aloud as you write.
5. Find your trouble spot in a word and create a gimmick to help you remember.
6. Keep a list of your commonly misspelled words.

Explanations and Examples

1. **Learn only one spelling rule.**

   The only spelling rule worth memorizing is: "I before E except after C or when sounding like A as in neighbor and weigh."

   The reason this is the only rule we recommend memorizing is because it covers over 3,000 words in the English language—and has fewer than 20 exceptions. It is that low number of exceptions that makes this rule so worthwhile. You can almost always count on it.

   The common exceptions include the words *their, weird, foreign* and *scientist*. And those are words you have used often enough that you probably know how to spell them, rule or not.

   If you haven't already done it, memorize this one rule today: I before E except after C or when sounding like A as in neighbor and weigh.

2. **Use your word processor's spell-checker.**

   But know that it isn't perfect. It will certainly earn its electricity just by finding transpositions and typos you might have missed. Words like *the* and *to* have a funny way of showing up as *teh* and *ot*. Worse yet, the person who typed them can rarely see them as errors.

   So your spell-checker will save you lots of embarrassment. Two words of caution are in order, however:

   a. *Your spell-checker isn't reading for meaning.* So if you transpose the word *form* into the word *from*, your spell-checker won't tell you about it. As long as the words it finds are words, the spell-checker assumes them to be correct.

   b. *Adding words to the dictionary can be dangerous.* What if you add a word that you are certain of—but it turns out you were incorrect. Now, every time you use your spell-checker it lets you get away with your common error. It assumed that you added only the correct spelling of a word to its dictionary. Double-check all words that you add to your spell-checker's dictionary.

3. **Use a dictionary or a thesaurus to find correct spellings of words.**

   Most of the time you can probably make a good enough start on a word to find it in a dictionary. If your question is whether the word *separate* is correct, or if it should be *seperate*, you can get to the *sep* section of the dictionary and browse from there without too much work.

   In a good dictionary, you will also be able to find the correct spelling of any word with a suffix or prefix. In the main listing for the root word, look for the alternate spellings at the end of the entry. For example, when you look up the word *cancel*, you also will find at the entry the correct spellings of *precancel, cancellation, canceled (or cancelled), canceling (or cancelling)*. No, you are not hallucinating. In many cases, a dictionary will tell you there is more than one accepted spelling of a word. The one the dictionary lists first is considered to be preferred.

   But when your trouble word is *hors d'oeuvre* and you don't even know if it begins with an *h* or an *o*, a thesaurus is a better resource. What is a synonym for *hors d'oeuvre? Appetizer? Snack?* If you look up either of those words in a thesaurus, you will find the word *hors d'oeuvre*—spelled correctly—in the entry.

4. **Write the word ten times, saying it aloud as you write.**

   And mispronounce it, if you think that will help you remember.

   You could quickly learn how to spell the word *separate* with this trick. You see, by using more than just your mind reading silently to yourself—by using your hand to write the word, your voice to speak it, your ears to hear it and your eyes to read it you are increasing the odds of the correct spelling taking root in your brain by four times.

   ▶ SEP - AY - RATE, SEP - AY - RATE, SEP - AY - RATE

   Psychologists tell us this will help you remember that correct spelling forever.

5. **Find your trouble spot in a word and create a gimmick to help you remember.**

Let's say you can never remember if the word *cemetery* ends with -ery or -ary. Your trouble spot is the final vowel:

> cemet **?** ry

Here's a gimmick to help you remember that *cemetery* ends in -ery. There are three E's in cemetery:

> c<u>e</u>m<u>e</u>t<u>e</u>ry—Because if you're stuck in a cemetery after midnight, you might just be screaming, "Eeeeeeeeeeee!"

Okay, it made you groan. But that's a sign you'll never forget it!

6. **Keep a list of your commonly misspelled words.**

This makes it easier for you to look them up. Instead of logging on, going to a dictionary Web site and typing in your best guess … instead of looking it up in a huge dictionary with hundreds of thousands of words, your simple customized list contains only the words you will need often. It will be much quicker for you.

Alternatively, most word processing programs have an automatic correction feature. Learn how to use it in your program—and remember, make sure the word you add is correct before you add it!

Business Writing

Commonly Misspelled Words

absence
accommodate
accompanying
achievement
acquaintance
across
advantageous
aisle
all right
analysis
analyze
answer
apparently
appreciable
approximate
arbitrary
architect
attorney
autumn
bankruptcy
basically
beginning
believe
beneficiary
benefited
calendar
campaign
canceled
catalog
category
cemetery
changeable
chronological
coincidence
collateral
colonel
column
commitment
committee

concede
conscience
conscientious
conscious
consensus
continuous
criticism
debt
debtor
defendant
deficit
definite
descendant
describe
detrimental
develop
development
dilemma
disappoint
dissatisfied
dissimilar
ecstasy
eighth
eligible
embarrass
emphasize
empty
enumerate
environment
exaggerate
exhaustible
exhibition
existence
exorbitant
experience
extraordinary
facsimile
familiar
fascinating

February
foreign
foresee
forfeit
forty
fourteen
fourth
government
grammar
grievous
guarantee
guardian
harass
hemorrhage
hors d'oeuvre
hygiene
hypocrisy
innocuous
inoculate
irrelevant
itinerary
judgment
(OR judgement)
labeled
laboratory
leisure
liable
liaison
library
license
lieutenant
likable
maneuver
mileage
miniature
miscellaneous
mischievous
misspell
mortgage

necessary
negotiate
neither
ninety
ninth
occasionally
occurrence
omelet
omission
opinion
pamphlet
panicky
parallel
partially
pastime
permissible
perseverance
persuade
phenomenal
physician
picnicking
plausible
possessions
prerogative
pretense
privilege
procedure
proceed
programmed
pronunciation
psychiatric
psychological
publicly
quantity
questionnaire
receipt
receive
recipient
recommend

reference
relevant
renowned
rescind
restaurant
résumé (or resume or resumé)
rhythm
schedule
separate
sergeant
siege
similar
simultaneous
skillful
sponsor
strength
subpoena
subtlety
subtly
supersede
surgeon
surprise
surveillance
susceptible
technique
temperature
theater
thoroughly
through
totaled
tragedy
transferred
unmanageable
Wednesday
wholly
wield
yield

SUBJECT LINES

Subject lines are mostly used in memos and e-mail. In both places they are important previews for the reader of what is to come. In e-mail, they could determine whether or not the reader even opens the message.

Although subject lines are covered in three formatting sections (Memos, pages 115 – 117; Letters, pages 110 – 112; and E-mail, pages 72 – 75), they are so important to the likelihood of whether or not your reader will read your document that they warrant their own section here as well.

Rules

1. Write subject lines that communicate the main idea of the memo, letter or e-mail—not just the topic.

2. Keep subject lines short.

3. Choose a format for your subject lines and stick with it.

4. When replying or forwarding an e-mail, delete all but one RE: or FW:.

Explanations and Examples

1. **Write subject lines that communicate the main idea of the memo, letter or e-mail—not just the topic.**

   Especially in the case of e-mail, your subject line may be your only chance to send the message you need to send to your reader. So be specific.

   > **Not helpful:** Company Picnic
   >
   > **Meaningful:** Company Picnic Canceled

2. **Keep subject lines short.**

   E-mail has disciplined us on this count. Back when our subject lines were on paper, we had the ability to make them as long as we wanted. Traditionally, the subject line for a letter could be up to two lines long and the subject line for a memo was a maximum of one line long. Unfortunately, long subject lines probably turned off our readers.

   A word about the differences between "Subject" and "RE": Subject is used when the topic is broad; "RE" (Latin for "thing") is used when the topic is more specific. For example, a letter about the dress code for a training session would use "Subject"; a letter about the dress of a particular person in that class would use "RE."

   Today, your e-mail program won't allow you to go on too long. So you need an economy of words, choosing only the most important ones to include. Typically, a good subject line is a maximum of 50 characters. Remember, a space counts as a character.

   > **Wordy:** Processing Plant in Alberta Being Closed Due to a Lack of
   > Revenue from Soy and Canola, Effective 12-31-09
   >
   > **Concise:** Alberta Plant Will Close 12-31-09—Soy/Canola Revenues Down

3. **Choose a format for your subject lines and stick with it.**

   Some writers capitalize the first letters of all important words in a subject line, other writers capitalize only the first letter of the first word. Either of these options is fine, but be consistent.

   Do not use ALL CAPS for a subject line—your reader might think you are angry.

4. **When replying or forwarding an e-mail, delete all but one RE: or FW:.**

   Have you ever received an e-mail that had been forwarded or replied to so many times the only thing in the subject line was FW: FW: FW: FW: FW: or RE: RE: RE: RE: RE:?

   Delete all but one of these abbreviations so your reader will see the meat of your subject line.

   Also, when forwarding, remove the addresses of the recipients the e-mail was previously forwarded to.

TECHNICAL WRITING

Technical, scientific and engineering writing differs from general business writing in two important ways:

1) The material covered in technical documents tends to be more analytical or detailed in nature than general business writing. This means that it could contain more difficult language, more difficult concepts or maybe just more language and concepts about a specialized area.

2) The readers of technical documents also tend to be more technical than the readers of more standard business writing. Therefore, they tend to be more concerned about the writer's accuracy, thoroughness and correctness.

By following the guidelines listed here, even a nontechnical writer can write convincingly to a technical or scientific audience.

Rules

1. Be accurate.
2. Be complete.
3. Organize your writing in a logical, easy-to-follow format.
4. Use language appropriate to your readers' needs; define all technical terminology.
5. Use short, simple sentences.
6. Keep paragraphs short and well-structured.
7. Summarize frequently in longer or more complex documents.
8. Employ the principles of graphic design to communicate clearly and quickly to your readers.
9. Keep a personal file of model technical documents.

Explanations and Examples

1. Be accurate.

The surest, quickest way to destroy your credibility as a writer and an expert in the eyes of technical readers is to be inaccurate in your reporting of facts. Before you do anything else, make certain that every detail you present is correct—whether in a sentence or a graphic. Double-check (maybe even triple-check) all statistics, dates, times, names and results you write about. Also double-check all graphics for accuracy.

Also, whenever possible, reference any supporting data that can be found elsewhere in either parenthetical notes or footnotes. This allows your reader to check your accuracy if so inclined.

2. Be complete.

The best technical writers always create documents that stand independently. While footnotes referencing side issues or further support of your writing can be useful, all information that directly relates to your document should be included within it. Sometimes the information will appear where it is referenced, other times it can appear in an appendix at the end of the full document, with a clear note in the body of where it is located.

Your reader should never have to put your document down to refer to another one, though, in order to understand the points you are making in your writing.

3. Organize your writing in a logical, easy-to-follow format.

This rule, of course, applies to all writing you do. In technical or scientific writing, however, it becomes even more important because of the potential complexity of the information you are communicating.

Writer's Tips:
For more complete information about Organizing Your Writing, see pages 127 – 128.

Many technical reports are organized in a *Cause and Effect* format or a *General to Specific* format. But as long as the format you choose makes sense for the material you are covering, any format can work well.

Remember: No matter what format you use to organize your writing, make sure to provide your bottom line information up front. In longer technical documents, this section usually bears the heading *Executive Summary*.

4. Use language appropriate to your readers' needs; define all technical terminology.

You may remember that in general business writing, we suggest that you stick to clear simple English words whenever possible. We encourage you to use words like *use* and *help* instead of words like *utilize* and *facilitate*.

In technical writing, though, many times your readers are themselves technical. Perhaps they have a specialized education or background that guarantees they speak a specialized language. When writing to this type of audience, it is a good idea to use their specialized language so they will be confident you know what you are writing about.

By the same token, make sure you define all technical terminology that is included in your document just in case a reader does not understand it. These definitions can be placed either in the document where they occur (in parentheses) or at the end of the document in a glossary. When adding a glossary to the end of a document, ensure that the first time you use technical terminology, that it is defined in that glossary. It can also be a good idea to visually format the words that can be found in the glossary in a certain way throughout the document (for example, in **boldface** or *italics*), after telling the reader in the beginning that you have done this.

5. Use short, simple sentences.

Once again, this is a guideline that we recommend to all business writers. And once again, it is even more important for technical writers to follow because of the complexity of the material they are writing about.

Short sentences are sentences that do not contain too many words. Simple sentences are sentences that contain only one major idea.

Many technical and scientific readers frequently read very complex material that contains both long sentences and sentences with many ideas in them. But this is no excuse for you to do it to them as well. (As a matter of fact, if you are a technical writer who has been a technical reader for a while, you may have to fight your tendency to "write like you have read.")

Even technical readers are busy. If they find themselves having to re-read particular sentences or paragraphs just to understand them, they will get tired. And that could mean they will stop reading before you have finished making your point.

In technical writing, we recommend that you keep your average sentence length to between 8 – 12 words. This is lower than the 10 – 17 average we recommend for general business writing. (Remember, you can figure the average sentence length of any body of writing by counting the total number of words in all the sentences and dividing that number by the total number of sentences or have your word processing software do it for you.)

The reason for shorter sentence length is simple: Technical writing contains a higher proportion of long words because of the technical, scientific or engineering jargon that is inherent in it. If you're going to be using words that are already six or seven syllables long, it just makes sense that you compensate for them in the total length of your sentences so your reader doesn't become overwhelmed.

The same principle holds for the number of major ideas you can afford to place within one sentence. When you are attempting to communicate technical, scientific or analytical material, be gentle with your reader—even your expert reader. Using transitional words at the beginnings of some of your sentences will give you both the benefits of shorter, easier-to-understand ideas and a smooth logical flow among those ideas.

6. Keep paragraphs short and well-structured.

Even if there is no real reason (content-wise) to break a paragraph, break it anyway before it gets longer than ten printed lines. Your reader needs the white space between your ideas in order to rest and check his or her understanding up to that point. Long, rambling paragraphs—even when they contain only one major topic—discourage your reader and contribute to his or her general feeling of being confused or overwhelmed.

7. Summarize frequently in longer or more complex documents.

By occasionally including a paragraph or sentence that summarizes what has been covered so far, you give your readers a touchstone upon which they can verify their understanding. It also provides what could be a needed moment to rest or digest what they have already read.

The summaries you provide can be presented in several different ways:

• Insert a sentence or paragraph beginning with words like *So far in this document, we have illustrated ...*

• Ask a question like *What are the most persuasive points in our position?* Then, of course, you would answer it in a paragraph summarizing those points.

• Provide a chart, table or graph that illustrates the points you wish to summarize.

8. **Employ the principles of graphic design to communicate clearly and quickly to your readers.**

It is imperative that your readers easily follow the information you are presenting because this is what enables them to understand it most clearly. One of the best sets of tools you have in order to make your writing easy to follow comes from the field of graphic design.

There is an entire section in this very manual devoted to the topic of graphic design for this exact reason. You will find it starting on page 272. For our purposes here, though, consider your answers to the following questions as you prepare your next technical, scientific or analytical document:

- Are the margins on the sides of your page large enough to make your document look clear?
- Is the print dark and clear?
- Is the typeface large enough to be easily read but small enough to look like it contains accurate and informed information?
- Is the typeface a style that is easy to read but still professional in appearance?
- Are your paragraphs of varying lengths to give your document visual interest?
- Have you included charts, graphs, illustrations, photographs or tables to illustrate your points?
- Have you accurately labeled all graphics presented in your document?
- Is the paper clean, or is the e-mail message formatted in a way that you are sure your reader will quickly grasp? (And will the formatting you have included in your e-mail translate to your reader's e-mail system?)

Thinking about questions like these will help you create the most beautiful and clear document you can.

Remember: The more beautiful the document looks, the more likely your reader will eagerly read it and give its author the benefit of the doubt.

9. **Keep a personal file of model technical documents.**

You know your technical writing needs better than anyone else, so keeping a personal file of good examples you've seen or received is a logical way to always have some good examples available to model from.

Of course, only you know the material that you need to present. That's why you're the one who is doing this writing to begin with! But formatting and style that has appealed to you can be copied.

Keep a file of technical writing you have appreciated when you received it from others. Also, keep a file of the technical writing you have received from the people you tend to correspond with. This will give you an indication of the styles they prefer. And, of course always keep copies of the writing you do yourself. You will be able to look back on the pieces that got you compliments and learn from the pieces that were less successful.

TONE

Different business documents may have different requirements for formality or lack of formality, but just about every business document needs to convey a warm and positive tone.

Tone in writing is similar to attitude in a conversation. Have you ever spent much time around negative people? Did you ever notice how even when they speak about good news it tends to depress you? Well, the tone of your writing has the same kind of effect. When you write in a style that is cold or negative, your reader won't want to be around you or your writing.

On the other hand, when you write in a conversational and courteous style you will probably automatically achieve the warm positive tone you should be looking for.

Rules

1. Use a conversational tone throughout most business writing.
2. Use a formatting style that is approachable.
3. Use personal pronouns and simple contractions freely in your writing.
4. Keep your tone reader-oriented, not writer-oriented, by using more references to *you*, *your* and *the reader's name* than you do to *I*, *me*, *we* or *us*.
5. It's absolutely okay to have personal references and information in most memos, e-mail and business letters.

Explanations and Examples

1. **Use a conversational tone throughout most business writing.**

   Conversational tone is the tone you would use on the phone or over lunch with your reader. You would probably speak to different readers in slightly different tones (some you might approach more formally, while others more informally), but the rule stands: Write to your reader the way you would speak to your reader. Again, when in doubt, err on the side of formality.

2. **Use a formatting style that is approachable.**

   This includes using the more readable serif typefaces like Times New Roman or Garamond, using letterhead that is attractive, using the indented style for letters and memos (as opposed to block style) and using warm salutations even in your e-mail messages.

   Your reader is overcommunicated—he or she gets way too much mail. Give that reader something to look forward to—a warm, positive relationship with you.

3. **Use personal pronouns and simple contractions freely in your writing.**

   > ▶ It has come to our attention that the security alarm located in the vicinity of the department within which the staff you manage works is in need of repair. We have contacted a repair company that will be working on the alarm next Tuesday morning. Please be prepared for the possibility of the alarm being activated throughout that morning. The repair company has notified us that this may in fact be necessary to recalibrate the system. Thank you for being understanding in this situation.

   The use of personal pronouns like *I*, *you*, *me*, *mine*, *yours*, *theirs* and the like make your writing conversational. So does the use of simple contractions.

   > ▶ Please don't be surprised if your department's work is interrupted next Tuesday morning by our security alarm. We've called a repair company to recalibrate the settings on our general alarm system and we can't be sure they won't need to set it off a few times to find the problem. Thanks for your understanding.

   That's much better than the more formal, less conversational version!

4. **Keep your tone reader-oriented, not writer-oriented, by using more references to *you, your* and *the reader's name* than you do to *I, me, we* or *us*.**

   This is a simple but critical guideline. Most business readers (including you, no doubt) have had the misfortune of reading a document that sounded egotistical—as though the writer didn't care at all about the reader. Avoid this trap by doing a quick count: How many first person references are there in your document? First person references are references to *I, me, we, us, mine* and *our*.

   Compare that number to the number of references you find to *you, your, yours* or *the reader's name* or *company name*. There should be at least twice as many references to the reader as there are to the writer. Edit and make it so.

5. **It's absolutely okay to have personal references and information in most memos, e-mail and business letters.**

   Reports and proposals, of course, should not include personal information—except in the cover letter or memo accompanying them. But for memos, e-mail and letters some appropriate personal references can help warm your reader's mood and regain their attention. It is okay to mention the reader's name in a sentence, for example.

   > Another point we need to make, Mr. Rand, is that our organization has been losing money on this project for ten months.
   >
   > Marika, please respond to me by Friday about this situation.

You can also mention other off-topic items briefly if they relate to your business relationship with the reader.

> Dear Jack,
>
> Our lunch together last Friday helped me to clarify several major ideas we've been discussing this past month.
>
> First, ...

TRANSITIONS

Transitions are words and phrases used by a writer to logically connect the ideas within sentences, paragraphs and documents. Placed between phrases, clauses, sentences or paragraphs, transitions communicate how the ideas expressed are related. Transitions also help the reader keep reading by providing a smooth flow between ideas.

In other words, coherent writing contains transitions that help connect ideas smoothly and logically. Some of the most commonly used examples of transitions are listed in the chart below. Notice that they have several different communication functions:

Common Transitions

To show chronological order:

after	finally	next
afterward	first	now
at last	formerly	previously
before	last	soon
during	later	then
earlier	meanwhile	until
eventually		

To show consequence:

accordingly	hence	then
as a result	otherwise	therefore
consequently	so	thus

To show order of importance:

also	furthermore	next
another	least	one
even greater	more	second
finally	moreover	third
first	most	
for one reason	most important	

To show concession:

anyway	however	nevertheless
at any rate	in any case	of course
even so	in any event	still

To illustrate:

as an example	for example	for instance

To summarize:

after all	in any event	in summary
all in all	in brief	namely
briefly	in conclusion	on balance
by and large	in essence	to summarize
finally	in short	that is
in any case	ultimately	

To show comparison or contrast:

also	instead	on the other hand
although	just as	similarly
besides	like	similar to
both	likewise	so also
but	nevertheless	whereas
however	on the contrary	yet
in contrast		

To show spatial order:

above	beneath	in the distance
ahead	beyond	near
around	in front of	next to
away	inside	outside
behind	in the center	to the right
below		

Rules

The rules for using transitions are simple and straightforward:

1. Use transitions to smooth the flow of your writing.

2. Use commas to separate transition words that interrupt the flow of thought in a sentence and to separate transitions from the main thought of the sentence.

3. Do not use commas to separate a transition word or phrase from the main sentence if that word or phrase is essential to the meaning of the main idea of that sentence.

4. Keep your transitions consistent in form.

Explanations and Examples

1. **Use transitions to smooth the flow of your writing.**

   Remember, one of the main tenets of business writing philosophy is to keep your sentences simple. That means that most sentences should contain no more than one major idea. Therefore, your sentences will be shorter and more straightforward than you are accustomed to. Transitions will help your writing sound less choppy to your reader while preserving the clarity that having only one major idea per sentence provides.

   Of course, transitions also often provide needed meaning in your sentences and paragraphs.

   Notice the difference in meaning between these two sentences ▶

   > Lara has demonstrated an excellent technique for staying on top of the multiple demands of this job. *Likewise,* Stu has created an interesting technique for handling his workload.
   >
   > Lara has demonstrated an excellent technique for staying on top of the multiple demands of this job. *In contrast,* Stu has created an interesting technique for handling his workload.

   The first sentence sounds plain and clear, the second one sounds sarcastic—all because of a different choice of transition words.

2. **Use commas to separate transition words that interrupt the flow of thought in a sentence and to separate transitions from the main thought of the sentence.**

   Whether the transition word comes at the beginning, in the middle or at the end of a sentence—if it is not a part of the main idea of that sentence, it must be separated from the main sentence with a comma or commas.

   > *Ultimately,* Robert and Lorenzo will need to decide the course this project must take.
   >
   > Robert and Lorenzo, *ultimately,* will need to decide the course this project must take.
   >
   > Robert and Lorenzo will need to decide the course this project must take, *ultimately.*

3. **Do not use commas to separate a transition word or phrase from the main sentence if that word or phrase is essential to the meaning of the main idea of that sentence.**

   > ▶ We will take that win *however* we can get it.
   >
   > It is *as a result* of your efforts that these bonuses are possible. Thank you.

4. **Keep your transitions consistent in form.**

   When using the words *primary* and *secondary*, express the third level as *tertiary*, not *third* or *thirdly*.

UNDERLINING

The use of underlining in business writing has declined with the easier availability of italics in word processing software programs. When typewriters were the tools of choice, underlining signified to a typesetter that the author wanted the underlined material to appear in italics.

Today, underlining can still be an effective tool for highlighting important or special information—if it is used in moderation.

Rules

1. Use underlining to emphasize words and short phrases.
2. Proofread carefully to ensure that the underlining you have used has been correctly toggled on and off in your word processor.
3. If you do not have the ability to use italics, use underlining for the titles of complete works (including the names of ships and airplanes), foreign words and phrases and words being used as examples of words.

Explanations and Examples

1. **Use underlining to emphasize words and short phrases.**

   Never underline any section of your writing that is going to be longer than three quarters of one printed line.

   Underlined text is terribly difficult to read quickly. When you (and your reader) learned how to read, it was with most lowercase letters strung together into words. As you became more and more experienced with reading, you built a mental library of what commonly used words looked like. This mental library allowed you to read more and more quickly as you became more and more experienced as a reader. Instead of sounding out each word every time, once you were certain that the combination of letters b-e-f-o-r-e meant *before*, you became a sight reader of that word.

   When those same letters are underlined, your mental library doesn't contain a match for them. So your brain has to work just a little bit harder to understand them as the word *before*.

   This is the same reason that ALL CAPS can be very difficult to read—as a young reader, you learned the skill on most lowercase letters. **Boldface** is your best option for emphasizing longer passages in your writing because it does not interfere with the ability of your brain to find the combination of letters it has already learned.

2. **Proofread carefully to ensure that the underlining you have used has been correctly toggled on and off in your word processor.**

   Because underlining, italics and boldface are toggle switches in your word processor, it is easy to invert them. You may have *thought* you toggled underlining to the *ON* position, but actually you may have toggled it to the *OFF* position. This would reverse the entire document.

3. **If you do not have the ability to use italics, use underlining for the titles of complete works (including the names of ships and airplanes), foreign words and phrases and words being used as examples of words.**

   When possible, of course, italicize these things instead. It is what your reader has come to expect.

   For more information, see Italics, pages 106 – 107.

She has taken a <u>laissez-faire</u> attitude toward her job.
How old were you when you read <u>Illusions</u> the first time?
My son was stationed on the <u>USS Franklin Roosevelt</u> for his first year in the Navy.
The word <u>parameters</u> is a popular one among technical writers.

VERBS

Verbs are the words in sentences that express action or state of being. This section will be devoted to the special issues many writers encounter when dealing with verbs, for example how to use tenses correctly and how to use irregular verbs correctly.

There are four principal forms of all verbs: the present, the present participle, the past and the past participle.

Examples of the verb talk in all four forms ▶

Present:	I often *talk* at branch meetings.
Present Participle:	They *are talking* about the plans for our new Web site.
Past:	You *talked* to the mortgage broker yesterday?
Past Participle:	She *has talked* about leaving before.

Of course, it is the present form of verbs that you find in a dictionary. A comprehensive dictionary will include the other forms of that verb in the listing under the present form. The key concept to remember is that the participial forms of a verb always require a helping verb to accompany the main verb.

▶ They *are* talking.
She *has* talked.

When the verbs you are dealing with are *regular verbs* (most verbs in English are), the way of making those verbs into their different forms is predictable. The past and past participle of regular verbs are made by adding -ed or -d to the end of the present form of the verb. To make the past participle, you also insert the appropriate past tense form of the verb *to be* in front of the main verb. (When the present form of the verb already ends in -e, add just a -d to make the past or past participle.)

Example ▶

Past:	Gene *copied* last quarter's invoices.
	I *welcomed* the new staff members before the meeting started.
Past Participle:	Gene *has copied* last quarter's invoices for the report.
	I *have welcomed* the new staff members already.
OR	I've *welcomed* the new staff members already.

The present participle of most verbs is made by adding the appropriate form of the present tense of *to be* before the verb and an *-ing* suffix to the end of the verb.

I *am saving* money for our future.
He *is recuperating* from his surgery.
They *are delving* deeper into the issue.

It is with irregular verbs that even sophisticated business writers frequently have trouble. The most difficult of all irregular verbs is the verb *to be*.

The good news, though, is that most native English speakers have used the various forms of *to be* so frequently that they know the correct forms by *instinct*.

Present:	I *am* hungry.
Present Participle:	They *are being* foolish.
Past:	You *were* smart to accept their proposal.
Past Participle:	She *has been* lonely in the past.

▲ *Example*

Now that we have covered some of the most difficult points about verbs, here are a few simple guidelines to keep you correct when using them.

Rules

1. If you can't find it in this style guide, check a comprehensive grammar guide or a recent dictionary to determine the form of any verb you are unsure of.

2. Don't worry about keeping an entire document in one tense. It is normal to need more than one tense to clearly communicate your message.

3. Make sure that every verb agrees with its subject.

> *Writer's Tips:*
> *For a description of how to build effective sentences with verbs, see Sentence Structure, pages 181 – 183.*

Explanations and Examples

1. **If you can't find it in this style guide, check a comprehensive grammar guide or a recent dictionary to determine the form of any verb you are unsure of.**

   When in doubt, look it up. This style guide will provide the answers to most of your verb questions, but in case you find yourself needing an irregular verb not listed in this section, check a very detailed grammar guide, an on-line dictionary or a comprehensive printed one.

2. **Don't worry about keeping an entire document in one tense. It is normal to need more than one tense to clearly communicate your message.**

   Many adults remember that they heard somewhere not to change tenses in a document. This advice refers to formal report writing only. It is advice an 11th grade English teacher probably gave you, and it was meant for a report you were writing about *Othello*.

Correct:	As Iago *betrays* Othello, Othello's relationship with Desdemona *falls* apart.
Incorrect:	As Iago *betrayed* Othello, Othello's relationship with Desdemona *falls* apart.

   But in typical business writing, any writer needs more than one tense to express the whole story:

   > Yesterday, the directors held a meeting about where the company needs to focus its energies in the future. It was decided that starting in January, we will devote 50% of the operating budget to the acquisition of new business.

3. **Make sure that every verb agrees with its subject.**

   The easiest way to accomplish this is to keep your subjects and verbs close together in your sentences. It is when many words or phrases come between the subject and verb that the writer can become confused:

NOT:	Marie, one of our most senior *employees, have* applied for the open job in the Administrative department.
BUT:	*Marie*, one of our most senior employees, *has* applied for the open job in the Administrative department.

Irregular Verbs—Present, Past and Participial Forms

Irregular Verbs with the Same Past and Past Participle Forms

Present	Present Participle	Past	Past Participle
bring	(am) bringing	brought	(have) brought
build	(am) building	built	(have) built
buy	(am) buying	bought	(have) bought
catch	(am) catching	caught	(have) caught
fight	(am) fighting	fought	(have) fought
find	(am) finding	found	(have) found
get	(am) getting	got	(have) got OR (have) gotten
hold	(am) holding	held	(have) held
lay	(am) laying	laid	(have) laid
lead	(am) leading	led	(have) led
lose	(am) losing	lost	(have) lost
pay	(am) paying	paid	(have) paid
say	(am) saying	said	(have) said
sit	(am) sitting	sat	(have) sat
spin	(am) spinning	spun	(have) spun
stick	(am) sticking	stuck	(have) stuck
swing	(am) swinging	swung	(have) swung
teach	(am) teaching	taught	(have) taught

Irregular Verbs with Same Present, Past and Past Participle

Present	Present Participle	Past	Past Participle
bid	(am) bidding	bid	(have) bid
burst	(am) bursting	burst	(have) burst
cost	(am) costing	cost	(have) cost
hurt	(am) hurting	hurt	(have) hurt
put	(am) putting	put	(have) put
set	(am) setting	set	(have) set

Irregular Verbs That Change in Other Ways (The Most Irregular of Verbs)

Present	Present Participle	Past	Past Participle
arise	(am) arising	arose	(have) arisen
be	(am) being	was	(have) been
begin	(am) beginning	began	(have) begun
blow	(am) blowing	blew	(have) blown
break	(am) breaking	broke	(have) broken
choose	(am) choosing	chose	(have) chosen
come	(am) coming	came	(have) come
do	(am) doing	did	(have) done
draw	(am) drawing	drew	(have) drawn
drink	(am) drinking	drank	(have) drunk
drive	(am) driving	drove	(have) driven
eat	(am) eating	ate	(have) eaten
fall	(am) falling	fell	(have) fallen
fly	(am) flying	flew	(have) flown
freeze	(am) freezing	froze	(have) frozen
give	(am) giving	gave	(have) given
go	(am) going	went	(have) gone
grow	(am) growing	grew	(have) grown
know	(am) knowing	knew	(have) known
lie	(am) lying	lay	(have) lain
ride	(am) riding	rode	(have) ridden
ring	(am) ringing	rang	(have) rung
rise	(am) rising	rose	(have) risen
run	(am) running	ran	(have) run
see	(am) seeing	saw	(have) seen
shake	(am) shaking	shook	(have) shaken
sing	(am) singing	sang	(have) sung
sink	(am) sinking	sank	(have) sunk
speak	(am) speaking	spoke	(have) spoken
spring	(am) springing	sprang	(have) sprung
swear	(am) swearing	swore	(have) sworn
swim	(am) swimming	swam	(have) swum
take	(am) taking	took	(have) taken
tear	(am) tearing	tore	(have) torn
throw	(am) throwing	threw	(have) thrown
wear	(am) wearing	wore	(have) worn
write	(am) writing	wrote	(have) written

Aside from *form*, verbs also have *tense*. *Tense* is a form of a verb that shows the time of action or state of being. In English, there are six tenses. Each of the six tenses has two kinds of forms—there are six *basic* forms and six *progressive* forms.

The six basic forms make use of the present, past and past participle forms of verbs. Notice this in the chart below:

Tense	Basic Form	Principal Verb Form Used
Present	I sing	Present
Past	I sang	Past
Future	I will sing	Present
Present Perfect	I have sung	Past participle
Past Perfect	I had sung	Past participle
Future Perfect	I will have sung	Past participle

Notice also that four of the verb tenses require helping verbs (future, present perfect, past perfect and future perfect).

The six progressive forms of a verb use only the present participle form of the main verb (ending in *-ing*), combined with the appropriate form of the verb *to be*.

Tense	Basic Form	Principal Verb Form Used
Present	I am singing	Present participle
Past	I was singing	Present participle
Future	I will be singing	Present participle
Present Perfect	I have been singing	Present participle
Past Perfect	I had been singing	Present participle
Future Perfect	I will have been singing	Present participle

And finally, a note about conjugating verbs. To conjugate a verb is to list all the singular and plural forms of a verb in a particular tense. To illustrate, and to provide a helpful list you can use when putting together less frequently used tenses, here is a chart that conjugates the verb *to be* into all six basic tenses.

Conjugation of the Basic Forms of *To Be*

Tense	Singular	Plural	Tense	Singular	Plural
Present	I am	We are	Present Perfect	I have been	We have been
	You are	You are		You have been	You have been
	He, she, it is	They are		He, she, it has been	They have been
Past	I was	We were	Past Perfect	I had been	We had been
	You were	You were		You had been	You had been
	He, she, it was	They were		He, she, it had been	They had been
Future	I will be	We will be	Future Perfect	I will have been	We will have been
	You will be	You will be		You will have been	You will have been
	He, she, it will be	They will be		He, she, it will have been	They will have been

Now, conjugating the progressive form of a verb becomes easier. To conjugate the progressive forms of a verb, add the present participle of the main verb (with the -*ing* ending) to the appropriate conjugation of the basic form of *to be*.

Therefore, to make the past perfect of *write,* start with the past perfect form of *to be*, then add the -*ing* form of *write*.

I *had been* writing	We *had been* writing
You *had been* writing	You *had been* writing
He, she, it *had been* writing	They *had been* writing

WORD PROCESSING

Most every writer in today's workplace uses a commercially produced word processing software program to prepare written documents. The rules for using the various available programs vary, but the guidelines for using word processing programs in general are clear:

Rules

1. Learn the most important elements of the word processing software program you use.

2. Keep an easy-to-use reference manual close by for less frequently used instructions.

3. Decide on a filing format for all documents you save on your hard drive.

4. Make separate backup disks or CDs of your important documents.

5. Pre-write on paper before writing a document in a word processing file.

6. Plan the formatting and design of your document before writing.

7. Use your word processing software to help you proofread and edit your document. But don't take its advice as the final word—always proofread it yourself as well.

8. Remember that not all readers use the same software programs as you do. When sending attached documents in your e-mail, check to make sure your reader has the ability to open them in the format you've sent them. Alternatively, use text files.

Explanations and Examples

1. **Learn the most important elements of the word processing software program you use.**

   You will probably find yourself automatically knowing the elements of your program that you use frequently. But be sure to work at it a little bit too.

2. **Keep an easy-to-use reference manual close by for less frequently used instructions.**

   Rarely is the manual that came with the software the easiest one available. Look into the simpler and more straightforward books available in major book shops and on-line bookstores. Take the time to learn the functions you use at least once a week so you know them without having to look them up. Also, when in doubt, use the Help menu provided in the program. You can usually keep it displayed while you follow the instructions in your written document.

3. **Decide on a filing format for all documents you save on your hard drive.**

   Do you have a consistent way of naming your files? For example, is the date included in the name? Is it the last name of the reader? How about a company name? Do you have separate virtual folders set up for various subjects? Or is everything just dumped together in one large folder, organized only by the alphabetical order the titles of the files fall into?

   Maybe you need a folder for every major client, or a folder for each major project. Perhaps you need subfolders in subfolders! Map it out before writing, when possible. If you are already working with a system of folders that isn't working for you, take the time to reorganize. See our section on Filing (pages 319 – 324) for more information about the methods you can employ in setting up a filing structure.

4. **Make separate backup disks or CDs of your important documents.**

You never know for sure whether or not your hard drive could be vulnerable to a virus that erases important documents, or to a power failure that causes you to lose them. Stay on the safe side. Make frequent backups of your most important documents onto USB flash drives, CDs or DVDs. Store the external backups in an area away from your computer. (We don't mean to be alarmists, but this will keep you safe even if there is a fire or flood.)

5. **Pre-write on paper before writing a document in a word processing file.**

Do you remember mind mapping (pages 117 – 119)? Mind mapping should be done on a blank sheet of paper. Organizing can then be done on that same page, just by writing numbers into the circles of your mind map and adding necessary or deleting unnecessary topics.

Many writers make the mistake of thinking that their computers can speed up their writing process because it is so easy to edit as they write. Of course, you know better now that you have used this style guide. Attempting to edit while you write only leads to writer's block—and a lot of wasted time.

6. **Plan the formatting and design of your document before writing.**

What visual formatting strategies will you use for main headings? Subheadings? How large will indents be and will you use any alternate fonts for emphasis of important ideas? If so, which ones?

These are the kinds of questions to address *before* you randomly begin making choices. Deciding upon these things ahead of time will keep you consistent and clear. Making your choices in the middle of the writing will produce a scattered and confused message.

7. **Use your word processing software to help you proofread and edit your document. But don't take its advice as the final word—always proofread it yourself as well.**

Your spell-checker is a worthy tool for helping you to be accurate, even if it doesn't catch everything (like *from* instead of *form*).

Any grammar checking software is also worth using, although be prepared: Most likely, it will be a better *editor* than *proofreader*. Grammar checking programs are great at telling you that your sentences are too long and that you are using jargon or words with a negative tone. But you will have to be the final judge of correctness in structure and most real grammar.

You can also use the Find command to look for your most frequent errors. If you have a tendency to mis-type *form* as *from*, you can use the Find command to find all the *forms*, then all the *froms* to double-check them.

8. **Remember that not all readers use the same software programs as you do. When sending attached documents in your e-mail, check to make sure your reader has the ability to open them in the format you've sent them. Alternatively, use text files.**

Your document can only be effective if it can be read. And so many computer users do use programs like Microsoft® Word, it can be tempting to forget that not every reader has a copy of that program to open your Word document in. Ask first. Alternatively, you can send a text file.

WORDINESS

Wordiness is the habit of using too many words to express simple ideas, and it is a bad habit.

Most writers were readers before they ever became writers. They probably became used to reading wordy writing, because many business writers have been using it for years. At first, they probably thought it made them sound more intelligent. Now, of course, they are addicted.

It's time to break the habit. Wordy phrases carry no interesting pictures to your reader's brain. They just look like snow does on a cable television connection that has gone down. You know what happens when your television picture turns into snow—you change channels. Don't tempt your reader to push your document away unread.

There is really only one guideline you need to limit wordiness: Edit your writing ruthlessly and substitute a conversational style for all wordy phrases you find.

To help, we have compiled a list of many of the most unnecessary wordy phrases (and some conversational substitutes) business writers have shown us.

In place of ...	Use ...	In place of ...	Use ...
a great deal of	much	in most cases	usually
a large quantity of	many	in other words	or
a majority of	most	in reference to	about
a number of	many	in respect to	about
a sufficient amount	enough	in the absence of	without
all of a sudden	suddenly	in the amount of $200	for $200
along the line of	like	in the event that	if
as a matter of fact	in fact	in the majority of cases	usually
as of this date	today	in the neighborhood of	about or near
as of this time	now	in the proximity of	near
as per	about or regarding	in the vicinity of	near
at a later date	(name the date)	in view of the fact that	considering
at all times	always	is of the opinion that	believes
at present	now	it is clear that	clearly
at the conclusion of	after	it is plain that	plainly
at the present time	now	it would appear that	apparently
at this time	now	last of all	last
based on the fact that	because	make application to	apply
based on the experience of this writer	in my experience	make a purchase	buy
		off of	off
basic essentials	basic or essentials	on account of	because
brought to a sudden halt	stopped	on a few occasions	occasionally
by means of	by	on an ongoing basis	continually
called attention to the fact that	noted	on behalf of	for
come to an end	end	on the grounds that	because
despite the fact that	despite or although	ought to	should
draw to a close	end	owing to the fact that	because
due to the fact that	because	period of time	period
during the course of	during	pertaining to	about
during the time that	while	please do not hesitate to call	please call
enclosed please find	here is	prior to	before
except in a small number of cases	almost always or usually	pursuant to our conversation	as we discussed
		refer back to	refer to
exhibits a tendency to	tends to	relative to	about
few in number	few	repeat again	repeat
for a period of 30 days	for 30 days	revise downward	lower or decrease
for the purpose of	to	seldom if ever	rarely
for the reason that	because	since the time when	since
giving further credence to	supporting	subsequent to	after
in accordance with	under	taking this into consideration	therefore
in addition to	also	there is no question that	unquestionably
in a large number of cases	many times	to be cognizant of	to know
in close proximity to	near	until such time as	until
in consideration of the fact that	because	with regard to	regarding or about
in light of the fact that	because	with the exception of	except
in many cases	often		

YOUR WRITING SPACE

Successful business and technical writers take the time to create a writing space that is comfortable and complete. Make sure you include as many of these components as possible in your normal writing area:

- Good light
- Your preferred computer and writing software
- A fast printer
- This guide
- Any other grammar or style guides you use often
- A fast connection to the Internet
- A good five-pound dictionary
- A reference library
- Plenty of blank white paper
- Some colored paper
- Letterhead, envelopes and any other forms
- Colored pens for proofreading—but not red
- An opaque ruler
- Ideally: A door to close

Good light. A window to the daylight can be ideal for light and to improve your mood, but make sure you also have enough light in your office to comfortably read both from paper and on your computer screen. Requisition a lamp if you need to, but stay in the light.

Your preferred computer and writing software. If you have more than one computer, which one is most comfortable for you to write with? Perhaps you have a very sophisticated desktop computer in your office, but to be honest you prefer your old laptop for writing. In that case, keep your laptop in your writing space. What word processing program do you use? Do you have any specialized writing software, for example a specialized spell- checker for a particular technical or foreign language that you use often in your writing? Have what you need.

A fast printer. You can't judge the quality of something you have just written unless you are reading it on paper. Make it easy to print out your rough drafts and you will find more to correct and more to improve. Your reader will be thrilled.

This guide. It provides a quick and easy reference for your most common questions about style, grammar, graphics and formatting.

Any other grammar or style guides you use often. For example, if you write in the world of academia occasionally, make sure you have a *Chicago Manual of Style*, a *Modern Language Association Handbook*, a *Gregg Reference Manual* or some other very detailed grammar guide. If you write with a particular technical vocabulary, keep handy a reference that defines and spells those words.

A fast connection to the Internet. This saves shelf space. Your best dictionaries are on-line, to say nothing about other reference materials you may need in the course of your particular work.

A good five-pound dictionary. The Internet connection is easier and takes up less space. If you don't have one, you must have a large current dictionary.

A reference library. Information is your lifeblood and you'll come to depend on easy access to a reference library.

Plenty of blank white paper. For mind mapping and organizing your ideas in the pre-writing process and for printing your rough drafts.

Some colored paper. Proofreading on colored paper sometimes helps a writer separate from it enough to be able to spot the errors.

Letterhead, envelopes and any other forms. So you don't have to get up and look for them when you need them.

Colored pens for proofreading—but not red. We recommend green. Find a color or colors that stand out from the page so you will be sure to see the corrections. But avoid red ink—it carries a negative connotation.

An opaque ruler. For reading down a page line by line in proofreading. Reading sentence fragments helps a proofreader stay more focused on the mechanics of the writing than reading whole sentences.

Ideally: A door to close. Privacy is the ideal environment to write in. Realistically, though, you may have to deal with frequent interruptions. In that case, is there a place you can retreat to for your most important writing assignments? Or could you post a sign telling your potential visitors not to interrupt you but that you will be available in 30 minutes? (If you ask for more than 30 minutes, it's unlikely your visitor will wait—he or she will just go ahead and interrupt you.) If you are interrupted, it is usually better to stop writing mid-sentence than to complete that sentence. Your brain will hold on to the rest of your unfinished idea more reliably than it will pick up with a new coherent thought after an earlier finished one.

MODEL BUSINESS DOCUMENTS

E-MAIL

In general, the formatting of e-mail is as much up to the designers of the particular software a writer uses to send the e-mail as it is up to the writer of the e-mail. But there are some formatting ideas that may help you convince your reader to open your e-mail—maybe even convince your reader to read it.

Rules

1. Use concise but clear subject lines in all e-mail. Make sure you tell the reader your most important idea before that reader ever opens the e-mail.

2. Consider using a salutation at the beginning of the body of your e-mail.

3. Use the indented style for the body of your e-mail document and keep your paragraphs short. No paragraph should be longer than eight printed lines.

4. Be sensitive to the limitations of e-mail communication.

5. Finally, keep most e-mails short (one full screen worth).

Explanations and Examples

1. **Use concise but clear subject lines in all e-mail. Make sure you tell the reader your most important idea before that reader ever opens the e-mail.**

   Just like you, your reader probably gets too much e-mail. He or she is most likely shopping for items that don't have to be read. The more appealing and clear your subject line is, the more likely your reader will choose to read yours.

   This topic is also covered in our E-mail section (pages 72 – 75) and our Subject Lines section (page 192). To sum up, don't just tell your reader the topic—tell your reader your most important point about that topic.

   > Astrophysics Budget Increased by Double
   >
   > **NOT**
   >
   > Astrophysics Budget

2. **Consider using a salutation at the beginning of the body of your e-mail.**

   It will warm up your e-mail. Certainly, there are some cases where a *Dear Jim* just wouldn't be appropriate. For example, if you and Jim have been e-mailing back and forth all day about a project you are working on together it would probably be a distraction.

   When you and Jim correspond via e-mail more rarely, it might just help Jim see that you are glad to be in touch with him.

   And, of course, if you start an e-mail with *Dear Jim*, make sure to end it with some kind of informal complimentary close and a signature (usually your typed name). If you have addressed your reader as *Jim* in the salutation, sign your own first name in the closing.

3. **Use the indented style for the body of your e-mail document and keep your paragraphs short. No paragraph should be longer than eight printed lines.**

   This means you should indent the first line of each paragraph and be willing to start new paragraphs even if the subject is the same. Not only will your e-mail be more readable (it's easier to find your place) but it will look more friendly to your reader. E-mail has a reputation for being brusque and even (occasionally) angry. The thoughtful writer does everything he or she can to keep it friendly.

   By keeping your paragraphs no longer than eight printed lines, it is likely that your readers will always be able to see a paragraph break within the window they are reading your e-mail in. This helps them stay energized and allows them to make it to the bottom of your message.

4. **Be sensitive to the limitations of e-mail communication.**

Many elegant formatting changes do not travel well through modems and multiple ISPs. For example, you could use all kinds of wonderful colors in the e-mail you compose on AOL® and it will never get to your reader who is reading it on a private company server. Realize that when your readers range across multiple ISPs, your safest bet for emphasizing particular words is to use ALL CAPS. But as you remember, ALL CAPS for sustained reading is not recommended—it is perceived as shouting.

Also be sensitive to limitations your reader may have in downloading attached files. Does your reader have a copy of the program the file was written in? If not, it may be difficult to open. Does your reader have security limitations imposed by his or her organization? Maybe downloading files is not allowed.

Also, be sensitive to the size of files you attach. Some e-mail programs have limitations on how large the files that are attached can be—to send and to open.

5. **Finally, keep most e-mails short (one full screen worth).**

E-mail, by its very nature, is meant to be for quick and relatively simple communication. If the message you need to send is long or more complex, consider letting your reader know in e-mail that it is on the way and then send it via fax or overnight delivery. Long, complex documents are more easily read by most readers on pages of paper. It is easier for those readers to find a section they'd like to read again or study more thoroughly. Plus it is more portable. Their options for reading it elsewhere or showing it to someone else are increased.

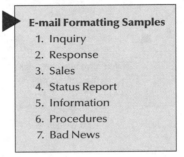

E-mail Formatting Samples
1. Inquiry
2. Response
3. Sales
4. Status Report
5. Information
6. Procedures
7. Bad News

E-mail Format #1: Inquiry

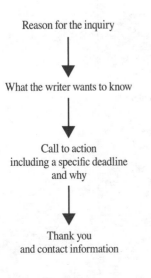

Reason for the inquiry

What the writer wants to know

Call to action
including a specific deadline
and why

Thank you
and contact information

Inquiry Sample

Roger,

Janice and I are going to be designing a new curriculum guide to go with the Project Management Training program you've been presenting for us this past seven months.

Could you forward us a list of the questions you are asked most often, as well as any suggestions you have for what should be included in this guide? As you know, both of us have always valued the comments you've made over these past months.

We were hoping to get started on the pre-writing of the guide at the beginning of March so it will be available to the trainers by April 30, when the new evaluation procedure is set to go into place.

Thanks for your help. Let me know sometime next week if this deadline is reasonable for you. And, as always, call either Janice or me anytime with your questions, concerns or comments.

Have a good week,

Mark

E-mail Format #2: Response

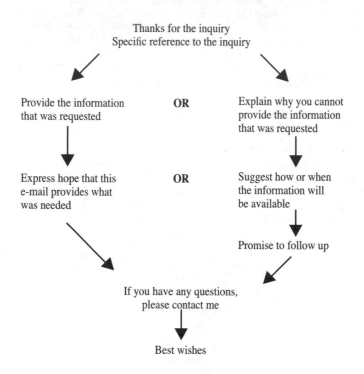

Thanks for the inquiry
Specific reference to the inquiry

Provide the information
that was requested

OR

Explain why you cannot
provide the information
that was requested

Express hope that this
e-mail provides what
was needed

OR

Suggest how or when
the information will
be available

Promise to follow up

If you have any questions,
please contact me

Best wishes

Response Sample

Hi Mark,

Thanks for asking for my input into the Project
Management curriculum guide.

As you know, there are several questions that come up
among participants more often than the rest. But I think I
will be able to do better than that for you. If you can give
me until March 15, I could compile about 50 pages that
you could include in your guide to help the other trainers
be prepared for *everything*.

I am quite busy traveling and teaching these next three
weeks, but I do have the beginning of March free to put it
together for you.

Let me know if my time frame will work for you, or if I
don't hear from you I'll give you a call next Monday.

Roger

E-mail Format #3: Sales

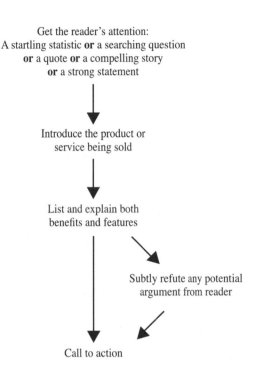

Get the reader's attention:
A startling statistic **or** a searching question
or a quote **or** a compelling story
or a strong statement

Introduce the product or
service being sold

List and explain both
benefits and features

Subtly refute any potential
argument from reader

Call to action

Sales Sample

Have you ever felt like you were wasting your potential? Henry Ford once said, "Whether you think you can or you think you can't—you're right!"

As many successful individuals of his generation did, Mr. Ford knew the secret to true success: positive thinking.

Now, the book that Henry Ford—and a large group of his contemporaries—helped to write, the book that has been a consistent bestseller for over 30 years is available to you on CDs. *Think and Grow Rich*, on 12 CDs, will see you through a month's worth of your commute AND change your life at the same time.

This is the easy way to absorb the most important information you could possibly have—how to control your thinking to produce the success you desire. The set also includes a paperback copy of the book itself, so when there are points you'd like to study more closely (and there WILL be), the information will be at your fingertips.

Do yourself—and the world—a favor. Achieve your dreams. Don't listen to the negativist who tells you that self-help books and CDs don't work. Think about it: Is THAT person's life working the way you want yours to? To get a better result you need to feed your mind better information.

To order your copy, risk-free, reply to this e-mail and ask us to ship you a trial copy. Or call us at 1-800-555-1212 with your questions. Don't wait another day to become the person you know you can be.

E-mail Format #4: Status Report

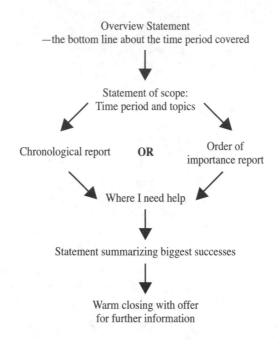

Overview Statement
—the bottom line about the time period covered

↓

Statement of scope:
Time period and topics

Chronological report   **OR**   Order of
importance report

Where I need help

↓

Statement summarizing biggest successes

↓

Warm closing with offer
for further information

Status Report Sample

Bob,

The Customer Service department has had an exceptional week in all three areas I normally cover in this report: Sales, Service and Courtesy.

Most important, we sold 232 new subscriptions to customers who already subscribe to another of our publications. This is an improvement over last week of over double, and an improvement over last year at this same time of 35%. I believe we are on a roll!

The service calls were down this week, which is always good. Of the 192 service calls that came in, we were able to resolve 183 of them here. The other nine were forwarded to our software support contractor. This is also an improved statistic—I think it shows that our reps are becoming more and more knowledgeable about how to help our customers themselves.

We logged only one complaint about a customer service rep this week, a call that I took myself. The individual's complaint concerned the tone of voice he perceived as coming from our rep. I have spoken with this rep and am convinced that the problem will not occur again. (I gave him a mirror to put on his desk and told him to look into it and smile while he was talking to our customers on the phone. As you know, it works every time.)

By the way, could you forward me a copy of the speech Jack gave at the awards banquet last week? I've told some of my staff about it and they'd like to see it.

Well, it's been a week I'm proud to write about. Those sales statistics really impressed me!

Let me know if you need any more details about any of this. See you Monday morning at the staff meeting.

Lee

E-mail Format #5: Information

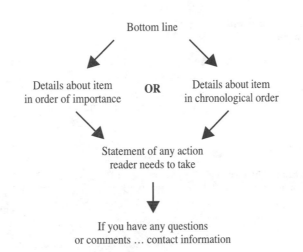

Bottom line

Details about item
in order of importance

OR

Details about item
in chronological order

Statement of any action
reader needs to take

If you have any questions
or comments ... contact information

Information Sample

Dear Customer Service Reps,

Just to let you know, there will be an awards banquet held on the first Thursday of next month during our normal lunch hour—which will be expanded to a full hour.

The Customer Service awards for April will be presented and Gary Sanderson, the Training Director, will give a presentation about listening skills. I have heard he is very funny and informative.

Please make plans to attend—remember, we buy lunch. There's a sign-up sheet posted in the break room. Please let us know you'll be there by March 23.

Stop in and see me if you have any questions.

Lee

E-mail Format #6: Procedures

Statement of what the procedure will
give reader the ability to do

When the reader may not want
to do the task: Compelling
reasons for doing it, unsettling
consequences for not doing it

Step One:
How to do it
What you will see when it is finished
Likely troubleshooting notes

Step Two:
How to do it
What you will see when it is finished
Likely troubleshooting notes

All steps, in order, in this format

List of other resources to check,
including writer's contact information

Quick reminder of reader's ability
or the benefits of following the procedure

Procedures Sample

To: Project Management Trainers

From: Mark Cohen and Janice LeBlanc,
       Curriculum Coordinators

RE: Project Management Curriculum Guide

Hi everyone,

This e-mail details the procedure we need you each to follow
in order to get a copy of the brand new Project Management
Curriculum Guide.

First, send us an e-mail right away and let us know that you are
interested in having a copy. We will send you a confirmation
of your request within the day. Please SAVE that confirmation.
You might need to show it to the Publications Department if
you pick the guide up there yourself.

Second, visit our Web site and download the rough draft of the
guide. You can do that by pressing the green button in the upper
left-hand corner of the Web page that says DOWNLOAD NOW.
It will take close to ten minutes—don't panic.

Third, once you have downloaded the guide, glance through
it for us and make sure it contains everything you want and
need—within reason, of course. Let us know via e-mail BY
FRIDAY, MARCH 22 if there are any changes you think must
be made.

The completed guides will be printed and ready to go by
April 25, according to Joann Montero over in Publications.
We will let you know then how to get your copy in time for
your programs that next week.

Thanks for your contributions to this guide. You, after all, are
the experts who meet our employees across the U.S. every
day and you are the ones who hear their questions, needs and
concerns in the area of Project Management.

Have a great month. We'll be in touch soon.

Mark and Janice

E-mail Format #7: Bad News

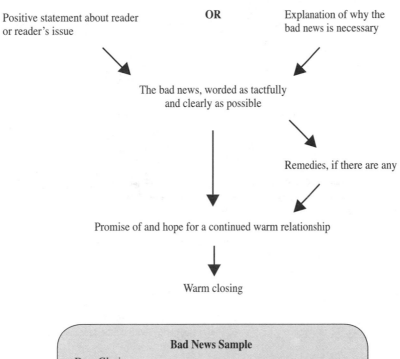

Positive statement about reader or reader's issue

OR

Explanation of why the bad news is necessary

The bad news, worded as tactfully and clearly as possible

Remedies, if there are any

Promise of and hope for a continued warm relationship

Warm closing

Bad News Sample

Dear Gloria,

You have been a great asset to this department every day that you have been here, for the past nine years.

That's why it hurts me to tell you that your request for a 20% pay increase has been denied by the Vice President of Finance. As we discussed last week, I was doubtful about it from the start. But I did express my support for you to the Vice President.

She suggested that if we changed your title from Administrative Assistant to Management Liaison and added a few duties to your job description that relate to project management, she might be able to swing 10%.

It's not that your actual job would change, of course— you already are the best project manager we have in the department. But maybe it's worth a try. What do you think?

As always, I treasure our relationship—both professionally and personally. If you need a shoulder, I'm here.

Margie

LETTERS

Although the formatting guidelines for business letters are moderately flexible, there are certain parts or elements that they all contain. Other elements are optional. Here's the full list:

Element	Status	Element	Status
Letterhead	Required	Subject Line	Optional
Date	Required	Body	Required
Reference Line	Optional	Complimentary Closing	Required
Delivery Notation	Optional	Signature Block	Required
Inside Address	Required	Administrative Notations	Optional
Attention Line	Optional	Postscript	Optional
Salutation	Required	Continuation Sheet Headings	Optional

On the following pages you will see an example letter that contains all of these elements. The first version of pages one and two of this letter appear in the *indented style*. Then, we show you the same letter in the *block style*. Either one of these formatting styles works. Use the one you are most comfortable with.

Of course, as you examine these letters, please keep in mind that you would probably never write a letter that needs every single one of these elements! (Letter formats are continued on pages 222 – 237.)

Element Guidelines

Letterhead

- Use letterhead for the first page of every business letter. Use blank pages (with continuation sheet headings) for all following pages.
- Center your letter within equal left and right margins that line up well with the printed letterhead.
- Leave at least three lines between the bottom of the letterhead and the date of your letter.

Date

- Place the date either flush left (block style) or five to ten spaces to the right of center (indented style). When using the indented style, your complimentary closing and signature block will be typed at the same tab position as the date. Type the date at least three lines below the bottom of the letterhead.
- Fully spell out the month and use the full year (January 23, 2010 or 23 January 2010, not Jan. 23, '10).
- The only comma needed in a date is a comma between the day and the year. Do not put a comma between the month and the year. (January 23, 2010 is correct. 23 January, 2010 is not.)

Reference Line

- Use a reference line if your reader needs a quick notation to help him or her find a file number, a customer number or the like.
- If you use a reference line, always include it as part of any continuation sheet heading.

Delivery Notations

- If the letter is sent in any other way but First Class mail, note the method in ALL CAPS above the inside address. (Examples: BY FAX, BY HAND, FEDERAL EXPRESS.)
- If any special restrictions or other notes apply to the letter, they can also be placed in ALL CAPS in this spot. (Examples: CONFIDENTIAL, PERSONAL.)

Letter Format: Indented Style

Perfect Letters, Inc.
12900 South Lake Avenue, Lakewood, OH 44107
Phone (216) 555-5211 • E-mail perfect@letters.let

May 8, 2010
Reference: Job #32-345

FEDERAL EXPRESS

Attn: Mr. Stanley Lupinski, Auditor
American Comma Company
987 East Comma Way
New York, NY 10017

Dear Mr. Lupinski:

SUBJECT: Rush Order—1,000,000 Commas Needed by June 1, 2010

This letter follows up on our phone conversation this morning. We at Perfect Letters, Inc. are ordering 1,000,000 commas that must be delivered to us by June 1, 2010. We have agreed to pay express delivery charges and our standard rate of $49.95 per 100,000.

Please call me by May 12, 2010 if you will be unable to fill this order on time.

Grammatically yours,

John

John F. O'Malley
President

JFO/mfp
cc: Purchasing Department

P.S. Thanks again for accepting this rush order—as you know, our clients' sentences have been getting longer and longer, so our need is pressing!

The continuation sheet headings (known as headers in your word processing software package) would look like this:

American Comma Company
May 8, 2010
Page 2

Letter Format: Block Style

Perfect Letters, Inc.
12900 South Lake Avenue, Lakewood, OH 44107
Phone (216) 555-5211 • E-mail perfect@letters.let

May 8, 2010
Reference: Job #32-345

FEDERAL EXPRESS

Attn: Mr. Stanley Lupinski, Auditor
American Comma Company
987 East Comma Way
New York, NY 10017

Dear Mr. Lupinski:

SUBJECT: Rush Order—1,000,000 Commas Needed by June 1, 2010

This letter follows up on our phone conversation this morning. We at Perfect Letters, Inc. are ordering 1,000,000 commas that must be delivered to us by June 1, 2010. We have agreed to pay express delivery charges and our standard rate of $49.95 per 100,000.

Please call me by May 12, 2010 if you will be unable to fill this order on time.

Grammatically yours,

John F. O'Malley
President

JFO/mfp
cc: Purchasing Department

P.S. Thanks again for accepting this rush order—as you know, our clients' sentences have been getting longer and longer, so our need is pressing!

When using the block style, the continuation sheet headings (known as headers in your word processing software package) would look like this:

American Comma Company
May 8, 2010
Page 2

Attention Line

- Use an attention line to bring a letter addressed to a whole organization or a whole department to the attention of a particular individual in that organization or department. This is most likely the individual who will carry your message through his or her organization.

- An attention line can be placed on the top line of the inside address OR after the inside address, following one blank line.

Inside Address

- The inside address contains as much of this information as you have:

  Your reader's courtesy title and full name

  Your reader's job title

  Department name or routing code

  Organization name (full and formal)

  Street address

  City, state and zip code (or for foreign countries: city, post code)

  (Foreign only) Country

- Fully spell out all first names, last names, titles, department names and organization names, street names, cities and countries. Spell out the word instead of using the symbols + or &. Like this:

  Mr. Jonathan K. Larson

  Assistant Director of Human Resources

  General Motors Corporation

  But not like this:

  Mr. Jon Larson

  Asst. Director, HR

  GM

- Use numerals for all street numbers and addresses. In general, use numbers for all numbered streets and avenues that are at least two digits. Use spelled out words for single digit numbered streets and avenues. (Example: 234 West 42nd Street; 876 Second Avenue.)

- Spell out *North, South, East* and *West* when they appear before a street name. Use abbreviations when they come after the street name. (Examples: 67 South Jewell; 13256 Gary Avenue SW)

- The correct spacing on the city, state, zip code line is:

  City, (one space) STATE CODE (two spaces) ZIP code

Writer's Tips:
You will find a listing of state abbreviations on page 19.

Salutations

- Always use the correctly spelled specific name of your reader whenever possible. Make a phone call to discover it, if you must.

- Use a comma after the salutation if you've used their first name. Otherwise, use a colon.

- If you must use something other than the correctly spelled specific name of your reader in your salutation, here are your best options:

  Single reader, name unknown:

Options	**Examples**
Dear Job Title:	Dear Human Resources Manager:
Dear Department:	Dear Credit Department:
Dear Company Name: (only for small companies)	Dear Utah Metals: (not Dear General Motors)

Multiple readers:

Which title would apply to all of the readers?

Dear Employee:

Dear Parent:

Dear Voter:

Dear Client:

Avoid complimentary adjectives when using these generic titles. They make you sound insincere.

AVOID:

Dear Diligent Employee:

Dear Busy Parent:

Dear Concerned Voter:

Dear Valued Client:

The American Management Style

Another option available to today's business writer is to leave out the salutation altogether. Replace it with a subject line. Be cautioned that some readers will be offended. But that number is dwindling.

If you can accept that one of the main reasons to use a salutation is to make sure your letter reaches the right desk very quickly, using a subject line could be your most logical choice. Some examples:

SUBJECT: Payment of 2009 Income Tax, SS# 123-45-6789

RE: Base Road Closures Effective 11-1-09

Of course, the other good reason for a salutation is to begin the rapport building process, which always seems to work better with a name.

Subject Line

- If you use a subject line and a salutation, the subject line can be placed either above the salutation (after the inside address) or below the salutation (above the body of the letter). In either case, there should be a single blank line both above and below the subject line.

- Place your subject line either flush left, indented one tab position or in the center of the line. (Once you choose, by the way, be consistent in all the letters you write.)

- Introduce your subject line with an introductory word or abbreviation. Use the word SUBJECT or the abbreviation RE followed by a colon (see page 192 for an explanation of the difference). When centering the subject line, it is permissible to leave off the introductory word.

- Choose a style for presenting your subject line and stick with it. All of these are acceptable:

    SUBJECT: Base Road Closures Effective 11-01-09

    SUBJECT: Base Road Closures Effective 11-01-09

    SUBJECT: BASE ROAD CLOSURES EFFECTIVE 11-01-09

    Subject: Base road closures effective 11-01-09

    RE: Base Road Closures Effective 11-01-09

The choices you need to make are:

Boldface or not?

All caps or not?

Initial caps or not?

Which introductory word will you use?

Make the choices that appeal to you and then *be consistent*.

- A subject line may be up to two lines long in a letter.
- Finally, use subject lines that sum up the most important elements of your letter. But don't make them too long. Try to keep them under one printed line.

Body

- Choose either the block style or the indented style for the body of your letter. In the block style, every line starts flush left. In the indented style, every paragraph begins with a line that is indented 5 – 10 spaces.
- Keep your message concise, but remember that clarity is your number one goal. It is better to have a two-page document that has plenty of white space than a one-page document that looks cramped.
- Keep your paragraphs shorter than ten printed lines, but do your best to vary their lengths. This keeps your reader interested.

Complimentary Closing

- Use a complimentary closing before your signature. Your reader expects it and it helps to create rapport.
- Use an appropriate complimentary closing—one that matches the message of your letter. Don't be afraid of *Sincerely* just because it seems overused, but consider other options: *Yours truly*, *Respectfully*, *Sincerely yours*, *Regards*, *Best regards* are some options.
- When using a complimentary closing longer than a single word, capitalize only the first letter of the first word.
- In a block style letter, place the complimentary closing flush left. In an indented style letter, line up the complimentary closing (and the signature block) with the date.

Signature Block

- Sign your name under the complimentary closing and above your typed name and perhaps job title or department (if they are not printed on the letterhead). If you have a close relationship with the reader and the letter is casual, sign just your first name above your full printed name.
- In a block style letter, place the signature block flush left. In an indented style letter, line it up with the complimentary closing and the date.

Administrative Notations

- Place all notations like the initials of the author, initials of the typist, copies and enclosures flush left at least two lines below the last line of the signature block.

    Examples:

    RD/mc

    cc: Roger Davis

      Mark Cohen

    Enclosures: 2010 Lease

            Contract Addendum

Postscript

- A postscript, especially a handwritten one, can be a great way to reaffirm your most important point in your reader's mind. It is often said by readability experts that if your reader reads nothing else, he or she tends to read a handwritten PS.
- Never make the first mention of something important in a postscript. You look disorganized or forgetful.
- The PS should appear at least two blank lines below your last administrative notation, flush left. You may use either the abbreviation PS or P.S.

Continuation Sheet Headings

When your letter is longer than one page, put headings on each continuation sheet to help your reader stay organized. These headings will contain the page number, as well as other identifying information about your letter. Usually, this is the date of the letter and the person whom it is addressed to. If there is a reference line on the first page of the letter, that reference line could also be a part of the continuation sheet headings.

Your word processing software makes it easy to produce these headings. Check the Help files in your software package and use the headers it provides. The Help files will give you tips on how to use them.

Letter Formatting Samples

1. Information
2. Request
3. Complaint
4. Response
5. Employment Reference
6. Sales
7. Resume Cover Letter
8. Bad News

Letter Format #1: Information

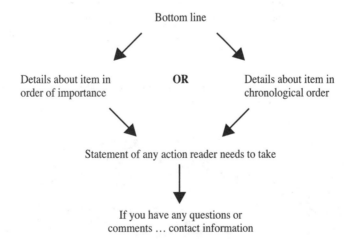

Sample Information Letter

Perfect Letters, Inc.
12900 South Lake Avenue, Lakewood, OH 44107
Phone (216) 555-5211 • E-mail perfect@letters.let

March 16, 2010

Ms. Marilyn McHale
Marketing Manager
Exel Corporation
1231 S. Main St.
Seattle, WA 66139

Dear Ms. McHale:

This is to let you know that the 50,000 brochures you ordered from us on February 25 will be ready to ship on March 23.

We were delighted that a few of our part-time employees agreed to increase their hours for these past few weeks to help us accommodate your short deadline. We're sure you're going to be quite pleased with the quality as well.

Unless we hear from you, we will assume that you still want these brochures delivered to your Lenexa office via UPS.

Please call me if you have any questions or concerns. Thanks for your ongoing confidence in us.

Sincerely,

John Nicholson
Service Representative

JN/cac

<u>Letter Format #2: Request</u>

Reason for the request

A statement of what the writer wants the reader to do

Call to action including a specific deadline and why

Thank you and contact information

Sample Request Letter

John and Marie Papadapoulos
12900 South Lake Avenue
Lakewood, OH 44107

(546) 555-5211

October 14, 2009

Harborview Interiors
Attn: Floor Coverings
45 Canal Street
Cleveland, OH 44102

Subject: Price Quote—Polished Oak Flooring

I am planning to replace the floors in three rooms of the house my wife and I are currently living in with Sanderson Polished Oak Flooring (#32498). The room measurements are 14 x 20 (great room), 12 x 12 (kitchen) and 12 x 18 (nook/dining area). The great room is presently carpeted and the kitchen and nook are covered with linoleum.

Could you please give me a rough idea of the costs I can expect? Certainly, I am hoping to know how much the boards themselves will cost. But could you also give me an idea of the costs I am facing in preparing the floors ahead of time?

Please e-mail me or call me with your best estimate sometime before the end of this week. We hope to purchase the materials this weekend and get started by next Monday.

Thanks for your help.

John

John Papadapoulos
JPapa@mine.com
(440) 555-0904

JP/mis

Letter Format #3: Complaint

Introduce and give background of complaint

↓

Describe events surrounding the complaint itself

↓

Express the emotion and the effect on the relationship

↓

Action writer is suggesting to rectify the situation

↓

Contact information

Sample Complaint Letter

Jeffrey McCrea
4322 S. Downing Street
Englewood, CO 80119
(216) 555-5211

October 3, 2009

Mr. Michael Torkelson, Manager
Patty's Pancake Pan
78099 Marginal Highway 80
Indianapolis, IN 46201

Dear Mr. Torkelson:

Last Sunday, October 1, my family stopped at your restaurant for breakfast. We were on the way home to Denver from a visit with my wife's parents in Chicago and had driven all night.

We were treated very well up until we received our food. Our waitress, Bonnie, was cordial and polite. She wrote our order down carefully. Apparently, her shift ended before our meal was ready to be served. So, I flagged down another waitress 20 minutes later and asked about our order. That waitress, who was not wearing a name badge, told us that we had already received our food.

Obviously, this was not the truth. When I explained (politely), she rolled her eyes and said, "It's not my problem."

Ultimately, our breakfasts did appear 10 minutes later, brought to us by a cook. And the food was fine. But quite frankly, our appetites had already been spoiled by the rude treatment we received at the hands of that other waitress.

I would appreciate it if you would respond and let me know that you have received this letter and tell me what you can do to make sure that no other tired traveler has to face this kind of treatment at your restaurant.

You can reach me at the address or e-mail address listed below.

Sincerely,

Jeffrey McCrea
4322 S. Downing Street
Englewood, CO 80119
JeffreyMcC@isp.com

JM/es

Letter Format #4: Response

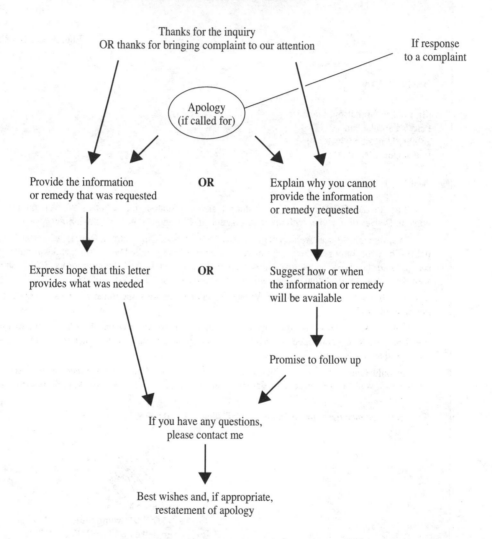

Thanks for the inquiry
OR thanks for bringing complaint to our attention

If response
to a complaint

Apology
(if called for)

Provide the information
or remedy that was requested

OR

Explain why you cannot
provide the information
or remedy requested

Express hope that this letter
provides what was needed

OR

Suggest how or when
the information or remedy
will be available

Promise to follow up

If you have any questions,
please contact me

Best wishes and, if appropriate,
restatement of apology

Sample Response Letter

Patty's Pancake Pan

78099 Marginal Highway 80 • Indianapolis, IN 46201
Phone (317) 562-0299 • E-mail michael@pancakes.let

October 7, 2009

Mr. Jeffrey McCrea
4322 S. Downing Street
Englewood, CO 80119

Dear Mr. McCrea:

Thank you for writing to tell me of the way one of the waitresses here at Patty's Pancake Pan treated you last Sunday. I hope you will accept my apologies—we know that it is families like yours that provide us with the great reputation we've had in the "Dining on the Road" community for 12 years.

I've discovered who it was that treated you in such a rude manner and we have had a talk. I also have the other waitresses watching her occasionally to make sure that the incident you told me of is not repeated—in any way.

I have also enclosed a $40 gift certificate good at any of our locations anytime within the next year. (I understand there is a Patty's Pancake Pan near the junction of I-225 and I-70 in east Denver.)

If you have any further comments or any questions, please do call me collect any morning Tuesday—Saturday between 5 a.m. and 1 p.m., Central Time.

Best wishes to you and your family and thank you once again for letting me know about your experience.

Yours truly,

Michael

Michael Torkelson
Restaurant Manager
MT/kl

P.S. Your original waitress, Bonnie, asked me to tell you how sorry she is that this happened to you as well. She remembers you and what she says is a charming family and asked me to tell you that your four children were some of the best behaved she's seen in a while. She told me that not one of them hit or punched any of the others for the entire 15 minutes she knew them. (That's something we don't usually see at the Pancake Pan.)

Letter Format #5: Employment Reference

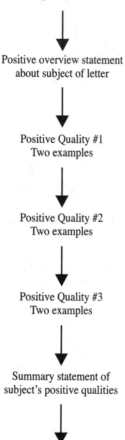

Reference to why writer is writing
(including name of referrer)

Positive overview statement
about subject of letter

Positive Quality #1
Two examples

Positive Quality #2
Two examples

Positive Quality #3
Two examples

Summary statement of
subject's positive qualities

Warm closing and contact information

Sample Employment Reference Letter

⪢ COUNTY GENERAL ⪡
SURGERY CENTER

June 24, 2010

Dr. Lorenzo Mazano
Director of Surgery
Faith Community Hospital
New Bedford, MA 07877

RE: Reference for Dr. Charles R. Christopher

Dear Dr. Mazano:

Dr. Charles Christopher has asked me to write this reference to you. He and his wife Cathy have decided to move to New Bedford and—sadly for me—there's nothing I can do to talk them out of it. He is the most qualified, careful and calm surgeon I've had the pleasure of working with in the past ten years.

Dr. Christopher came to us from the Cleveland Clinic, where he had risen to become the head of the Emergency Surgery department. He started here as a Trauma Team Surgeon, but within a year had become Director of Surgery for us, a position he has served in for nine years. You probably have copies of his transcripts from Harvard Medical, but did you know he graduated number three in his class?

The concern he shows in three areas has always been remarkable. First, and most important, Dr. Christopher is a meticulously careful surgeon. I can think of three occasions in the past year alone where his attention to detail saved a patient from a second surgery.

Second, Dr. Christopher is one of the few surgeons we know who will take the time to carefully file the ever-increasing load of paperwork the HMOs have been demanding. I'm sure you work with many surgeons who leave that job to the nursing assistants.

And third, he brings his meticulous nature to the training he provides the other doctors and staff. He is patient with people, and doesn't give up on anyone.

We hate to see him go, but at least the Faith Community Hospital can benefit from our loss. If you need any further information, please call me anytime. I'm always happy to tell the stories we've accumulated here about Dr. Christopher.

Sincerely,

Dr. Steven Ross
Hospital Administrator

SR/bkm

5548 HOLLYWOOD BOULEVARD • LONG BEACH, CA 90802 • (301) 366-8315

Letter Format #6: Sales

Get the reader's attention:
A startling statistic **or** a searching question
or a quote **or** a compelling story
or a strong statement

↓

Introduce the product or
service being sold

↓

List and explain both
benefits and features

↓

Subtly refute any potential
argument from reader

↓

Call to action

Sample Sales Letter

Book End Club
72902 Blair Street, Seattle, WA 98111 • (206) 955-5211

July 2, 2010

Ms. Nancy Patrick
132 Cherry Lane
Middleford, IA 56544

Dear Ms. Patrick:

Have you ever felt like you were wasting your potential? Henry Ford once said, "Whether you think you can or you think you can't—you're right!"

As many successful individuals of his generation did, Mr. Ford knew the secret to true success: positive thinking.

Now, the book that Henry Ford—and a large group of his contemporaries—helped to write, the book that has been a consistent bestseller for over 30 years, is available to you on CDs.

Think and Grow Rich, on 12 CDs, will see you through a month's worth of your commute and change your life at the same time.

This is the easy way to absorb the most important information you could possibly have—how to control your thinking to produce the success you desire. The set also includes a paperback copy of the book itself, so when there are points you'd like to study more closely (and there will be), the information will be at your fingertips.

Do yourself—and the world—a favor. Achieve your dreams. Don't listen to the negativist who tells you that self-help books and CDs don't work. Think about it: Is that person's life working the way you want yours to? To get a better result you need to feed your mind better information.

To order your copy, risk-free, reply to this letter and ask us to ship you a trial copy. Or call us at 1-800-555-1212 with your questions. Don't wait another day to become the person you know you can be.

Yours truly,

Susan C. Smithson
Fulfillment Representative

SCS/ma

P.S. These will go quickly—act today!

<u>Letter Format #7: Resume Cover Letter</u>

I am applying for
_____ position

My resume is enclosed

I am a good match for this
position because
(list three reasons)

Contact information

I will call you
(date and time)

Thank you

Sample Resume Cover Letter

Susan Prendergast
123 Main Street
Baltimore, MD 21201

May 28, 2010

Mr. Jackson Reinhart
Human Resources Director
Cargill Institute
P.O. Box 5
Moline, IL 62122

Dear Mr. Reinhart:

I am applying for the position of Technical Writer that was advertised in Sunday's *Moline Register*. My resume is enclosed.

I've been a technical writer with the Cleveland Institute of Electronics for eight years and am the author of their top-selling Degree Program correspondence course. My husband was recently transferred to the Quad Cities and the opening you have seems ideally suited to me.

I will be in Moline starting June 1. You can reach me on my cell phone at (410) 555-3432 or via e-mail at techiewrite@isp.com. If I haven't heard from you, I will call you with our phone number and address in Moline once we have established ourselves.

Thank you.

Yours truly,

Susan

Susan Prendergast

Enclosure

Business Writing

Letter Format #8: Bad News

Positive statement about reader or reader's issue   **OR**   Explanation of why the bad news is necessary

The bad news, worded as tactfully and clearly as possible

Remedies, if there are any

Promise of and hope for a continued warm relationship

Warm closing

Sample Bad News Letter

 Good Credit
Mortgage Co.
123 Broadway
Los Angeles, CA 92323

April 20, 2010

Mr. and Mrs. Paul Riveras
2312 Hilltop Drive #2
Lawrence, CA 93212

Dear Mr. and Mrs. Riveras:

We have reviewed your mortgage application, checked your references and looked over the information you provided about your outstanding negative credit items.

Unfortunately, we are not able to approve the application you have made for the purchase of the property on Oak Street. Although your references are great, and your explanations about the negative items on your credit report seem logical, the formula our bank uses to determine loan eligibility just doesn't allow us to write your 95% loan.

If there is a way you could increase your down payment to 10%, or find a co-borrower who already owns a home, chances are good we could fund a mortgage.

Thanks for coming to us, and please let me know if we might be able to help you in the future.

Yours truly,

Michael

Michael Dillon
Mortgage Specialist

MD/jm

MEMOS

Since the advent of e-mail, interoffice memos are not as common as they used to be. But they are still sometimes necessary and useful. The formatting requirements of most memos are relatively flexible and certainly dependent upon the conventions of the organization the writer works in.

In general, though, a memo contains these parts:

- Heading
- Body
- (Signature line)
- Reference initials
- Attachment notation
- Courtesy copy notation

Heading: The heading of a memo must contain the date, the names of the people the memo is being sent to, the name of the person the memo being sent by and a subject line containing a capsule version of the most important point of the memo.

Most of this is very straightforward. Be vigilant about using subject lines that accurately and clearly communicate your most important point. The topic is not enough: What is the point about the topic?

One line is the maximum length of a subject line for a memo.

Body: The body contains your message. Make sure to put your most important idea in the first paragraph and to use some logical organizing format to communicate the rest of your information.

(Signature line): A memo does not require a signature line, but a little handwriting on any printed document can get your reader's attention in a positive way. It will also make your memo look more personal.

An alternative to a signature line is for the author to initial next to his or her name in the heading.

Reference initials: The author's initials are typed in capital letters, the typist's initials are typed in lowercase letters with a slash or a colon separating them.

Attachment notation: As in a letter, a list of any attached items is presented.

Courtesy copy notation: Also as in a letter, a list of all other parties who will be receiving a copy of this memo and who were not listed in the **TO** line of the heading. In some cases, the copy notation is listed after the subject line of the heading.

Again, memos are simple and a little flexibility with this format is to be expected in most organizations. As always, keep a file of memos that have been well received in your own organization to use as samples and model documents.

Memo Formatting Samples

1. Inquiry
2. Response
3. Status Report
4. Information
5. Procedures
6. Bad News

Here's an example:

DATE: March 31, 2009
TO: Don Jameson, Margot Dimitri, Fred Aguerra
FROM: John Eastman
SUBJECT: Possible Need to Postpone Employee Reviews Until 4-15-09

As you may know, the Human Resources department has recommended that we update our procedures for reviewing all employees. The new forms will be available by April 15. (A proof copy is attached to this memo.)

If possible, please postpone any reviews you may have scheduled between now and then so that you can use the new forms for all reviews from April 15 on.

As soon as the forms are ready, I will bring each of you a set and point out the differences between them and the older ones. I will also answer any questions you may have about them or about the necessity for the changes.

Call or stop in if there is anything you want to discuss.

John

JE/edh
Att: Proof copy of employee review sheet, effective 4-15-09
cc: Dolores Harris, Human Resources Director

Memo Format #1: Inquiry

Reason for the inquiry

↓

What the writer wants to know

↓

Call to action—include a specific deadline and why

↓

Thank you and contact information

Sample Inquiry Memo

DATE: February 15, 2009
TO: Richard Campbell
FROM: Michael Cohen
SUBJECT: We Need Your Input—Project Management Curriculum Guide

Susan LeBlanc and I are going to be designing a new curriculum guide to go with the Project Management Training program you've been presenting for us this past seven months.

Would you forward us a list of the most frequently asked questions, as well as any suggestions you have for what should be included in this guide? As you know, both of us value the comments you've made over these past months.

We were hoping to get started on the pre-writing of the guide at the beginning of March so it will be available to the trainers by April 30, when the new evaluation procedure is set to go into place.

Thanks for your help. Let me know sometime next week if this deadline is reasonable for you. And, as always, call either Susan or me anytime with your questions, concerns or comments.

Have a good week!

Michael

Memo Format #2: Response

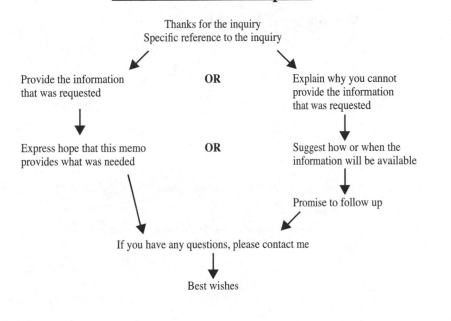

Thanks for the inquiry
Specific reference to the inquiry

Provide the information
that was requested   **OR**   Explain why you cannot
provide the information
that was requested

Express hope that this memo
provides what was needed   **OR**   Suggest how or when the
information will be available

Promise to follow up

If you have any questions, please contact me

Best wishes

Sample Response Memo

DATE: February 16, 2009
TO: Michael Cohen
FROM: Richard Campbell
SUBJECT: How I Can Help with Your Curriculum Guide

Thanks for asking for my input into the Project Management Curriculum Guide.

As you know, there are a number of questions that come up among participants more often than others. But I think I will be able to provide more than just a list for you. If you can give me until March 15, I will compile about 50 pages that you could include in your guide to help the trainers be prepared for everything.

While I am quite busy traveling and teaching these next three weeks, I do have the beginning of March free to put it together for you.

Let me know if my time frame will work for you, or if I don't hear from you I'll give you a call next Monday.

Richard

Memo Format #3: Status Report

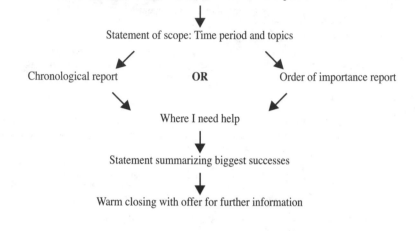

Overview Statement—the bottom line about the time period covered

↓

Statement of scope: Time period and topics

↙   **OR**   ↘

Chronological report   Order of importance report

↘   ↙

Where I need help

↓

Statement summarizing biggest successes

↓

Warm closing with offer for further information

Sample Status Report Memo

DATE: August 12, 2009
TO: Bob Romano
FROM: Lee McLaughlin
SUBJECT: Status Report for Week of August 8

The Customer Service department has had an exceptional week in all three areas I normally cover in this report: Sales, Service and Courtesy.

Most important, we sold 232 new subscriptions to customers who already subscribe to another of our publications. This more than doubled last week's numbers. It also shows more than a 35% improvement over last year's numbers at this time. I believe we are on a roll!

The service calls were down this week, which is always good. Of the 192 service calls that came in, we were able to resolve 183 of them in our department. The other nine were forwarded to our software support contractor. This is also an improved statistic—I think it shows that our reps are becoming more and more knowledgeable about how to help our customers themselves.

We logged only one complaint about a customer service rep this week, a call that I took myself. The individual's complaint concerned the tone of voice he perceived as coming from our rep. I have spoken with this rep and am convinced that the problem will not occur again. (I gave him a mirror to put on his desk and told him to look into it and smile while he was talking to our customers on the phone. As you know, it works every time.)

By the way, could you forward me a copy of the speech Jack gave at the awards banquet last week? I've told some of my staff about it and they'd like to see it.

Well, it's been a week I'm proud to write about. Those sales statistics really impressed me!

Let me know if you need any more details about any of this. See you Monday morning at the staff meeting.

Lee

Memo Format #4: Information

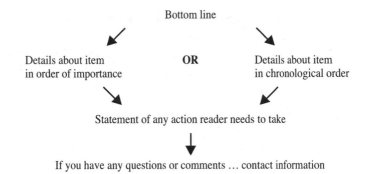

Bottom line

Details about item
in order of importance

OR

Details about item
in chronological order

Statement of any action reader needs to take

If you have any questions or comments … contact information

Sample Information Memo

DATE: March 8, 2009
TO: All Customer Service Representatives
FROM: Lee McLaughlin, CS Manager
SUBJECT: April Awards Banquet

Just to let you know, there will be an awards banquet held on the first Thursday of next month during our normal lunch hour—which will be expanded to an hour and a half.

The Customer Service awards for April will be presented and Gary Sanderson, the Training Director, will give a presentation about listening skills. I have heard he is very funny and very informative.

Please make plans to attend—remember, we buy lunch. There's a sign-up sheet posted in the break room. Please let us know you'll be there by March 23.

Stop in and see me if you have any questions.

Lee

Memo Format #5: Procedures

Statement of what the procedure will give reader the ability to do

When the reader may not want to do the task: Compelling reasons for doing it, unsettling consequences for not doing it

Step One: How to do it, what you will see when it is finished, likely troubleshooting notes

Step Two: How to do it, what you will see when it is finished, likely troubleshooting notes

All steps, in order, in this format

List of other resources to check, including writer's contact information

Quick reminder of reader's ability or the benefits of following the procedure

Sample Procedures Memo

DATE: March 2, 2009

TO: Project Management Trainers

FROM: Michael Cohen and Susan LeBlanc, Curriculum Coordinators

RE: Project Management Curriculum Guide

This memo details the procedure we need each of you to follow in order to get a copy of the brand new Project Management Curriculum Guide.

First, send us an e-mail right away and let us know that you are interested in having a copy. We will send you a confirmation of your request within the day. Please save that confirmation. You will need to show it to the Publications Department if you pick the guide up there yourself.

Second, visit our Web site and download the rough draft of the guide. You can do that by clicking the green button in the upper left-hand corner of the Web page that says "DOWNLOAD NOW." It will take close to ten minutes—don't panic.

Third, once you have downloaded the guide, glance through it for us and make sure it contains everything you want and need—within reason, of course. Let us know via e-mail or by phone by Friday, March 22 if there are any changes you think must be made.

According to Joann Montera in Publication, the completed guides will be printed and ready to go by April 25. At that time, we will let you know how to get your copy in time for your programs that following week.

Thanks for your contributions to this guide. You, after all, are the experts who meet our employees across the U.S. every day and you are the ones who hear their questions, needs and concerns in the area of Project Management.

Have a great month. We'll be in touch soon.

Susan   *Michael*

Memo Format #6: Bad News

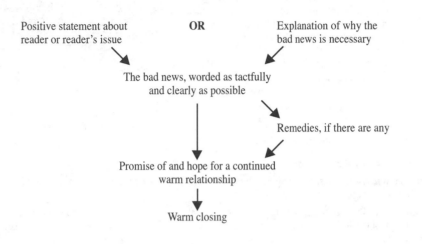

Positive statement about reader or reader's issue

OR

Explanation of why the bad news is necessary

The bad news, worded as tactfully and clearly as possible

Remedies, if there are any

Promise of and hope for a continued warm relationship

Warm closing

Sample Bad News Memo

DATE: June 18, 2009
TO: Gloria Ali
FROM: Susan Luna
SUBJECT: My Conversation with the VP of Finance

I think you know how sincere I am when I tell you that you have been a great asset to this department every day that you have been here for the past nine years.

That's why it hurts me to tell you that your request for a 20% pay increase has been denied by the Vice President of Finance. As we discussed last week, I was doubtful about it from the start. I want you to know, though, I did express my support for you to the Vice President.

She suggested that if we changed your title from Administrative Assistant to Management Liaison and added a few duties to your job description that relate to project management, she might be able to swing 10%.

It's not that your actual job would change, of course—you already are the best project manager we have in the department. But maybe it's worth a try. What do you think?

As always, I treasure our relationship—both professionally and personally. If you need a shoulder, I'm here.

Susan

PROPOSALS

The instructions presented in the Request for Proposal (RFP) usually determine the format used for the proposal. If an RFP has been received but no instructions are given, it is a good idea to mirror the format of the RFP itself as much as possible.

> *Writer's Tips:*
> *If no RFP has been received, follow the instructions presented in this section and in the Report Formats Section on pages 252 – 259.*

Rules

1. If there is a written Request for Proposal document soliciting your proposal, follow any instructions it gives for preparing your proposal—*to the letter*.
2. If specific formatting instructions are not stated in a Request for Proposal, follow the formatting style of the RFP.
3. If there is not a written Request for Proposal soliciting your proposal, use a format that puts your ideas and your sales points close to the beginning.

Explanations and Examples

1. **If there is a written Request for Proposal document soliciting your proposal, follow any instructions it gives for preparing your proposal—*to the letter*.**

   This will often be the case when you are preparing a formal proposal. Think of it as you used to think of the instructions your high school teachers gave you for preparing a research report: What they ask you to do *might* sound peculiar, but they want it that way. Consider their instructions the hoop you need to jump through in order to get in the door.

2. **If specific formatting instructions are not stated in a Request for Proposal, follow the formatting style of the RFP.**

   If the author of the RFP uses boldface to emphasize headings, then you should use boldface to emphasize your headings. If the author of the RFP uses headers on each page that contain specific references to the project name, then you should use headers on each page that contain specific references to the project name. And this goes right down to whether the author of the RFP used serial commas or not.

3. **If there is not a written Request for Proposal soliciting your proposal, use a format that puts your ideas and your sales points close to the beginning.**

   When you have no guidelines to follow from the reader you are making your proposal to, we recommend you use the simple business format of a report with just a few modifications:

   - Letter of Transmittal
   - (Cover)
   - Title Page
   - Table of Contents
   - List of Charts, Tables and Figures
   - Executive Summary
   - Body
     - Conclusions
     - Recommendations
     - Discussion
     - Methods
     - Costs
   - Bibliography
   - Appendixes

   Letter of Transmittal: Even if your proposal is more informal, it should be introduced by a letter or memo that briefly sums up your intent in sending it. This letter or memo can also contain any side information that you may be hesitant to put in the proposal itself. For example, that a discount could be available if you can prove the potential for future orders to your boss.

   (Cover): It's not essential, but now that it is relatively easy to produce a nice looking cover, we would recommend you do. It will help your proposal get the attention it deserves.

   Title Page: This page contains the title of the proposal, your name, your company name and contact information and the date of the proposal. Any reference numbers or materials that were a part of the Request for Proposal may also appear on this page.

Table of Contents: Let your reader get a good overview of your proposal by glancing at the Table of Contents. As always, use visual formatting strategies like indents and page leaders across the page to help the reader quickly find what he or she may be looking for.

List of Charts, Tables and Figures: If there are more than five of them throughout your proposal, provide a list. Otherwise, include them in your general table of contents.

Executive Summary: Make a statement of what you are proposing and back it up with a statement that the full proposal will provide compelling reasons that you have the winning proposal. If there is a down side, briefly and positively mention it with an assurance that the down side can be greatly diminished by following your plan.

Body: This is the meat of your proposal.

Conclusions: This is your statement of proposal. What have you concluded is the best plan? How will you carry it out? What exactly are you proposing?

Recommendations: This is a more detailed statement and explanation of what you just communicated in your conclusions section. Here you may include why you have proposed what you have as well as other available options. The less formal your proposal, the more likely the conclusions and recommendations sections will be combined into one.

Discussion: As in a report, this will be the largest section of your proposal. This is where you will offer all the proof for your statements and present arguments against the potential drawbacks your reader might see. Make sure to use subheadings throughout this section so your reader can easily find a specific topic he or she may be looking for.

Methods: This is where you will list any special methods or materials that will be used to fulfill the proposal. For example, you may have made reference in the conclusions and recommendations section to a survey that will be taken. This section is where you will explain the methods you will use to take that survey.

Costs: Most proposals include a section that specifically lists the costs associated with the various elements of the proposal. Of course, you should mention these costs much earlier than this in the proposal. By the time your reader gets here, he or she should be prepared for and sold on the benefits of paying these amounts.

Bibliography: If outside sources were used in producing any part of this document, you must note those sources.

Appendixes: You can add extra evidence, supporting documentation or pertinent charts, tables, graphs or illustrations to the end of the proposal as appendixes. Make sure to reference them in the body of the proposal itself so your reader knows why they are included. Also, use as many as you need.

Proposal Format #1: Letter of Transmittal

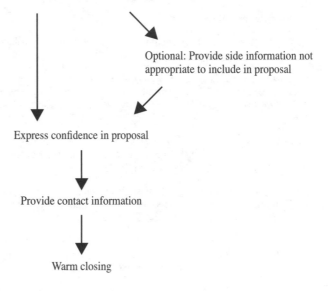

Introduce proposal, refer to any RFPs or reference numbers

Optional: Provide side information not appropriate to include in proposal

Express confidence in proposal

Provide contact information

Warm closing

Sample Letter of Transmittal

ALL ABOUT TRAINING
2349 N.E. 91st Street
Detroit, MI 48180
(313) 555-7898

June 1, 2009

Mr. Frederick J. Gustafson
Director of Training and Development
General Motors Corporation
1 Camaro Circle
Detroit, MI 48180

Dear Mr. Gustafson:

Enclosed is our organization's <u>Proposal to Provide Communication Skills Training</u>, in response to your Request for Proposal, dated May 10, 2009. Your Contract Reference Number is 78-65456.

As you and I discussed today on the phone, further discounts than the ones quoted within the proposal would be available when the training program moves into the GM divisions.

Our team has worked diligently to keep your company's needs and constraints in mind as we prepared this proposal. We are sure you will be pleased.

You can reach me at (313) 555-7898, ext. 233 if you have any questions or would like more detail about any item in our proposal. Or if you would prefer, e-mail me at MKline@isp.com.

Thanks for giving us this opportunity to provide training for your organization. We look forward to working with you soon.

Sincerely,

Michael

Michael Kline
Faculty Coordinator

MK/sl
Enclosures

<u>Proposal Format #2: Proposal</u>

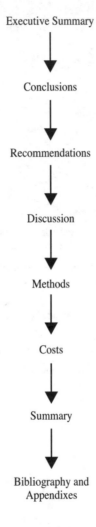

Executive Summary

Conclusions

Recommendations

Discussion

Methods

Costs

Summary

Bibliography and
Appendixes

Sample Proposal

Executive Summary

All About Training proposes to supply General Motors, Glass Division, with 100 presentations of the GM program "Communication in the Workplace" at a cost of $3750 per presentation session. Each program would include 50 GM Glass Division employees and would last for two consecutive six-hour days. Workbooks and audiovisual materials would be supplied by General Motors.

Conclusions

Because the program is already designed and the workbooks and audiovisuals are being provided by General Motors, All About Training will be providing only the facilitators and the training services themselves. For this reason, we have cut our normal fee in half.

We have found, while studying the workbook provided with General Motors' Request for Proposal, that only a moderate amount of staff training is required. As it turns out, All About Training has actually facilitated a program very similar to this one for another of the Big Three automakers here in Detroit.

We will be ready to begin training on July 15, 2009.

Recommendations

All About Training suggests that we offer the first class at no charge as a pilot program sometime in the last week of June. We would encourage General Motors to fill this pilot class with a sampling of supervisors from the Glass Division, whom we will then poll for ideas as to how we can further customize this program for their needs. We will provide you with an original of the customized materials by July 3. This will give you time to prepare the workbooks for July 15.

Discussion

General Motors and All About Training have had a long and positive relationship. Over the past six years, our company has presented training programs to General Motors for over 2,875 employees.

Etcetera. The Discussion portion of a proposal offers every selling point and detail that could help the bidder win the contract.

Methods

General Motors Glass Division employees will travel to the Corporate Training Headquarters on Camaro Drive to attend the training. Each program will have two trainers, provided by All About Training. Both trainers will be present both days. The topics of interpersonal communication, assertiveness and conflict management will be covered on day one. The topics of nonverbal communication, meetings, presentation skills, teambuilding and handling pressure will be covered on day two. The class will be a mix of lecture, group activities and audiovisual presentation.

Costs

All About Training will charge $3750 per two-day session, to be invoiced at the end of each month. If General Motors needs to add more attendees than 50 to any one presentation, we will charge $100 per additional person for the two days.

Summary

All About Training has proposed to supply General Motors, Glass Division, with 100 presentations of the GM program "Communication in the Workplace" at a cost of $3750 per presentation session. The programs would each include 50 GM Glass Division employees and would last for two consecutive six-hour days.

All About Training has also proposed to offer one pilot program at the end of June at no charge for Glass Division supervisors in order to get the feedback we need to customize the program to their specific needs.

We would provide an original of any customized materials as part of our fee. Workbooks and audiovisual materials would be supplied by General Motors.

REPORTS

There are many different kinds of reports that writers produce. Some are simple reports that actually look more like memos: for example, a weekly status report or a short trip report. Others are mid-sized reports that do indeed look like reports. They have sections and titles throughout covering a wider range of information: for example, a major project report or a corporate technical report. There are also mega-reports—large enough to be books in themselves, such as the final report of a major project or a detailed status report covering an entire year.

All of these reports have several features in common. The longer a report gets, the more features it has.

The list below shows all the possible parts of a major report. Don't worry, most reports do not contain all of these.

- Letter of Transmittal
- Cover
- Abstract
- Title Page
- Preface
- Table of Contents
- List of Charts, Tables and Figures
- Executive Summary
- Body
  - Introduction
  - Conclusions
  - Recommendations
  - Methods
  - Discussion
  - Summary
- Bibliography
- Appendixes

The section below shows three types of reports and the sections most commonly found in each one.

Recommended Report Formats

Simple Business	Formal Business	Scientific/Technical
Executive Summary	Letter of Transmittal	Letter of Transmittal
Body: Introduction	Cover	Cover
Discussion	Title Page	Abstract
Conclusions	(Preface)	Title Page
Recommendations	Table of Contents	Preface
(Bibliography)	List of Charts, Tables and Figures	Table of Contents
(Appendixes)	Executive Summary	List of Charts, Tables and Figures
	Body: Introduction	(Executive Summary)
	Conclusions	Body: Introduction
	Recommendations	Methods
	Discussion	Discussion
	Methods	Conclusions
	(Summary)	Recommendations
	Bibliography	(Summary)
	Appendixes	Bibliography
		Appendixes

Simple Business Reports

Most people in the world of work need to write some simple business reports. While the format is not carved in stone, the recommendations we make will assure you of a credible and complete report. Note that in the simplest of reports, these sections may not even have titles.

Executive Summary: Every clear business report begins with a statement of the bottom line of that report. In report writing parlance, this is called an executive summary. Whether the heading *Executive Summary* is used or not, always begin every report (and memo and letter and e-mail, as a matter of fact) with a paragraph that sums up the most important idea(s) of that document.

Introduction: In a simple business report, the introduction could include a telling of background of the topic as well as define any special terms being used throughout. It is also a good place to set the limits of the report and to specify the scope that is being covered.

Discussion: This section fully states and explains the relevant information that is being reported. It is generally the longest section of a simple business report.

Conclusions: This section ties everything in the report up to this point together and states your findings and beliefs. Often, at least a part of the conclusion is a restatement of the executive summary.

Recommendations: This section states your suggestions for future action based on the information in the report. The more informal the report, the more likely this section of recommendations will become a part of your conclusions.

(Bibliography): If you used reference sources, you must make note of those sources in the bibliography. In a less formal report, you could simply reference the sources in parentheses following the material used in the text.

(Appendixes): You can add any charts, tables, graphs, listings or extra material that is not part of the report itself in an appendix. However, the material must be applicable to the topic of the report and of interest to the reader.

Formal Business Reports

From time to time, people must produce a formal business report. This type of report will most certainly have a cover, a title page and headings throughout the document, to name a few. Again, you will need to be careful to check with the authority the report is being prepared for to make sure of the formatting guidelines he or she may need to follow. But when in doubt, here is the most traditional format used for formal business reports explained in detail.

Letter of Transmittal: Letters of transmittal are called cover letters in less formal applications. It is placed on top of the report before it is delivered and introduces the report to the reader. When the same report is presented to different readers, either different transmittal letters are used for each person or a letter is written to the entire group. For this reason, a letter of transmittal is often a perfect place to present information that is tailored to one particular reader which might not be appropriate for all readers of the report. In general, this letter is short and conversational. It includes the topic of the report, why the report was written and any special information the reader may need to understand the report.

Cover: Welcome to the information age. Now that most people in the work world have access to computers that produce graphics, the expectations your readers have for covers are much greater than they were years ago. You do need to produce a cover that takes advantage of your publishing software and your color printer. The cover will also include most of the information from the title page. But make certain it is beautiful. First impressions are extremely important.

Title Page: The title page is printed on the same type of paper, in a similar typeface as the rest of the report. It is not as beautiful as the cover. Centered down the page, it contains:

- The title of the report
- The author of the report
- The person or group the report was prepared for
- The date of presentation
- The name of the company, division or group the author represents
- Any special numbers or codes necessary for identifying or filing the report, if applicable
- A copyright notice, if applicable

(Preface): The preface is sometimes called the *foreword*, literally meaning words that come before the main report. A preface is more often not used than it is used. Most often, prefaces are used to acknowledge other contributors or sources, to make personal comments regarding the contents of the report, to provide background information that is so far removed from the content of the report it wouldn't be appropriate in the introduction, or to note financial implications or other unusual results.

Table of Contents: The table of contents tells readers where they can find the various sections and topics covered in the report. Carefully prepared, it can also provide an excellent overview of the report for a busy reader. Make sure to include every heading from the report as an entry in the table of contents, even the second and third level subheadings. Determine a format that will be visually helpful (for example, indent all second level subheadings to the same point and all third level subheadings to a different point). Finally, use a trail of periods (called dot leaders or page leaders) across the page to help the reader connect the topic to its page number.

List of Charts, Tables and Figures: Include this separate table of contents if there are more than five charts, tables, figures or other visual aids presented in your document. On the other hand, if there are fewer than five, include them in your main table of contents. If you have used many visual aids, make sure to assign each an identifying number and a title in the document and re-state that number and title in the list of charts, tables and figures.

Executive Summary: Just as in a simple business report, the executive summary is very important. This is where your reader finds your bottom line—the most important ideas you have to share. In a formal report this section will most likely carry either the title *Executive Summary* or, if the word *executive* seems inappropriate for your reading audience, you can use *Overview* or *Summary*.

Introduction: In a formal business report, the introduction will include the background about the topic and will define any special terms being used throughout the report. It is also where the thoughtful writer sets the limits of the report, specifies the scope that is being covered and provides instructions the reader may need to understand the report. These are often called "conventions."

Conclusions: The conclusions section states the writer's findings and beliefs. Often, at least a part of the section restates the executive summary. One of the differences between a simple and a formal business report is where this section is placed in the report. In a longer, more formal business report, this section comes before the discussion. Your reader needs as much bottom line information as close to the beginning of the report as possible. In a simple report, the reader doesn't have as much information to get through to reach the conclusion, so it can follow the discussion.

Recommendations: The writer's suggestions for future action based on the information in the report are stated in this section. Even though the reader will know the writer's conclusions, the recommendations will still need to be elaborated on in the discussion.

Discussion: This explains and discusses the information already provided in the conclusions and recommendations sections and does so in all the detail the reader may need. It is generally the longest section of a formal business report.

Methods: This section explains the methods used to acquire the information in the report and also lists any materials that were used. If the methods or materials used in preparing the report were conventional and familiar to most readers, this section is not necessary. In the case of conventional and familiar methods and materials, list them briefly in the introduction.

(Summary): Many writers (and readers) find a summary section redundant in a report that contains an executive summary, conclusions and recommendations. After all, your reader can easily page back to one of those sections if he or she has forgotten your bottom line points. In a formal report, however, sometimes the authority that has asked you for the report is comforted by the presence of this section—even if it is unnecessary.

Bibliography: In a formal business report, it is highly likely that you used reference sources. They should be made note of in a bibliography. Ensure that every reference item listed does get a mention at some point in your document to keep your reader from having to guess why it was presented only at the end. In the most formal of formal reports, those references would probably appear as footnotes. In less formal reports, you could simply use the author's name in parentheses following the point in the text where you used that reference.

Appendixes: Any charts, tables, graphs, listings or extra materials not made a part of the report itself that are applicable to the topic—and of interest to the reader—can be added as appendixes. Each appendix should be a separate entry in the table of contents.

Scientific and Technical Reports

Most of the suggestions we have for scientific and technical reports are very similar to the ones we have for formal business reports. The biggest difference between them is the *order* in which the information is presented, not in the contents of the various sections.

Scientific and technical readers tend to want a more logical approach to the information they read—they want to build to a conclusion rather than start with one.

It may also be helpful to explain several small differences between scientific and technical reports themselves.

While scientific reports are almost always read by people who understand the scientific language and theories the writer uses, technical reports are often read by readers who are not as familiar with the technical language and background. More often, technical reports tend to be internal reports, prepared by a technical department for another less technical department. Also, it is more possible (but still not likely) that the reader of a technical report cares only about the conclusions, and not about the process the writer used to reach them.

For these reasons, we recommend that technical writers use an executive summary more often than we recommend scientific writers use one.

Letter of Transmittal: In the case of scientific and technical writing, everything stated in the previous description of Letters of Transmittal is applicable. In addition, the letter of transmittal is a good place to give needed scientific or technical background that a less experienced reader may not know. In general, this letter is short and conversational. It includes the topic of the report, why the report was written and any special instructions the reader may need to understand the report.

Cover: Now that most people in the work world have access to computers that produce graphics, the expectations your readers have for covers are much greater than they were years ago … even highly analytical readers. You do need to produce a cover that takes advantage of your publishing software and your color printer. The cover will also include most of the information from the title page, but make certain it is beautiful. First impressions mean a lot.

Abstract: Scientific and technical reports are the only reports that could require an abstract. An abstract is separate from the report itself and contains the most distilled version of the writer's conclusions, recommendations and summary as possible. Ideally, an abstract is one to two paragraphs long; if you can't limit it to that length, an abstract is never more than one page long. A properly written abstract will tell a potential reader whether or not he or she needs the information the entire report contains. Abstracts are kept on file as part of academic and scientific card catalogues in libraries and data centers for exactly this reason.

Title Page: The title page is printed on the same type of paper, in a similar typeface as the rest of the report. It is not as beautiful as the cover. Centered down the page, it contains:

- The title of the report
- The author of the report
- The person or group the report was prepared for
- The date of presentation
- The name of the company, division or group the author represents
- Any special numbers or codes necessary for identifying or filing the report, if applicable
- A copyright notice, if applicable

Preface: The preface is sometimes also called the *foreword*, literally meaning words that come before the main report. A preface is more often not used than it is used—even in scientific and technical reports. Most often, prefaces are used to acknowledge other contributors or sources, to make personal comments regarding the contents of the report, to provide background information that is so far removed from the content of the report it wouldn't be appropriate in the introduction, or to note financial implications or other unusual results.

Table of Contents: The table of contents tells readers where they can find the various sections and topics covered in the report. Carefully prepared, it can also provide an excellent overview of the report for a busy reader. Make sure to include every heading from the report as an entry in the table of contents, even the second and third level subheadings. Determine a format that will be visually helpful (for example, indent all second level subheadings to the same point and all third level subheadings to a different point). Finally, use a trail of periods (called dot leaders or page leaders) across the page to help the reader connect the topic to its page number.

List of Charts, Tables and Figures: Include this as a separate table of contents if there are more than five charts, tables, figures or other visual aids presented in your document. On the other hand, if there are fewer than five, include them in your main table of contents. If you have used many visual aids, make sure to assign each an identifying number and a title in the document and re-state that number and title in the list of charts, tables and figures.

(Executive Summary): Just as in both simple and formal business reports, the executive summary is very important to the reader who needs your important information quickly. It is where your reader finds your bottom line, the most important ideas you have to share. Be aware, however, that in some scientific and technical reports, it is unnecessary. Remember—The more analytical your reader (and the more time available to that analytical reader), the more likely he or she will want to build to your conclusion in the same way you did: step-by-step.

Introduction: In a formal business report, the introduction will include the background about the topic and will define any special terms being used throughout the report. It is also where the thoughtful writer sets the limits of the report, specifies the scope that is being covered and provides instructions the reader may need to understand the report. These are often called "conventions."

Methods: This section explains the methods used to acquire the information in the report and also lists any materials that were used. In most scientific reports, the writer will need to make a careful list of both materials and methods to satisfy the analytical reader. In technical reporting, this section may not be necessary depending on the familiarity of any methods or materials used in the course of acquiring the information being reported. In the case of conventional and familiar methods and materials, list them briefly in the introduction section of the report.

Discussion: This explains and discusses the information already provided in the conclusions and recommendations sections and does so in all the detail a reader may need. In a scientific or technical report, it will most likely give a blow-by-blow description of any experiments, processes or research undertaken. As in the previous types of reports, it is generally the longest section of a scientific or technical report.

Conclusions: The conclusion section states the writer's findings and beliefs. Often, at least a part of the section restates the executive summary. Again, notice that one of the differences between a scientific or technical report and a formal business report is where this section is placed. In a formal business report, this section comes before the discussion. The reader of that type of report needs as much bottom line information close to the beginning of the report as possible. In a scientific or technical report, the analytical nature of the topic and thinking of your reader make it more likely that the reader would prefer to build to the conclusion in a more logical manner.

Recommendations: The recommendations section is where you state your suggestions for future action (based on the information in the report). While the reader will already know the conclusions you have drawn from the information you gathered, you must also prove, in the discussion, what you are recommending.

(Summary): Many analytical writers (and readers) find a summary section redundant in a report that contains an executive summary, conclusions and recommendations. After all, the reader can easily page back to one of those sections if he or she has forgotten your bottom line points. In a scientific or technical report, however, the authority that has asked you for the report often wants this section—even if it may seem unnecessary. And as you know, an important rule of business writing is "what's in it for my reader," so if the reader wants this section—provide it.

Bibliography: In a scientific or technical report, it is very likely you got some of your information from reference sources. It is important that you create a bibliography to note any reference you used. Make sure that every reference listed is mentioned at some point in your document. This keeps your reader from having to guess why the reference was presented only at the end. In the most formal of formal reports, the references would appear as footnotes. In a moderately formal report, you can simply put the author's name in parentheses following the point in the text where you used that reference.

Appendixes: Any charts, tables, graphs, listings or extra materials that are not a part of the report itself can be added as appendixes. Information in any appendix must be applicable to the topic and of interest to the reader. Each appendix is a separate entry in the table of contents.

<u>Report Format #1: Simple Business Report</u>

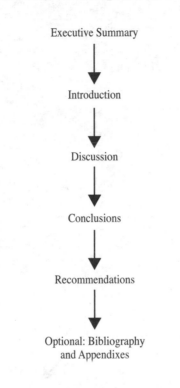

Executive Summary

Introduction

Discussion

Conclusions

Recommendations

Optional: Bibliography
and Appendixes

Report Format #2: Formal Business Report

Executive Summary

Introduction

Conclusions

Recommendations

Discussion

Methods

Summary

Bibliography
and Appendixes

<u>Report Format #3: Scientific or Technical Report</u>

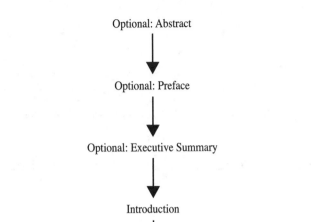
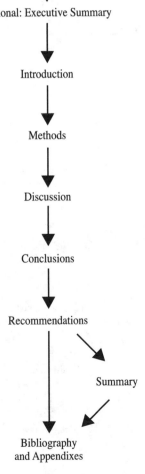

Optional: Abstract

Optional: Preface

Optional: Executive Summary

Introduction

Methods

Discussion

Conclusions

Recommendations

Summary

Bibliography
and Appendixes

Business Writing

OTHER BUSINESS DOCUMENTS

While most of the documents you will be writing fall under the categories of e-mail, letters, memos, proposals and reports, you will occasionally need to prepare more specialized documents. In this section, we will present examples and a few notes about preparing a variety of these more specialized documents:

1. Job Description
2. Meeting Minutes
3. Newsletter
4. Organizational Mission Statement
5. Performance Review
6. Press Release
7. Resume

The guidelines for each of these documents are very different from each other, so they are presented as models first.

Other Business Document Format #1: Job Description

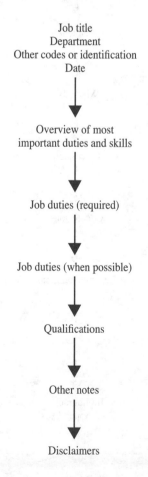

Job title
Department
Other codes or identification
Date

↓

Overview of most
important duties and skills

↓

Job duties (required)

↓

Job duties (when possible)

↓

Qualifications

↓

Other notes

↓

Disclaimers

Sample Job Description Format

Administrative Assistant II

Field Sales Department

January 1, 2010

The primary job responsibility of the Administrative Assistant II in the Field Sales department is to support the Field Sales Director in acting as the liaison between the Company and the outside sales representatives.

Major Job Duties:

- Answer all incoming phone calls from Sales Representatives
- Call Sales Representatives as determined by Field Sales Director
- Plan and schedule all travel and hotels for Sales Representatives visiting home office
- Write letters and memos to Sales Representatives as needed
- Send weekly information and accumulated mail to Sales Representatives
- Report any non-routine communication to or from Sales Representatives to Field Sales Director

Other Job Duties:

- Keep all Field Sales files organized and current
- Train Field Sales Assistant as needed
- Maintain positive communication with Sales Representatives

Qualifications:

- Outstanding people skills
- Excellent writing skills
- Familiarity with Microsoft® Word and Excel®
- Two years of college
- Previous work experience with salespeople

Other Notes:

The Field Sales department Administrative Assistant II is often asked to participate in various Field Sales promotional events that may include travel for up to four days. Also, if the Field Sales Director agrees that another department urgently needs the help of the person in this position, he or she may occasionally be asked to work in another department for up to one full day.

All employees of McMahon Insurance are required to take a yearly drug test.

Other Business Document Format #2: Meeting Minutes

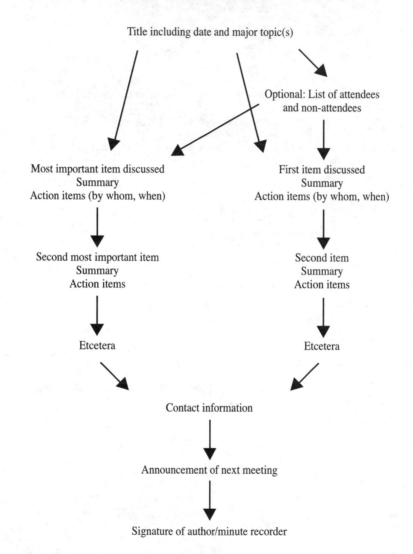

Sample Meeting Minutes Format

Minutes of June 15, 2010 Managers' Meeting

Topics Discussed: New Health Insurance Provider and Customer Care

Attendees: All managers were in attendance.

New Health Insurance: Beginning July 1, Healthcare Mutual will be our health insurance provider. The HR Department has submitted all paperwork necessary to seamlessly transfer all employees and their dependents to the new plan.

> **Action Item:** Hanna LaRue, Manager of Benefits, will send a memo announcing the change, along with new ID cards to all employees on June 18.

Customer Care: Bob Achman led a discussion of how each department can improve customer care. While some suggestions were particular to specific departments, most of the ideas were determined to be so good they were worth publishing.

> **Action Item:** Bob Achman, Customer Service Manager, will compile the suggestions in a memo to be sent to all employees. He will tape a peanut butter cup to each memo to better get the employees' attention and he will send these memos on June 20.

If you need more details about any item, please e-mail me at shunter@isp.com.

Our next managers' meeting will be held on June 30 at 10:30 a.m. in Conference Room A.

Respectfully submitted,

Susan

<u>Other Business Document Format #3: Newsletter</u>

Masthead

↓

Major story
(with top headline)

↓

Other stories and announcements
(make sure everyone's interests are addressed)

↓

Box listing the names of
the people who wrote, assembled
and published the newsletter

Sample Newsletter Format

Newsletter

Volume 12, Issue 4   May 24, 2010

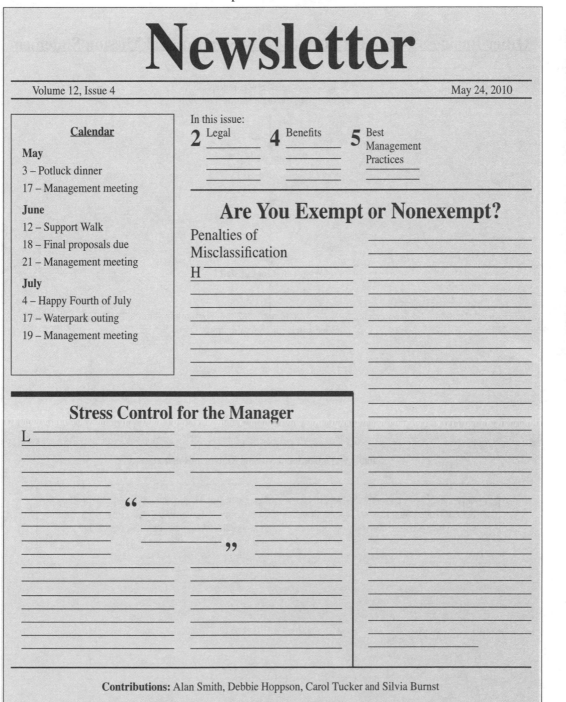

Calendar

May

3 – Potluck dinner

17 – Management meeting

June

12 – Support Walk

18 – Final proposals due

21 – Management meeting

July

4 – Happy Fourth of July

17 – Waterpark outing

19 – Management meeting

In this issue:

2 Legal   **4** Benefits   **5** Best Management Practices

Are You Exempt or Nonexempt?

Penalties of Misclassification

H

Stress Control for the Manager

L

"   "

Contributions: Alan Smith, Debbie Hoppson, Carol Tucker and Silvia Burnst

Other Business Document Format #4: Organizational Mission Statement

Clear, concise overview paragraph that
fully expresses the organization's mission

Why are we here?

What's in it for our clients?

What's in it for our staff?

What's in it for our community?

Sample Organizational Mission Statement Format

Patty's Pancake Pan serves the largest variety of fresh, wholesome pancakes available to travelers across the United States. It is the goal of our associates to provide travelers and traveling professionals with an inexpensive, hearty and comforting dining experience. As investors in our restaurants, our associates are our first and best resource in fulfilling this mission.

Other Business Document Format #5: Performance Review

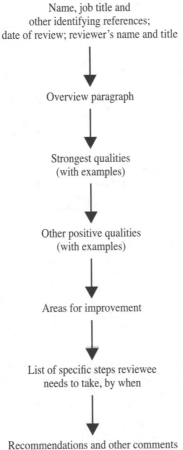

Name, job title and
other identifying references;
date of review; reviewer's name and title

Overview paragraph

Strongest qualities
(with examples)

Other positive qualities
(with examples)

Areas for improvement

List of specific steps reviewee
needs to take, by when

Recommendations and other comments
(end with something positive)

Sample Performance Review Format

Performance Review of: Kelly Martini

Job Title: Supervisor, Quality Assurance Department

Payroll #:   KM0018

Date of Review: January 16, 2010

Reviewed by: Giles Marchand
        Executive Vice President

Kelly displayed great determination in learning the Supervisor job that she was promoted into last July. Her ability to manage her employees effectively is her strongest point. While she needs to further develop her product knowledge over the next review period, Kelly's overall job performance is superlative.

She has met or exceeded all the objective performance criteria set for this position, most notably in the decrease (by half!) of the return rate on our Model 4200 Toaster. It was her careful training of her staff that alerted them to the most common problem associated with that toaster. Furthermore, she took it upon herself to have the engineering department teach her the simple fix, which Kelly then taught to her staff.

Her management skills have been developing every day. It appears that the employees in her department respect her and trust her. Some of them have visited me to thank me for putting such a reasonable and intelligent person in charge of the department!

As mentioned above, my only request is that Kelly immerse herself now into more of the technical background of our product line. I have recommended she visit with Bob Beck in Engineering for some advice about how best to begin. She will report back to me about an informal training program by January 20.

I recommend that Kelly receive the standard 10% pay increase a new employee receives after the first review. She has proven herself a dedicated supervisor and is a true asset to Thomas Brothers Inc.

<u>Other Business Document Format #6: Press Release</u>

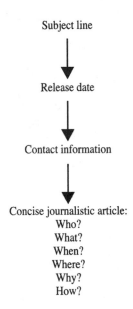

Subject line

Release date

Contact information

Concise journalistic article:
Who?
What?
When?
Where?
Why?
How?

Sample Press Release Format

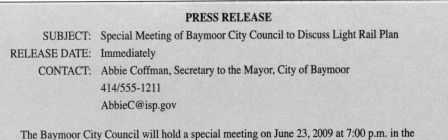

PRESS RELEASE

SUBJECT: Special Meeting of Baymoor City Council to Discuss Light Rail Plan

RELEASE DATE: Immediately

CONTACT: Abbie Coffman, Secretary to the Mayor, City of Baymoor

414/555-1211

AbbieC@isp.gov

The Baymoor City Council will hold a special meeting on June 23, 2009 at 7:00 p.m. in the Council Chambers, Baymoor City Hall. The public is invited to attend to ask questions and comment on the Light Rail Plan received from GR Construction. No vote will be held; the meeting is for discussion only.

Other Business Document Format #7: Resume

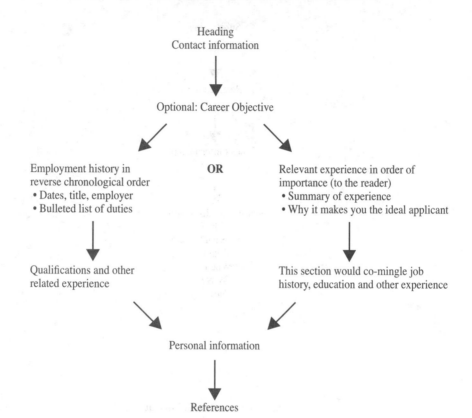

Heading
Contact information

Optional: Career Objective

Employment history in
reverse chronological order
• Dates, title, employer
• Bulleted list of duties

OR

Relevant experience in order of
importance (to the reader)
• Summary of experience
• Why it makes you the ideal applicant

Qualifications and other
related experience

This section would co-mingle job
history, education and other experience

Personal information

References

Business Writing

Sample Resume Format

SHANE J. LARSON

1423 W. 325th Street

Lake Village, Ohio 44181

440/555-6776

E-mail: massageman@isp.com

I have been a licensed massage therapist in the State of Ohio since 1998. It is my goal to relieve the pain and stress of critically injured hospital patients to facilitate their physical and emotional recovery.

Employment History:

1998 – present: Massage therapist, Gates Rehabilitation Hospital, Lake Village, Ohio
Duties: Provide massage therapy to spinal cord injured and brain injured patients in residence. Work with the physical therapy team and the medical team to determine the massage program for each patient. Work with the psychological team to recommend and design a massage program for some patients as a remedy for emotional issues common to SCI.

1994 – 1998: Part-time massage therapist, University of Denver Health Center, Denver, Colorado. Duties: Provided massage therapy to students and staff members to provide relief from physical and emotional stress.

Education:

BA, University of Denver. Major: Philosophy. Minor: Biology. Graduated March 1998.

Massage Certification Program, Denver General Hospital 1994 – 1995. Certificate received June 1995.

Other qualifications:

Licensed Massage Therapist, State of Ohio – License #98 04567

(Unofficial) Massage therapist to the DU Pioneers hockey team, 1994 – 1998

Personal:

Born and raised in Appleton, Wisconsin. My hobbies include playing hockey, reading and learning.

References:

Dr. Paul Oslatchovicz, Rehabilitation Director, Gates Rehabilitation Hospital, Lake Village, Ohio 440/555-9000 ext 122

Elnora Michaelson, Physical Therapy Manager, Gates Rehabilitation Hospital, Lake Village, Ohio 440/555-9000 ext 134

Professor Albert J. Potter, Chair, Philosophy Department, University of Denver, Denver, Colorado 303/555-7600 ext 2321

GRAPHICS

ALIGNMENT/RELATIONSHIPS

Design involves the arrangement of visual elements on a page. Elements used in designing documents should relate to each other in a natural, organized way.

Typical elements include headlines, photographs, blocks of body copy, borders, space and the page itself. But each element may break down into smaller parts. A headline, for example, may contain a number of words. Each word is made up of a number of letters. In this example, each letter of each word could be considered a visual element, as well as each word in the sentence. Elements may combine together to create other elements. A caption and photograph fit together to form a single element.

Priority of relationships between elements is established by their proximity. The closer the elements are to each other, the stronger the relationships. For example, a caption should relate to a photograph in such a way that the two become one element. Any other elements such as headlines, subheads or body copy should not be closer to either the caption or the photograph than the two are to each other.

The article on the left shows the correct relationships while the article on the right shows incorrect relationships

Relationships can be established by their alignment. In the case of the photo and caption above, the relationship is created from not only proximity, but by the fact they are aligned on center. Elements can line up on center, to the right or to the left as in the business card examples on the facing page.

In some cases, relationships can be established by changing alignment from element to element in a seemingly random way. This complex way of establishing relationships can create a powerful attention-getting affect.

272

Graphics, Prepress and Printing

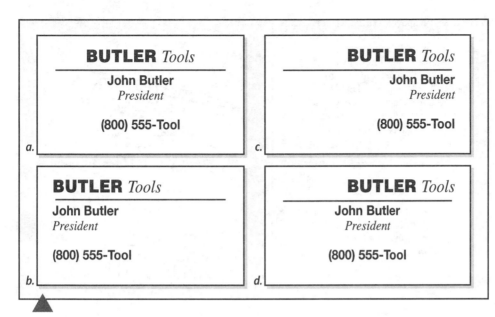

Business cards (a), (b) and (c) are examples of center, left and right alignment respectively. Card (d) demonstrates the awkwardness of mixing alignments.

Other ways of creating relationships between elements involve use of color, texture or size. In the example to the right, the elements which form an interesting relationship are neither aligned with each other or close to each other. The relationship is established by color, or value, alone.

Often when two or more elements relate on a page, one element should dominate another. In the case of a caption and photo, the caption will subordinate the photo. Subordinance can be established by size and order. Dominance is given to an element which is on top, or bigger, than another element.

In this example each word relates to the next word by proximity, but not by alignment. Nevertheless, the randomness of the relationships creates a pleasing pattern.

The best tools.
The best prices.

The screened back type creates a relationship between the two phrases in this example

Graphics, Prepress and Printing

As with every rule, there are exceptions. When exceptions are made, the designer must be aware of the exception and compensate accordingly. For example, captions often are positioned on top of photos instead of below or to the side. In this case, it is important to make sure the size of the caption does not overpower the photo which should be dominant. In this case of caption on top, the photo would need to be larger in relation to the caption than it would normally be if the caption were positioned below. The increased size ensures dominance by the correct element.

In the top example, dominance is established by order. In the next two examples, the largest element dominates despite its position.

BACKGROUNDS AND SCREENS

Backgrounds and screens may be used to organize, add emphasis and/or communicate a message.

When a screen or background is used behind body copy, a density of no more than 20% gray is recommended. Different colors will have different neutral or gray scale densities when screened back. For example, process yellow at 100% density has a relative neutral density of only 16% and is therefore suitable behind body copy.

To find out if a color you have chosen has a neutral density of less than 20%, take the following steps:

1. Create a square and fill it with the target color.
2. Create a second square next to the first and color it with a 20% black.
3. Send the file to print. In the printer dialog box choose the option to print the document as a "grayscale."
4. Compare the target color to the 20% black. If the target color is lighter or the same as the 20% square then it is less than or equal to a neutral density of 20%.

Use plain, solid color or gray screens to organize a document or chart. Assign a particular meaning to the different colors or different densities of screens to be used. A key may be necessary to explain the system of organization.

A screen can add emphasis to an article or part of a page. If the screen is used more than two or three times on a single page or spread, the power of the screen to attract and emphasize is diluted. Because screens add weight to a layout, they may create a focal point or provide a balance to a focal point. Overuse of screens to attract attention can quickly make a composition appear cluttered.

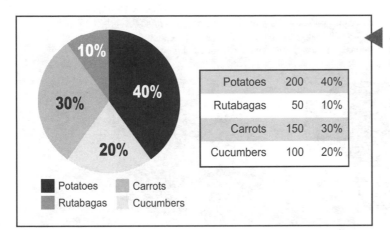

A variety of screened backgrounds creates easy readability and organization

Potatoes	200	40%
Rutabagas	50	10%
Carrots	150	30%
Cucumbers	100	20%

If the purpose of the screen is to emphasize, bright colors or graduated backgrounds can add graphic flair to the page.

Screens may also be applied to a design element to deemphasize the element if it competes too strongly with a focal point. A screen of 50% density can greatly reduce the amount of weight—and attention— the element receives.

Subtle visual communication can be achieved by using a ghosted image or watermark in a document. If the image or watermark is used behind copy, make sure the neutral density is no more than 20% gray. Using the eyedropper tool in Adobe® Photoshop®, a measurement may be made of the darkest part of a ghosted image to determine if text will be readable on top of the image. It may be necessary to use a text box with a plain background on top of a ghosted image to ensure readability.

Example of a good use of a screened background to emphasize versus an overuse of screens which dilutes attention-getting ability

Screening back an element can reduce its emphasis

Emphasis Lessened with Use of Screens

Screens may also be applied to a design element to deemphasize the element if it competes too strongly with a focal point.

Emphasis Lessened with Use of Screens

Screens may also be applied to a design element to deemphasize the element if it competes too strongly with a focal point.

Color is a strong factor in determining the messaging property of a ghosted image. Keep in mind that bright colors in an image become soft and muted when ghosted and will change the message of the image. A photograph of a speeding race car in bold reds and yellows becomes pink and cream once ghosted and may contradict the very nature of the image.

Another way to communicate a subtle message is to use a textured background. Using textured backgrounds such as marble, woodgrains, stone or even an abstraction can visually enhance a written message or send a visual message by itself. The more abstract the background, the more subtle the message sent. Representational backgrounds can get in the way of a written message and decrease readability of the text because the brain is forced to recognize the image. Abstractions bypass conscious recognition and don't impede readability.

Two different backgrounds using representational and abstract images. Note how the representational image on the left tends to attract the eye, in comparison to the abstract background which tends to make the type more prominent.

BLEEDS

When a design element runs to the edge, or off the edge, of a page it is said to "bleed." Filling a page with an image and bleeding it off the edge is a good way to create drama and graphic appeal.

When bleeding an element, make sure to extend it 1/8 of an inch outside the finished size of the document to allow for mis-trimming at the printer.

Be aware of the "live" area of the page, which is approximately 1/2 inch inside the finished size of an 8.5 x 11 page and will vary depending on page size. Larger pages require relatively larger margins and live areas to keep the page in balance.

The focus of the photograph should fall within the live area of the page as demonstrated correctly in the left example and incorrectly in the right example. The live area is indicated by the small dashed line. The trim size of the document is indicated by the solid line and the 1/8 inch bleed by the large dashed line.

Examples of a partial bleed (a) and full bleed (b). The right example (c) shows the correct way to position a photo which bleeds off the cover but does not extend to the back cover of a publication.

BORDERS AND RULES

A border is the outline of a shape, usually rectangular, which contains either written or visual information. The border is secondary to and should not overpower what it contains. A rule is any mark that connects two points. Usually the mark is straight but does not have to be.

Borders and rules are used for three primary reasons: to organize, to emphasize and in some cases to communicate a visual message.

The best way to organize a page is to use the appropriate amount of space between elements to create good relationships. However, sometimes space is in short supply in your document. When it is, a border or rule works nicely to separate elements or to establish relationships between elements.

When used for organization, the border or rule should be simple and understated. A single hairline rule or even a simple row of dots can effectively create a visual separation between elements.

A simple rule may also be used to relate one element to another when they cannot be related by either alignment or proximity.

Aid Given to Physicians

City Medical Center's Home Health Department has been helping physicians take care of their patients since 1985. Whether a patient is terminally ill or only in need of occasional assistance, we provide safe, comfortable and economical care in the comfort of home.

Home care works with the patient and the physicians to ensure the highest level of quality care. Our skilled staff includes registered nurses licensed vocational nurses; physical, speech and occupational therapists social workers and home health aids.

Our broad scope of services allow appropriate levels of care in response to each patient's needs. Home Care's professional services and staff help contain costs, prevent or shorten hospital stays, allow patients to return to work quickly and prevent terminally ill people from spending

Smith Recognized

Chuck Smith, Director of Plant Operations for City Medical Center, was recently awarded admission into the international Ambassador's Club by Acme, Inc. Smith, an Acme employee who works on-site at City Medical Center through a cooperative agreement, earned this special recognition for his "outstanding contributions in carrying out the Acme Vision of Creating Customer Value." For Acme employees, the Ambassador's Club represents the highest, most respected level of recognition within the company's Home and Building Control Division. Over the last two years, City Medical Center has become an international example of successful working partnership with Acme. Last year alone, Smith's department helped the Medical Center save more than $880, 000 in energy and operational cost with minimal over time applied to this

Aid Given to Physicians

City Medical Center's Home Health Department has been helping physicians take care of their patients since 1985. Whether a patient is terminally ill or only in need of occasional assistance, we provide safe, comfortable and economical care in the comfort of home.

Home care works with the patient and the physicians to ensure the highest level of quality care. Our skilled staff includes registered nurses licensed vocational nurses; physical, speech and occupational therapists social workers and home health aids.

Our broad scope of services allow appropriate levels of care in response to each patient's needs. Home Care's professional services and staff help contain costs, prevent or shorten hospital stays, allow patients to return to work quickly and prevent terminally ill people from spending

Smith Recognized

Chuck Smith, Director of Plant Operations for City Medical Center, was recently awarded admission into the international Ambassador's Club by Acme, Inc. Smith, an Acme employee who works on-site at City Medical Center through a cooperative agreement, earned this special recognition for his "outstanding contributions in carrying out the Acme Vision of Creating Customer Value." For Acme employees, the Ambassador's Club represents the highest, most respected level of recognition within the company's Home and Building Control Division. Over the last two years, City Medical Center has become an international example of successful working partnership with Acme. Last year alone, Smith's department helped the Medical Center save more than $880, 000 in energy and operational cost with minimal over time applied to this

A dark, heavy rule which is meant to merely separate can overpower the headline in these two articles. A thinner rule, shown in the bottom example, separates the articles without detracting from the headlines.

Chuck Smith, Director of Plant Operations for City Medical Center, was recently awarded admission into the international Ambassador's Club

City Medical Center

555 Hospital Drive
Parkside, KS 66666

Relationships created by a simple rule

A border or rule may also be used to emphasize an element on a page. In this case, it may be useful to use a thicker or more decorative border to call attention to the element. The border should never overpower the element it contains and should be appropriate to the element.

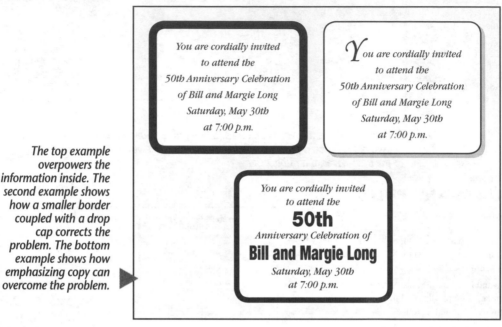

The top example overpowers the information inside. The second example shows how a smaller border coupled with a drop cap corrects the problem. The bottom example shows how emphasizing copy can overcome the problem.

Remember, emphasis is created by departing from an established pattern. In the example above, only one border uses a drop shadow to establish emphasis. If all the borders used drop shadows, no emphasis would be established for any of the elements.

A rule or border may be used to communicate in some cases. A dashed line around a coupon, for example, communicates the message that the coupon should be cut out. When using a rule or border to communicate, it is acceptable to make the border more prominent or illustrative. Decorative borders around the edge of certificates communicate importance, for example.

An illustrative effect is best if it is less representational and more abstract. Representational borders tend to attract too much attention and detract from what they contain. (See also "Emphasis.")

The top three borders, although heavy, are abstract and will not detract from any information placed inside. The three borders on the bottom are representational and may overpower any text placed inside.

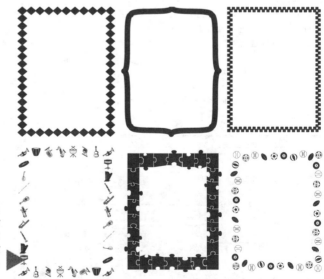

CAPTIONS

A caption is a body of text used next to a graphic element such as a photo or chart. A caption should closely relate to the graphic by both proximity and alignment. No other element should be more closely related to a graphic than its caption. The graphic element and the caption should appear to be one element.

Captions will normally be one to three points smaller than the body type in the same document. This size difference makes a clear distinction between caption and body. However, even with a size distinction, it is a good idea to emphasize the caption by using boldface, italics or both. Captions also may be emphasized by using color, boxes or copy warmers to attract attention. In these cases, make sure the emphasis does not overpower the graphic element.

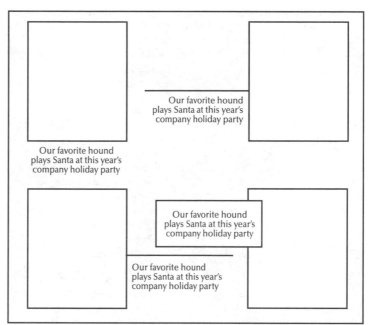

Our favorite hound plays Santa at this year's company holiday party

Our favorite hound plays Santa at this year's company holiday party

Our favorite hound plays Santa at this year's company holiday party

Our favorite hound plays Santa at this year's company holiday party

CHARTS, GRAPHS AND TABLES

Charts, graphs and tables satisfy both the reader's need for visual stimulation and the reader's need for specific, written information. For a chart, graph or table to communicate effectively it must be designed to accomplish two goals. First, it must visually represent data in an organized, easy-to-see fashion. Second, the specific information detailed by the graph, chart or table must be precisely represented and easily understood. The key to accomplishing both goals is simplicity.

Printer's Tips:
See Copy Warmers on page 286 for more information.

A visual trend represented by a simple design is quickly and easily recognized. Unfortunately, many designers sacrifice simplicity by trying to make the design more visually compelling. Not only does this destroy the immediate readability of the design, it may also distort the specific information or make it difficult to understand.

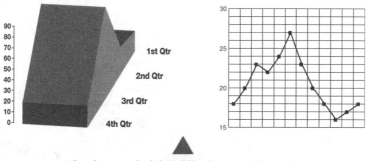

The chart on the left is difficult to read due to the overuse of the 3-D effect. The chart on the right is two dimensional and easier to read.

Another way to simplify a design is to regroup the information into broader categories. Broader categories result in less data which need to be demonstrated and clearer visual representations. For example, a line graph illustrating the amount of sales for a company in a year would be better if the months were charted instead of the weeks. Keep in mind the reader's need for specific information, however. Charting every quarter of the same graph may be too broad.

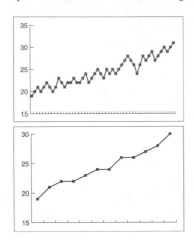

The bottom graph shows how visually simplifying the information makes it easy to read and understand yet still attractive

Choosing the correct format for the graph, chart or table is also necessary. The following visual syntax will apply to most designs:

1. Chronological data usually works best when charted left to right. However, it can be charted left to right or bottom to top with the earliest date appearing in the bottom left and progressing to the latest date either to the right or the top.

2. Amounts of any kind, either monetary or otherwise, should be charted left to right or bottom to top with the lowest number appearing in the bottom left and progressing higher to the right or the top.

3. Flow charts demonstrate the order of events, or cause and effect, from left to right or top to bottom, with the first event occurring on the left-hand side or the top and progressing either to the right or the bottom.

4. Organizational charts demonstrate rank from top to bottom with the highest rank appearing on top and progressing to the lowest rank on bottom. Direct reporting is indicated with a solid line and indirect reporting is indicated with a dashed line.

Flow charts demonstrate work flow or organization (a).

Pie graphs demonstrate parts of a whole (b).

Bar graphs make comparisons (c).

Stacked bar graphs display parts of a whole that contribute to a comparison (d).

Line graphs indicate up and down trends (e).

Styles can be combined to demonstrate more data.

Tables display data without visual emphasis.

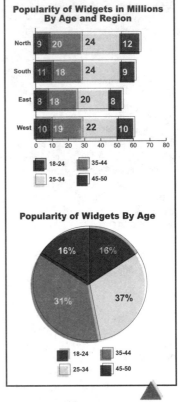

Different types of information require different types of graphs

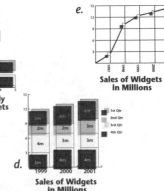

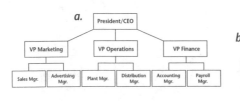

Graphs making comparisons should use devices which show contrast between the different information. Color and tints of color are preferable over patterns, which can often be visually confusing. Shapes may be used in flow charts to clarify organization. The maximum amount of contrast between parts should be used when possible. More contrast equals clearer communication.

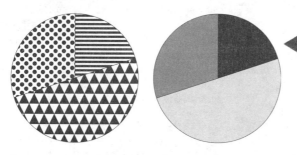

The variety of patterns may show different sections of the graph, but their busyness creates confusion between the divisions

When using representational objects, such as images instead of bars or lines, keep them simple and easy to understand. The same image should be used throughout a graph and only the size changed to demonstrate the data.

Using different objects can confuse the audience if the objects illustrated have varying size differences to begin with. For example, a graph comparing sales of trees, shrubs and flowers that uses the actual objects would be confusing because of the relative differences in the size of the objects. The fact that the reader already knows flowers are smaller than shrubs, which are smaller than trees, is a hindrance to communicating the information effectively.

To further clarify communication, always make sure your graph, chart or table has a descriptive title to tell the reader exactly what is being illustrated. An explanation of the data can be included in a caption, and a key to the chart makes it easier for the reader to understand the information. Additionally, it may often be necessary to label certain charted data instead of making the reader scan across or down to find the information. This is also useful if specific data needs to be communicated. Shaded rectangles or lines can aid the reader in matching data across and down or help highlight specific information.

This graph contains a strong heading and consistent use of shapes within to represent different numerical quantities

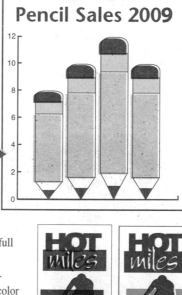

COLOR

Color is light and the reflection of light from printed material. Color ranges from black, which is the absence of color, to white, which is the reflection of the full range of color.

Color can be used to attract, add emphasis, communicate a message and organize.

When attracting or adding emphasis, color should be used sparingly. Overuse of color spoils its ability to attract attention or emphasize. Use the color on a focal point or balance to the focal point for maximum emphasis.

Colors have long been used to communicate emotions or set a tone of voice for a design. Color choices are usually made intuitively, however, there are general guidelines for choosing colors which will convey specific meanings. Keep in mind that different cultures may have different meanings for certain colors. For example, in Western culture the color used to symbolize death is often black. But Eastern cultures often use white to symbolize death.

Yellow	Cheerful, surprising, bright, positive, happy; also intellectual, educational, intelligent; **Light:** elegance, sophistication
Orange	Friendly, warm, casual, inviting, open honest; **Dark:** earthy, natural; **Light:** soft, relaxing
Red	Powerful, forceful, bold; also passionate, emotional, exciting; also danger, warning; **Dark:** wealth, richness; **Light:** romantic
Green	Fresh, healthy, natural, relaxing; **Dark:** prosperous, traditional
Blue	Refreshing, invigorating, relaxing; also traditional, classic, professional, dependable
Violet	Nostalgic, romantic, subdued; **Dark:** regal, royal, magical, mysterious
White	Purity, cleanliness, perfection, elegance, professionalism
Black	Mysterious, magical, elegance, simplicity, basic, professional

The use of colors in different contexts will also change the meaning. Generally, red is considered the color of passionate emotion. It is used as such for Valentine's Day or to communicate strong emotions like anger. On a stop sign, however, red means you must "stop."

No matter how color is used, consideration should be given to its meaning in context. Even when designing a chart, color choices should make sense.

When using color to organize communication, different colors may be assigned certain meanings. A key, or guide describing the meaning of the colors, may be necessary to help the reader understand the organization. Choose colors which all fit sensibly within a set. For example, use all pastels or all bright colors or all dark colors to create your organization for a single document or section of a document. If you mix different sets of colors without a reason, your audience will instinctively relate them even if you don't mean them to be related.

For example, if you use green, red, blue and soft pink to organize four sections of a book, your audience will assume the soft pink section is different in some way from the other three sections. Unless this is the desired response, another bright color such as orange should be used to maintain the consistency in the organization.

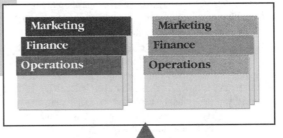

Sensible colors create organization for the separate documents without confusion

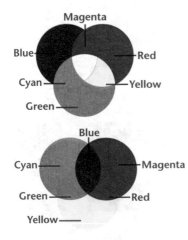

Choosing color for printed material is not the same as choosing color for Web sites or presentations. The difference between the two often causes a great deal of confusion. Print materials use cyan, yellow, magenta and black (CMYK) inks while computer monitors and projectors use red, green and blue (RGB) light. Many colors which can be produced using RGB color cannot be reproduced using CMYK.

Choosing color for print based on what is represented on a computer monitor will usually yield unexpected results. To accurately choose color for printed materials, use a print color guide which shows every possible combination of the four process colors (CMYK).

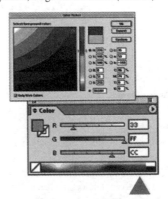

Using Web-safe colors will ensure your Web site will show up accurately

Choosing colors for Web sites may also yield unexpected results on different monitors. Using Web-safe colors will ensure your Web site will show up accurately on most computer monitors.

One way to more accurately display colors on your monitor is to calibrate your monitor to display for print or Web. The popular photo editing software Adobe® Photoshop® comes with additional software and a step-by-step guide for calibrating monitors. Other software is also available for calibrating monitors.

Sometimes printing from a desktop color printer will yield different colors than those printed on a traditional offset press. Accurate color can be produced from some printing devices using ICC (International Color Consortium) profiles provided by the manufacturer. ICC profiles use software to ensure accurate densities of CMYK are printed from your computer. Check with your printer's manufacturer to see if your printer has this capability.

In addition to the four process colors, printers will also use "spot" color to add color to a document. When a printer uses spot color, an ink is selected using a system such as the inks system created by PANTONE®. The actual colored ink is printed instead of a combination of process colors which would yield a similar result.

For example, if you wanted an item printed in green, the customer or printer could choose to print a spot color, say PANTONE 361, to print the green. Process color could also be used to print the green, but instead of an actual green ink, a combination of the process colors cyan and yellow would be used to create the illusion of green using halftone dots.

Keep in mind, process color buildups simulate color while spot color inks are real. For this reason, spot colors are often more attractive than the illusion of color created by CMYK. However, images such as photographs can only be reproduced using CMYK inks.

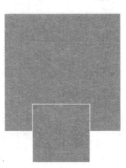

Example of color buildup ▶

CONSISTENCY

Consistent graphic styles used in communication pieces originating from a company or organization create an easily identifiable look and feel. This consistency sends a single, clear message to the audience concerning the company's underlying theme or brand.

Consistency is established by applying a standard to all communication from a company or organization. Advertisements, brochures, Web sites, reports and even memos and business correspondence should all be related by the way they look.

The following factors should be considered when establishing consistency in design materials:

Color

Choose colors which communicate your identity (see Color). Keep it simple by choosing a set of no more than three. One way of building flexibility into your standards is to choose a single color which appears on all documents and to combine it with a number of different colors for different reasons. For example, a company with three different products may use yellow for all three and green, blue and red for the respective products.

When choosing a specific ink color such as a PANTONE® color, keep in mind the color can appear differently in different venues. It may be useful to choose three similar spot colors for different reasons. For example, the same spot color will look different when used on coated or uncoated stock, and also when the color is used in outdoor signage. It may be necessary to pick a brighter, more saturated color for uncoated stock and for outdoor signage.

Web sites also present a particular challenge because colors chosen for display need to fit into the palette of Web safe colors. Choose a Web color first and follow with colors for print to ensure consistency.

Typography

Choose a type family which is broad enough to provide options for complex documents. A type family is a collection of type faces or fonts which have similar visual characteristics, such as the Helvetica type family. The type you choose should include not only Roman, or normal, but bold and italic faces as well. To increase flexibility, the family may also have black, extra black, light or thin. Some type families include both serif and sans-serif versions, providing even greater flexibility in design while maintaining consistency.

Stone Sans	Garamond	Helvetica
Stone Sans Bold	**Garamond Bold**	**Helvetica Bold**
Stone Sans Semibold	**Garamond Bold Condensed**	**Helvetica Heavy**
Stone Sans Italic	*Garamond Light Italic*	*Helvetica Ultra Light Italic*
Stone Sans Bold Italic	**Garamond Ultra**	**Helvetica Bold Extended**

Sometimes two families may be chosen to go together to create flexibility. This is usually used in styles for publications. When using two families, choose those with a great deal of contrast to increase the usability. For example, a delicate serif type such as Garamond works well with a strong sans-serif such as Futura.

Logo

Your logo acts as a signature to your documents and should be as consistent. Make sure the logo appears in the same location and size in like documents. Both multicolor and single color versions should be developed to cover all production situations. The logo may be accompanied by a company name, an address line, or a slogan or tag line. How these elements relate to the logo should be clearly defined and used in the same way on similar documents.

> **Understanding and using your home computer**
> - Available to people of all ages
> - Convenient times and locations
> - All levels of training available throughout the course
> - Computers available on-site for use both during class and after hours
> - All learning materials provided

Imagery

Photographs and illustrations say as much about your company or organization as the copy you use. Create guidelines for choosing illustrations and photos to ensure consistency. For example, guidelines for choosing photos could include not only subject matter, but color, lighting, exposure and type of film used. One way to create these guidelines quickly is to use a stock photo book to find photographs which show the style you are looking for. Another way to ensure consistency is to use the same photographer or illustrator whose style matches your message.

Layout

Layout consistency can be created by using a common grid system on similar documents (see Grid). This is particularly useful in publications to establish a look which distinguishes editorial from advertising sections. In publications, headers and footers can be added to the grid to further define the publication's style.

Use of space and balance is another way to establish a layout style. Both an economical and extravagant use of space can be a distinguishing characteristic of your company's style. Choosing between symmetrical and asymmetrical balance also defines your layout style.

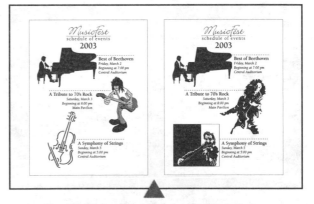

Varying illustration styles can send a confusing message to the viewer. Keep your clip art selections consistent as illustrated on the right.

EMPHASIS

Visual emphasis is added to a document by creating contrast between elements. In the case of emphasis, contrast is added by departing from an established pattern.

For example, adding emphasis to text within body copy is often achieved by italicizing the part of the copy which requires emphasis. In this case, the pattern is established by the use of Roman, or normal, type of the body copy and the contrast created by using italics and departing from the pattern.

Emphasis is used to set up a priority of elements on a page, showing the reader what to look at first and directing eye flow through the page. The more contrast used, the greater the emphasis on the element. Greater emphasis makes the element more prominent. Care should be taken regarding how much emphasis is placed on every element on a page or spread to establish the priority. The element with the most emphasis becomes the "focal point" of the page or spread. No other element should have as much emphasis as the focal point. A second, and possibly a third, element should be emphasized to create a balance on the page for a strong focal point and direct the eye flow.

Emphasis may also be used to organize a page. This can be achieved by using subheads or a graphic element such as a box or border. In this case the contrast and departure from the pattern will be less than when creating a focal point. A slight difference is all that is required to show the reader a change in a topic or idea. More emphasis than is necessary can create conflict with the focal point. Remember, when everything is emphasized, the pattern on the page is destroyed and nothing is emphasized.

Emphasis can be created in a variety of ways using one or a combination of techniques described below.

- Size: Larger elements attract attention.
- Space: Adding space around or between elements emphasizes the elements.
- Value: The darker the element, the more it attracts the eye
- Position: Elements at the top of the page tend to get noticed first

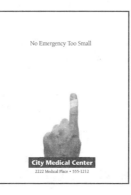

These two illustrations show examples of emphasis on the headline. In the first example, the headline appears at the top of the page (position) and is surrounded by a lot of space (space). In the second, the headline is at the bottom, but is reversed out (value) and is larger (size).

In example (a), the lack of a grid creates misalignment of elements and can be confusing. To create emphasis, apply a grid (b); then depart from the grid to emphasize elements (c). The grid aligns the elements and creates a pattern for the reader. Departures from the pattern make the design more attractive.

Graphics, Prepress and Printing

Copy Warmers

Copy warmers are graphic elements that direct the reader's eye to the beginning point of the copy. They should be strong enough to attract attention without detracting from the message. Usually, abstract elements have the most subtlety, but different types of communication may benefit from less subtle symbolic elements. A copy warmer adds emphasis and is subject to the same guidelines. (See Emphasis, Borders and Rules, Initial Caps.)

Drop Caps (Initial Caps)

A drop capital letter is a type of copy warmer that uses an enlargement of the first letter of the first word of an article or body of text. It is used to attract the reader's eye to the beginning point of an article and, in some cases, set the tone of voice for the message. Because it is used as a device to attract, it should conform to the rules of emphasis (see Emphasis).

Use drop caps sparingly, at the very beginning of a work, and occasionally at the beginning of long chapters or sections. If the beginning point of a piece is obvious, a drop cap becomes more decorative than functional.

When using a drop cap to help set the tone of voice, choose a novelty typeface which feels like the message of the piece.

There should be a significant amount of contrast between a drop cap and the rest of the body copy. Size and weight will create the primary difference in almost every case. However, differences in the font itself are appropriate and can create a more interesting drop cap.

A drop cap should be as wide as necessary to accommodate the letter and about three to four lines deep. It should usually conform to the left and top margins of the body copy, however, it may extend into those margins to create better alignment relationships.

Relating the drop cap to the letter which follows is the greatest challenge in using this technique. Pay close attention to this relationship to ensure readability. A box or other shape may be necessary to create the right relationship. Also, adjustment of the first line of text may be necessary.

> *U*se copy warmers to direct the audience's eye to the beginning point of the copy. This is helpful when dominant visual elements lead the eye away from the copy block.
>
> Use copy warmers to direct the audience's eye to the beginning point of the copy. This is helpful when dominant visual elements lead the eye away from the copy block.
>
> Use copy warmers to direct the audience's eye to the beginning point of the copy. This is helpful when dominant visual elements lead the eye away from the copy block.
>
> Use copy warmers to direct the audience's eye to the beginning point of the copy. This is helpful when dominant visual elements lead the eye away from the copy block.

*C*ity Medical Center's Home Health Department has been helping physicians take care of their patients since 1985. Whether a patient is terminally ill or only in need of occasional assistance, we provide safe, comfortable and economical care in the comfort of home.

Home care works with the patient and the physicians to ensure the highest level of quality care. Our skilled staff includes registered nurses licensed vocational nurses; physical, speech and occupational therapists social workers and home health aids.

Our broad scope of services allow appropriate levels of care in response to each patient's needs. Home Care's professional services and staff help contain costs, prevent or shorten hospital stays, allow patients to return to work

*C*huck Smith, Director of Plant Operations for City Medical Center, was recently awarded admission into the international Ambassador's Club by Acme, Inc. Smith, an Acme employee who works on-site at City Medical Center through a cooperative agreement, earned this special recognition for his "outstanding contributions in carrying out the Acme Vision of Creating Customer Value." For Acme employees, the Ambassador's Club represents the highest, most respected level of recognition within the company's Home and Building Control Division. Over the last two years, City Medical Center has become an international example of successful working partnership with Acme. Last year alone, Smith's department helped the Medical Center save more than $880,000 in energy and operational cost with minimal over time applied to this.

FOCAL POINT (SEE EMPHASIS)

HEADLINES (SEE TYPOGRAPHY)

ILLUSTRATIONS AND PHOTOGRAPHS

Illustrations and photographs are used to direct the reader's eye, attract attention, convey a tone of voice or clarify or replace a written description.

The placement of an illustration or photograph in a document has an effect on the way the reader views the document. Imagery tends to attract the passive interest of the viewer and can pull the reader's eye from corner to corner. For example, eye flow usually begins in the upper right corner of a two-page spread and immediately begins to scan back to the upper left corner. In a document with no imagery, the eye will not travel nearly as far as in a document with strategically placed imagery. See the example on the right.

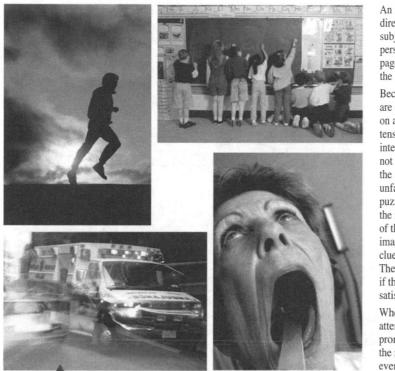

An illustration or photograph can also direct a reader by the orientation of the subject matter. A photograph of a person looking off the page or into the page will direct the reader to follow the subject's example.

Because illustrations and photographs are often the first item a viewer sees on a page, they may be used to create tension and, therefore, attract the interest of the reader. Imagery may not be immediately recognizable, or the subject of the imagery may be unfamiliar or unusual. This visual puzzle creates tension in the mind of the reader. The reader seeks resolution of the tension by examining the imagery more closely or looking for clues in the headline or body copy. The imagery creates the desired effect if the tension is resolved in a way that satisfies the reader.

When using imagery to attract attention, make the imagery the most prominent part of the page. Making the reader seek out the copy creates even more tension and a more dynamic design.

Each of these photos convey a different message or "personality" based on the way they look

The tone, or personality, of your communication can be established by using an appropriate illustration or photograph. Illustrations may be rendered using a huge variety of styles and techniques, each communicating a particular tone.

Photographs use a variety of films, angles, lenses and lighting techniques to achieve the desired tone. Choosing imagery by the way it "feels" is subjective and usually done intuitively. However, there are certain techniques which can be relied on to deliver the appropriate tone.

Showing an image rather than describing it with words is one of the most effective forms of communication. A written description of the Grand Canyon will never be as effective as a photograph of the Grand Canyon. The latter communicates in an instant while the former must be read and translated to a mental picture.

Illustrations are effective in showing how something works or is assembled. In this case, a combination of words and pictures creates the desired communication.

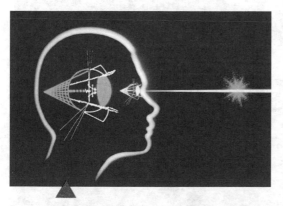

This illustration is effective in showing light entering into the human eye without the use of supporting text

Whether your illustration or photograph directs the reader's eye, attracts attention, conveys a tone of voice or clarifies or replaces text, it should be used to communicate, not decorate.

Poor use of imagery often involves overusing or misusing ready-made art or stock photos. Visual imagery is perceived by the brain faster than written messages. Using too many pictures can overload the reader and crowd the document. In most cases, an illustration or photograph needs to be prominent and given the space it deserves. The exception is a simple illustration used to direct the eye to a particular piece of copy. These "copy warmers," although illustrative, do not command the same attention as a piece of art or a photograph. Make sure the art chosen for this type of effect is very basic and directs instead of attracts the eye.

The overuse of art in the second example has caused the focus to turn from the information to the abundance of imagery

Mixing different styles of ready-made art in one document is another poor use. The style of an illustration will set the tone for the communication. Using a cartoon, a realistic drawing and a stylized design all in one piece can be confusing. Choose art which looks like it was created by the same illustrator using the same style to create consistency and power in your communication.

Photographs and illustrations should be cropped to focus attention on the subject matter. Information in the photo which is not part of the communication should be cropped out. On the other hand, a crop which is too tight can remove necessary information.

Photos may be cropped to balance the subject matter in the rectangle either symmetrically or asymmetrically. Symmetrical balance focuses the reader on the subject matter but may be too static. Asymmetrical balance is often more natural and pleasing to the eye. Deciding on which type of crop to use will depend on the message you are sending.

Simply cropping an image can change the emphasis and feeling of a photograph

ITALICS (SEE TYPOGRAPHY)

LEADING (SEE TYPOGRAPHY AND SPACE)

LISTS (BULLET POINTS)

Lists are excellent ways to dispense information quickly and efficiently. Bullet points, boxes or some other copy warmer should be used to delineate the beginning of a new point or idea. Only one space is necessary after the bullet point or copy warmer to establish a good relationship between the thought and the graphic element. Avoid the word processing types of indentions which are unnecessary and hinder readability. When a list has two or more lines per point, the copy should align under the first line of copy, not the bullet point.

<table>
<tr>
<td>
• Apples, pears, peaches, plums, bananas, pineapples
• Oranges, lemons, grapefruits, tangerines, limes
• Strawberries, blueberries, raspberries, boysenberries
• Watermelons, cantaloupe, honeydews, pumpkins
</td>
<td>
•Apples, pears, peaches, plums, bananas, pineapples
•Oranges, lemons, grapefruits, tangerines, limes
•Strawberries, blueberries, raspberries, boysenberries
•Watermelons, cantaloupe, honeydews, pumpkins
</td>
<td>
• Apples, pears, peaches, plums, bananas, pineapples
• Oranges, lemons, grapefruits, tangerines, limes
• Strawberries, blueberries, raspberries, boysenberries
• Watermelons, cantaloupe, honeydews, pumpkins
</td>
</tr>
<tr>
<td>a.</td>
<td>b.</td>
<td>c.</td>
</tr>
</table>

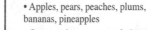

In the three examples listed above, (a) and (b) illustrate improper spacing and alignment, while (c) demonstrates correct formatting

LOGOS (SEE CONSISTENCY)

MAPS

Maps serve two primary functions in business communication. A map may show directions to a location. A map may also be used to show differences in particular areas as in the amount of population by state, or the weather forecast across the country.

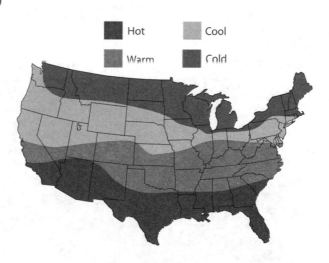

When creating any map, make sure the map is oriented with the north at the top. It is a good idea to include a marker or arrow indicating that north is at the top of the map. Use an accurate map as a starting point, and simplify the map to clarify the information. Accurate maps are available from map companies or on-line. These maps are usually too detailed for good, clear communication, especially if the map will be reproduced small in a document.

A directional map should include major landmarks such as the intersection of main highways. Make sure to create the map to be understandable no matter which direction the reader will be traveling from. A reader from south of the location may not be familiar with a landmark to the north, for example. The map should include landmarks to the south as well as north, east and west.

Directional maps may be simplified by eliminating minor roads or landmarks which are unnecessary. It is acceptable to make the roads straighter than they may actually be to simplify the look of the map. Keep in mind, a simplified map may require written instructions, particularly indicating distance from one point to another.

Maps illustrating differences in various geographical regions do not need highways, railroads, bodies of water or other geographical indicators unless they are relative to the information to be communicated. Using colors or tints of colors to indicate differences is preferable over patterns, which can be visually confusing. Use as much contrast as possible when indicating differences. Contrast equals clearer communication.

A key which tells the reader what the various colors mean may be necessary. If symbols are used to indicate certain characteristics, make sure to provide a key for the symbols as well. Titles, captions and labels also help clarify the information.

MARGINS (SEE SPACE)

PAGE LAYOUT/GRID SYSTEMS

One of the best techniques for organizing a document, creating consistency and setting up natural relationships of elements on a page is to create a grid for your document. When an element such as a photo, headline or block of body copy is placed on the grid, it must conform both horizontally and vertically to the grid. This conformity aligns elements in a natural, organized fashion. The consistent structure of the grid plays into the reader's natural recognition of patterns, making a more pleasing, easy-to-read document and establishing consistency among pages.

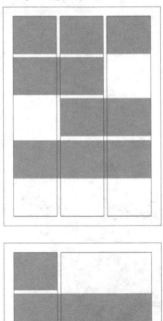

The best way to create a grid is to work traditionally using a pad of paper and a pencil. Begin with a proportional rectangle about half the size of the eventual document. Sketch a simple two-column grid and block in shapes to represent where headlines, body copy, photos, logo and other elements will go. These sketches are called "thumbnail" sketches. Use the two-column grid as an understructure to complete five or six thumbnails. Experiment using one column and progress to three or more columns. Combine ideas to create more complex, unique grids. You may have a grid with two columns on the top and three on the bottom, for example. Try both usual and unusual ways of positioning elements on each grid. Keep in mind the more thumbnails you complete, the better your eventual layout will be.

A good technique is to pick one element to be the focal point, or main attention-getting device, on the page. Block in that element first. (For more information see Emphasis.) Select a second point as a balance to the focal point and block it in. Lay the rest of the elements into the document using the grid as a guideline.

One benefit of the grid system is the way it creates a recognizable pattern on the page. Departure from the grid, and therefore the pattern, creates a strong attention-getting device. After choosing which elements will be the focal point and balance, determine how much of a departure is needed to attract attention.

Sketching your initial layout through the use of thumbnail sketches will help you breeze through the process of getting from general ideas to actual concepts for the finished design

The combination of focal point, balance, and grid should organize the page to direct the reader's eye from a beginning to an ending point. Designing around the natural eye flow of the reader is a good way to ensure the structure you create will work. Among theories concerning eye flow are the "Z" theory, reader gravity and golden means. All are very similar and can be combined in a single layout.

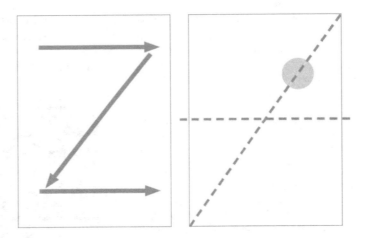

PULL QUOTES

The goal of most designers is to compel the audience to read the information in the document. Getting the audience to begin reading is a first step. Many designers use pull quotes to achieve this crucial first step.

A pull quote is a short block of copy, usually no more than a sentence or two, which is emphasized and positioned prominently on the page. The quote is usually an interesting bit of information chosen from the body copy of the document. The idea is to create enough tension with the quote to compel the reader to find it within the context of the body copy.

"Over the last few months, nearly 3000 widgets were sold each day."

"Over the last few months, nearly 3000 widgets were sold each day."

"Over the last few months, nearly 3000 widgets were sold each day."

There has been much debate on where in the body copy the pull quote should be taken from. Some have proposed the pull quote should be taken from the later part of the article. This presumes the reader reads the copy up to the pull quote, then reads the pull quote before continuing on with the rest of the copy. This opinion overlooks the original purpose of the pull quote altogether. If the pull quote does its job, it is one of the first items read on the page. If it compels the reader to locate it within the body copy, it is better for it to be taken from the early parts of the text, giving the reader an earlier start in the article.

Whether you choose the pull quote from the earlier or later parts of the article, it is a good idea not to position the quote too close to its source. Making the reader search for the context of the quote ensures greater readership. However, I have seen many designers who pull the quote from a completely different page than where it appears. This can frustrate the audience and lead to a loss of readership.

SPACE

Space is everything you don't see when you look at a document. You see text, photos, headlines, captions, logos and other elements. The area around and between those elements is the space. Becoming aware of the space in a document is the first step in using it effectively.

Space is used to create visual relief, provide emphasis and organize a page. Space may also be used as a communication device lending drama or elegance to a layout. Not being aware of space in a layout may create "captured" space, or space which does not make sense and establishes poor relationships between elements.

Nutrition for Growing Children

100% juice provides lots of vitamins and minerals

"A daily multivitamin is a great idea for kids."

Two principles work in tandem to govern the amount of space between and around elements:

1. Space provides visual relief and maintains the integrity of elements on a page. An element should be surrounded by enough space to be recognized as an individual element.

2. Elements should also be close enough together to form good relationships. The closer elements are to each other, the more they relate. A caption should be closer to a photograph than to any other element on a page, for example.

By creating space based on the two principles, visual relief as well as a natural organization of elements on a page will be established. But the use of space goes beyond being merely functional. Use of space can also create powerful messages. When using space to create a message, the principles which govern the organization of your page are often ignored. Crowding elements together can give a number of impressions, just as using an extravagant amount of space can give a number of opposite impressions.

How much space to add between elements will be based on the type of relationships you want to establish and the message of the document. However, some space is standard and measurable. The following guidelines for space are standard:

1. Use one space after a period, comma, colon or semicolon. Two spaces, used with typewriters, is unnecessary on computers.

2. No space is necessary either preceding or following a dash.

3. The margin on a standard 8.5 x 11 page should be at least 3/8 of an inch. Any less creates trimming problems and compromises the integrity of any element close to the edge.

4. A paragraph indention should be from 1/4 to 3/8 of an inch—just enough to make a distinction. The first paragraph of a chapter or section needs no indention.

The arrows point out the spacing issues present within the previous document before being proofed

TABS AND INDENTS (SEE SPACE)

TYPOGRAPHY

Type is the most powerful communication tool a designer uses. Type not only contains the written message, but also communicates a visual message by the way it looks. Careful consideration should be given to the choice of type style used to convey the message. A message conveyed using different type choices can take on different meanings as demonstrated.

Type is used to communicate written messages in headlines, subheads, captions, pull quotes and body copy. Each conforms to certain rules of legibility, readability, organization and visual appeal.

You're Invited

You're Invited

You're Invited

Visual appeal and legibility often work against each other. The more visually appealing the type the less legible it often becomes. Simple serif or sans-serif Roman, or normal, type has been shown to be very legible. More visually appealing fonts such as script or novelty typefaces hinder legibility. Additionally, setting type on a curve, outlining type, condensing or extending type too much or applying other dramatic visual effects also hinders legibility while making the type more interesting.

Emphasis and readability also work against each other. Many studies have shown that adding color or using boldface and italic type hinders readability. However, emphasizing type is necessary in many cases.

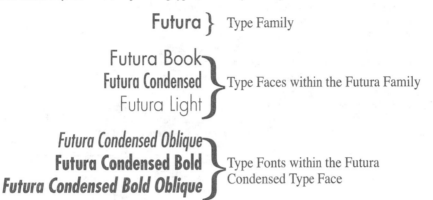

Knowing when to make the trade-off between legibility and readability and visual appeal and emphasis is the job of the designer. Generally, the fewer words used to convey a message, the more visual appeal and emphasis the type can have. Body copy should be readable, headlines should have visual appeal. Subheads, pull quotes and captions will fall somewhere in between depending on the amount of information communicated and the importance of the information.

Visual appeal and emphasis are added by using italics, boldface, all capitals, small capitals and larger sizes of a given typeface. Additionally, contrasting typefaces and novelty or script typefaces add both visual appeal and emphasis.

Italics are the best choice for emphasizing type within body copy. Because the italic font of a typeface is often the same weight as the Roman, or normal, font of the typeface, they do not attract the eye as boldface font would. Attracting the eye to a phrase or word in body copy would cause the audience to read the copy out of context.

Italics may also be used to add elegance to headlines, subheads and pull quotes. When used in captions or subheads, they provide a good contrast to the typically Roman headlines and body copy.

Our broad scope of services allow appropriate levels of care in response to each patient's needs. Home Care's **professional services** and staff help contain costs, prevent or shorten hospital stays, allow patients to return to work more quickly and prevent premature institutionalization. **Furthermore, studies show that patients recover more rapidly in the familiar surroundings of home.**

Our broad scope of services allow appropriate levels of care in response to each patient's needs. Home Care's *professional services* and staff help contain costs, prevent or shorten hospital stays, allow patients to return to work more quickly and prevent premature institutionalization. *Furthermore, studies show that patients recover more rapidly in the familiar surroundings of home.*

The bold words attract the eye first causing the audience to read the copy out of context

One of the best ways to emphasize type is to choose boldface. The extra weight attracts attention and tells the reader the text is important. Boldface can be used in headlines, subheads, pull quotes and captions but should rarely be used within body copy.

A typeface may have a number of bold fonts including bold, extra bold, black and extra black. The heavier the stroke of the letter, the more commanding it becomes. When using various bold fonts to organize a document, use the heaviest for the more important elements, such as headlines and subheads, and the less heavy boldface for pull quotes and captions. Studies have shown headlines using boldface are easier to comprehend.

In addition, boldface may be combined with size, italic, extended or condensed looks to help organize the page. Generally, extending a boldface will give it more importance while condensing it increases the drama, but not necessarily the importance of it. In every case, making type bigger will increase the dominance of that type over another. Bold italic indicates text is subordinate to bold while increasing either the drama or delicate nature of the information.

When using a number of fonts to organize a page, make sure the contrast between the fonts is substantial enough to clearly distinguish most important to least important.

Using all caps to emphasize type is the visual equivalent of shouting. The larger the size of all caps the louder the type seems to shout. This is a good way to indicate excitement or urgency and is used a great deal in retail advertising. All caps has been shown to reduce legibility more than boldface or italic and is best used in headlines and sparingly in subheads.

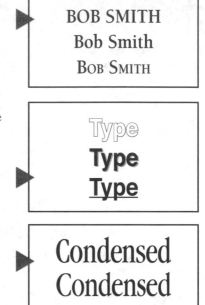

Small caps may be a suitable replacement for all caps when an understated emphasis is required. Small caps do not attract as much attention as all caps and don't darken the page as much as all caps. For the same reason, small caps are a good replacement for capitals in acronyms. When given the option of setting the proportion of small capitals to capitals, set small capitals at 80% to 90% of the size of capitals.

Emphasis created by outlining, underlining or using drop shadows should be used sparingly, if at all. These three choices are vastly inferior to using bold, italic, and even the use of all capitals both in terms of the amount of emphasis created and readability of the type. However, these techniques may be used on an individual type treatment for one or two words to create a departure from a standard style.

Use of computers in design has made it possible for the designer to condense or extend any typeface. This possibility has disadvantages and advantages.

Traditional fonts created by designers as condensed or extended versions of a normal typeface are superior both aesthetically and in terms of readability. These fonts should be used in place of digitally condensing or extending a normal font.

Using a computer to condense a typical font used for headlines by 90% has shown to improve the readability of the headline. However, condensing more than 70% or extending more than 120% creates such a deterioration of the original font it is not advisable. The key is moderation when using a computer to artificially create these variations.

Adjusting the space used between letters and lines of copy is crucial in creating legible and aesthetically pleasing text. The space between lines is referred to as *leading*. It is measured from a descender in one line to a descender in the line above it. Leading is increased as the type size becomes smaller. For body copy, two points of space between an ascender in one line and a descender in the line above it is the most legible choice. In larger type however, it is common to close the space up to improve both the look of the type and the legibility.

The adjustment of space between letters is known as *tracking* and *kerning*. Tracking is the equal adjustment of space between all letters in a selected body of text. Kerning is the adjustment of space between individual letter pairs. Rounded letters tend to need less space between them than do letters with a single vertical stroke. Some letter pairs such as a capital *T* with any lowercase letter needs a great deal of kerning to establish good relationships.

Ascender
X-height
Descender

Examples of tracking and kerning

Some typefaces, such as Helvetica, are available in more than the usual Roman, bold and italic versions. You may encounter versions such as Ultrathin, Thin, Black and Extra Black. These versions allow the designer to create dynamic contrast in type while using the same typeface. Keep in mind that any departure from normal, Roman type reduces legibility. The more severe the departure, the more legibility is compromised. Using these extreme versions can have a dramatic effect, but use them sparingly as a way of attracting attention in headlines or type treatments to reduce legibility problems.

Contrasting two type styles in a headline or type treatment is one of the best ways to attract attention. The more contrast between the styles, the more attention it attracts. Two similar type styles create only subtle contrast which seems more confusing to the reader than attractive. Contrast may be created in a variety of ways including use of differences in size, weight, color and font or a combination of these. For two contrasting type styles to work together, there must be harmony created in the space and alignment relationships. Notice how the examples below use contrasting type styles which relate to each other.

Type treatments and headlines may also use a graphic element as an integral part of the design to attract attention and communicate an idea. This is very similar to using contrasting type styles and the same rules apply. Specifically, the type should relate to the graphic by proximity and alignment.

Combining different type styles can create contrast and attract attention

Using color in type is another way to attract attention and communicate a message. However, colored type is not as readable as black type and should be used sparingly. Even a shift from black to dark blue can have an effect on the readability and retention of the information. For this reason, body copy should always be black, although color may be used on headlines and type treatments, and to some degree on subheads and pull quotes.

White or colored type on dark backgrounds also pushes acceptable standards of readability. But the dramatic effect created is often worth the loss of readability in headlines or type treatments. As with color, use this effect sparingly.

Legibility of body copy is of major importance to the designer. As described above, many techniques which create emphasis can affect the readability of body copy. The following guidelines are for creating body copy with maximum readability. It isn't necessary to follow every rule; if it were, all body copy would look the same. It is essential, however, to know how far you are departing from the rules when creating body copy.

1. Serif typefaces are more readable in body copy than sans-serif. In headlines, there is little difference.

2. For body copy, use 10 to 12 point type with two points of space between lines. 10 point type on 12 points of leading, 11 on 13, and 12 on 14 are the best choices.

3. Justified copy improves both readability and retention of information. The next best choice is flush left. Flush left is a good compromise when using small columns and larger type, both of which can cause space and hyphenation problems when justified. Flush right and centered copy are difficult to read and should be reserved for headlines, subheads, pull quotes and captions.

▶ **Flush left ...**

Our broad scope of services allow appropriate levels of care in response to each patient's needs. Home Care's professional services and staff help contain costs, prevent or shorten hospital stays, allow patients to return to work more quickly and prevent premature institutionalization. Furthermore, studies show that patients recover more rapidly in the familiar surroundings of home.

▶ **Flush right ...**

Our broad scope of services allow appropriate levels of care in response to each patient's needs. Home Care's professional services and staff help contain costs, prevent or shorten hospital stays, allow patients to return to work more quickly and prevent premature institutionalization. Furthermore, studies show that patients recover more rapidly in the familiar surroundings of home.

▶ **Justified ...**

Our broad scope of services allow appropriate levels of care in response to each patient's needs. Home Care's professional services and staff help contain costs, prevent or shorten hospital stays, allow patients to return to work more quickly and prevent premature institutionalization. Furthermore, studies show that patients recover more rapidly in the familiar surroundings of home.

▶ **Centered ...**

Our broad scope of services allow appropriate levels of care in response to each patient's needs. Home Care's professional services and staff help contain costs, prevent or shorten hospital stays, allow patients to return to work more quickly and prevent premature institutionalization. Furthermore, studies show that patients recover more rapidly in the familiar surroundings of home.

---

4. Use black type with a white background where possible. If you are using type on a screened background, make sure the background is no more than 20% neutral gray density.

Type also may be used to organize a page, showing the reader by choice of style and size which information belongs together and which is separate. When using type to organize, make sure the contrast between elements is sufficient to show the reader an obvious difference.

1. Begin by choosing body copy. Your body copy should be Roman, or normal, and will probably be between 11 and 13 points.

2. Usually your body copy will be serif. You may choose a second typeface in sans-serif to contrast with the serif copy.

3. Make your captions 1 to 3 points smaller than your body copy. If using the serif face, make the caption bold and/or italic or use another device to distinguish between caption and body copy. Be careful when reversing small, serif type because the serifs may be too small to show up when reversed. If sans-serif type is used, that difference may be sufficient.

4. Choose a font for pull quotes which is 2 to 6 points larger than the body copy. Bold italic is a good choice for pull quotes, particularly if it uses the same typeface as the body copy. Make sure to distinguish between pull quotes and subheads, which can be very close in size. If the pull quote and subhead use the same typeface, make one bold and the other italic. You may also use all capitals or small capitals on the subhead, although this wouldn't normally be a good choice for pull quotes.

5. Headlines will be the largest size. A good way to determine headlines is to double the size of your pull quotes. Keep in mind subheads will be sized between the headline and the pull quote and there needs to be enough difference between all three to create an obvious contrast. If the sizes are close to the same, a great deal of contrast needs to be applied either by changing color or font, or using capitals, italics or bold in different ways to establish obvious differences.

TITLE	**34 pt. Berkeley Black All Caps**
Headline	**26 pt. Berkeley Black**
Subhead	**22 pt. Berkeley Bold Italic**
Pull Quote	**16 pt. Berkeley Book Italic**
Body Copy	**12 pt. Berkeley Book**
Caption	**10 pt. Berkeley Bold Italic**

Punctuation in Body Copy

Dashes

There are three typographical dashes used in design: hyphen, en dash and em dash. A hyphen is used between two parts of a word when it is necessary to separate the word for a line break. An en dash is a slightly longer dash used to separate numbers. An em dash is used to replace a comma when the pause requires more emphasis. Neither en dashes, em dashes nor hyphens require space to be added either before or after the dash. Double dashes, often used on typewriters, are inappropriate in modern design and should not be used.

> **Hyphen:** 10-18-03
> **En Dash:** 14th – 15th
> **Em Dash:** Sally bought a dog, a collar and a food dish—all for less than $1.

Commas and Periods

Only one space is required after a period, comma or colon in modern typesetting. This rule conforms to the rule of relationships. Two spaces, used only on typewriters, can create poor relationships, especially in justified copy.

WATERMARKS (SEE BACKGROUNDS)

PREPRESS AND PRINTING

Understanding how a design moves from the your computer to an actual printed piece is important to creating successful communication. The following articles will aid you in working with your printer and ensuring top quality reproduction.

RESOLUTION

Understanding resolution and how it affects your work is the first step in creating digital files which will print successfully.

All images meant to be printed will have to be interpreted by a printing device of some kind. This device may be your color inkjet printer or your black and white laser printer. The device may also be an expensive "imagesetter" used by your printing company to make press-ready plates or film. All printing devices must interpret the digital information you have created on your computer. These devices use a RIP or Raster Image Processor to interpret and reproduce the digital information. The information you send to the printer will be in either a "vector-based" or a "pixel-based" form.

The image you see on a computer screen is created by pixels. A *pixel* is the building block used by the digital world to reproduce an image. In certain software such as Photoshop®, you can enlarge an image to more clearly see these actual pixels. The resolution of a digital image is determined by the number of pixels per square inch, or ppi, in the image. If an image is 300 ppi, it contains 300 x 300 pixels, or 90,000 total pixels per square inch. An 8 x 10 inch image at 300 ppi would contain 7.2 million pixels—90,000 x (8 x 10) = 7,200,000.

Each pixel contains numerical data which can be interpreted by a printing device. An image interpreted in this manner is considered to be a pixel-based image. These images are also called *rasters* or *bitmaps*, although neither is as precise as the term *pixel*. A *raster* is another name for a row of spots or dots and a *bitmap* is a visual map of bits of information. Both can mean something other than pixel-based images. Photographs seen on your computer monitor are good examples of pixel-based information.

A *vector* is an image which is defined by a path or curve represented on screen as an outline. The path itself contains an equation which is interpreted by the printing device. If you have ever created a piece of art using a "pen" or "path" tool, you were creating a vector. The vector may be changed by altering the path, and therefore the equation. When you set type in most programs, you are working with vectors. Although these images are interpreted on your computer screen using pixels, a printing device uses the path to determine how to recreate the image. For this reason, the pixel resolution (ppi) of a vector is unimportant. Vectors are said to be "resolution independent."

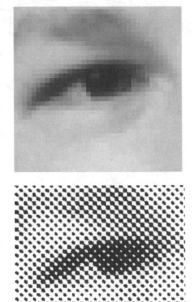

The top picture is an example of pixels per inch or ppi and the bottom picture shows lines per inch or lpi used for halftone screens

Whether you send a vector-based image or a pixel-based image to a printing device, the image is reproduced in much the same way. First, the device will determine how the information will be mapped, or placed on a "bitmap grid," when it is printed.

Each cell of the grid will either contain black or solid, or white or none, depending on how the RIP interprets the images. The number of cells in a square inch of the grid is termed *dots per inch* or dpi. A printer which is 1200 dpi has 1200 x 1200 cells or 1,440,000 total dots (cells) per square inch.

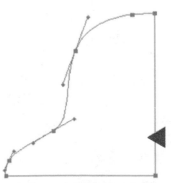

The graphic illustrates a vector path making the resulting image resolution independent

Graphics, Prepress and Printing

Many people confuse the dpi of a printing device with the halftone dots used to recreate photos in print. They are not the same although there is an important relationship between the two. Because printing ink can only be laid down as a solid, tones of color must be recreated using halftone dots. The larger the dot and the closer they are together, the darker the tone appears. The smaller the dot and the farther they are from each other, the lighter the tone appears.

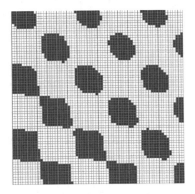

Before digital imaging, the halftone dots were created using screens and a photomechanical process. Today these halftone dots are created using the cells on a bitmap grid of a printing device. Digital dots are no longer a perfect ellipse as they were a few years ago, but the effect is still the same. Note how the dpi of the printing device creates the halftone dot in the illustration below.

How fine an image is reproduced using halftone dots is measured by the screen frequency or *lines per inch* (lpi) of the halftone. Lines per inch actually refers to the number of rows, or lines, of halftone dots used to create the halftone. A halftone with 150 lpi uses 150 rows of halftone dots in an inch. The higher the lpi, the more halftone dots are used, and the finer the halftone appears. Many commercial printers use 150 lpi while newspaper printers use 85 lpi.

Halftone dots use either AM (amplitude modulated) or FM (frequency modulated) screening to recreate the tones of an image. AM screening uses halftone dots of varying sizes placed at regular intervals to recreate tone. FM screening, also called "stochastic" screening, uses smaller, randomly placed dots to recreate tone. The magazine you get in the mail and your newspaper most likely use AM dots, while many inkjet printers use FM dots.

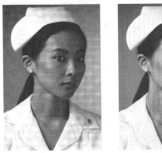

Full color is reproduced using the same halftone dots and lpi except that three additional colors are added to the black to create the illusion of multiple colors. These four colors are known as process colors and include cyan, magenta, yellow and black (CMYK). Imagine four halftones

The different line screens used in the photographs can easily be seen

printed on the same page, each in one of the four process colors, and you will have a good idea of how color printing works. To keep the colors from printing on top of each other, the colors are turned at four different angles which allow the halftone dots to lay beside each other instead of on top of each other.

Traditional printing requires four separate plates to create the color build up demonstrated above. When a color, digital file is sent to a printer's imagesetter, four separate halftones are imaged on four separate plates. Each plate is inked with the appropriate process color and a single sheet of paper is printed with the four plates. The result is a recreation of the image in full color.

An inkjet or other color printer uses fountains of cyan, yellow, magenta and black ink to recreate the color in the same way. Only the plates are missing from the process.

PPI, DPI and LPI

It is as important to understand how the different resolutions relate as it is to know what they mean. Creating good quality images hinges on knowing how the image is going to be used. The first bit of information you must know is which lpi will be used to create the halftones. As mentioned earlier, general printers use 150 while newspapers use 85. If you are printing to your laser printer or inkjet printer, you can usually set the lpi of the printing device through your layout software.

How high of an lpi you can print is determined by your printing device's maximum dpi. Using the formula below you can calculate the number of different tones which can be created from your printer at different lines per inch.

(dpi ÷ lpi) squared

For example if your printing device will print at 1200 dpi and you want to use a 100 lpi halftone: 1200 ÷ 100 = 12 and 12 x 12 = 144. Your printer can create 144 different tones. Although some photos call for at least 200 different tones, 144 tones will be adequate for many purposes. The maximum number of tones that can be digitally produced is 256. The following chart demonstrates different reproduction capabilities of different resolution printing devices.

Printer's Dots Per Inch

Line Screen	300	600	1200	2400
65	21	85	256	256
85	12	50	199	256
100	9	36	144	256
133	5	20	81	256
150	4	16	64	256
175	3	12	47	256
200	2	9	36	256

Possible Shades of Gray

Another important relationship exists between lpi of the halftone and the ppi of the image. To create a good image, the pixels must be invisible when the job prints. In order to ensure the quality, make sure your image is at least 1.5 times the lpi.

lpi x 1.5 = ppi

Many printers will tell you to double the lpi, but a sample of only 1.5 is enough to ensure the pixels will not be visible when reproduced.

SCANNERS

Scanning Resolution

Another resolution that is important to know about is the capture resolution of your scanner. Many people, including the manufacturers of scanners, call scanning resolution *dpi*. As we learned previously, dpi is the resolution of a printing device. In technical circles, scanning resolution is more accurately known as *samples per inch* or SPI. Further confusion is created by the fact that some choose to call the output resolution of printing devices *spots per inch* or spi. Others will also call halftone dot resolution *spots* OR *dots per inch*—instead of the more common *lpi*. Below is a list which attempts to clarify the confusion without creating more.

- Scanning Resolution—dpi, more accurately known as spi (samples per inch)
- Image resolution—also erroneously called dpi, more accurately known as ppi
- Output resolution—dpi, this is correct
- Halftone resolution—sometimes called dpi, more commonly known as lpi

Samples per inch (spi) refers to the number of actual samples a scanner can capture using a CCD or charged couple device in a square inch. A 600 spi scanner can capture 600 x 600 or 360,000 samples in a square inch. The good news is there is no math in determining the relationship between scanner spi and image ppi. There is a simple one-to-one relationship between the two. If you scan an image at 600 spi, it will show up on your monitor at 600 ppi. For this reason, some choose to call capture resolution ppi! More confusion.

Scanning Tips

A scanner is a mechanical device which is limited by its optics. A CCD may only scan at its true optical resolution, or spi. To scan at any other resolution creates interpolation of the image. *Interpolation* is the reconfiguration of original pixels captured by the scanner. In other words, if you instruct a 600 spi scanner to scan at anything other than 600 spi, it will scan at 600 and then reconstruct the original scan to provide what you asked for. Interpolation generally degrades the quality of the image and should be avoided. An exception to this fact is that it is possible to scan at the true optical resolution of the scanner divided by any whole number without sacrificing quality. So a 600 spi scanner can capture at 600, 300, 150, and 75 spi without too much degradation of quality. Many argue convincingly that such stringent guidelines for scanning apply only to line art and aren't necessary for color or gray photos. Try an experiment in your studio and you be the judge.

One rule that many stick with when scanning is to capture only at 100% of the actual size of the image. This also reduces interpolation and captures the image more accurately. Resizing is done in an image editing software such as Photoshop®. The following formula will help you determine the actual capture resolution to use on your scanner.

> ▶ lpi x 1.5 x reproduction scale (round sum up to nearest optical resolution)

For example, a 3 x 5 inch photo which you wish to print at 6 x 10 inches and at 150 line would be captured at 600 ppi. 150 x 1.5 x 2 (200%) = 450 spi. This sum would be rounded up on a 600 spi scanner to 600 spi. The resulting image would be resized in Photoshop® by halving the resolution and doubling the size.

STEP-BY-STEP GUIDE TO PREPARING A FILE FOR PREPRESS

1. Before design and production begins, the following information needs to be gathered:

   a. What line screen, or lines per inch (lpi), will be used by the printer? Knowing the lpi is necessary to determine both the capture resolution of a scanned image and the resolution of the photographs and illustrations to be reproduced.

   b. What computer platform (PC or Mac®) is used by the service bureau? Although it is possible to print Mac® files from a PC or vice-versa, this "cross-platform" approach is not recommended. Check with your printer or service bureau to see which format they prefer.

   c. What software will be used to print your file? The most efficient way to print your film from an imagesetter is to run the file using the same software in which it was created. Most service bureaus will use QuarkXpress®, Adobe® PageMaker® or Adobe® InDesign®. Some service bureaus will also accept and use Microsoft® Publisher 2000. Check with your service bureau to see if your software is compatible. Keep in mind files created in illustration or photo editing software are often placed in a page layout document by a service bureau before sending the file to the imagesetter. Common illustration and photo editing software includes Adobe® Illustrator®, Adobe® Photoshop®, Adobe® Freehand® and CorelDRAW®.

   d. How will your service bureau handle fonts? You should provide copies of the original fonts used to create your document to ensure error-free output. This is generally an acceptable extension of the license you purchased when you paid for the fonts. Allowing your service bureau to substitute fonts can create unexpected results and is not recommended.

   e. Will the job be printed in black ink only, spot color, process color or process color plus one or more spot colors? How you define colors in your software's color editing tool will affect output. A process color job requires all colors to be built from CMYK (process color) only. Using any model other than CMYK in a process color file will result in color which will not separate to film correctly. Almost every color editing tool allows you to choose whether a color will be spot or process color.

   f. Who will be responsible for trapping the job? Traps can be created in most desktop publishing software. However, many jobs are trapped by the service bureau or printing company using software to apply traps as the job prints. Ask your printer if you need to create the traps according to their specifications. Refer to your software manual to determine how to set traps for a document.

2. All raster and vector images must conform to the
   following guidelines:

   a. Raster images should be saved at a screen resolution
      (ppi, or pixels per inch) high enough to hide the pixels
      when the image prints. Generally the lpi used by the
      printer multiplied by 1.5 to 2 is sufficient. For example,
      a photograph printed at 150 lpi should have a screen
      resolution of 225 to 300 ppi. This resolution can be set
      in the Image Size box in Photoshop®. Images saved in
      the Bitmap mode should be saved at a resolution of at
      least 600 ppi.

      Vector images are resolution independent. As long as the
      vector image is saved and placed from its native software,
      resolution is not a factor.

   b. Raster images should be saved in one of the following modes:

      • CMYK—process color images

      • Grayscale—black and white photos or gray images

      • Duotone—black and white photos using a spot color tint

      • Bitmap—black line drawings or black only artwork

      • RGB, Lab, HSB and other color modes will not separate correctly from an imagesetter

      Vector images are not saved in a color mode. The color of the output is determined when colors are created using a
      color editing tool. Use only CMYK, grayscale or spot color to create your images.

   c. A raster should be saved as either a TIFF or EPS. Check with your service bureau to see which they prefer. JPEG,
      BMP, PICT, PNG and other file formats are unacceptable in high-end imagesetting. Vector images may only be
      saved as EPS files.

   d. Images should be placed into page layout software using a "place" or "get picture" command. Copying and pasting
      an image into the software will not embed the information needed to create good quality, high-resolution output.

   e. Don't resize a raster image in page layout software. Doing so creates a degradation of quality of the image and can
      have negative effects on output. Reopen the image in a photo editing software such as Photoshop® to resize it. A
      vector image may be resized in page layout software without any adverse effects.

3. When choosing type for your document follow these guidelines:

   a. It is best to use Postscript Type One fonts. These fonts will always
      print correctly as long as both the printer and screen font is provided
      to the service bureau.

   b. Truetype fonts may be used if your service bureau is using a Postscript
      Level 3 imagesetter. However, check with your service bureau first
      to see if they accept Truetype fonts. Truetype fonts require only one
      font instead of a printer and a screen font. This font will need to be
      supplied to your service bureau.

   c. Any font may be outlined in an illustration program to avoid potential
      font problems. Generally, the larger the type, the better outlining
      works. Type below 16 points or delicate typefaces may appear
      bloated if outlined. Also, large amounts of outlined copy may
      create files which are too complicated for some printing devices.

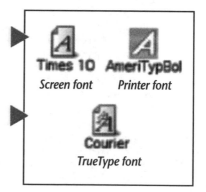

302

Graphics, Prepress and Printing

Where to find outlining tools in Illustrator® and Quark®

4. Find out if you need negatives or positives. Commercial lithographers, or offset printers, mostly use negatives to burn metal plates. Quick printers, silkscreeners and some other printers, however, may use positives. When using film, your printer may also specify "right" or "wrong" reading and "emulsion up" or "emulsion down." Check with your vendor to see which is required.

5. Print a hard copy of your document to send to your service bureau. The hard copy will be compared to the screen version when the file is opened at the service bureau. This helps the service bureau visually identify any potential problems before the file is printed.

6. Preflight your document before sending it to the service bureau. Preflighting is available in most page layout software. It is a way of checking the file to see if all of the images have been saved correctly and are in place and all of the fonts are available on the system. Preflighting may also copy files, images and fonts to a target disk, eliminating the need to search for them. Third-party preflighting software is available which goes beyond the ordinary preflighting available in Quark® and PageMaker®. Your service bureau will also preflight your document before it prints. However, preflighting before you send it provides an extra measure of security which ensures error-free jobs.

7. Copy your TIFF and EPS images into one folder and label it "Links." Copy your printer and screen fonts to a second folder and label it "Fonts." And copy the page layout file to a third folder and label it "File." By setting up your disk in this manner, you ensure the service bureau will know exactly which file should be printed and where all the necessary links are located. This organization will speed the prepress process.

Tips on Checking Proofs

After your job is sent to a service bureau, the next stage is to check a proof. A proof is a full or single color print which will give you an idea of what the job will look like once it is printed.

Both traditional and digital proofs are being used today. A traditional proof is created from the film after it is output from an imagesetter. A digital proof is made from the file before print is created. A traditional proof is generally more accurate because it is shows the actual halftone dot which will be used to print the job. However, a digital proof from a properly calibrated proofer can be very accurate, and in some cases, more accurate. Because a digital proof is made before the film, any errors discovered on the proof can be easily changed without incurring film and stripping costs.

The following tips will help you achieve an error-free job:

1. Find out from the printer exactly what kind of proof you have. If it is a traditional proof made from film, such as a Matchprint or Cromalin, it is an accurate color proof. If it is a digital proof, ask your printer if the press operator will be using it as a guide to adjust color on the press. Ask the printer, "Is this an accurate representation of what I will see on a press check?" The answer should be yes. Keep in mind no proof will show exactly what will happen when ink hits the paper. But a good color proof should be close enough to be used as a guide.

303

Graphics, Prepress and Printing

2. Make sure you have a place with good light to check the proof. A color correct light is preferable, but a well lit room will do.

3. Make sure you are in a place where distractions are minimalized. Tell your printing rep you would like to look at the proof alone. Interruptions can cost dearly.

4. Look at the proof three times. The first look should be a quick, casual scan of the proof, similar to the way your audience will look at it. The second look should be more detailed. Here are a few tips of what you should look for:

   a. Check the white areas of one or two photos for a color cast. You may do this by comparing the white to a white sheet of paper. If the white in the photograph appears a little blue, yellow, green or pink, it has a cast to it. This may have happened during the scanning, color correction, film output or even during the creation of the proof. In any case, it's a good idea to isolate the problem and correct it before it goes to press.

   b. Check the perceptual color of the images. Make sure your sky is blue, your grass is green and the skin tones are natural.

   c. Check each page against the hard copy you originally provided to the printer. Look for missing graphics, images which may have linked incorrectly and are low resolution, or images which may have linked with the wrong file. Check the bottom of each page, or anywhere the copy stops, to see if the bottom line is still in place. Sometimes the window of a text box may close and send the last line to the top of the next page or paragraph or cut it off completely. This is called "rewrapping" and is a common problem when fonts are substituted or file preferences are replaced. Check the relationships of margins, drop caps, captions and photos, gutters and other graphic elements to make sure they haven't moved or been deleted.

   After giving the proof a thorough second look, leave the room and take a five- to fifteen-minute break. When you come back into the room, turn the proof upside down or put it at an unusual angle. Give the proof another look from this new perspective. Often, obvious mistakes which were missed the first two times become apparent from a different angle.

   After checking the proof, sign it and return it to the printer. You will see this proof again if you do a press check. During a press check, you will check a press sheet against the proof. If your first proof was digital, you may double check the items in number 4 above. You will also check registration of the printing by using a small glass called a *loupe*. Place the loupe on the edge of a photo, piece of type or other image where you know all four process colors are being used to build the color. You should see a smooth edge with none of the color "hanging" or out of alignment. Check all four sides of the press sheet to ensure registration throughout the document. If the color is accurate and the job is in register, you will sign the proof and take two or three press sheets with you to compare to the final printed piece.

Descriptions of Printers

Quick Printer

Quick printers are classified as those printers using either paper or polymer plates instead of metal plates for the press and using small format presses. The primary reason you use a quick printer is because they are fast and inexpensive. However, quick printers generally have some limitations which create quality problems if not understood. Usually, a quick printer will have trouble with close registration and, therefore, with four-color printing. For that reason, CMYK is not listed as an acceptable color mode. To run the job correctly a quick printer will need a positive RC paper slick or a high resolution positive laser print (1000 dpi or above). A quick printer may also accept your disk to create the necessary plate for their press.

- Required Color Modes: grayscale, bitmap
- Lines Per Inch: 100 to 133 lpi
- Required Resolution of Raster Images: lpi x 1.5, except bitmap which requires a resolution of 1000 dpi
- Acceptable Art Work: vector or raster
- Acceptable File Types for Art: TIFF or EPS

Commercial Sheetfed Printer

These printers employ larger presses and metal plates to print your job. This high-quality option is the most popular and most used process in the world for printing. These printers use one-color, two-color and four-color process, and may add spot color and varnishes to the job. There are commercial offset presses capable of printing 10 colors at a time. A commercial sheetfed printer will require a high-resolution (1270 dpi and up) color separated negative, usually right reading emulsion side down. These negatives cannot be produced from a standard laser printer and require a service bureau to create.

- Acceptable Color Modes for Photos: grayscale, bitmap, CMYK, duotone
- Lines Per Inch: 133, 150, 175, 200 and up to 400 lpi. Make sure to ask your printer for specifics.
- Required Resolution of Raster Images: lpi x 1.5, except bitmap which requires a resolution of 1000 dpi
- Acceptable Art Work: vector or raster
- Acceptable File Types for Art: TIFF or EPS

Commercial Web Printer

These printers employ even larger presses and metal plates to print your job. This high-speed option is often not as high quality as sheetfed but saves a considerable amount of money in longer runs of 50,000 or more copies. These printers use one-color, two-color and four-color process. A commercial web printer will require a high-resolution (1270 dpi and up) color separated negative, usually right reading emulsion side down. These negatives cannot be produced from a standard laser printer and require a service bureau to create.

- Acceptable Color Modes for Photos: grayscale, bitmap, CMYK, duotone
- Lines Per Inch: 85 to 120 lpi depending on paper. Web printers using newsprint will use a lower line screen. Make sure to ask your printer for specifics.
- Required Resolution of Raster Images: lpi x 1.5, except bitmap which requires a resolution of 1000 dpi
- Acceptable Art Work: vector or raster
- Acceptable File Types for Art: TIFF or EPS

Silkscreen Printer

A silkscreen press transfers ink to a substrate (paper, cloth or other material) by pressing the ink through a mesh directly to the material below. A slower process than offset lithography, it is usually used to print signage or t-shirts. These printers use multi spot colors but may have trouble with four-color process images because the line screen used is often very coarse. A silkscreen printer will require a high-resolution (1270 dpi and up) color separated positive, usually right reading emulsion side down or a color separated paper laser print.

- Acceptable Color Modes for Photos and Art: grayscale, bitmap, CMYK, duotone are all used but the best results come from bitmapped images with no halftones or screens
- Lines Per Inch: around 65 lpi. Make sure to ask your printer for specifics.
- Required Resolution of Raster Images: lpi x 1.5, except bitmap which requires a resolution of 1000 dpi
- Acceptable Art Work: vector or raster
- Acceptable File Types for Art: TIFF or EPS

Digital Printing

Technically, any printing device which will print your job directly from your disk could be considered a digital press. However, most of the time, digital presses are considered those presses which create multiple copies of printing in full color. These presses are made by Indigo, Heildeberg, AB Dick and a variety of other manufacturers to directly compete with traditional printing presses. Digital presses use a variety of processes most of which conform to the standards of traditional presses. A digital printer will require only your disk prepared properly.

- Available Color Modes for Photos and Art: grayscale, RGB, CMYK. Check with your printer for acceptable color modes.
- Lines Per Inch: around 133 lpi. Make sure to ask your printer for specifics.
- Required Resolution of Raster Images: lpi x 1.5, except bitmap which requires a resolution of 1000 dpi
- Acceptable Art Work: vector or raster
- Acceptable File Types for Art: TIFF or EPS

Color Proofers

These printing devices are close cousins of digital presses but are usually used for single copies, limited quantities or proofs. Some, such as the Iris Proofer, are capable of such fine quality and detail that even experts cannot often tell the difference between the Iris and an original. Only a properly prepared file on disk is required by the printer.

Acceptable Color Modes for Photos and Art: grayscale, bitmap, CMYK. As digital technology improves, more printers will begin to accept RGB files which is a superior color space than CMYK. Check with your printer to see if you can provide files in this mode.

GLOSSARY OF PREPRESS TERMS

Bitmap

One of the many work or color modes used to edit and save raster images. Bitmap is used when dealing with line art or simple black and white images. Unlike most of the other modes, bitmap is one-bit, meaning a single pixel can only be either black or white.

Color Management

A development in desktop publishing which allows users to define color space for monitors, scanners and printing devices through software. If used correctly from a calibrated system, color management allows you to accurately see the color of your document on your monitor before it prints. Although it was originally theorized many years ago, it has only recently been practically applied to typical desktop publishing systems.

Color Mode

A work mode for editing and saving color images. The three major modes are CMYK (cyan, magenta, yellow, black), RGB (red, green, blue) and LAB (lightness, *a* and *b* coordinates).

Color Proof

A color print of your work from any number of devices which will show you what your job will look like once printed from an offset press. To be accurate, the printing device must be calibrated to the press. There are both traditional and digital color proofs. A traditional color proof is made from film. A digital color proof is made from a digital file.

Color Separated

The process of sending a CMYK image to an imagesetter where it will be printed as four separate pieces of film. The imagesetter uses halftone dots to simulate various light and dark areas in each of the four colors. See Bitmap, CMYK.

Color Space

The way a particular device interprets color data. A monitor uses RGB, a printing device will use CMYK, for example. Within each realm are a number of different color spaces which may be chosen. For example, a monitor may use one of many spaces including sRGB and Colormatch RGB. A printing device may use SWOP Coated, SWOP Newsprint or SWOP Uncoated to print a document. Each space has different characteristics and advantages. If devices are properly calibrated, it is possible to define color spaces consistently across different monitors and printing devices to ensure accurate color from device to device.

Continuous Tone

Also called Contone, this refers to any art where a visible change cannot be noted between smooth transitions in color or value. If you enlarge a halftone, for example, you can see how the dots only create the illusion of color and value change. On a monitor, enlarging a photo shows transitions between pixels. Neither the halftone or the monitor demonstrates continuous tone. However, in the digital world, a multi-resolution gray or color image may be called Contone Raster Data because it is as close to continuous tone as the digital world will ever get. Only photographs and original pieces of traditional art are truly continuous tone.

CMYK

One of the many work or color modes used to edit and save raster images. CMYK stands for cyan, magenta, yellow and black. The four colors are actually four grayscale images which create the illusion of full color when printed. Each color has eight bits of information per pixel. This allows the pixel to be manipulated and changed in many ways. For this reason, a CMYK image is said to be multi-resolution, meaning the resolution can be changed up or down. When a CMYK image is sent to an imagesetter, it is separated into four pieces of film, each with a bitmap interpretation of the light and dark areas using various densities of halftone dots. The CMYK image will print at the resolution of the printing device. For example a CMYK image saved at 300 ppi and sent to a 1270 dpi imagesetter will print at 1270 dpi.

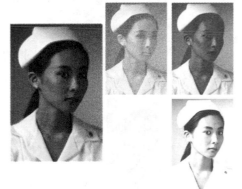

This mode is used for almost all printing devices (some use RGB).
Of the three major color modes (RGB, CMYK and LAB), this mode has the most restricted color gamut, or range of colors which can be represented.

Digital Press

A printing device which will print multiple color copies directly from a computer. A variety of processes are used to create the image from inkjet, to laser, to actual printing plates imaged on a press.

Duotone

One of the many work or color modes used to edit and save raster images. Duotones are made up of a two grayscale images, one of which is usually gray and the other a spot color using PANTONE® or some other color system. Like CMYK, RGB and grayscale, duotones are also multi-resolution images which are turned to bitmaps by an imagesetter. Duotones cannot be printed from a desktop printer or color proofer. Duotones can only be printed on a traditional press.

EPS

Encapsulated postscript is one of two widely accepted file formats used in graphic arts along with TIFF. An EPS file may be a raster or vector graphic. It may also be an RGB, CMYK, grayscale, duotone or bitmap. Only EPS files support spot color. Not to be confused with a postscript or PS file.

Film Negative

Output from an imagesetter on a clear piece of film. On a negative, everything that will print is clear and everything that will not print is black. Used in offset lithography.

Film Positive

Output from an imagesetter on a clear piece of film. On a positive, everything that will print is black and everything that will not print is clear. Used in silkscreen printing.

Four-color Process Printing

Printing ink on paper using CMYK and halftones to create the illusion of full color. Photos and art are reproduced using this process.

GIF

Graphics Interchange Format. One of two primary file formats used on the Web. GIF format works best on line drawings, icons and images with a small number of flat colors.

Grayscale

One of the many work modes used to edit and save raster images. Grayscale images are used to represent black and white photos. A grayscale image has eight bits of information per pixel. This allows the pixel to be manipulated and changed in many ways. For this reason, a grayscale image is said to be multi-resolution, meaning the resolution can be changed up or down. When a grayscale image is sent to an imagesetter, it is bitmapped using halftone dots to create the illusion of lightness and darkness of the image. The grayscale image will print at the resolution of the printing device. For example, grayscale image saved at 300 ppi and sent to a 1270 dpi imagesetter will print at 1270 dpi.

Interpolation

The process a software uses to reconfigure pixels in an image that has been resampled. Interpolation causes degradation of a raster image whether it is downsampled or upsampled. However, sometimes resampling is necessary, and therefore interpolation is unavoidable. In Photoshop® there are three types of interpolation available: Bicubic, Bilinear and Nearest Neighbor. Of the three, Bicubic is superior and should be used exclusively. Damage to an image from interpolation can be partially corrected by using an Unsharp Mask Filter.

JPEG

Joint Photographics Expert Group. One of two types of files used to save graphics for the Web along with GIF. Although sometimes used in printing, it isn't recommended because JPEG files are lossy, which means they subtract information from the photo to compress the space. For this reason, a visible degradation of quality can occur when a file is changed to a JPEG. Most imagesetters will not recognize and print a JPEG file.

LAB Color

One of the many work or color modes used to edit and save raster images. The *L* stands for Lightness. The *A* and *B* have to do with combinations of red and green, and yellow and blue respectively. Of the three major color modes (RGB, CMYK and LAB), this mode has the broadest range of color gamut, modeled after what the human eye can see. No method exists to simulate LAB color either on a monitor or in print. It is useful both in archiving and in some color correction and photo editing.

Line Art

Black and white images with smooth black lines and areas of solid blacks. The best way to create and save line art is as a vector image. However, a piece of line art that is scanned becomes a raster image. It is best scanned as a multi-resolution grayscale which can then be converted to a bitmap at a resolution of 600 ppi or above.

Lithography

A high quality printing process based on the principle of water and grease (ink) not mixing. Also called offset and planographic, or single plane, printing.

PDF

Portable Document Format. PDF files allow the recipient of the file to view a document in full color with fonts and graphics intact without having the native software or fonts resident on their computer. More recently, many have been using PDF files to send documents to an imagesetter or color printer. It has been widely accepted that this format will eventually become the file format of choice for transferring complex documents between computers. The technology is improving rapidly. Check with your printer for specifics on creating PDF files.

Plates (paper, polymer, metal)

The material used to transfer an image to a blanket, and eventually to a piece of paper on a traditional offset press. Paper and polymer plates are often used in the quick print industry because they are inexpensive and easy to produce. However, they tend to stretch and create registration problems as well as wear out quickly. Commercial sheetfed printers use metal plates which are more durable and stable and create better quality images.

Postscript

The language used by computers, printers and software within the graphic arts world.

Raster

A raster image is one that is built of individual pixels. Those pixels may be CMYK, RGB, LAB, grayscale or bitmap. Rasters are unlike vectors in that vectors, although demonstrated on screen using pixels, do not use pixels to print. For more information, see Vectors.

Registration

The process of printing one color on top of another in perfect alignment on the press. It is particularly crucial in four-color process printing where photos are being reproduced. If the colors are not aligned, or off registration, the photo will look fuzzy or soft. Registration has been greatly improved by the development of digital prepress which automates the process of creating film and plates. However, registration problems can still occur due to a faulty imagesetter or film stretch. Most often, registration problems occur on press and can be corrected by adjustments to the press.

Resampling

The reconfiguration of pixels using interpolation to change the resolution of an image independently of its size. Usually size and resolution are linked. As resolution decreases, size increases and vice-versa. When an image is resampled, however, the resolution or the size may be changed without affecting the corresponding size or resolution. If an image is made larger either in size or resolution it is called *upsampling*. If an image is made smaller either in size or resolution it is called *downsampling*. Either of these relies on interpolation to reconfigure the pixels which causes a degradation of quality to an image. Of the two, upsampling is more damaging.

Resolution

Refers to how fine or coarse an image is captured, saved or printed. Input resolution is measured in spi or samples per inch, which are interpreted by the computer as ppi or pixels per inch. This resolution is then output to an imagesetter using dpi or dots per inch to recreate the image using halftone screens measured as lpi or lines per inch. Although each measurement is related, they are really separate parts of an entire process. In every case, the higher the number the finer the resolution and the better the image quality.

RC Paper

White photosensitive paper which, when exposed to a laser and processed, holds a digital image. It is used in imagesetting devices instead of film for different reasons.

RGB

One of the many work or color modes used to edit and save raster images. RGB stands for red, green and blue. The three colors are actually three grayscale images which create the illusion of full color on your monitor. Each color has eight bits of information per pixel. This allows the pixel to be manipulated and changed in many ways. For this reason, an RGB image is said to be multi-resolution, meaning the resolution can be changed up or down. RGB is used primarily to represent color on monitors. It is also a fairly good mode to work in when archiving color photos and art. Of the three major color modes (RGB, CMYK and LAB), this mode has a wider gamut range than CMYK, but is more limited than LAB.

Right Reading Emulsion Down

The most common standard for producing film negatives for the printing industry. Emulsion is affected by exposure to light. In a negative, the emulsion comes off of the exposed part of the film during processing leaving a clear area which will let light through. If you are holding a negative emulsion down, the emulsion would be on the bottom of the negative. If the emulsion were up, it would be on top of the negative. If a negative is right reading, you can read the type just as you are reading the type on this page. Wrong reading means the type is backward. Right reading emulsion down is the same as wrong reading emulsion up. Also sometimes called RR E-down.

Service Bureau

A business that uses imagesetters or other printing devices to print your job to film, paper or color proof from your disk. Many printing companies have this capability in-house and call it their prepress department.

Sheetfed Press

An offset press which uses sheets of paper cut to a standard size as opposed to a web press which runs off of a continual roll of paper.

SPI

Samples per inch. The true optical resolution of a scanner using a CCD or charged couple device. SPI is often called dpi (dots per inch) which can be confusing because output to an imagesetter is also called dpi. The two are not related as one has to do with input and the other with output. A scanner with 1200 spi can capture 1200 samples per inch off of a continuous tone photograph or piece of art. The capture directly relates to ppi or pixels per inch in that the capture is turned into pixels for your monitor. For best results, a scan should be captured at the true optical resolution of the scanner or the true optical resolution of the scanner divided by any whole number. For example, a 1200 spi scanner can capture at 1200, 600, 300, 150 and so on.

Spot Color Printing

Printing using one of the color ink systems, such as PANTONE®, as opposed to process color, which uses cyan, yellow, magenta and black inks. For example, to print a specific color of green, you would choose an ink from a color swatch book and the printer would either buy that color ink or mix it using guidelines provided by the ink company. The green ink is added to the ink tray for printing. Various shades of green are created by using screens, or halftones, to create the illusion of lightness or darkness. Spot color is often used in combination with black on a single job or combined with process color for a five-color printing.

TIFF

One of the two acceptable file formats used in high-end graphic arts. The other is EPS. TIFF stands for tagged image file format. TIFFs are reserved for raster images only and are usually color or grayscale photos, although a bitmap can be saved as a TIFF as well.

Vector

All graphic images are either rasters or vectors. A vector uses a series of curves and anchor points to create an outline around an image. The outline itself is actually a complex mathematical formula which tells a printing device how to redraw the image on film or paper. Unlike rasters, pixels do not play a role in the printing of a vector and therefore resolution is unimportant. A vector is said to be resolution independent and will reproduce with smooth outlines at any size. Type fonts are created from vectors.

Web Fed Press

An offset press which uses a continual roll of paper as opposed to individual cut sheets.

CAREER SUCCESS HANDBOOK

ASSERTIVENESS

Assertiveness is a much misunderstood communication skill. Its purpose, though, is simple: to get what you want, both in the short term and in the long term.

Of course, once you've made the decision to be assertive (and it is your decision), it is clear you have a short-term goal to resolve whatever issue you have with the individual you intend to approach assertively.

These issues could be large or small. Perhaps, for example, you are asking an employee to change his or her work habits to become more productive. Or maybe a co-worker has been avoiding you and you want to find out why, and perhaps work to resolve the issue. Or possibly a loved one at home hasn't been paying enough attention to you and you want to make your discomfort known and request better treatment. Those are what most people would call larger issues.

Smaller issues need your assertiveness skills, as well. For example: a co-worker who smacks gum all day long in a way that truly annoys you; a spouse who fails to change the seat adjustment in your car back to your preferred settings when he or she returns from a quick trip to the grocery store; or, even a new acquaintance who insists on calling you by your full name instead of your preferred nickname.

Your short-term goal in these examples is clear. You want to get immediate change in someone else's behavior.

But assertiveness also must have a long-term goal, and it is important: To maintain as positive a relationship as possible with the person you are being assertive with. And it is for this reason that the number one rule of assertiveness is what it is.

Rules

1. Never be assertive at the spur of the moment if you can help it.
2. Carefully consider what you will say—and how you will say it.
3. Be so clear your listener (or reader) can make no mistake about the meaning of your message.
4. Pay people in a currency they can spend.
5. Maintain the relationship.

Explanations and Examples

1. Never be assertive at the spur of the moment if you can help it.

We are social animals and because of this we usually don't mention our mild dissatisfactions right away. When someone steps on your toe for the very first time, you're hardly going to be assertive right then. You wouldn't want to be rude.

Most of us recognize that we have at least a mild case of passive aggression we feed and nurture every day. See if this example seems familiar:

Day One: Someone steps on Kathy's toe. She's probably going to say, "Oh—don't think another thing about it—it's really okay." But twenty minutes later when she notices that her toe is still throbbing, she's probably going to take a tiny little grain of a highly explosive material and stuff it deep inside her psyche—for later. In some cases, for much later.

Day Two: The same person steps on Kathy's toe again. Maybe you are like Kathy on Day Two—still in control, still an understanding and forgiving adult. Probably Kathy would say something like, "You know, my feet are so large—it's probably my fault!"

Day Three: Aren't most of us still okay on Day Three? That same person steps on Kathy's toe again, but she says, "Why can't this person see that my foot is attached to the end of my ankle?"

For most people, it's Day Four where patience runs out. And the really sad thing about Day Four is that it doesn't even have to be the same offending person stepping on Kathy's toe or your toe, does it? In fact, it probably isn't—more likely, it's a brand-new person, maybe even a person you or Kathy have never met before. And this poor soul doesn't even need to step on a toe! All he or she needs to do is look at your toe in a manner you find offensive. BOOM! All the pent-up frustration of the past three days explodes on an easy target. And that easy target most likely didn't even step on your toe.

But think it through. What inevitably happens next? You apologize, right? Maybe you even go so far as to set yourself up for more discomfort:

"Oh, I am so sorry! Please, why don't you step on my toe? That would make us even."

Because of a huge tendency toward passive aggression in normal adults, we recommend waiting. When you feel the need to be assertive, take a timeout. Vent your anger or frustration or fear or shame or you-name-the-negative-emotion privately first—somewhere you can't do irreparable damage to your positive reputation. Think now of some effective venting techniques for you.

Does a brisk walk help you regain control? How about some journaling? A talk with a trusted friend? How about a half-hour of mindless (but necessary) work, like filing? Or maybe if you have the luxury of some time at home, how about a hot bath? Or do you find relief by cleaning? Or maybe getting in your car and listening to some really loud music? Make your own personalized list of venting strategies.

Then vent.

Afterward, consider for a few moments what you want to say to the person you need to be assertive with. Use one of the formulas presented here to help you find the right words—and the right way to say them.

As a note, it is true that occasionally you won't have the opportunity to think before you talk. Every once in a while, your assertiveness is needed at the spur of the moment—and if you fail to act now, the opportunity disappears forever.

Generally, though, when you need to be assertive at the spur of the moment you can take comfort from the fact that you will probably never see the person you need to be assertive with again. But please do remember that other people judge you by how they see you treat not just themselves, but the people around you. If you lose your temper with a gate agent at the airport in a particularly aggressive way, I would bet your traveling partners will remember it for a long time—and change their opinion of you for just as long. This most likely will also impact your dealings with the security staff at the airport.

2. Carefully consider what you will say—and how you will say it.

As you have probably noticed, different people can have very different personalities. This usually means that they will also have very different needs and expectations in relationships. Some people only feel comfortable in a relationship where they have control. Others are afraid to assert any control, ever. Most are somewhere in between.

In short, it is your job (as a great communicator) to divine the needs and preferences of the people you hope to influence. Because only then can you indeed influence them.

Here's an example: Mary's boss Angie is very insecure in her recent promotion. Secretly, Angie believes Mary is much more qualified to be the boss than she is. This makes her very wary of Mary and very sensitive to her own fear that Mary might want to take over.

In this scenario, do you see that if Mary approaches Angie assertively, Angie might just shut her out completely? Not because Mary isn't competent, but in fact because she is. Sometimes it's best to realize that there's more than one way to get your needs met assertively.

There are three main approaches to assertiveness that work. One starts with the bottom line, with your expression of the need or request you are making of the individual. The second one starts more gently, with a discussion of the way things are now. The final approach is halfway between the two—and the one you will likely use most frequently.

The First Approach to Assertiveness: Be Direct

Imagine that assertiveness could be measured on a continuum with passivity and aggression. Here's how that continuum would look:

Passive _____ **Assertive** _____ **Aggressive**

Notice that assertiveness is not in only one spot, but in the entire middle range.

The direct approach of this first method is what many people think of when they think of assertiveness: It falls slightly to the right of center, like this:

Passive _____ **Assertive** _____ **Aggressive**

It is a very direct, bottom-line-first method. We call it the **ERRRR** Technique:

E xpectation

R eason

R espect for the person you're being assertive with

R espect for yourself or for your "side"

R eward

The *Expectation* statement contains your bottom-line message.

Example 1:   Andrea, I need you to refrain from making personal telephone calls from your desk during the hours we are counting on you to answer the customer service calls.

<u>**OR (in a personal situation)**</u>

Example 2:   Honey, can we talk for a few minutes about what's going on with us? It seems like we aren't spending a lot of time together and I'm hoping we can discuss some ways to be closer.

<u>**OR EVEN**</u>

Example 3:   I'd really prefer if you'd call me Ned.

The *Reason* statement explains the WHY behind your bottom line.

Example 1:   You see, when I hired you my thought was you would be able to answer at least 15 customer calls per hour. Yet when you make personal calls, I notice that many times our customers' calls end up going unanswered and that's just not okay with me.

<u>**OR**</u>

Example 2:   I think you know how much I treasure you and our relationship. If there's a problem developing I want to deal with it now, before it gets any worse.

<u>**OR**</u>

Example 3:   I prefer people to call me by my first name because we're all part of the same team. Besides, my mother calls me Mr. Anderson when she's upset with me!

***Respect for them* is necessary so they know you are not out to get them.**

Example 1:   What was it, two or three weeks ago, Andrea? Do you remember that customer who called in and screamed at you for half an hour straight and you didn't get upset with him? You turned him around; do you remember? He had just needed to vent and you stayed on the line, you didn't take it personally and when he was done you were able to calm him down and actually get him laughing. He called back the next day and placed another large order with us. You are really great with even our angriest customers.

<u>**OR**</u>

Example 2:   One of the best things about our relationship is that you have always been open to talk about things. I really appreciate that.

<u>**OR**</u>

Example 3:   I know you probably just don't want to be rude.

***Respect for yourself or for your side* makes it clear that you are not a pushover—that your request deserves attention.**

Example 1:   Andrea, our customers invest a lot of capital with us when they contract for our services. Can you imagine how angry they could feel if they call, hoping we will resolve an issue and all they get is a ringing phone? They deserve to have their calls answered—and quickly.

<u>**OR**</u>

Example 2:   I have always been honest in this relationship too. And there are some things going on with us that I truly need for us to fix.

OR

Example 3:   But I have always hated that name—it makes me feel like a stuffy old man and actually, I'm enjoying my life as an open-minded and responsible younger man!

Finally, your *Reward* statement is where you offer the person you are being assertive with something that will make them feel rewarded if they do as you ask. In some cases (not many, actually) you will be offering a negative consequence if they don't do as you ask.

Example 1:   I'll tell you what: I am going to update your personnel file. If you have turned around on this behavior in three weeks and eliminated the personal phone calls by then, I will remove any mention of this issue from your file. That way, it won't affect you down the road as you move up in this organization.

In this example, you might also find it necessary to offer a negative consequence:

If you don't turn around on this behavior, I will need to start the process of terminating your employment in three weeks.

OR

Example 2:   Maybe after we talk, we could go out to dinner and see a movie—you've wanted to see that new sci-fi thing, right?

OR

Example 3:   And you know, I look forward to a very warm and productive relationship with you. I think teams work better together if we're on a first-name basis.

Use this approach when you are dealing with:

1. Most healthy adults. By "healthy adult" we mean people who don't have control issues and who aren't overly sensitive emotionally.

2. The busy, straightforward people in your life who would prefer to not spend too much time building up to a bottom line.

But remember—this is not the only approach we have to recommend. Using the E-R-R-R-R technique on a control freak, for example, is a recipe for disaster. It would make matters much worse instead of much better.

A better choice for the control freaks in your life, and several other classes of people, would be the Five Steps of Positive Assertiveness.

The Second Approach to Assertiveness: Gently Proving Your Case

Some of the people in your life just aren't healthy or confident enough to be able to deal positively with your directness. For cases where your message needs to be framed in a gentler way, try the Five Steps of Positive Assertiveness:

Step One: I see

Step Two: I think

Step Three: (I feel)

Step Four: I want

Step Five: I will

Notice where the Five Steps of Positive Assertiveness show up on the continuum we have been using throughout this section:

Passive _____ **Assertive** _____ **Aggressive**

314

Career Success

Although well within the bounds of assertiveness, this approach is closer to the passive end of the spectrum than it is to the aggressive end.

Let's try this approach with our three earlier examples:

Example 1:   Your employee, Andrea, makes too many personal telephone calls and doesn't take enough customer service calls—which is her job.

Example 2:   You want to schedule a serious talk with your spouse or significant partner.

Example 3:   You want a newer co-worker to call you by your preferred name.

Step One: I see.

The main difference between this approach and the more direct ERRRR Technique is that this one builds up to the bottom line, while the ERRRR starts with it. This first step is where you lay out all of the proof you have for what you are about to state. And you should take the word *proof* literally. The things you mention must be verifiable in an objective way. They can't be based on your assumptions or your feelings.

Example 1:   Andrea, I've noticed this past month and a half that when you get here in the morning you immediately begin making calls. I've also noticed that most of those calls last for at least 30 or 45 minutes, and that you laugh quite a bit during them. At the same time, I notice that the customer service lines into your office are ringing but you aren't answering them.

Example 2:   I have noticed these past two weeks, honey, that when things are quiet here in the evenings you go to the computer room and spend four or five hours on-line and then go right to bed.

Example 3:   I've noticed that since you were hired last week, when you come to talk to me you always call me "Mr. Anderson."

Step Two: I think.

Most likely, this is the first thought you had—the one that caused you to want to become assertive in the first place. But it also must be the logical conclusion that your evidence from Step One leads to. It's just that you usually know these two steps in reverse order. In fact, sometimes it takes a good amount of careful thinking to come up with the evidence that leads to the assumption you will be stating in Step Two.

Example 1:   I think that the time you are spending making personal phone calls is keeping you from answering your share of the customer calls.

Example 2:   I think that you might be avoiding me.

Example 3:   I think you figure I prefer that you call me that.

Step Three: (I feel).

The parentheses around Step Three indicate it is an optional step. In some situations it is appropriate and effective to talk about your feelings. In others it is not. In your close personal relationships, of course, your feelings are always important. In some business relationships, your emotions can help you communicate your needs more persuasively to your listener. In others, they could guarantee that your listener would shut down totally. Carefully consider the needs and personalities of your listeners and then use your best judgment.

Example 1:   What do you think? Does Andrea's boss really need to express an emotion? Or does he or she have enough legitimate power in the relationship that the emotion is unnecessary? It would sound rather ridiculous for the boss to say, "And I feel so betrayed when you do this."

But what if you're not Andrea's boss? What if you are her co-worker, with no legitimate power to make her change? Wouldn't a statement of your feelings potentially give you a little more power? "And I feel used and taken advantage of because I end up taking the extra calls."

Example 2:   I feel frightened when you avoid me and I fear our relationship is failing.

Example 3:   I feel that you perceive me as unapproachable when you call me that.

Step Four: I want.

Finally, (notice how long it takes to get here), you tell the person what it is you want them to do or what it is you want them to stop doing. But you need to be specific. Present your listener with your request in a way that is so clear he or she will have no doubt about how to go about doing it. You can't tell Andrea merely to be more productive: that is too vague. Specify what she needs to do.

Example 1: I want you to refrain from making personal telephone calls from your desk during the hours you are working in this department and I want you to answer at least ten customer calls per hour.

Example 2: I want us to talk about our relationship sometime within the next couple of days. Let's take a minute right now and figure out when we can do that.

Example 3: Please call me Ned.

Step Five: I will.

What can you offer to this person to make it a good deal for them? And of course, when you have the power and it is appropriate that you use it, what can you offer in the form of negative consequences if they fail to make the change?

Example 1: Andrea, I will be updating your personnel file in three weeks. If you have turned around on this behavior, I will eliminate any mention of it from your file so that it doesn't have to follow you through your career here. However, if you don't make this change, I will need to start termination procedures at that point.

Example 2: And honey, maybe if we have that talk tomorrow after work we could go out for dinner and see that new sci-fi movie you've been wanting to see.

Example 3: And I hope this is just the beginning of a good and supportive relationship for as long as we both work here. As a matter of fact, how about if I teach you how to use this new program—I used it at my last job.

This approach to assertiveness is much gentler and less direct than the ERRRR Technique. Use it in three important situations:

1. Any time you are hoping to persuade someone with control issues to do something your way.

2. Any time you need to show deference to the person you are talking to—for example, a client.

3. When you hope to make an impact on one of your teenaged children. (Teenagers are by definition dealing with control issues. This is a great way to look reasonable to them.)

Finally, there is one more approach we can recommend. We call it the USA Approach.

The Third Approach to Assertiveness: A Reasonable "No"

As you can tell by the title, this is a method that works best when you need to limit someone's behavior or when you need to say a polite (or political) "no." It is also the simplest technique, made of only three steps.

U nderstand

S ituation

A lternate Action

It is also the approach that shows up closest to the center on our continuum:

Passive _____ **Assertive** _____ **Aggressive**

Let's use the same three illustrations: Andrea, the significant partner and Ned Anderson. Then we will also illustrate how to use this technique to say a polite "no."

Understand. Here you explain your understanding of why the person does what it is he or she does that is annoying you.

Example 1: Andrea, I understand why you make the personal calls that you do. You have a lot of friends and you are very popular. And frankly, sometimes our incoming lines are not busy at all—it must seem like you have plenty of time.

Example 2:   Honey, I understand how tired you must be when you get home from work. And I know that the stresses there have doubled for you since your co-worker Gary resigned last week.

Example 3:   I understand that you have probably always been encouraged to call your supervisors by a more formal name.

Situation. Now you explain the situation you find yourself in because of that person's behavior. This could include your feelings, or it could be a more straightforward statement that explains how the other person's behavior is damaging you or others.

Example 1:   Our situation, though, is that we have promised our customers that they will be able to reach us 24-7. When you are busy on a personal call, I notice that you don't even answer the customer line. Can you imagine how frustrated that caller must get? When we hired you, we made it clear that your number one priority was to answer every call, and preferably within the first two rings.

Example 2:   I've also had an increased workload these past several weeks. And for me, the most relaxing thing I could do is come home and spend time with you doing something fun. When you isolate yourself in the computer room, I feel lonely and rejected. It seems that you don't care about me.

Example 3:   Ever since I have been in management, though, I have always encouraged people to call me by my first name. I think the best way for us to work well together is to have a casual, warmer relationship.

Alternate Action. Here you suggest what you would rather have the person do. Keep in mind that you could get better results if you allow them at least a small amount of leeway, so they feel as though they have been treated in a generous way. (This is hard to do if you have been extremely frustrated with their behavior for a while. But that's still not a reason to avoid doing it.)

Example 1:   So I'll tell you what: If you will agree to refrain from making any personal calls between 8:30 and 11:30, and if the phones get quiet before lunch it would be okay with me if you make a short call between 11:30 and noon. The same is true for the afternoon. As a matter of fact, maybe it would be a positive thing for the whole department. We should figure out a schedule. Each of you should get a pre-scheduled 30 minutes in the afternoon where the rest of the department will cover your phone for you so you can each make a few calls. Everyone could probably use the break.

(*Note:* Many supervisors roll their eyes when they read this. "Why should I have to let her make any personal calls?" they ask. Well, to be honest, they don't have to allow her any personal calls. It just might make for a more positive organization—if it's practical. Obviously, if the phones are always busy with incoming customer calls, this is probably not an option available to explore.)

Example 2.   So why don't we go out to DeMarco's for dinner and then go see that new sci-fi movie you've wanted to see. I think it would do us a world of good to do something special.

Example 3:   So please call me Ned. If it makes you feel any better, you can call me Mr. Anderson when we are together in meetings with clients.

Because this is such a simple method to remember, and a simple one to use, we recommend it for just about every situation where it would be practical. The main difference between the USA Approach and the ERRRR Technique is in directness. The ERRRR Technique starts with the request you have of the other person, the USA Approach does not. The USA starts with you trying to see it from their side—a very gracious approach.

The difference between the USA Approach and the Five Steps to Positive Assertiveness is in tone. The USA does state some evidence (in the situation statement), but in a subtler way than the Positive Assertiveness *I see* statement. The USA is a more casual, less formalized approach.

Finally, the USA Approach can also be used to tell someone "no" in a very polite and political way. For example, perhaps your boss has asked you to take on more than you had the time or ability to handle. And you felt that to say "no" would be inappropriate—even if it was necessary. Here's how it works.

Early today, your boss and you agreed on your "to-do" list. It is a full list. But now, at 2 p.m., your boss tells you, "I've decided I want you to call all our clients this afternoon to tell them about our new product line."

317

Career Success

You still have three hours worth of work on your to-do list. And you don't want to stay three hours late to get it all done. Here's how you could use the USA Approach:

Understand: I understand why you want me to make those calls—you have that major project due at 5:00, so you don't have the time to make them yourself. You know how much I enjoy talking with the clients on the phone and how much most of them enjoy talking to me. And it is important that they hear about our new product line soon.

Situation: Here's my situation. Of course, I am going to do whatever you determine I need to be doing, whatever you determine the most important and most urgent priorities are. It's just that before I start making those calls, would you look at this to-do list with me? This is the one we agreed on earlier today. Is there anything you see on it that is more urgent or more important to you than these phone calls?

(*Note:* And this is where you need to have an understanding of your boss's personality. Is your boss reasonable? Would he or she look at your to-do list sincerely and perhaps tell you of one or two things that are more important? And tell you to do those but forget the rest of the list and make as many of the client calls as you can in your remaining time? If so, you are done. You don't even need to go into Alternate Action. If, however, you think your boss would look at your to-do list quickly and say, "Why can't you just stay and do all of it?" then you'd better have Alternate Action ready to go.)

Alternate Action: (After the boss has glanced at the to-do list for just a moment, you interrupt with something like this.) I just remembered something. You've always told me that ten of our clients are worth 95% of our annual revenue. Why don't you give me those ten names? I'll call them right away because they are clearly the most important ones. As far as the other 125, why don't we just have the customer service department call them over the next week?

Do you see how offering an alternative makes you look like a hard worker? It's much more responsible and credible than a flat "no." It is also more credible than you taking on all the calls and the "to do" list and being unable to finish either. That would be a case of over promise/under deliver.

3. Be so clear your listener (or reader) can make no mistake about the meaning of your message.

When you are finished talking (or they are done reading your memo), the people you have been assertive with should have no doubt of what you are asking them to do (or what you are asking them to stop doing). And not just in general terms. Notice that Andrea's boss didn't tell her, "Andrea, I need you to be more productive at work."

That simply isn't specific enough. And if you've ever worked with someone like Andrea, I'll bet you'll also know that Andrea—believe it or not—believes she is productive. Your statements need to be so specific, so clear, that people could check the items off of a list as they complete them.

It's also important that the person you are talking to knows how to do what you are asking. Do you need to provide them with instructions or training? Is it possible that one of the reasons Andrea makes so many personal phone calls is because she is insecure about how to talk to the customers who call? Perhaps her boss could provide her with training or scripts to use.

The same is true of how specific you need to be when spelling out the rewards and consequences you have to offer. You must make sure that your listener knows exactly and specifically what's in it for them if they agree to your request—and what's in it for them if they don't. It is never very effective to tell your children that if they don't do something "right now" that you want them to do, then they'll be in trouble. What exactly is the trouble they'll be in? To say nothing about how much further you would get by promising a reward than you will by threatening a negative consequence.

There is an important note in all this talk of reward, though, and it's best not to miss it. A reward will only work if the person you're offering it to sees it as a reward.

4. Pay people in a currency they can spend.

This is just a catchy way of saying *always offer people rewards they appreciate*. By the same token, don't offer negative consequences unless you absolutely must—but when you do, always make sure they are seen as negative by the person. In either case, make sure you follow through.

Some people enjoy attention, like a round of applause at a meeting. It makes them feel bigger, more appreciated and more powerful. Other people shy away from public displays of attention—even positive attention—because it embarrasses them.

Many people enjoy chocolate—others are allergic. Some people get a real charge out of trophies. To others, they're useless.

In today's work world, there are only two rewards you can count on, two rewards that everyone appreciates:

1. Money
2. Time off

Everything else is a matter of preference. To be a more powerful person, make a study of the people around you. Notice their tastes; notice their preferences.

The other half of this rule goes back to basic child psychology. If you have children, have you ever gotten so frustrated that you over promised on a consequence:

"If you kids don't quiet down, you're going to be grounded for six months!" Just who's getting punished with *that* one? They're too loud so you're going to keep them in the house? For six months?

Not only is it a punishment that doesn't make sense, it is a promise that you will never keep. The people you have relationships with need to be able to count on you. You must be predictable. And that means you must keep every promise you make. So don't over promise.

5. Maintain the relationship.

This can be hard advice to follow. Most adults dread conflict, even if it has been necessary and even if they have been responsible enough to be assertive. But many adults find that once the conflict has been talked out, it is sometimes tempting to avoid each other for a while—there's just too much of a negative memory.

In fact, this is the worst choice on earth. By avoiding each other, these adults make it much more likely they will have another bad moment, another conflict sooner rather than later.

Go out of your way to keep in contact with anyone you have had an assertive conversation with. You don't need to bring up the conflict, of course, keep it lighter than that. Perhaps you could poke your head around their cubicle wall and ask them if you can bring them a soda back from the vending machine.

By maintaining the relationship—even if it's difficult—you will help guarantee a more positive relationship between you in the long term.

FILING

Filing's a chore most of us dread. But it's a chore that could make a huge difference in whether you are seen as a credible professional or not.

All of us keep some files. While it is true that some of us keep only a very few files, have you considered that the list of names and phone numbers that you keep in a day planner or smartphone is a file? Or how about the memos, printed e-mail and mail that you keep in your in-basket? That in-basket could also be called a file.

This section illustrates the few down-to-earth and common sense tips that all members of the world of work can use to quickly and effectively organize their files.

Rules

1. Never forget: The purpose of filing is easy retrieval.
2. Use the filing system most appropriate for the information you must archive.
3. The cardinal rule of filing is consistency.
4. The cardinal sin of filing is a duplicate file.

5. Make order from the chaos that presently surrounds you.

6. Become aware of the rules and constraints governing the files you keep and then heed them.

7. Create a record retention plan, a record retention schedule and a destruction schedule for your files.

Explanations and Examples

1. Never forget: The purpose of filing is easy retrieval.

If you keep just this in mind your files will definitely be organized in a way that is useful to you. It's easy to forget this concept, though. Especially when your desk is overloaded with paper that hasn't been sorted or filed for close to a month, the purpose of filing can certainly look like it's *to get that junk off my desk!*

But think about it: The purpose of filing is to be able to find something again if you need to. Will you need to find every piece of filing you save? No, let's hope not. But better *save* than be *sorry*.

When creating a filing system, ask yourself where most people would look first for a certain item, then file it in that spot.

Also, beware of mixing too many inactive files into the files you use more regularly. While you may not be able to dump or destroy the inactive files (at least not yet), there is no rule that says they must be stored in the same place as the ones you do use often.

The Association of Records Managers and Administrators (ARMA) claims that in an active filing system, the ideal ratio of files stored to files used should be 5:1. Yes, that does mean that 80% of the files you store will probably never be used at all. Good! But that 5:1 ratio also keeps you safe in the event that you do need some of them.

Of course, it would be lots easier if we could all be psychic. All we would need to do is hold a potential file up to our foreheads to see if we will need it ever again or not.

Until that skill becomes possible, stick with the 5:1 ratio.

On the other hand, most people report that the files they work with have a much higher retention ratio than 5:1. Does it ever feel to you that you need to look through 100 files in order to find the one you're looking for?

Or have the tightness of the files you keep ever caused your cuticles to bleed? Start an inactive file for all those files you hardly ever need. Have you ever experienced the pain of all those deep knee bends when the most active files you use are consistently in the bottom drawers? Keep inactive files in the bottom drawers and active ones in the top drawers.

Always remember: The purpose of filing is easy retrieval. Use that as your guiding principle in every aspect of organizing your files and you will suffer much less.

2. Use the filing system most appropriate for the information you must archive.

The five most common systems used to organize files are:

- Alphabetical
- Subject
- Chronological
- Numerical
- Geographical

Note that within the subject and geographical systems, the files may be in alphabetical order.

Even if you keep a relatively small number of files, it is likely that not all your files are stored best in the same format. Some files naturally fall into alphabetical order (like address and phone number lists or files of clients). Others fall best into subject order (like reference material in a training department). Still others are stored most logically in a chronological order—whether descending (oldest first) or ascending (newest first). Other methods include numerical (like by social security number) or geographic (like by territories of sales reps in a Sales Office).

When building your files, consider the logical order into which each set of those files naturally falls. Don't be shy about storing different types of material in different systems.

For example, in a Human Resources department it is conceivable that some of the files would be subject oriented: Benefits flyers about health care would be in a separate file from benefits flyers regarding life insurance.

Employee files could be filed alphabetically by last name, or perhaps for security purposes numerically by social security number.

There could also be a geographical system set up to distinguish the employees of one branch office from another branch office in a different state.

Originals of the standard office operating procedure memos routinely generated by this department would be stored in ascending chronological order in a binder, one binder for each year.

3. The cardinal rule of filing is consistency.

Make sure that the filing rules you are using in your organization are published and easily available to anyone using the files. Even filing experts disagree about some of the rules of filing, especially alphabetic filing rules. But that shouldn't matter to you once you have set the rules your organization will be using.

For example, if you have an alphabetic file of company names, where would you put the file for 3M Corporation? Some people would put it at the beginning of the alphabet, following a rule many people are aware of that says *All numbers come before all letters*. Other people, though, might put it in the file where the word *Three* would appear, following a rule that says *Spell out all symbols and figures and file alphabetically*. Still others might file it under *Minnesota Mining and Manufacturing*, following an old rule that said to *Spell out all abbreviations and acronyms and file alphabetically*. And we haven't even touched on the number of people who would probably just forget about the 3 and file it at the beginning of the *M's*.

Again, it doesn't matter where you file it—as long as all the people you work with file it in the same spot. Decide on the basic filing rules that will be used in your filing system, publish them and make sure there are copies kept near the files for anyone who needs to use them.

4. The cardinal sin of filing is a duplicate file.

Many people balk at this concept, thinking that the true cardinal sin of filing is the misfile. Here's why they're misled. A misfile can be very annoying, even dangerous. But at least when you can't find a file, you know you have a problem. When you find a duplicate file, you are probably unaware that it is indeed a duplicate. Yet because it is a duplicate it's likely to be incomplete and inaccurate.

And that is very dangerous—at least to your ability to retrieve what you want when you want it.

Control the potential for developing duplicate files in one of a couple ways. Either use "out cards" or restrict access to the files.

"Out cards" are pieces of card stock that are placed into a filing system at the spot a file is removed. The out card lists who has the file and what day (and perhaps time) it was taken.

Not only does this system let another person looking for that particular file know where it can be found, but it also lets that person know that there is a file. Now that person won't be inclined to create a second file. Another benefit is that an out card makes re-filing easier—the out card serves as a bookmark in the file drawer.

The other option you might want to explore—depending on the responsibility level of the people in your organization who use the files—is to limit access to the files. Put a few file clerks or other employees in charge of retrieving all the files anyone needs, and make them responsible for correctly re-filing them once the people who have used them are finished with them.

Yes, that is an extreme step. But consider your legal liability if the files in your system have a tendency to disappear.

5. Make order from the chaos that presently surrounds you.

Sometimes, no matter how many tips you receive about filing, it seems that you just can't get organized. Maybe the whole system should be re-built. And it's truly not as overwhelming a task as it may seem to be.

There are five simple steps to making order from chaos. Whether the chaos you find is in a file cabinet, an office, a junk room at home or even on your computer's hard drive, here is the process to use:

Step One: Brainstorm a list of everything you think you have in whatever area it is you are attempting to organize.

Step Two: Make no more than ten categories that encompass all of those items.

Step Three: Physically sort the area into boxes or piles. Include a box to put more urgent items in.

Step Four: Organize the urgent box.

Step Five: Now, organize each of the other boxes (or piles) into a file that makes sense for that topic.

Step One: Brainstorm a list of everything you think you have in whatever area it is you are attempting to organize.

If you are organizing a file cabinet or a roomful of file cabinets, make a list on several sheets of paper. What do you think you have in those cabinets?

This list shouldn't be absolutely specific. You don't need to list every memo that you have received from the Legal Department about trademarks and patents. All you would need to list is *Legal Dept. memos re: trademarks and patents*. Maybe you have a lot of old magazines—some of them about home decorating, some about engineering. List those as two: *Magazines—home decorating, magazines—engineering*.

When you have finished it is probable you will have missed a few things. This is fine—you have thought of enough to do a good Step Two.

Step Two: Make no more than ten categories that encompass all of those items.

And these categories should be about content, not about medium. For example, using the magazine example above: If I am an engineer, I probably have a good number of professional journals and magazines about engineering. The home decorating magazines are about a hobby of mine, decorating. Those magazines would be included in two separate categories: Engineering, Professional and Home Decorating.

If you end up with more than ten categories, you will be overwhelmed. Remember that you can always further subdivide inside a particular category when you get to the last step and begin filing that category.

By the same token, if you end up with fewer than four categories you have probably not differentiated among them enough to be truly helpful. Depending on the size of the area that you are attempting to organize and the breadth of the material to be found there, aim for between four and ten categories.

Step Three: Physically sort the area into boxes or piles. Include a box to put more urgent items in.

Once you have determined your categories, acquire one box, basket or folder for each category. Make sure that the container you choose will be large enough to hold however many items you will end up with.

Have one extra box labeled urgent. Also, have a garbage can or recycling bin nearby. Then, choosing a time you are least likely to be interrupted, take your boxes (or baskets or folders) into the chaos and physically sort it. Shred, throw away or recycle anything that is no longer needed. Put into the urgent box anything that you know must be handled immediately. As for everything else, put it all in the box that seems most appropriate.

Will you do this sorting perfectly? Probably not. But you will get close enough, and you can always fix the problems in Step Five.

Step Four: Organize the urgent box.

Obviously. When the chaos you have been living with has become long-term it is inevitable you will find at least a few things that surprise you. (*"Wow! I still have this?!?!?"*) Now that you have found it, make sure to handle it first. Then, after you've handled it, place whatever remains for your file into the appropriate category box.

Step Five: Now, organize each of the other boxes (or piles) into a file that makes sense for that topic.

Start with the category that you use most often or the one that is most important to you or your organization. Empty the box you created for that category in Step Three and look for the logical way to organize it.

Realize as you do this that most files break down into more than one level of filing. For example, perhaps I am filing all the reference material I have ever used in creating training programs and workbooks. The first level of distinction would be by topic: Some of the programs I have written are about communication skills, some about peak achievement, some about business writing and still others about self-esteem. So let's make those my four main filing categories. That would be subject filing.

But inside those four subjects, there are lots of different items. Some are magazine or journal articles, some are notes I have developed over the years, some are photos and diagrams, some are CD-ROMs, others are audiotapes or videos. Obviously, these different media require different kinds of storage. That could be another sublevel of the filing. And then, there are of course sublevels within the topics themselves. In business writing, for example, there's information about grammar, style, spelling, proofreading, the creative process and reference books. Within each of those subtopics are even more subtopics. Grammar, for example, contains: the difference between American and British English, the difference between a business style and an academic style, common errors and how to fix them, funny stories about how grammar rules have changed and separate topic files for various grammar rules.

Eventually, most files will subcategorize themselves into alphabetical filing. The common grammar problems, for example, could be filed alphabetically. Dangling participles would come before split infinitives.

Just remember that as long as each category maintains its own filing integrity, the method you use to organize one category doesn't necessarily have to be the method you use to organize all categories.

6. **Become aware of the rules and constraints governing the files you keep and then heed them.**

If you work for a government agency or a business (or nonprofit) organization that is governed by a regulatory agency, there is a pre-set list of what you must keep, and for how long you must keep it. Even many organizations who are not legally bound to a regulatory agency do have a list like this, commonly referred to as a records retention schedule. Find any that your organization currently has on file.

Everyone knows that you and your organization can get into trouble for getting rid of documents too soon. But did you know that it is just as dangerous to keep files too long as it is to keep them not long enough? If you hold on to something too long, it could demonstrate to an investigating authority that you have selectively discarded other items that were the same age. Even if you could have thrown away all of it!

Become aware of the rules that you need to follow to stay within the law, whether that law is one made by a government or by your organization.

Here's a quick test for you: How long are you supposed to keep copies of your personal income tax returns? What does the Internal Revenue Service say?

Was your answer seven years? That's what most people say. But it's not correct. The IRS says three years—unless they suspect fraud, in which case they can ask you for records from perpetuity (that's forever!).

7. **Create a record retention plan, a record retention schedule and a destruction schedule for your files.**

If no such records retention plan is already in existence in your organization, spearhead the effort to create one. Check with your supervisors and their supervisors. What do they know about the requirements for keeping and destroying the kinds of records you are the steward of? Are there any government agencies that would have something to say about your records and how long they should be kept?

Once you have done your best to determine the correct retention periods, prepare a document that lists these things:

- Type of document (employee personnel file)
- How long to keep (three years after that employee's separation)
- Where it is kept (inactive files, Human Resources Department)
- Who is the steward of those files (Human Resources Director)
- How they are disposed when it's time to get rid of them (shredded)
- Who gets rid of them (Human Resources Records Staff Supervisor)

Have the document signed by officials of your organization, and have it certified or notarized as well. Keep several copies in various safe locations.

This document will protect you in the event that someone does have a complaint about a document being destroyed too soon or too late. As long as your record retention schedule has been followed—even if it turns out to be incorrect in a small way, you can probably defend yourself from horrible consequences. Especially if you have had that schedule reviewed and certified by a records expert.

GOALS

The first step in accomplishing anything is to know what you hope to end up with when you have finished. And the self-help and human development movements have spent many years teaching simple, coherent strategies for goal setting. (And, to be honest, a few that were less simple and coherent.)

The topic of goal setting includes more than just the setting of goals. It also includes the determining of one's main purpose in life, the clarification of one's values and the establishment of the rules for the living of life.

And this indeed is how we will approach the topic here: in four main parts. First we will address values clarification, then goal setting itself. Third will come planning, and finally we will end this section with a rousing pep talk on the single most important step toward any goal: take action.

Our tips for this section, then, are simple:

Rules

1. Clarify your values and your purpose.

2. Set goals for your immediate future, your medium-range future and your long-range future, for each important area of your life. Write them down.

3. Plan the details of how you will achieve your goal. Think about the actions you need to take, the resources you need to acquire, the people you need to meet and the education you need to get.

4. Be relentless—take action until you are finished. Monitor and adjust as you go, but make sure to finish.

Explanations and Examples

1. Clarify your values and your purpose.

What are you living for? Do you believe your life has a specific purpose? Do you have a combination of talents and preferences that allow you to make a particular contribution to your life and the lives of others? What's your life about?

Perhaps these may seem to be heavy questions but better to challenge yourself about them now than to live the bulk of your life and then worry about them! As the best-selling author Rabbi Harold Kushner says: Of all the deathbeds he has visited in his vocation as a rabbi, not one dying person has ever said to him, "Why didn't I spend more time at the office?" (*When Bad Things Happen to Good People*).

Use the Values Worksheet on page 325 to help you get started. We recommend you actually use this worksheet several times over a few days. This will help you gain access to all the different parts of you that deserve a say in your future.

We're not suggesting that you are seriously schizophrenic, just that most people have several different personalities that need expression. Maybe you're adventuresome enough to want to climb mountains on one day, but comfort-oriented enough to want to curl up in front of a fire with a good book and a hot cocoa on another day. There are no wrong answers to any of the questions we pose. They are just meant to give you some things to think about—and some patterns to discover.

We have included both a blank form for you to use and an example form with sample answers, to give you an idea of how it can be used.

VALUES WORKSHEET

Ask yourself the following questions and write down all answers that come to mind. Do this worksheet several different times over the next few days, so as to gain access to all the different parts of yourself that want a voice.

1. Who do you want to be? (Think about this question in terms of the last years of your life: What do you hope to be able to say about yourself?)

2. What do you really want to do? (You probably have some long-term goals already in place that can serve as part of the answer to this question. Also consider any one-time goals you might have, or a list of places you would like to visit, books you would like to read, education you would like to acquire or people you want to meet—just as some examples to get you started.)

3. Whom do you admire? Why? What qualities do they possess that you admire? (The people on this list can be from your own life, or they can be public figures, historical figures—or even fictional characters. What we are really after here is to find your values and the *why*.)

4. List some favorite books, movies, plays, inventions, pieces of art, etc. Why do you like them?

5. If you could have only one, but you could have all of it that you wanted, which would you choose: Money or power? Why?

SAMPLE WORKSHEET

1. Who do you want to be? (Think about this question in terms of the last years of your life: What do you hope to be able to say about yourself?)

    A success, a hero, someone who overcame obstacles, an example to others

2. What do you really want to do? (You probably have some long-term goals already in place that can serve as part of the answer to this question. Also consider any one-time goals you might have, or a list of places you would like to visit, books you would like to read, education you would like to acquire or people you want to meet—just as some examples to get you started.)

    Build a house from the ground up for my family, climb some major mountains, retire young, learn Greek, travel to Greece, learn to fly

3. Whom do you admire? Why? What qualities do they possess that you admire? (The people on this list can be from your own life, or they can be public figures, historical figures—or even fictional characters. What we are really after here is to find your values and the *why*.)

    My father—he was kind, a hard worker and almost totally self-sufficient.
    Rudy Guiliani — he stepped up, even though he had his own problems.

4. List some favorite books, movies, plays, inventions, pieces of art, etc. Why do you like them?

    Armageddon — heroic, but with a sense of humor
    Fountainhead — a true individual who never compromises himself and wins in the end

5. If you could have only one, but you could have all of it that you wanted, which would you choose: Money or power? Why?

    Power—power over myself, over my limitations and fear

Once you have completed the Values Worksheet (you may have to do this several times) read over your answers and find the patterns. Notice that in our example, there are many answers about adventurousness and risk taking. Use highlighters of different colors to mark what you find, and attempt to name the values important to you.

This would also be a good time to give some thought to the areas of your life that you value, and how much. How important is it to you to be a successful professional? A great parent? A loving spouse? A friend? A Scout leader? A member of a formal support group? A gardener? A health and exercise enthusiast? (These are just a few examples— let your mind and your heart go to help you find your personal list.)

After you have come up with your list of important life areas, use a pie chart to balance the interest (and sense of commitment) you have to each in light of the others. Realize that some days you will necessarily be more focused on one or two of your areas—we're not trying to balance each day, we're trying to balance a *life*. Think in terms of a week or a month at a time when assigning relative priority.

Sample:

LIFE AREA CHART

The life areas I am committed to:

A. *Father*

B. *Husband*

C. *Stock Investor*

D. *Author*

E. *Mountain Climber*

F. *Director of Sales for XYZ, Inc.*

G.

H.

PIE CHART:

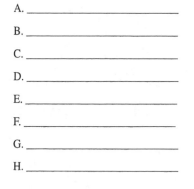

Your turn:

LIFE AREA CHART

The life areas I am committed to:

A.

B.

C.

D.

E.

F.

G.

H.

PIE CHART:

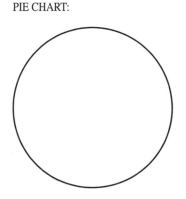

327

Career Success

2. **Set goals for your immediate future, your medium-range future and your long-range future, for each important area of your life. Write them down.**

   Now that you have thought about and determined the values important to you and the areas of your life that you need to focus on, your next step will be to set goals for each of those areas that are in line with the values you find important. Set some short-term goals, some medium-range goals and some long-term goals in the various areas of your life. Write them down on the following worksheet or in your own goal book. (We do recommend you purchase a beautiful blank book to make your goal book.)

   Short-term goals (S) are the ones you hope to accomplish within a week to a month.

   Medium-range goals (M) are to be accomplished from within a month to a year.

   Long-term goals (L) will take a year or longer to accomplish.

SAMPLE WORKSHEET

LIFE AREA	GOALS
Father	S: Take each child out for a few hours at least once a week
	M: Plan a great family vacation for next summer
	L: Get to work on their college fund
Husband	S: Take Emma out at least once/week
	M: Join that painting class with her next spring
	L: Make the marriage last
Stock Investor	S: Re-think portfolio, make changes
	M: Set up direct deposit, figure formula
	L: Retire in 10 years
Author	S: Start a journal
	M: Begin a novel before summer/write every day
	L: Sell a novel
Mountain Climber	S: Read some books, rent some videos
	M: Climb an easy one next summer
	L: Climb a major mountain within 5 years
Director of Sales for XYZ, Inc.	S: Set up meeting schedule w/ managers
	M: Double sales of add-on items within year
	L: Promotion within two years

Your turn:

LIFE AREA   GOALS

_____   S: _____

                            M: _____

                            L: _____

_____   S: _____

                            M: _____

                            L: _____

_____   S: _____

                            M: _____

                            L: _____

_____   S: _____

                            M: _____

                            L: _____

_____   S: _____

                            M: _____

                            L: _____

_____   S: _____

                            M: _____

                            L: _____

_____   S: _____

                            M: _____

                            L: _____

Once you have established your goals, you are well on your way to success. Just the fact that you wrote them down serves to program a subconscious part of your brain that will now be on the lookout for the people, places, things and opportunities that could help you achieve those goals.

But wait! We can (and will) do better.

First, let's consider the qualities of a powerful goal. We call them the ACTION tips:

- Achievable
- Compatible with your values
- Time-specific
- In writing
- Owned by you
- Negotiated

Is your goal *Achievable*?

Do you believe that it can indeed be done, and that you are the one who can do it? Is the time frame realistic? If you work every day a little bit, can you get there on time?

How about control? Do you have control over enough of at least one of the constraints influencing your goal that you will indeed be able to move forward? Do you have flexibility with the budget, whether in money, supplies or human resources? Or, if you have little control over budget constraints, how about time frame? Can you adjust the time frame according to your needs? Or if neither budget nor time are flexible, how about the quality specifications? Can you modify them according to the reality of your budget and time constraints? If you have control over any one of these constraints, you will probably feel that what you are aiming for is doable. If you have little control over any of them, you may only feel trapped.

And what about your habits, your current comfort zone? Are you aware that psychologists tell us that most human beings would rather stay with a life they know that is far from ideal than take a risk on a different life that could be better—but a life that they have never experienced before? Human beings want to feel comfortable. And to feel comfortable, sometimes we sacrifice the new, the untried. Pay attention to your tendency to stay inside a comfort zone that no longer provides you with the happiness you want and deserve.

Compatible with your values?

We've discussed values already in this section on goal setting (page 324). But when your goals match your values, you free up a natural energy source. No one really does anything he or she doesn't want to do. Even those negative people who complain to you every day that they didn't really want to come in to work today are lying. Of course they wanted to—for one reason or another—or they wouldn't have come!

You know what motivates them to show up, don't you? Money! Or perhaps fear of some kind of negative consequence (like losing that source of money). How many of those negative people do you suppose come in daily just for the pleasure of complaining to you about the miserable state of their lives and the world? Perhaps they are even motivated by a secret belief that by sharing their negativity with you and as many people as possible, they might just lure one or two more of you over into their unhappy state. Remember, misery loves company.

Ask yourself if the goals you have established accurately reflect your most important values, as you examined them and clarified them back on page 327. Make sure they do.

Time-specific?

Many of us need deadlines in order to act. How about you? If you had various goals and priorities in front of you but none of them were due at a particular time, wouldn't you just sit back and have another donut? Or two?

If you don't have assigned deadlines, create them yourself. And if the assigned deadline looks less than achievable, break it down roughly into its milestones. Milestones are the steps along the way to your goals where you can measure how far you have come and how far you need yet to go.

If the assigned deadline is not achievable, the process of mapping out the milestones will make that apparent—to you and to whomever gave you the less-than-realistic deadline. You will have a stronger position from which to negotiate.

In writing?

Mark Victor Hansen, the best-selling co-author of the *Chicken Soup for the Soul* books has a great and simple saying for this: "When you think it, ink it."

By writing down your goals, you are programming the subconscious parts of your brain so they can now look full time for solutions, strategies and opportunities for success. Yes, even while you sleep!

Check our Worksheet on page 333 and the sample on page 332. Notice that we ask you to be much more specific in describing your goals. How will you know you have achieved your goal? What is the measurable, verifiable proof? What is your deadline? Where will you need to be by halfway, and when will that be? Where will you need to be by the end of this week? The end of this day?

Think about what kind of training you will need to achieve this goal. Who can help you? Who can encourage you? And then, the questions that will help you visualize your success, see your outcome before you get there. What will you be able to see when you get there? Hear? Touch? Feel? Taste? Smell?

Yes, we know. You may be saying that this is a lot of work. You bet it's a lot of work. But the time it will save you in working your way toward the goal makes it an investment you really must make. Let your brain help you work smarter not harder. Try it and let us know how it goes for you. We're eager to hear your success stories.

Owned by you?

Most of us are experienced with working toward the goals others have given us. At work, it is often necessary to involve ourselves in other people's priorities. But have you ever had the experience of working on a goal that you thought was foolish? Pointless? Not worth your time?

If you have, you know how deadly it is to feel no ownership of the goal you are completing. Each of us has a large supply of energy we can tap into. In order to tap into that energy, it is essential to find something in every goal that you can call your own. This must be something that you believe in.

And the truth is this: No one does anything he or she doesn't really want to do for one reason or another.

Have you ever worked with a negativist? One who complains every day that "I didn't really want to be here today"? You know why they came in! Most of them came because they wanted the paycheck or because they didn't want to lose their jobs. A few of them even came in because they see themselves as missionaries, working hard to convince their co-workers to become negative with them. But they do want to be there after all.

You can tap into your desire to do anything if you can sell it to yourself on the benefits of what it will do to advance you or the people you care about. This is where the rubber of your values hits the road of your goals.

Negotiated?

Your goals need to be negotiated in terms of the priorities you have established as well as in relation to the goals others may have for you—and how seriously those other goals impact your life. It is also important to consider the control you have (or don't have) over the budget, the time frame and the quality standards that the goal has been presented with. Can you modify the budget to accomplish your goal in a shorter time frame? Or do you have some flexibility in quality to accommodate a budget cut?

Carefully consider the resources you have available—including your own time, priorities and energy. Then establish what's important to you. Perhaps one of your goals needs to be placed on a back burner for a few months to make the time for another goal that your boss requires.

Or perhaps in this case, the negotiation you need to have is with that boss. Can you get a longer deadline? Or perhaps help from others? Either of those would make your own goal more doable in the present.

Sample:

PUTTING MY GOAL AND PLANS IN WRITING

My Goal: *Writing & selling a novel. Having it be successful*

Four ways I will know for sure I have achieved my goal:

1. *Hard bound books w/ my name and picture on them in every major bookstore*

2. *Large quarterly royalty checks coming to me*

3. *Oprah wants me on her show*

4. *We need to move and get an unlisted number*

My deadline: *5-31-10*

Halfway to my deadline: *5-31-10*

Where do I need to be by halfway (fill in date)?
   Novel written, agent hired

A quarter of the way to my deadline:
   11-30-09

Where do I need to be by a quarter of the way (fill in date)?
   Novel written, in hands of friends and editors. Agents being queried.

Where do I need to be by the end of the week?
   Writing

Where do I need to be by the end of today?
   Writing – 1500 words per day minimum

What training or resources do I need?
   A laptop computer with a good word processor

Who can help me?
   Emma – can help me lock myself in the den for several hours each night

Who can encourage me?
   Emma, Jack, Bob, Gerard, the kids

What will I *see* when I have achieved this goal?
   My book, piled high in bookstores; long lines of people waiting when I pull up in limo

What will I *hear* when I have achieved this goal?
   "It's him, LOOK!" The gears of the fast cash machine cranking out my unlimited funds

What will I be able to *touch* when I have achieved this goal?
   The crowds at book signings, cool feel of freshly printed books, stickiness of money

What will I *feel* (emotionally) when I have achieved this goal?
   Pride & financial security

What will I be able to *smell* when I have achieved this goal?
   The coffee/paper smell of the bookstores, the smell of money, the smell of the crowd

Your Turn:

PUTTING MY GOAL AND PLANS IN WRITING

My Goal: _____

_____

Four ways I will know for sure I have achieved my goal:

1._____

2._____

3._____

4._____

My deadline: _____

Halfway to my deadline:_____

Where do I need to be by halfway (fill in date)?_____

A quarter of the way to my deadline: _____

Where do I need to be by a quarter of the way (fill in date)? _____

Where do I need to be by the end of the week? _____

Where do I need to be by the end of today? _____

What training or resources do I need? _____

Who can help me?_____

Who can encourage me? _____

What will I *see* when I have achieved this goal? _____

What will I *hear* when I have achieved this goal? _____

What will I be able to *touch* when I have achieved this goal? _____

What will I *feel* (emotionally) when I have achieved this goal?_____

What will I be able to *smell* when I have achieved this goal? _____

3. **Plan the details of how you will achieve your goal. Think about the actions you need to take, the resources you need to acquire, the people you need to meet and the education you need to get.**

There are six steps in the planning process:

1. Brainstorm everything you can think of related to achieving your goal.

2. Organize the chaos of your brainstormed list.

3. Assign jobs and acquire needed resources.

4. Train, motivate and inspire yourself and your team.

5. Act.

6. Monitor progress as you go.

Let's give you the skills to use each one of these planning steps in the most practical and positive way.

1. *Brainstorm everything you can think of related to achieving your goal.* Make a list of everything you can think of related to achieving your goal. This list is random and long. Don't limit yourself. Give yourself permission to write down everything that crosses your mind. And also give yourself permission to cross any items out later. For more information about using the creative process, see pages 61 – 65.

2. *Organize the chaos of your brainstormed list.* For this step you will need to move back into the more logical and organized left hemisphere of your brain. Find the items from your brainstormed list that are related to each other and put them together into separate categories. Then, try to organize things consecutively within each category. Add anything you forgot earlier and subtract anything you find to be nonessential.

3. *Assign jobs and acquire needed resources.* Do you have a staff you can delegate to? Are there resources you need to acquire in order to achieve your goal? Assign tasks as you can and get what you need.

4. *Train, motivate and inspire yourself and your team.* Anyone working toward a goal needs a pat on the back occasionally. And in many cases, they need some training too. Training someone provides them with the *how to* of a particular job. But providing just the *how to* might not be enough; most of us need to be *motivated*. What's in it for the person doing the job? Communicate this information and give some thought to occasionally *inspiring* those delegatees too. The difference between motivation and inspiration is the difference between understanding something logically, in your head (motivation) and understanding it more deeply, in your heart (inspiration).

5. *Act.* While this is a list of the steps of planning, eventually all those plans need to bear fruit. This is where they will. Certainly, plan: But then act on your plan. Never leave the spot you were sitting when you planned a goal without having taken at least one small step toward achieving it. Get moving.

6. *Monitor progress as you go.* This will allow you to adjust where necessary as you move forward. Keep checking in to see how you're doing. Are you getting the results you had hoped for? Don't wait until you are months past the point you could have fixed something. Monitor every day or at least every few days.

4. **Be relentless—take action until you are finished. Monitor and adjust as you go, but make sure to finish.**

Plan tomorrow's action today and tell someone about it. Hold yourself accountable. It doesn't have to be a big thing—even a small step will do because it will keep you moving forward. Don't go to bed at night until you have done that one small thing that you promised yourself.

LISTENING

Listening is the undervalued communication skill!

Everyone knows it is considered important to be a good listener. But so many of us just have so little time and so very much we need to say to really focus our energies on it.

Yet being a good listener opens doors: doors in your relationships, doors in your career, doors in your community. And it isn't that hard, if you remember to do it.

Rules

1. Make time to listen to the people in your life.
2. Tune in to listen.
3. Eliminate distractions.
4. Be quiet until the speaker has finished.
5. Take notes.
6. Ask clarifying questions and summarize what the speaker has said to check for understanding.
7. Thank the speaker for taking the time to talk with you and compliment him or her in some honest and specific way.

Examples and Explanations

1. **Make time to listen to the people in your life.**

   Maybe it seems apparent, but with everyone's busy schedule this is truly the primary tip we can offer. Build time into your workday for short, informal meetings with your supervisor, your co-workers, your employees and your customers. Build time into your home life for your family, your friends and the people of your community.

   By establishing yourself as a listener, you enhance your reputation as someone who cares. And when people know you care, they tend to do a better job of caring about you (and your ideas and needs) too.

   At work, realize that your open-door policy might not be attracting all the people who you should be listening to. Sometimes people are busy themselves, or sometimes just too shy to take advantage of your offer, "Stop by anytime—I'm available." Make a point to seek out the people you don't often talk—and listen—to. It means actually making eye contact with the person you're listening to.

   At home, use the same advice. Find times that are convenient for your loved ones and then be prepared to listen as they tell you about their day, or about their thoughts and feelings. But make the time.

2. **Tune in to listen.**

   Tuning in means that you have eliminated all possible distractions and focused your full attention on the people talking to you. It means pushing your computer keyboard to the side, so you are not tempted to start typing while your co-worker is telling you about the dilemma she is facing in her project. It means turning your body to fully face your supervisor who has caught up with you on your way to the photocopier. It means muting the television and turning your body away from it when your teenager asks you if you have a minute.

   And tuning in looks so good! If you do just this, your communication partners assume you are paying attention—even if you're not! (Of course, we recommend that you do pay attention.)

   Eye contact, **body position** and **facial expression** are all key components of tuning in.

   Eye contact: While you wouldn't want to be staring into the eyeballs of your communication partners, you do need to be looking them in the face for most of the conversation.

   Body position: Turn both your face and the rest of your body toward anyone who is speaking to you. Keep your posture open and relaxed. People interpret (sometimes accurately and sometimes inaccurately) very quickly what your body language is saying to them. Beware of the natural human tendency to close your body posture—whether by crossing your arms in front of you while standing, or by crossing your legs in front of you while sitting. Lean into the conversation slightly—this sends an important subliminal signal that you are eager to hear what the speaker has to say.

   Facial expression: Do you know what your neutral face looks like? Most people assume that because their emotional state is neutral, their facial expression looks neither positive nor negative. This is usually not the case. Most facial expressions that require no effort look either bored, tired or angry. Guard against this possibility by checking your neutral face in a mirror. Then, to make it look more open and positive, do two things: 1) Open your eyes a little wider and 2) Turn the corners of your mouth up until you stop frowning. See? Isn't that better? Practice making this kind of face while you are listening neutrally to other people. They'll see you as a more positive person.

3. Eliminate distractions.

Do what you can to have your conversation in a quiet, comfortable place. Make sure that interruptions are cut to the minimum and that the environment is positive. Is there too much background noise that could interfere with your ability to pay attention? Is the temperature of the room comfortable? Is there a television or a computer on that could distract you? How about a phone? Can you set your phone to be answered by voice mail?

The more attention you can focus on a speaker, the more easily you will correctly hear and understand that speaker's message.

4. Be quiet until the speaker has finished.

Sometimes this is the hardest listening tip of all to follow. After all, what if you think of something exciting or important that you want to add to the conversation before the speaker has finished?

Well, the answer is obvious: Be quiet anyway. This shows respect for the other person, and if you follow our next tip you will not risk forgetting what you want to add—when it is your turn.

5. Take notes.

There are four good reasons that note-taking makes you a superb listener:

1. You will have a record of what was said, should you need to check it.

2. You will avoid the tendency to think ahead and to finish the unspoken thoughts of the speaker before he or she has had the opportunity to say them. Because the process of writing takes so much more time than the process of listening, you will focus better on the conversation that is really happening instead of the one that you may be predicting in your mind.

3. You will have a place to keep track of your own thoughts so you won't find it necessary to interrupt. You can write them in the margins of the notes you are taking about what the speaker is saying.

4. In cases where you are in conflict with the person doing the talking, you can use your notes to keep track of areas of agreement (perhaps you can mark them with stars)—no matter how large or how small. Then, when it is your turn to talk, you can start with those agreements: "Gee, we seem to agree on more than I thought … "

6. Ask clarifying questions and summarize what the speaker has said to check for understanding.

Once the speaker has finished, ask any questions that you have. (Maybe you have included them in your notes.) Then, sum up briefly your understanding of what was said. Use any of the buzz words that the speaker used, but also try to re-word things in your own conversational style so he or she can be confident that you do get the message. This rephrasing is especially important because people often have a different concept of what a word means.

7. Thank the speaker for taking the time to talk with you and compliment him or her in some honest and specific way.

Even if the conversation was less than totally positive, two people being willing to discuss something—especially something difficult—is a very positive thing. For that reason alone, you do need to thank your communication partners for the effort they made and the time they took to be clear with you. Then, give them the extra reward of a sincere and specific compliment about the way they communicated: Maybe something like, "Thanks for being willing to answer my questions so thoroughly," or "Thanks for being so enthusiastic about this project as you explained it to me." A sincere and specific compliment will make it easier for the two of you to speak together again—no matter what the circumstances.

MEETINGS

Meetings are one of the most frequently complained about phenomena of workplace life. The complaints range from they don't start on time, to they're too long, or we don't get anything done. And that doesn't even scratch the surface of the complaints that exist about the personalities of the people in attendance!

Reigning in your workplace meetings is easy to do. Use the strategies listed here and you will be well on your way to actually looking forward to the time you spend in meetings.

Rules

1. Create an organized and practical meeting plan before the meeting. Distribute it to all attendees at least 24 hours in advance of the meeting.

2. Appoint revolving roles of Secretary, Facilitator, Timekeeper and Conscience to keep the meeting (and future meetings) running smoothly.

3. Start the meeting on time. No matter who's there and who's not.

4. Handle meeting problems in a routine and predetermined manner.

5. Have meetings at times that make sense so as to make the best use of the energy levels of all attendees.

6. Have at least one forced participation question or comment in every meeting to keep everyone involved.

7. Include action items (highlighted for each participant) in any minutes distributed after the meeting.

8. Evaluate your meetings periodically and adjust them as needed.

9. Make sure you take good meeting minutes.

Explanations and Examples

1. **Create an organized and practical meeting plan before the meeting. Distribute it to all attendees at least 24 hours in advance of the meeting.**

   Most meetings are run from an agenda. But an agenda doesn't normally contain enough information to be useful in controlling the meeting. Most agendas merely list the time the meeting is supposed to begin, the topics that will be covered and the time the meeting will end.

   Try a more detailed meeting plan instead. Use the form below:

   MEETING PLAN

   Meeting date:

   Attendees:

   Start time:

   Location:

   Contact person:

TOPIC	TIME	TOPIC LEADER	OUTSIDE GUESTS	HANDOUTS ATTACHED?
1.				
2.				
3.				
4.				
5.				

Here is an example of how this meeting plan could be filled out:

SAMPLE MEETING PLAN

Meeting date: *February 5*

Attendees: *HR Dept, VP of Marketing, Sales Director,*
Customer Service Manager and
Administrative Liaison

Start time: *9:30 a.m.*

Location: *Conference Room 3, 2nd floor*

Contact person: *Annalee Romero, HR Director ext. 153*

TOPIC	TIME	TOPIC LEADER	OUTSIDE GUESTS	HANDOUTS ATTACHED?
1. *Customer Service Training*	*10 min.*	*Ann J.*	*––*	*yes - training outline*
2. *Communication Training Update*	*10 min.*	*Bob P.*	*––*	*no*
3. *Marketing Plan for 2nd Qtr.*	*15 min.*	*Jean L.*	*––*	*no*
4. *Valentine's Day Company Party*	*5 min.*	*Sam B.*	*potential DJ Mark Cohen*	*no*
5.				

The TOPIC list is obvious: What topics are going to be discussed at the meeting?

Then, how much TIME will be allowed for that topic?

Who will be the authority on that topic present in the meeting? That is the TOPIC LEADER. It's not that this individual will do all the talking about this topic, just that he or she will be a good resource to turn to if there are questions or problems.

It is also a good habit to publish a list of OUTSIDE GUESTS who will be attending this meeting. It's possible that one of these guests could be expecting something from another attendee at the meeting. If that other attendee isn't notified that the guest will be present, someone could be embarrassed and maybe even appear incompetent.

Finally, are there any handouts attached to this meeting plan—or could there be—that will further help prepare the attendees to spend their time in the best possible way once they get to the meeting? Have you ever attended a meeting where the attendees received the handouts they needed to be familiar with for the discussion as they walked in the door? What a waste of time that is! You have better things to do in that meeting room than to turn it into a reading room.

Put someone in charge of getting this meeting plan together and make sure it is distributed to all attendees so they receive it—and the attached handouts—at least 24 hours in advance of the meeting. It's not that all attendees will use it to responsibly prepare themselves for the meeting. But at least they had the opportunity to, so it isn't the fault of the person who called the meeting if some attendees aren't prepared.

2. **Appoint revolving roles of Secretary, Facilitator, Timekeeper and Conscience to keep the meeting (and future meetings) running smoothly.**

Yes, this is an idea from the field of Total Quality Management, which was popular in the middle 1990s. And it is one of the best ideas to this day about how to keep meetings running smoothly.

Appoint four attendees at each meeting to play the four roles of Secretary, Facilitator, Timekeeper and Conscience. These roles are assigned for one meeting only and then they revolve to other attendees at the next meeting. This guarantees that everyone gets some ownership of making the meetings better and you'll see positive results very soon.

The **Secretary** has a role you have probably guessed. This is the person who takes the minutes during the meeting and prints them up for everyone who attended. We recommend that this role last for the entire time period between meetings, as well. The Secretary is the logical person to assemble the meeting plan for the next meeting and get it distributed to the attendees. So this job begins with the taking of minutes in Meeting One and continues through the publication and distribution of the meeting plan for Meeting Two. (See Rule #9 for tips on how to easily take effective meeting minutes.)

The **Facilitator** will run the meeting. This individual calls on the various attendees to speak. The Facilitator does not do all the speaking, nor does the Facilitator change the constraints of the meeting plan without the willing vote of all attendees.

The **Timekeeper** has only two jobs, but they are very important. Job One: The Timekeeper calls the meeting to order at the time that was published as the start time—no matter who's there and who's not. *We teach people how to treat us by how we allow them to treat us.* This is exactly how we get people to attend meetings on time. We don't wait for them to show up, and if they're late we make them responsible for catching up on their own.

Job Two of the **Timekeeper**: End each topic on time. Let's say Topic One has been allotted 15 minutes. In minute 10, the Timekeeper should clear his or her throat and gently interrupt the meeting: "We have only five minutes left to discuss this topic. Can we sum it up here or should we schedule another meeting to finish discussing it?"

How do you think most sane people answer that question? Most people will be eager to avoid an extra meeting and they will work hard to sum up then and there. If you really do need another meeting, though, it can be scheduled.

Finally, the **Conscience**. The Conscience's job is to enforce the ground rules the group has already agreed upon (at a separate start-up meeting) during the course of the meeting. This, of course, assumes that the group has decided upon some ground rules. How long is one person permitted to talk before it is automatically someone else's turn? How many *times* is a person allowed to speak before all attendees have had a chance to speak? How much negative emotion is it okay to express honestly in the group? These are the kinds of questions you need to ask yourselves to determine the role of the conscience.

Maybe one attendee spoke way too much. Every time he opened his mouth, everyone else's eyes rolled. Finally, one of your co-workers snapped and yelled at this attendee: "Why don't you just sit down and stop talking?"

While it may have been true that most attendees were glad that someone said something, most likely the co-worker who made this comment is now the new Bad Guy in the meeting. And everyone is on edge. Most likely the meeting will end very soon, and not well.

When there is an appointed Conscience, and that Conscience is a different person every week, you get the best of both worlds. You get to control the poor behavior exhibited at the meeting and no one becomes the Bad Guy—because everyone knew going in that it was this individual's job for that meeting. Consider giving a nametag to the Conscience that says, "*Hi." I am the Conscience.*

3. **Start the meeting on time. No matter who's there and who's not.**

As mentioned in our discussion of the Timekeeper: We teach people how to treat us by how we allow them to treat us. If you start every meeting on time, how long do you think it will take before most attendees begin getting there on time?

If you still see a problem, think about adding some consequences for the late attendees. Perhaps they need to sing a couple bars of the company's theme song. Or perhaps there's a dollar jar at the door—deposit a dollar for every five minutes you are late (you can use the money for snacks at the next meeting).

We heard a story from a man who attended a meeting at an office of his company based in Tokyo. He was surprised to see that there was a credit card reader mounted on the doorjamb. It was for the latecomers: Have your card out, because you need to swipe it to get in the room—an equivalent of $50 American (your dollars) would be deposited in the Manufacturing Floor's entertainment fund.

4. Handle meeting problems in a routine and predetermined manner.

Once you have appointed people to play the four roles we recommend, it becomes much easier to handle most meeting problems. Check out our chart:

THE MOST COMMON MEETING PROBLEMS—AND HOW TO HANDLE THEM	
Latecomers	Start without them; Dollar jars; Make a latecomer the Secretary for the next meeting.
Irrelevant, unworkable suggestions	Conscience or Facilitator redirects back to topic.
Good points, but not related to topic	Conscience or Facilitator redirects back to topic.
Wallflowers	The Facilitator could call on the quieter people; be careful—this can backfire if the person is very shy. Another option is that every meeting should include one or two points that everyone comments on, around the table.
Ramblers	The Conscience interrupts and sums up the point.
Mockers, snipers and whisperers	The Conscience would handle these, but how about a better way? Break them up—preassign seats.
Arguers	The Conscience interrupts and redirects the group back to the positive topic.
Unprepared presenters	You have a choice to make here. Either they present anyway (recommended when this person is never prepared); or, postpone and reschedule (recommended for most other situations).
Inappropriate comments	The Conscience interrupts and redirects, giving the group time to process any hurt feelings if they have occurred.

5. Have meetings at times that make sense so as to make the best use of the energy levels of all attendees.

Most people experience a few hours in their day when they have a higher energy level. These hours are often referred to as *peak hours*. Work hard to schedule routine meetings during times when most of the attendees are not experiencing their peak hours.

Here's a hint: The majority of people who work a traditional daytime schedule of 8:00 a.m. – 5:00 p.m. tend to have morning peak hours. This means that in that environment, you're better off having your routine meetings in the afternoon, during most people's non-peak hours. When you are having more important planning, brainstorming and project meetings, they should be held during peak hours.

The rationale here is simple. Don't waste people's peak energy on routine tasks. Most of the people in your organization should be as free as possible to focus on their own most important priorities during their peak hours.

6. Have at least one forced participation question or comment in every meeting to keep everyone involved.

This guarantees that the more shy, the more quiet participants—who often have some of the most creative and best ideas—will be given time to speak, whether they would have volunteered or not. Make sure that everyone who regularly attends your meetings gets in the habit of speaking at least once or twice per meeting. Only in this way will you truly have access to all the genius that getting together provides in the first place.

7. Include action items (highlighted for each participant) in any minutes distributed after the meeting.

This is a written reminder to each participant in the meeting what he or she has committed to do. Not only does it actually remind a forgetful participant, but it also provides the rest of the attendees a "CYA" memo that clearly shows who is responsible for each action item.

Make it part of the secretary's job to highlight and customize the minutes like this.

8. **Evaluate your meetings periodically and adjust them as needed.**

   After all, they are your meetings. Make sure they are working for the majority of the people attending them. Once in a while, include a meeting evaluation as the last topic on your meeting plan and have everyone contribute one item they think is great and one item they want to make better.

   This takes time but, little by little, you will refine your meetings to a point where most people actually look forward to the time they spend in them.

9. **Make sure you take good meeting minutes.**

   Taking good meeting minutes can seem like a daunting task. However, it's really much easier than you might think.

   1. Remember that the minutes are a record of what happened at the meeting—not a transcription of all the discussion. They are a record of motions and decisions made, action items and who is responsible for them.

   2. Prepare a list of all invitees—as they come into the meeting, check them off. This saves sending around a sign-in sheet or having to remember who came. Leave room for uninvited attendees—staff members, guests, etc.

   3. Take whatever tools you need to the meeting. Tools might include a recording device, a laptop and paper and pens. If you use a recorder or laptop, make sure you have paper and pens along as well—they're your backup if a battery dies or something else happens.

   4. If you're not familiar with everyone who is coming to the meeting, consider creating a blank seating chart and filling in the names of the attendees as they choose their seats. Make sure you introduce yourself to everyone who comes that you don't know. If you're uncomfortable doing this, ask the meeting organizer to have everyone introduce themselves before the meeting starts.

   5. Ensure you have a copy of the agenda. It can help to take the agenda and prepare note-taking pages by leaving a blank area under each agenda item.

   6. At the top of the minutes, state the meeting title, the date and time, the location, a list of everyone invited, a list of invitees who actually attended and a list of uninvited attendees. Record who is filling each of the four rotating roles and who called the meeting to order.

   7. State that minutes from the previous meeting were read and whether they were approved or not.

   8. Record each motion made, who made the motion and any decisions reached. Remember, who said what in the discussion is not important.

   9. List items tabled until the next meeting, if any.

   10. Provide a list of action items and who is responsible for each one. List target completion dates and the status of each item.

   11. If another meeting is needed, and if the date and time is set during this meeting, report that as well.

   12. Transcribe the minutes as soon as possible after the meeting. Show the transcription to the meeting facilitator and ask if he or she would like to add, delete or modify anything in the minutes. Make changes as requested.

   13. Distribute the minutes at the earliest possible time.

ORGANIZING YOUR WORKSPACE

It's hard to work when the area you're working in is disorganized. While it is probably not necessary that you be able to see yourself in the reflection off the top of your desk before you leave each evening, it is necessary to reduce the clutter and chaos in your workspace as much as you can.

This section explores the very best advice available for keeping your workspace organized, every day. It's actually very simple advice. Find the time to use it and watch your stress level go down while your productivity level goes up.

Rules

1. Throw away as much as you can before even beginning to get organized.
2. Make a plan for how you want your space to be organized.
3. Keep the things that you use every day within your reach.
4. Keep the things that you use every week in drawers or on shelves, within your reach.

5. Keep the things you need within a month inside your office, cubicle or work area.

6. Put things you don't use at least once a month outside of your immediate work area.

7. Use some kind of visual charting system to track your major projects and responsibilities.

8. Work from a written to-do list.

9. Use the Internet to save yourself desk space.

Explanations and Examples

1. Throw away as much as you can before even beginning to get organized.

You won't be able to do this *perfectly*, but any start is a good one. Do you presently have a lot of clutter surrounding you? Have you found it difficult to concentrate on any one thing when all you see out of the corner of your eye is chaos?

Give yourself the time—and the permission—you need to throw away the things that you know are junk. And don't make a pile of that junk that you will throw away "later." Throw it away—now.

2. Make a plan for how you want your space to be organized.

We suggest the steps that are listed in our Filing section (pages 319 – 324) for making order from chaos. In those steps you will see that we ask you to make your plans from another location—not from the center of your chaos.

Step away from your workspace long enough to be able to imagine it organized in a totally different way, if necessary. (For some people, just imagining it organized at all will be totally different!)

3. Keep the things that you use every day within your reach.

Things like your computer, your stapler, maybe a pad of sticky notes. You shouldn't have to exert much effort to get to these items and others you use frequently. Keep as many of these items within plain sight and within as easy reach as possible.

If you are referencing a huge printout several times per day, make sure that it's located somewhere you only have to turn toward to find, for example on a shelf behind you. If there is a database in your computer that you use many times a day, make a direct link to it on the desktop.

4. Keep the things that you use every week in drawers or on shelves, within your reach.

The difference between these items and the ones you use every day is that you don't need these within your view. Put these things on shelves, in drawers or in file cabinets. Make sure that those shelves, drawers and file cabinets are within easy reach to save you the time and effort of getting up.

5. Keep the things you need within a month inside your office, cubicle or work area.

Anything you use as often as monthly can be kept in your immediate workspace, whether that is an office, a cubicle or a specified work area. The things you use *only* once per month should be kept at the greatest distance from you, the things you use every week and a half can be kept closer.

Your goal in this process is to reduce the amount of work you need to do to access the things you need.

6. Put things you don't use at least once a month outside of your immediate work area.

In our Filing section we mention that *the purpose of filing is easy retrieval.* And when we are talking about organizing your workspace, isn't that really a kind of filing?

Do you then see that if you use something more rarely than once per month, it would actually slow you down in getting to the something you need more often if they were both kept in the same spot?

Keep your less active files and less frequently needed resources in a general storage area, not in your valued workspace. Consider your workspace prime real estate. Use it wisely.

7. **Use some kind of visual charting system to track your major projects and responsibilities.**

   One of the simplest but most effective visual charting techniques available can be a calendar, one with a large page for each month, containing blocks for each day. There is plenty of room on a calendar like that for notes and scheduling information. Plus, when it is posted in a place that others can see it as they enter your office, they will also have a good idea—going in—of the priorities you are already committed to.

   For your more formalized or complex projects, use the Gantt charts and PERT charts recommended in the Project Management section (pages 346 – 352).

   Most people in today's workplace understand things best when they see them. Learning theorists refer to this as a *visual modality of learning*. Have you ever color-coded something to keep track of it? Most people have. It works well because it is an immediate visual cue to the way something is organized.

   But don't overdo it. If you were to post many different calendars, people (including you) would become confused. If you developed a color-coding system that used so many different colors you were into fuchsia and tawny burgundy, you've probably gone too far. Keep it simple: no more than eight major colors, and no more than two calendars.

8. **Work from a written to-do list.**

   A written to-do list keeps you focused and allows you a place to record any other priorities you may think of as you are working on the ones you thought of previously. No one can remember every thought that crosses his or her mind.

   Keep a notebook, a piece of paper, a pad of sticky notes, a hand-held electronic day planner or even a single file card handy. When you think of something you need to handle, write it down. You can always refer to the list later to schedule that item. But now, because you wrote it down, your brain won't be trying to remember it—and therefore it won't be acting like a snooze alarm distracting you from what you were doing to begin with.

9. **Use the Internet to save yourself desk space.**

   There are so many excellent resources available on-line, why bother with a huge dictionary on the corner of your desk? Who needs a five-pound dictionary when you can go on-line?

   Of course, in order to use this tip you do need the ability to go on-line at will. And it would be a good idea to bookmark those frequently visited sites so you don't repeatedly need to type in a URL.

   To find on-line resources to begin with, use your favorite search engine and type in what it is you are looking for. You will be able to find just about anything!

PRESENTATION SKILLS

The ability to present one's ideas publicly is a skill that most people in the world of work know they must have in order to get ahead. It is generally said that as a person is promoted through an organization, that person is asked to do two things more frequently: write and speak.

This section covers the basics of becoming a more confident public speaker.

It's true—most adults will tell you that their number one fear is public speaking. The Gallup poll has actually tracked it as a greater fear than death! Most people are only fearful of it because they don't do it enough. It's out of their comfort zone.

Here are the ten tips that—when you use them—can make you a more confident and poised presenter:

Rules
1. Prepare. Prepare your topic, prepare your audiovisuals, prepare for the audience you will be presenting to and prepare yourself to be seen as an expert.
2. Build rapport before the presentation.
3. Ask someone to introduce you. Provide him or her with a short paragraph that includes the most important information this audience should know about you.
4. Get the audience's attention first.
5. Tell them what you're going to tell them.
6. Make your presentation. Include appropriate audiovisuals or handouts.
7. Remind them what you told them. Summarize.

8. Get them laughing or get them crying.

9. Stick around to answer questions.

10. Speak more often.

Explanations and Examples

1. **Prepare. Prepare your topic, prepare your audiovisuals, prepare for the audience you will be presenting to and prepare yourself to be seen as an expert.**

    The more carefully you prepare for your presentation, the more confident you will be making it. We don't recommend going so far as to memorize the entire speech—that makes it too easy to forget the whole thing by forgetting just one word.

    But do your homework. Research your topic thoroughly. Prepare yourself for more questions than you could possibly be asked. Research the interests of your audience. Consider the interests of your audience when you prepare your presentation. Use those interests to help you create the examples you use.

    Take the time to prepare visually appealing audiovisuals that are clear, readable and appropriate to your message. Practice your presentation, using your audiovisuals. The last thing you need for your credibility is to be in the middle of the most important point of your presentation and not know what is on the next slide.

    Also, give some thought to how you will dress for your presentation. In general, the advice is to dress to fit in with the highest level people in the room. That would ensure that you will be looked up to by most participants. It's also important to think about where you will be while presenting. Will you be standing or sitting? (Standing is always better for your credibility). Will you be in the front of a room or at a certain spot around a table? Will some areas of the room give you more authority than others? (Yes, the front of the room or a spot near where the director would sit in this room give you more authority.)

    If you have time, do a dress rehearsal of your presentation for several trusted friends and get their comments.

    Remember: The more time spent in preparation, the more confident the presenter. It's worth the time.

2. **Build rapport before the presentation.**

    When you will be presenting, get to the meeting at least 30 minutes early to check any equipment you will be depending on (microphones, computers, etc.) and to introduce yourself around the room.

    Shake hands with as many of your audience members as possible. Introduce yourself and be sincere in your happiness to meet them. It will help you relax and it will help them like you even before you start speaking.

3. **Ask someone to introduce you. Provide him or her with a short paragraph that includes the most important information this audience should know about you.**

    Write a short paragraph and put it on a file card for the person introducing you. Focus on the parts of your resume or experience that will impress your audience about your expertise in the field you are speaking about. Make sure the one who introduces you knows how to pronounce your name correctly.

    In some cases, there will be no one available to introduce you. In that case, you will need to introduce yourself. Again, find a few things from your history that will convince your listeners that you are indeed an expert on your topic. The trick is to sound humble yet confident as you mention them.

4. **Get the audience's attention first.**

    Many people do this by telling an engaging story. Others show cartoons that are appropriate to the topic they are presenting (if you do this, make sure you have the creator's approval). Still others quote statistics, the more alarming or dramatic the better. Maybe there is an inspirational quote you could read from a credible source, or a tasteful but funny joke relating to your topic. Perhaps you could prepare a short but powerful audiovisual presentation to open with.

    Some people also use jokes as self-deprecating humor. Be careful with that—audiences tend to believe what you tell them. If you make too much fun of yourself early in your presentation you run the risk of convincing your audience that you don't deserve respect.

5. Tell them what you're going to tell them.

It's part of the formula for giving a speech, right? Tell them what you're going to tell them. Provide your audience with an overview statement that alerts them as to what they should be looking out for.

Something like this is very effective: "I have three creative ideas for doubling the income we get from add-on sales. Are you ready to hear them?"

6. Make your presentation. Include appropriate audiovisuals or handouts.

Everyone likes to get something extra—but most people don't like to get too much extra. Limit your handouts to only the most important and appealing ones you can develop. Be sure to provide an audiovisual presentation as you speak if you have the technology available. A simple PowerPoint® presentation that sums up your major points as you talk helps reinforce those points in your listeners' minds—especially if your handout consists of the PowerPoint® notes with three slides to a page. Putting three to a page gives each attendee room to take his or her own notes.

If you aren't expert with the technology that would allow you to use audiovisuals, find someone to help you.

As you make your presentation, be clear at your transition points. Overemphasize them. The difference between a speech and a letter is that your listener doesn't have the visual formatting you'd use in a letter readily available like your reader does. So make sure your listener can keep up:

"That was my first idea. But remember: I told you I had three. Are you ready for the second one?"

7. Remind them what you told them. Summarize.

At the end of your speech, you need to restate your most important points in a concise paragraph of information.

"I have presented three creative ideas for doubling the income from add-on sales. My first idea is to offer cash bonuses to our sales force for certain levels of add-on sales. My second idea is to send direct mail to our present customers selling them on the positives of purchasing the add-ons. And my third idea is to send the direct mail and have the sales staff follow up two weeks later with phone calls. What questions can I answer for you?"

8. Get them laughing or get them crying.

Motivational speakers always end their talks with some story or point that is guaranteed to either bring a tear to the eye or a laugh to the heart. You may be saying to yourself, *Yeah, sure, but I am no motivational speaker*.

Maybe not—but every listener likes to be moved in some way. The reason motivational speakers like the technique so much is because they know that most people are more likely to act from a strong *emotional* state than from a strong *mental* state.

Certainly, you need to be appropriate for your audience. However, consider ending with a touching or funny story that illustrates what you have said or moves your audience to act.

9. Stick around to answer questions.

If you stay late to talk to the stragglers after the meeting has ended, people will like you and trust you. Some of the stragglers may be arguers, but even dealing with the arguers can be a good thing. Consider that they just need some attention from you and this is the way they have learned to get it. Always assume the best intentions of the people you deal with and you will never treat them in a way you'd be ashamed of tomorrow.

10. Speak more often.

Public speaking is a job skill that will help you become more visible and more promotable. Is that a good enough reason for you to get better at it? Yes, and the single best way to become a better public speaker is to speak more often.

Most people fear public speaking for the sole reason that they don't do it often enough to become comfortable. Put yourself in a position where you will speak more often: Perhaps you could volunteer to lead some meetings of a club you belong to or to do some readings during a service at your church.

You could find a Toastmasters group to join. Toastmasters is an international group that allows you a support group of peers who are as interested in improving their speaking skills as you are. You learn in the best possible way: by speaking.

345

Career Success

PROJECT MANAGEMENT

Project management skills are necessary to anyone who manages large and comprehensive priorities. They provide:

1) A logical format for you to be able to proceed with working on the project.

2) A wealth of information about how to more effectively communicate to both the project team and the outside world about the status of the project at any given time.

There are college degrees available in this topic, so there is already a lot of useful and detailed information out there. Our goal in this section is to provide you with a quick but practical overview of the very best information.

Rules

1. Set a *clear* project goal.

2. Hold a brainstorming session to think of every project detail or potential limitation possible.

3. Break the project into logical subcommittees.

4. Determine a chairperson for each subcommittee. Then, with each chairperson's input, establish the priorities for and the constraints facing each subcommittee in more detail.

5. Use Gantt charts and PERT charts to describe and track the project.

6. Take action.

7. Have regular project team meetings and establish a routine communication procedure among team members.

8. Evaluate and adjust as you go.

9. Reward team members along the way.

10. Mark the moment the project is completed.

11. Once the project has ended, hold a debriefing session for all who worked on it. Take great notes.

12. Send thank you notes and congratulations.

Explanations and Examples

1. **Set a *clear* project goal.**

   Write it down and be specific.

   Have you ever worked on a project where no one bothered to write down the goal ahead of time? Most likely. If so, you've learned your lesson. Usually what happens in this case is that the project goes along fine for the first few weeks. Then it's time to have a regular project team meeting to discuss the project, but no one can discuss the project. They're all too busy arguing about what the project is to begin with!

   Write down the goal. Include the specifics of how many, by when and exactly what it will look like. Also write down the plans you have developed for achieving this goal and who will be responsible for which steps. It saves you a lot of headaches down the road.

2. **Hold a brainstorming session to think of every project detail or potential limitation possible.**

   Once you have put together your initial project team, get that team together to think of everything they can about the project. What resources will be needed? What details might be overlooked? Who would be good to get involved? Who wouldn't be so good to get involved? Is there anything else coming up on the schedule that could interfere with this project?

   Ask yourselves every question you can think of and take a lot of good notes about the answers that come up. Remember: This is a brainstorming session. You are not committed to anything that is mentioned, so it's better to mention everything that comes to mind. You can always dismiss the meaningless items later.

3. **Break the project into logical subcommittees.**

   Ideally, you will have enough of a team that you can form subcommittees. Even if your project team is small, and you figure that all of you will be doing all of the project, it's still useful to break the project into logical subgoals. It will help you be more organized.

You can use the list you brainstormed in Step 2 to help you figure out the most logical subgoals or subcommittees to develop.

Let's say your project is to put on a convention for the entire sales force your organization employs. Further, let's say you have a very generous budget. When your team gets together to brainstorm the particulars, it's likely you'll end up with a list something like this:

Convention for Sales Reps	
Location	Meeting room
Dates	Bar?
Hotels	Welcome gifts
Travel – Air	Raffle
Rental cars	Awards presentation
Food	Golf
Banquet	Keynote speaker
Entertainment	Budget
Family activities	Evaluation process
Program	Brochures
Speakers	Press releases
Breakout sessions	

Notice that on this brainstormed list, some of the items are repetitive (Speakers and Keynote speaker), other items could use their own brainstormed list (Program) and other items are questionable (Bar?). That's the way it's supposed to be.

When you get to the task of organizing the project, it becomes more important to group these items logically. Glancing at the brainstormed list, what logical major subcommittees do you see?

Here's a possible list:

- Travel
- Program
- Budget
- Entertainment
- Advertising and Public Relations

To make sure you have covered everything with these five subcommittees, go through the brainstormed list and assign each item on it to one of your major subcommittees. This is how you will both 1) organize the project by breaking it down into smaller, more manageable pieces and 2) determine if you have thought of everything that you needed to in the formation of the subcommittees.

Here's how:

Convention for Sales Reps

T- Location	P- Meeting room	
P- Dates	E- Bar?	
T- Hotels	E- Welcome gifts	
T- Travel – Air	E- Raffle	T–Travel
T- Rental cars	P- Awards presentation	P–Program
E- Food	E- Golf	B–Budget
E- Banquet	P- Keynote speaker	E–Entertainment
E- Entertainment	B- Budget	A–Advertising & PR
E- Family activities	P- Evaluation process	
P- Program	A- Brochures	
P- Speakers	A- Press releases	
P- Breakout sessions		

Some of the items in this list could've been assigned to more than one subcommittee. For example, Meeting rooms could have been handled by either Program or Travel. And there's no right or wrong way to decide who will have the responsibility. At some point, the person making the assignments becomes the ruler of the project. He or she says, "Let the Program Committee handle the meeting rooms," and so be it.

4. **Determine a chairperson for each subcommittee. Then, with each chairperson's input, establish the priorities for and the constraints facing each subcommittee in more detail.**

Put someone in charge of each subcommittee. Even when you are working with a smaller project team and you won't actually be using real subcommittees, it's still good to spread the responsibility around to the help you do have. This gives more people a feeling of authority that will serve to motivate them. It also helps the project stay on track and organized.

Then, to develop the strategy for tackling the project, the people with the authority for each subgoal should work with the project team leaders to determine what exactly each subcommittee will do—and when.

This should also include a careful consideration of potential obstacles and constraints.

In project management literature, much is made of the triple constraints that face every project. Here's what it looks like:

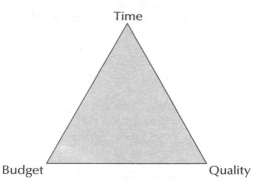

Each project has these three elements that can serve to either advance or constrain activity toward the goal.

Budget: The kind of budget most people think of first is the financial one. How much money is available and how flexible is that total? But also considered in thinking about budget for project management purposes are the supplies and resources that are available to help you complete the project. These include the human resources—the people available to help and how many hours those people can help.

Time: The deadline. When is the project due? Are there any other deadlines involved besides the final one? For example, when putting together a large convention, there will be many smaller deadlines. Airline tickets need to be purchased by a certain time in order to get the lowest prices. Hotel rooms need to be booked by a certain number of weeks or months in advance to guarantee their availability. Speakers need to be contracted by a certain time to be certain they will be available.

Quality: How good does it need to be upon completion to count as a finished project? In the case of an advertising brochure announcing a new product line to your clients, perhaps the quality needs to be better than if you were producing a specification sheet for internal use only.

These three elements—budget, time and quality—could be fixed or fluid. Have you ever worked on a project where the budget was fixed? No matter what happened, you knew there wouldn't be another dime available. How about the opposite? Most people have had experience both ways—sometimes more money can be found, other times it can't.

When you are working on a major project, you need to know as much as possible up front about which constraints are going to be fluid and which aren't. It's also helpful to discover which constraint is the *driving constraint*. In other words, which one is most important to the ultimate authority who has requested that this project be completed? Ask this question: If push comes to shove and we find ourselves in desperate circumstances, which item would give first? Would we be more likely to get more money or more time? Or would it be more likely that they would loosen the quality standards?

You see, the constraints are also flexible with each other. If you get more budget it's likely you would be able to complete the project in less time or at a higher quality. A change in one usually produces flexibility in the other two.

This is also what you need to keep in mind when one of the constraints is made tougher: Perhaps the budget gets cut halfway through or the deadline is moved up a week. If you have flexibility with either of the other two, you will probably be able to pull out a victory.

In the case of our convention for sales reps, once the people to lead each major subcommittee have been chosen, they and the project team leaders will need to do more brainstorming, and certainly more organizing. What comes first in the Travel subcommittee? Probably determining where the conference is going to be held. To make any definite travel arrangements, this committee will also need to wait for the Program committee to decide on the actual dates of the conference.

What about constraints? Once the date of the convention has been set, published and booked, the deadline will be fixed. How about the budget? Is it large enough? Is it flexible enough to handle a few emergency needs? And what about the quality specifications? What are the expectations of the people who have requested this convention? Which of these constraints is the driver?

Once these questions have been addressed, the project team leadership will have a very good idea of how to construct the charts in Step 5.

5. Use Gantt charts and PERT charts to describe and track the project.

Gantt charts are timeline charts. They list each activity of a project along with its time frame. Gantt charts can also include the name of the person responsible for each task. (The chart is named after engineer Henry Gantt, who used one and taught it to his friends and co-workers. Apparently, the chart helped everyone so much they named it after him.)

PERT charts are critical path diagrams. They are set up as flow charts so that anyone looking at one can easily see the order of the activities required. In the case of the Travel Committee for our convention, the location needs to be determined before any airfares are researched.

Examples of both charts are presented here. More information about these charts and other project management details can be found in *Practical Project Management*, published by SkillPath Seminars.

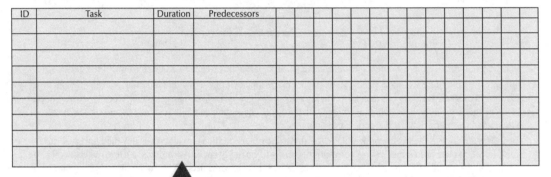

Example of a Gantt Chart

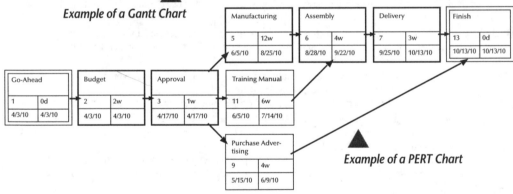

Example of a PERT Chart

6. Take action.

All the charting in the world won't lead to a completed project unless someone finally gets up and takes the action required to move forward. The charts will make it easier to know what to do, and it is more likely that the action will indeed get you closer to where you want to go. But there are many people who get this far in the process and quit. They love designing the charts, they just don't like getting up every day and moving forward. Because sometimes moving forward is hard work.

You aren't like those people, right?

Never let a day pass without moving every major priority in your life forward by even just a few inches. Keep your momentum going, have a habit of acting and eventually you won't be able to not act.

7. Have regular project team meetings and establish a routine communication procedure among team members.

Certainly, have the meetings you need to keep everyone informed. But don't over-meet people. Schedule a routine meeting for your subcommittee so that people will keep that time available. But if 24 hours before the meeting time you notice there just isn't enough to talk about, call the participants, thank them for keeping the time available but tell them you have canceled the meeting to save everyone the time.

When a project is due one year from today, how often do you think the team needs to meet? Maybe every month, maybe even every two months. As the deadline gets closer and during times when activity is heavier, the meetings could be held twice a month. And as you get even closer, once a week. Finally, in the last week of an intensive project, you may meet as often as several times a day.

The same general rule holds true for any other kind of communication lines you set up among the committee members. Does everyone need to write a status report every week? That could be overkill. Maybe once a month is often enough for written status reports in the earlier days of the project when the deadline is months and months away.

It is essential that project team members be aware of what everyone is doing—and of the results they are getting. This prevents anyone from doing the same thing a second time and allows the flexibility of revising goals that need to be revised as feedback is received earlier in the process.

Set up a project mailing list in your e-mail program and encourage everyone who has important results or changes to report to send an e-mail to everyone. Just be sure to define the word *important* carefully. You know how much the people in your life loathe getting too much of what they consider to be junk e-mail.

8. Evaluate and adjust as you go.

This will happen almost automatically when you keep the lines of communication open among your team members. Once you set out toward a goal, it is imperative to check the environment as you go to make sure you are moving in the right direction. If you're not, adjust as soon as possible to save you and your team from wasting time, energy and resources.

9. Reward team members along the way.

It is important to reward your team in a currency they can spend. Not all the members of your project team will have the same tastes. Some will do anything for a peanut butter cup, others need humorous cards and still others will need a round of applause occasionally.

When possible, of course, reward with money or time off. No one needs to be asked whether they appreciate either of those rewards.

Also, use good psychology. Make sure that when you offer rewards it is clear to those being rewarded exactly what the reward is for. This makes it more likely they will link their positive behavior with the reward. And that makes it more likely they will repeat the positive behavior.

10. Mark the moment the project is completed.

Psychologically, acknowledging the completion of a project is comparable to hitting the TOTAL key on a cash register. A bell rings and the cash drawer pops open.

The people who have worked with you long and hard will appreciate the moment when they get their pats on the back and the project itself is acknowledged.

The theory here can be found in the psychology of the productivity cycle. Once an individual decides to do something, that individual takes action. If all goes well, eventually that individual takes enough action to complete it. Upon completion, the individual reaps the sense of success and inner acknowledgment that comes from having completed something. *It is from this sense of inner acknowledgment that the individual gains the energy—and sometimes the courage—to go on, to make another decision, to take on something else. In other words, completion leads to productivity.*

Make sure everyone involved in achieving a goal gets a moment to cash in on this acknowledgment. When you do, they will be much more likely to have the desire and the energy to help you out again.

11. Once the project has ended, hold a debriefing session for all who worked on it. Take great notes.

After the party you have in Step 10, make sure to get together one last time to record any useful insights and experiences that will help you—or the next people in your organization who will be asked to tackle a project like this. Make sure the people who come after you have the information they need to be successful.

Who was great to work with? In the example of our convention, did the hotel you chose treat you well? Was there one particular customer service person in that hotel who was especially helpful to you in getting the things you needed— more quickly than the other people there?

Make a note of that person's name so you will be able to ask for his or her help from the beginning next time.

How about things that didn't go so well? Record some of your experiences so that the next project team doesn't have to waste the same weeks you did reinventing a wheel you already invented.

Make sure there are at least three people taking notes in this final session so you're sure you don't miss a thing. This project final report will become the most important document of all for the next people in your organization who have to do a project similar to yours. Remember, it might even turn out to be you.

12. Send thank you notes and congratulations.

Remember that excellent customer service person at the hotel? Why not send him or her a thank you note and maybe even a memento of some kind to express your appreciation? Think of everyone who was a great help along the way, and don't forget about the members of your project team. Send them some nice handwritten notes too. What about the people in your organization who assigned you this project to begin with? You may not have felt like thanking them during the long road of working on the project, but now that it's finished—it's a great gesture.

The same goes for congratulations. Offer congratulations to everyone involved who contributed to your mutual victory.

By remembering to share credit and to offer thanks, you strengthen the relationships you have developed through the course of working on the project together. Best of all, those relationships will be available to you in the future.

A Note About Project Management Software …

Is project management software necessary?

If we knew that elements of our project were going to be changing frequently, it would probably be a good idea to have some kind of computer program to help us print and reprint the charts as those things changed. It would save time.

Some project managers are responsible for so many elements of their very sophisticated projects, they probably couldn't keep on track unless they were using a software package.

Here's our only caution: Don't get in over your head.

There are three basic levels of project management software. Microsoft® Project is an example of what you could call a middle-level project management package. It has a lot of bells and whistles, even the ability to let the program determine whom you should hire for a particular task because he or she is more cost-effective. There is so much in it that it will take you longer than an afternoon to become comfortable with it. The only complaint with mid-level programs is that they are not as customizable as some project managers responsible for very complex and sophisticated projects may need.

For those needs, there are very expensive but totally customized programs like Primavera. When you purchase one of these, it comes with software engineers who build the program for you, according to your own specifications.

There are also very simple programs that don't have the sophistication of even a mid-level program but that can produce Gantt charts and PERT charts, as well as remind you of what you need to be doing each day when you log in.

For more advice, check with your software specialist for recommendations. Just understand that overbuying is just as unproductive as underbuying.

STRESS MANAGEMENT

The ability to manage stress is vital to anyone's success in life. A person can complete project after project and even earn millions of dollars, but if he or she is too tired or too sick to enjoy those successes, then what are they worth?

Nothing.

Life can be stressful. That is unavoidable. But stress management techniques encourage us to live balanced lives, to laugh more often, to nurture our friendships, to occasionally take a day off. Psychologists tell us that if an individual lives a more balanced life then that individual will more likely experience greater success in the long run.

See how many of the suggestions below you can implement in your life.

Rules

1. Develop or join a support group.
2. Find a hobby you care about and spend time on it at least once a week.
3. Eat good food.
4. Exercise regularly.
5. Treat yourself once in a while.
6. Find a place that is a retreat for you.
7. Do something positive for someone else and don't let anyone find out about it.
8. Breathe.
9. Reject perfectionism.
10. Use visualizations to reduce your physical, emotional and mental stress.
11. Focus on one task for 30 uninterrupted minutes.
12. Avoid the things (and people) that are toxic to you.

Explanations and Examples

1. **Develop or join a support group.**

   How many close friends do you have? If you are emotionally troubled, is there someone to call? Is there more than one person to call? Stress management experts recommend that we each have five close friends, five people we could call at the drop of a hat if we needed emotional support. How many do you have? What could you do to increase the list?

   If you don't have the time to find close friends, see about renting some. Seriously, is there a support group of some kind that you are eligible to join? Anything from a Parents Without Partners group to a church study group to a support group that helps you deal with an unhealthy habit could be useful.

   Don't let yourself get so busy that you neglect personal relationships. Develop your friendships and weave yourself into a society of people who care about you. Start today.

2. **Find a hobby you care about and spend time on it at least once a week.**

   Many people laugh at the thought of a hobby. "A hobby?" they ask. "When would I have time for a hobby?"

   Well, make time. All work and no play, you know the rest of that cliché, don't you? The other benefit of working at a hobby is that it sometimes provides you with a support group. Maybe you and your spouse or significant other decide to take a watercolor class. Some of the other members of that class could become good friends.

3. **Eat good food.**

   Eat the food that supports you both physically and emotionally. This means that while your whole diet cannot consist of chocolate, a small amount certainly won't hurt you.

   Of course, your physical needs must come first. Your body needs nutrients to stay healthy and alert. Are you getting enough vegetables, enough protein, enough grains and enough fruit? Those foods will take care of your body.

   What about your soul? Does an occasional bite of some very expensive chocolate make you feel well taken care of? Does a whole bag of potato chips help you deal with the end of a close relationship? (As long as it's just one whole bag!)

   In all things moderation, that's the best advice for stress management. And that means you even need some moderation in living healthy!

4. Exercise regularly.

There are two kinds of exercise: aerobic and anaerobic. Aerobic exercise increases the supply of oxygen in your body while anaerobic exercise increases muscle mass. Both kinds are necessary to be truly strong and vital.

If you are looking for a quick boost of energy and an overall feeling of well-being, get some aerobic exercise. The great thing about aerobic exercise is that you can do it anywhere! You could step out of your office and go for a brisk five-minute walk anytime. Even if you need to stay inside, that walk will do you wonders.

Regular exercise also improves self-esteem. You feel good about yourself because you are taking good care of yourself. Do you see the positive cycle this sets up? You exercise more because you feel good about yourself. That exercise makes you feel even better. Etc., etc.

5. Treat yourself once in a while.

When's the last time you did something truly special for yourself, something that you enjoy but don't do often? When's the last time you spent a weekend in the mountains skiing? When's the last time you went to hear the local orchestra? How about a weekend getaway out of town? Do you love the theater? When's the last time you went?

Plan a special time for yourself, whether you have anyone in your life right now to go with you or not. You deserve it.

6. Find a place that is a retreat for you.

This means it would be best if no one could find you there. Is there a spot in your house where people would leave you alone if you asked them to? How about in your workplace? Is there an empty office you can use when you need to get away to concentrate on something important? (We don't recommend the restroom—but it will do in a pinch.)

How about outdoors? When the weather is good, is there a park you especially enjoy? Or do you live near a beach or some woods or a mountain? Find some spots that give you a renewed sense of peace and awe. Visit them often.

7. Do something positive for someone else and don't let anyone find out about it.

There is nothing quite like doing anonymous good deeds to build your sense of how valuable you are as a person. Somehow when you are the only one who knows about them, the positive feeling grows bigger and bigger inside of you, making you happier and happier.

Look for opportunities to give.

8. Breathe.

Seriously. BREATHE. With your mouth closed, breathe in as deeply as you can. Hold that breath for ten seconds and then exhale through your mouth. Do you feel that? You have just increased the oxygen in your blood. And that blood will go to your brain and make you feel more peaceful and less stressed.

When you are in a moment of crisis, this same kind of breathing can keep you from going off on an adrenaline rush that would cause you to explode, cry or just change colors.

Adrenaline is the chemical that your body produces in response to perceived danger or crisis. Indeed, the symptoms you experience of stress are often the results of that adrenaline being in your system too long.

Make a habit of taking the time to breathe deeply, several times a day. It will oxygenate your blood and make you a much calmer and more collected person.

9. Reject perfectionism.

Perfectionism (and the rejecting of it) are covered in detail in our section on time management (pages 356 – 367). It is an essential part of managing your stress. When you believe nothing you do is good enough, you will keep beating your head against the same wall trying to make it better.

It's time to let yourself off the hook. Reign in your perfectionistic tendencies and enjoy your life. You will become more productive because you will more appropriately focus the energies, talents and time you have.

10. Use visualizations to reduce your physical, emotional and mental stress.

Visualizations could go with the breathing exercise you are going to start doing. No matter where you are, if you close your eyes and imagine yourself somewhere else, your brain will cause your body to react to the new place.

Have you ever had that scary dream that you were falling? Did it wake you up? Once you woke up, did you notice you had some physical symptoms of being frightened, of falling? Perhaps your heart was racing or your palms had become sweaty. Well, if you remember those symptoms, ask yourself another question: Were you really falling? Of course you weren't. But your body thought you were, so it created the physical response you would have experienced had you really been falling.

There's good news. Once your brain vividly imagines something—as in a dream or a visualization—it's as though you are really there, at least as far as your brain is concerned. Do you see why this is good news? You don't actually have to go to the beach to get the relaxation you would get by being there for a few minutes with your bare feet in the hot sand. All you really need to do is vividly imagine yourself there.

Build a relaxing visualization for yourself. Do this soon. It may take a few minutes to create it for the first time, but once you have created it you will be able to return at any time—very quickly.

Think of a place that makes you feel peaceful. Maybe it's a place in nature, or a comfortable chair in a comfortable room in your own home. Once you have decided on your spot, take a deep breath and relax. When you're ready, close your eyes. See yourself in the spot you've chosen. Notice the things you can see around you. Be sure to imagine yourself seeing this spot from your own eyes, as though you are really there. It is more likely you are seeing it like a movie of yourself at first—but do your best to move into your body.

After you have noticed all there is to see, try a visualization technique from the field of Neurolinguistic Programming (NLP). Make the colors brighter. Sharpen the focus. Move the image closer. Do you notice how these changes make your feelings more intense?

Now, add a soundtrack. What can you hear? Make sure you take the time to notice everything. If you are outdoors, can you hear birds? The ocean? Wind? Background noises?

How about some physical sensations? Work hard to actually feel the wind on your face or the sand between your toes. If you are imagining yourself in a comfortable chair, feel the fabric under your fingers.

And finally, can you imagine a smell? The beach has a smell—so do the mountains and the forest. Even a cozy spot in your home probably has a smell you can remember. If not, why not start lighting some scented candles there or building a fire in the fireplace? Or maybe you could imagine the smell of cookies baking.

Once you have built this entire visualization for yourself, stay there for several minutes. Return there every time you feel overwhelmed. Now that you have created this image, it won't take so long to re-create it. Even a minute or two spent there will lower your blood pressure and relax your mind.

11. Focus on one task for 30 uninterrupted minutes.

Have you ever become so stressed that you felt like a whirlwind, rushing from one unfinished item to the next at a high speed? Settle your mind by giving just one priority your undivided attention for a short amount of time.

If 30 minutes seems impossible, how about 10 or 15? Have some kind of symbol or sign that you could display to let people know that they can't interrupt you. Make sure you have told the people in your life what that symbol is and how it will work. Be sure to include a note that says what time you will get back to them—and a spot for them to leave a note.

The key to making these symbols work is your guarantee that you will be available at a certain time. And that certain time had better be within only 15 – 30 minutes—or the people who need you will never be able to wait.

Once your sign is posted, move forward on something important without an interruption for those minutes. The fact that you were able to make even a little progress will revitalize and de-stress you. You may even be able to take another 15 – 30 minutes—after you've checked in with those people who needed you of course!

12. Avoid the things (and people) that are toxic to you.

It's not that there is one list of "toxins" that works for everyone equally. Certainly, you've heard that tobacco and too much alcohol are not good for you. For some people, a combination of caffeine and sugar becomes toxic after an hour or two when the crash comes. But for others, a morning without caffeine and sugar is what's toxic.

Pay attention to the signals your own body sends you. What works for you and what doesn't? There are many books and training programs of all kinds available in the area of personal health and well-being—but you have to test each suggestion for yourself to make sure any particular one will work for you.

There are also relationships that may be toxic for you. Do you work with someone who is very negative? Do you feel yourself succumbing to negativity every time you are within ten feet of that person? Well, why not avoid that person? Or maybe even tell that negative person that you need to keep a distance because you value your positive attitude. Remember to review our section on Assertiveness (pages 311 – 319) before you attempt any conversation of this nature.

It's not that you're unsympathetic. It's just that you know how important your positive energy is to your sanity. When you allow yourself to sink into the depths of negativity and eventually, despair, you will quickly see that all your energy for getting things done has evaporated.

The same holds true for your personal relationships. Does your Aunt Matilda irritate you every time the family gets together? Well, why not offer to sometimes see your family members—the ones you get along with better—in another environment? This would be an environment that doesn't include Aunt Matilda.

Of course, you need to determine how important your attitude is to you. It can be very difficult to stand up for yourself and safeguard your own happiness. You may wonder, what if Aunt Matilda becomes offended?

Well, what if Aunt Matilda becomes offended? Have you ever considered that by putting up with her negativity you are enabling her to continue to be that negative?

We're not saying it's easy. We are saying it may be necessary. Make your positive state of mind a top priority.

TIME MANAGEMENT

Most people in today's work force will tell you that they have too much to do in too little time. They also say that the truly important things in their lives are occasionally left alone for too long because of the pressing demands of emergencies and diversions.

While it is true that some jobs have too much to do, and some environments are overridden with emergencies, most people can get at least a sense of control over their lives by practicing the basic principles of time and priority management.

Rules

1. Truly understand the value of your time.
2. Plan your day the day before.
3. Keep a master to-do list.
4. Stay balanced.
5. Never set a goal without deciding upon the first small steps you will take—on a daily basis—to get started.
6. Then, chart your goal to completion, setting milestones and deadlines along the way.
7. Learn to say "no"—appropriately.
8. Overcome your tendencies toward procrastination or perfectionism.
9. Get support.
10. Remain flexible.

Examples and Explanations

1. Truly understand the value of your time.

If you did just this, but did it all the way, you would never have a time management problem again.

Your time is irreplaceable. Once you have spent it, it's gone forever. When Harold from the cubicle next to yours pokes his head around the corner and asks, "Hey, do you have a few minutes?" you may indeed have a few minutes, but not for long. Once you allow them to be spent in a way you would rather not spend them, those minutes are gone forever. It would have been better to loan Harold $50.00—at least you might get that back!

When people truly get this concept—that time is the only commodity that cannot be replenished—they quickly become better at saying *no* to unwanted interruptions, assignments, demands and people.

Your time is precious. If you had a room full of gold bricks, would you guard it? Or would you allow people in there whenever they wanted to take those bricks away?

Guard your time—spend it where you want to spend it and where you need to spend it. Avoid giving in too easily to the requests and demands of others.

2. Plan your day the day before.

Most people acknowledge that they have heard this time management rule sometime in the past. And most people also acknowledge that they don't follow it. It seems time consuming, they say. Or they complain that they don't know what is going to happen the next day so it is impossible to plan.

Really, neither excuse works.

Once you get into a routine, planning your day the day before should take no more than 10 or 15 minutes. Even though no one knows everything that will be happening to him or her the next day, it is still possible to have some plans that will make the day run more smoothly. And even planning for the emergencies, allowing some time for them, will help you be more organized and in control.

Here's a simple process: Use a day planner or scheduling software program like Microsoft® Outlook®. At the end of your day at work (or if you prefer, at home before bed), take a look at your calendar and to-do list for today. Cross off the things you accomplished, pat yourself on the back for your successes and analyze the things you didn't get to.

How many of them need to be done tomorrow? Add those to your list for tomorrow. How many of them would be okay if they were held longer? Add those to later pages. Are there any priorities you could delegate to someone else? Make a note on the "tomorrow page" to do so. Finally, are there any items that you have found yourself moving forward day after day, week after week and that you suspect are neither important nor urgent enough to ever do? Dump them and congratulate yourself for being so wise.

Next, turn to the "tomorrow page." Some items are probably already there—meetings, phone calls you need to make and whatever you have already scheduled or moved forward. Consider your outstanding priorities (See Rule #3, Keep a master to-do list) and consider the important aspects of your life (See Rule #4, Stay balanced). What must be done tomorrow? What could be done tomorrow? What large or small thing could you do in a neglected area of your life to bring yourself into balance?

Add a manageable number of priorities to your day. Do not expect that you will necessarily finish everything, but be realistic. Committing to handle 50 items on a day you know will be hectic just sets you up for a case of extreme letdown later that night. You don't deserve it.

Try to establish a routine for the parts of your day that are time consuming but necessary—could you devote 20 minutes of your afternoon to filing, every day? Could you establish three or four callback times throughout your day so you won't be interrupting yourself every single time the telephone rings? Is there something useful you could do during your commute? Stephen King, one of the world's best-selling novelists, says he never goes anywhere in a car without books on tape or CD. What about you? Could you be learning something? Enjoying a novel? Listening to particular music that would help set your mood?

One more note: Once today becomes tomorrow, and you are now running your day from the plan you developed yesterday, be sure to add any unplanned interruptions or priorities to your dated calendar page before you tackle them.

This helps you in three ways: First, when you return from handling the unplanned priority, you will be able to cross it off your list. Perhaps it's a small victory, but it is a victory nonetheless. Second, you will have an accurate record of what you really did accomplish. So later that night, when you are reviewing your day and thinking of criticizing yourself for not finishing everything on your to-do list, you will be able to be more gentle and honest with yourself instead. And finally, if your boss has ever asked you, "Just what is it you do all day?" now you have an answer!

3. Keep a master to-do list.

If you use a professionally produced day planner, you can keep this master to-do list on the pages in it labeled *Remember* or *To Do* or *Action Items*. Or you could use a legal pad, your smartphone or even a 3 x 5 index card (if you write very small).

The point is to have an easily accessible place to write down every priority, goal or to-do list item that you think of—large or small, long term or short term—the minute it crosses your mind. This master list is by no means meant to be a prioritized list to act from. But it is meant to be the list you look over when deciding what to commit to for tomorrow.

Periodically, you will want to prune this list. Once a week or so, look through the items and cross out the things that have been done, remove the things that are no longer important or urgent and consciously look for things to delegate to others.

Do not, however, recopy this list daily. That would be a waste of time.

4. Stay balanced.

What are the important areas of your life? Many people work so much these days it is easy to forget that there are other priorities that matter to them. What matters to you? Try to list at least six areas of your life that are important to you or you wish you had more time for. Then, list the important functions of what you do to earn a living. Here's an example:

Gloria—Important areas of my life I wish I had more time for
Mom
Marriage
Writing
Reading
Volunteering at school
Redecorating house, room by room
Gloria—Important functions, work
Manager of 8 employees
Curriculum designer
Trainer of faculty members

Now it's your turn. Don't worry about being perfect or about thinking of everything. You can always add to or subtract from this list later.

Now that you have thought of some areas of your life you would like to focus on, think of two or three goals—both long term and short term—that you want to aim for in each area. For example:

Gloria

Mom	Read to the kids before bed at least three nights a week	Volunteer	Volunteer at school at least once per week for two hours
	Take each of them out for special time with me at least once a week		Make friends with other volunteers
	Play a family sport or see a movie once every two weeks	Redecorate	This month—Shane's room
			Next month—Faith's room
Marriage	Get a babysitter at least once every two weeks so we can go out	Manager	Have a weekly meeting for everyone
	Catch him doing at least three things right every day—and mention them		Meet once per week privately with each employee for 15 minutes
Writer	Write a novel this year	Curriculum	Present "Communicating Under Pressure" program—this month
	No matter what, write 1000 words per day		Establish list of curriculum to be revised
Reader	Read more—at least a couple books per month	Trainer	Train Jack in conflict management
	Listen to books on tape in the car		Train entire staff on priority management—new program

Now, how about you? Set some goals for each of the important areas of your life and your work.

Finally, break these goals into smaller pieces and begin working on them one piece at a time. Even if all you do this week toward redecorating Shane's room is buy the new wallpaper border and call the carpet installer, you did accomplish something. You will feel more in control and more balanced—to say nothing about the fact that you will also find yourself moving forward in all areas of your life instead of just a few!

5. Never set a goal without deciding upon the first small steps you will take—on a daily basis—to get started.

Have you ever had a goal that was so large, so all-consuming that you never worked on it? It was just too daunting to get started! Well, by thinking of your first small steps—the ones you can act on *immediately*—you begin turning your dreams into reality. Anyone can think of a long list of grand things that he or she wants to do. But once you begin acting toward a goal, that goal is no longer a dream. It is a project, a work plan set in motion.

Set goals (see pages 324 – 334 in our Goal Setting section). Don't go to bed that night until you have taken at least one small step toward completing each of them. In the beginning of your goal, make sure to act daily. The steps you take do not need to be big, they just need to be taken.

By working every day on a new goal, you establish a habit that will see you through even the tougher times you may face in the future. Plus you gain momentum as you progress.

6. Then, chart your goal to completion, setting milestones and deadlines along the way.

Once you have begun working on a goal, it will be easier for you to "guesstimate" the deadlines and milestones that are realistic for you. Plan them in detail. The closer the date of the milestone, the more detail with which you can plan it. Here is an example of a milestone chart for the production of a new training program:

MILESTONE CHART

Goal: Design New Communication Training Program Workbook

Deadline: December 31

Start Date: September 1

TASKS:	BY:
Research topic on Internet and in library	September 20
Organize and outline program	September 30
Prepare rough copy of workbook	October 15
Have HR Director review workbook	October 22
Revise, if necessary	October 29
Conduct pilot program	First week of November
Get comments of participants	November 15
Revise program based on comments	November 30
Have HR Director review new workbook	December 10
Make revisions	December 15
Send workbook to printer	December 15
Receive copies from printer	December 29

Now develop your own detailed chart for upcoming events on the Milestone Chart:

MILESTONE CHART

Goal:_____

Deadline: _____

Start Date: _____

TASKS: BY:

_____   _____

_____   _____

_____   _____

_____   _____

_____   _____

_____   _____

_____   _____

Once you have charted your plans, then, of course take action. If something changes along the way, be flexible. Perhaps a crisis occurs in another part of your job or another part of your life. Handle the crisis; but once you have, return to work on your goal. Modify your plans, but keep moving forward. Remember, the universe rewards action.

7. Learn to say "no"—appropriately.

Do you know what keeps many people frustrated and unproductive? The time they waste working on priorities that are not their own—priorities they should have turned away from. But what keeps us from turning away?

Our inability to say "*no*."

After all, it is scary. What if I say "no" and hurt someone's feelings? What if I say "no" and get called uncooperative? Or what if, in saying "no," I teach the people I count on for occasional help to say "no" to me?

Plus many of us have been told from the time we were children that we need to help others. And helping others is a great idea—but how can we help others while neglecting our own needs?

Saying "no" is uncomfortable for most of us. But that's no reason to avoid doing it. Here's a practical process:

1. Give yourself permission to say "no."
2. Learn some formulas and methods for saying "no."
3. Practice saying "no" in low-risk situations first.
4. Try out your "no"-saying skills on someone who loves you.
5. Say a small "no" in a more intimidating situation.
6. Measure the results of that "no."
7. Modify your approach if necessary.
8. Say "no" confidently in any appropriate situation.

Now, let's discuss each of these steps:

1. *Give yourself permission to say "no."* This could be the hardest step of all. Once you have tried and tried and tried to let go of the guilt you may feel when you do say "no," it may be time to just put your reservations aside and say "no" anyway. Ask yourself if taking on more than you can handle is helping you or hurting you. Then, make it real to yourself. Exactly how is it helping you or hurting you? And if those answers aren't compelling, try asking them five years out. What will my life be like five years from now if I don't start saying "no"? What will I miss out on? What goals of my own will have to be put on hold? Who in my life will suffer? How will they suffer?

Here's an example: If I don't start saying "no" to my client when he asks me to do extra work—for no additional payment—is that helping me or hurting me? Well, it helps me look good to that client, but it hurts me because it takes me away from my other clients. It helps me how? Well, my client is happy with me. And that is worth what? Well, nothing really—I don't make any more money. I guess it does help me keep his business. But it does hurt my relationship with my other clients—and those other clients have expressed interest in me doing more work for them. Plus they have offered to pay for that work.

Five years from now, if I keep working free for Client A, I will have less money and less time available to earn money from other clients. Yet I have three children whom I would like to be able to send to expensive colleges. Hmmmmmm.

See how it works? You need to convince yourself that to avoid saying "no" is to do yourself, your family, your friends and your career a disservice.

2. *Learn some formulas and methods for saying "no."* There are many options to choose from. Our favorite format for saying "no" is called the USA Approach.

> **U** nderstand
>
> **S** ituation
>
> **A** lternate Action

It starts with your explanation of "I understand why you want me to do this …" Then it moves into, "Here is the situation I am in …" Finally, it ends with your offer of what you can do or the help you can provide.

Let's say that a colleague comes and asks you to help with a project; perhaps your boss is out of the office and this colleague perceives you have little or nothing to do. However, before your boss left the office, you asked him if there was any priority work you were to complete before you left that day. Your boss assigned you some tasks and you have a number of your own. Here's how the USA Approach could help you.

UNDERSTAND: "I understand how important it is that this project (usually, you would just name it) gets done. And I'd love to help you with it."

SITUATION: "The thing is, my boss and I have set some priorities I have to get done before he returns."

ALTERNATE ACTION: "Here's what I can do. As soon as I'm finished with my priorities, I'll come and help you with your job."

Note: Sometimes the person who comes to you is asking you to do the type work for him or her that could be left with you. And they may just try to leave that work at your desk. Don't let them. Often, if you allow others to leave work with you, they'll start calling you (and calling you, and calling you) until you just give up and do the work so you can get your work done without all the interruptions. Be aware that you're teaching them that they can leave work with you and get you to put it in front of your boss-assigned priorities if they just bother you enough. In other words, if they leave it—you own it.

Prepare a reason as to why they can't leave the work with you. Something like this will work: "Thanks for being so thoughtful and willing to leave it. My concern is that I'm going to be sorting papers all over my desk today and I'm concerned I'd lose it. Go ahead and hang onto it and I'll come and get it as soon as I'm done. Thanks so much for understanding."

They may not understand, but your thanking them for their understanding will go a long way toward maintaining your professionalism and yet still not taking on the additional workload.

There are other ways of saying "no" as well. You could just smile politely and say it—"No." After you do that, be sure to keep from taking it back. Count to ten *very* slowly in your mind before allowing yourself to speak again. (Have you ever noticed how pathetically some people can look at you once you say "no"? And haven't those pathetic looks ever caused you to take back your "no"?)

Or maybe you could explain to them what would be involved if you took the time to fulfill their request. Sometimes just your explanation of how much is involved will convince the person doing the asking that the task is just not worth the time—not worth your time.

Here are some other strategies for saying "no":

- "I would if I could, but … " (including a reason you can't right now)
- "Which of these other tasks should I put aside?"
- "After looking at my calendar, I see I will have time to do that for you next week." (This can be used in response to a request for something to be done today).
- "Can I get back to you on that? I have to look at my availability."
- "I'd be glad to, but you might be better off asking Lisa. She's a much quicker typist." (With this strategy, you would also want to do something nice for Lisa.)
- "After realizing the scope of this project, I need to say 'no.'"
- "I would feel awkward doing this for you."
- "I'm sorry, but I just can't do it."
- "I'll do it if you … " add your own request. Barter.
- And finally, "No" (with a smile).

3. *Practice saying "no" in low-risk situations first.* If saying "no" is new to you, you will need some practice before you begin in earnest. Ask a friend to help you. Have the friend play the role of someone in your life who asks for too much and then practice several different ways of saying "no" to him or her. Definitely try the USA Approach as well as any others from the list above that sound genuine to you. Then, move on to other low-risk situations, like at a fast food restaurant when the kid in the window asks you, "Do you want fries with that?" Build your "no"-saying muscles in situations that won't get you into any trouble. Build your comfort zone safely.

4. *Try out your "no"-saying skills on someone who loves you.* This is the logical next step, don't you agree? Next time your husband asks you if you want to watch the news with him, or your wife asks you to take out the trash, or your good friend asks you to go out to dinner at a place more expensive than you can afford that week—try the USA Approach. Remember: Smile while you deliver it. See how it goes.

Most likely, anyone who knows you well is going to be slightly shocked to hear the New You. But stay calm and stay kind. You might even want to tell them what you're up to. "I'm practicing saying 'no.' I know you love me, so I thought I'd try it out on you first. But I am actually in the process of working up to … (tell them the situation you hope to say 'no' to soon)." Most of your friends and loved ones will be eager to help with such a noble cause!

5. *Say a small "no" in a more intimidating situation.* Yes, it's true that you are taking plenty of time to build this muscle. Now it is time to move up to a more intimidating person or situation. But nothing too big. Maybe you want to tell an intimidating co-worker that you don't want to go to lunch today. Or maybe you want to tell an understanding friend that you can't pay back the $20 until next week. Don't try telling the intimidating co-worker that you can't pay him back $100—that would be too much in this step.

6. *Measure the results of that "no."* Now that you have tried the new skill of "no"-saying, evaluate how it went. You might have felt uncomfortable. Your comfort zone is feeling violated and it is probably letting you know about it! But did you accomplish your goal? Did the intimidating co-worker accept your gentle refusal to go to lunch without becoming angry or abusive? Did your understanding friend accept your offer to pay back the $20 next week instead of this week? Or did you get a response that you didn't like?

If you experienced a response you didn't like, ask yourself what you could change in your approach next time around. Was your body language appropriate? Were you too passive (head down, avoiding eye contact) or too aggressive (too close, shaking finger)? How did your voice sound? Were you strong without sounding angry or defensive? Also, what about the words you used? If you were using our USA Approach, were you sincere? Did you offer an alternative that would be appealing to the person you were saying "no" to?

7. *Modify your approach if necessary.* Ask yourself how you could be more successful next time. Practice another approach or adjust your body language and vocal quality to become more appealing to your listener. Most of the

363

Career Success

time, when you have done your best to be responsible with the words you have chosen, any frustration or failure you experience in communication can be traced back to the nonverbal message. After you have adjusted your approach, try again in a low-impact situation: Go back to the understanding friend about the $20, or try again to refuse that lunch date. Practice until you are satisfied and comfortable—the more you practice, the more comfortable you will be.

8. *Say "no" confidently in any appropriate situation.* Now that you have worked to grow your comfort zone, and to find a tone and approach that works for you, you are ready to more confidently say "no" whenever you need to. Of course, don't risk going too far by saying "no" too often. Save this skill for the most important situations of your life. When all someone is asking for is if you could lend them a few paper clips out of your desk drawer to save them a trip all the way back to their own office, is it really worth exercising your "no"-saying skills? Remember: If you are helpful whenever you can be, the occasions you need to say "no" will be taken more seriously and more in stride by the people you need to say "no" to.

Saying "no" to requests that will waste your time is a key to being able to get more of your important priorities handled in the limited time you have available. It is one of the best options you have for becoming more productive and successful.

8. Overcome your tendencies toward procrastination or perfectionism.

Procrastination and perfectionism keep you stuck, unable to achieve your goals or complete your priorities. When you procrastinate, you guarantee you will never finish for two reasons:

1. Because you never start.

2. Because in your view, what you have done always needs more work.

You don't deserve to set yourself up that way.

To overcome procrastination, all you must do is the next right thing—right now. To overcome perfectionism, all you must do is allow your finished work to be excellent, rather than perfect.

Overcoming procrastination. Procrastination, of course, is the habit of putting off until tomorrow (or even further into the future) that which you really must do today. The cure? Never let another day pass without taking at least one small step toward the completion of your important goals and priorities. Please read that carefully—there is no need to take huge steps on a daily basis. Small consistent steps taken daily will get you far. You will create momentum and action will become a habit.

To be specific, there are three steps to overcoming procrastination:

1. Tell someone (or a large group of someones) what you are going to do. Make yourself accountable. Be sure to tell someone who will hold you to your word, someone you would be embarrassed to let down.

2. Sell yourself on getting the priority or goal handled. What's in it for you to do it? What's in it for you if you don't do it? Focus on the positive benefits of getting something done and the negative consequences of postponing.

3. Finally, break the priority down into the smallest pieces you can. What is the smallest possible first step you could take before you go to bed that night? Write it down and then do it. And do the next right thing every day. Eventually, you will be less intimidated by the goal and/or more in the habit of taking action and the steps you take daily can become bigger.

How would this process work for you? Let's say that you need to write a quarterly status report. But the task seems overwhelming to you, and besides: you hate writing.

First, tell someone that you are going to get started on this report today. Also tell that person when you hope to have it finished, and how excellent you expect it to be. (You don't have to lie there—stay tuned. We will be helping you overcome perfectionism next.) Ask them to give you a call the next day and ask how it's going.

Second, spend a few moments considering what is in it for you to get it done? Maybe in this case, it doesn't look like much. You'd get to meet a deadline. Maybe you are thinking that meeting that particular deadline is not such a big deal. Okay, why not try the other question? What's in it for you if you don't do it? Well, your boss is going to be upset. You will lose credibility and perhaps you will lose more—could you lose some of your budget? Or some responsibility? How about some promotability? Is it possible you could ultimately lose your job?

Finally, ask yourself what small step you could take before you go to bed that night to get started on this task. Could you print out your project notes from your computer and put them in the center of your desk to begin work with the next morning? Then maybe the next morning, could you organize them into major subject areas? Perhaps the day after that you could write the outline of the first subject … Do you see how this can work for you?

Overcoming perfectionism. Perfectionism isn't much different. Both procrastination and perfectionism are designed to keep you from finishing things. One by never starting, the other by never finishing. (Well, if it isn't good enough yet, how could it be finished?)

The secret for overcoming perfectionism is simple—not always *easy* (for a perfectionist, at least!) but simple.

Identify one thing in your life right now that you are perfectionistic about—preferably something small. Are you a nitpicker about keeping your large paper clips separated from your smaller ones in your desk drawer, for example? Or when you are cooking dinner, are you compulsive about measuring every ingredient in micro exactness? Or perhaps as you type in your word processing program you drive yourself nuts by going on-line for the correct spelling of every word you are unsure of as you type.

Whatever your particular perfectionistic peccadilloes may be, find one that you are going to let go of for now. Just one, the smaller the better. See—most of us who have suffered from some form of perfectionism know that it's not a good idea and know that we should be letting go of it. But we make the mistake of trying to let go of our perfectionism perfectly.

Start with one small thing and let go of that alone for just one week. At the end of the week, ask yourself if you made it through the week (don't worry, we will bet money that you did). You will probably feel great enough about this modest success that you will be willing to try something else the next week. Take it slowly and be sure to reward yourself with the good feelings you deserve to have.

Don't try to let go of too much too soon. Be patient with yourself.

9. Get support.

There are three kinds of support you may need if you feel overworked and unproductive. As a matter of fact, at least a couple of these will work to make anyone more productive and happier.

The first type of support we recommend is the support of a group of friends and peers. Next, we would recommend that you make sure you have the support of the tools and resources you need to accomplish your job (and the priorities of your life) within easy reach. Finally, we recommend the support you can get from a professional when stress begins to threaten your physical health or psychological well-being.

Friends and peers. Do you have five close friends? We're talking about the kind of friends you could call in a heartbeat if you were having a crisis in your life. And we aren't talking about a crisis like a flat tire—there's always AAA for that. We are referring to the emotional, social and political crises that often beset most of us. Do you have friends whose shoulders you can cry on for a while? Friends who will remind you of the good things about you? Friends who will just *listen* when you need it?

You should also look for co-workers and peers whom you can help when they seem overwhelmed. Those very same co-workers and peers would probably be available to provide you with some support at work as well.

Start today. Tithe your time. You have heard of tithing before, no doubt—probably in terms of the practice of donating a percentage of income to a church or charitable organization. Well, do the same with your time. Give away at least 30 minutes of your time every day to some co-worker or peer who hasn't asked you for the help. Do it casually— something like this: *Roger, I'm waiting for a phone call to come and I just don't have anything that I can get involved in for a few minutes at my own desk. How about if I do some of this filing for you while I'm waiting for the phone to ring? Would that be okay?*

Chances are excellent he is going to be delighted to let you help with his filing. And how do you think he is going to feel about helping you out some day in the future? He'll very likely be more than happy to help you.

As you tithe your time, spread it around to everyone. But don't give yourself credit for tithing if someone has actually asked you for the help. Tithing is a gift, given willingly. We understand you might not always be feeling willing, but act as if you are. You will be amazed at the positive reputation you will get, and the amount of help that will then be available to you.

Tools and resources: What resources do you need to do your job well? Are there certain office supplies, reference books, computer manuals, help-line phone numbers and the like that make it faster and easier to do your job? Have those resources within easy reach.

At first, you may need to gather them and find appropriate places to put them. Your important phone numbers, obviously, should be placed as near to the phone as you can get them. Or if you work more from a portable phone, program those frequently used numbers into the directory.

Resource guides should be on a bookshelf within reach of your main work area. The ones that you depend on in cyberspace should have direct links programmed into the memory of your Web browser. (Under Favorites or Bookmarks, for example).

The tools you use—everything from pens, sticky notes and printer cartridges—should be in your desk. Restock your desk once a week with the tools and supplies you are running low on. Don't wait until you are on the phone, balancing the receiver on your shoulder while looking in your top drawer, to discover there are no sticky notes there to write an important note on. Set aside time every week for restocking. If your job also includes supporting a boss, make sure to restock his or her desk weekly as well.

Professional support: When the stress in your life has caused you to become truly depressed, angry or out of control, it might just be time for a chat with a counselor or therapist. It is not a sign of weakness to seek help from a mental health professional, and—in some cases—it has been known to save lives. The chronic stress many people face can ultimately lead to physical symptoms of burnout and depression. Have you had trouble sleeping lately? Or have you had trouble waking up (more than usual, that is)? Have you lost your appetite, have you stopped laughing, have you stopped enjoying life? How about physical symptoms of stress? Has your blood pressure gone up, have you had more headaches than usual, have you noticed that you are grinding your teeth while you are asleep? These are some examples of the symptoms you should be on the lookout for.

Remember: Nothing is more valuable than your health and well-being. Do everything you can to safeguard them.

10. Remain flexible.

Life is unpredictable, and it's likely your job and your boss are too.

Have you ever become frustrated because competing priorities kept you from completing any one thing? It is human nature to at least *occasionally* need completion to feel worthwhile, to feel like a success. In fact, consider this productivity cycle:

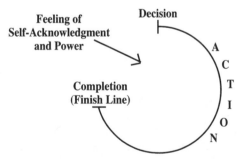

It all starts with your decision. Not that you were necessarily the one to think of a priority, goal or task originally, of course. Sometimes someone else has requested that you take something on that was *his* or *her* idea. But the minute you say, "Okay, I'll do that," you have made a decision. And remember: The decision you made was to *finish* the task, not simply to *work on it*.

After you make the decision, after you say "yes," the next step is action. Some tasks take just a small amount of action (*Please get me a box of paper clips from the supply cabinet*). Others require lots and lots of action (*We have been contracted to build a new international airport for the city.*).

Either way, once you have made a decision to take something on you begin to act. (See our tips earlier in this section for overcoming procrastination if you can't relate to starting action.) Once you begin to take action, you generally keep taking action until you get to the completion—the finish line—of your priority or goal.

Once you get to that completion, you feel a sense of success, a sense of self-acknowledgment. (Sometimes, you even get acknowledgment from the outside world.) It is this sense of success and accomplishment that fuels you with the energy to make a new decision, to take on something else.

Unless you have been interrupted along the way, that is, before you get to the finish line. And many times the interruptions you would face are so urgent or so important they cause you to put the current priority on a back burner—unfinished. It is in this way you deny yourself not only a finish line, but also the sense of success and the refueling of your energy that would come from completion.

Have you ever had a day like that? You had started off by working on one priority, then you got interrupted by a more urgent priority which itself was later interrupted by something even more urgent. Many people in today's workplace report that this happens often.

Of course, most people can handle a small amount of this kind of interruption and diversion. It's when the interruptions themselves become interrupted, and then even more priorities are on the back burner—and on and on until you no longer see any finish line for any priority within your reach because you are only *beginning* action and rarely finishing any one thing.

The secret to overcoming the frustration that accompanies these constant interruptions and newly emerging priorities is simple: Be flexible.

Flexibility is a state of mind. It is a state of mind that can save your life. This is how it works:

When your boss asks you to complete Project A, you are being asked to make a decision that will set the productivity cycle in motion. Instead of saying, "Yes, I will do Project A," why not make a decision that will allow you more flexibility? Why not say, "Yes, boss, I will do whatever you need me to do that you consider to be most important and most urgent at the particular time."

Now, no matter what else comes up you will still be working (taking action) toward the decision you made up front: To do whatever is considered most urgent and most important at the time.

There will never be another day that you can't walk away patting yourself on the back, feeling the acknowledgment and success that comes from making it to the completion of a decision. Even if a priority (or a large group of priorities) are unfinished, you have still accomplished what you set out to do: whatever was most urgent and most important at the time.